Certificate Book

OF THE

Virginia Land Commission

1779-1780

By The

Kentucky Historical Society

SOUTHERN HISTORICAL PRESS, INC.

The Rev. Silas Emmett Lucas, Jr.
President & Publisher

LaBruce Mortimer Seabrook Lucas
Vice-President & Associate Publisher

275 West Broad Street
Greenville, South Carolina 29601
803-233-2346

ISBN 0-89308-229-5

Library of Congress Card Catalog Number: 81-50453

CONTENTS OF VOLUME 21

OFFICERS

of the

KENTUCKY STATE HISTORICAL SOCIETY

SUBSCRIPTIONS.

Subscription, Yearly, $2.00 Current Number, 75c Per Copy.
Back Numbers, $1.00 Per Copy.

Subscriptions must be sent by check, or money order. All communications for The Register should be addressed to H. V. McChesney, Editor, Frankfort, Kentucky.

H. V. McCHESNEY, Editor and Business Manager.
MRS. JOUETT TAYLOR CANNON, Associate Editor

TO SUBSCRIBERS.

If your copy of The Register is not received promptly please advise us. It is issued in January, May and September.

Entered as second class matter September 17, 1919, at the Post Office at Frankfort, Kentucky, under the Act of August 24, 1912.

THE STATE JOURNAL COMPANY
FRANKFORT, KY.

REGISTER

Kentucky State Historical Society

Vol. 21. January, 1923. No. 61.

EDITOR'S PREFACE.

The September, 1922, issue of the Register carried an article from the pen of Mr. Lucien Beckner entitled "Captain James Harrod's Company." In this reference was made to what Mr. Beckner calls the "Doomsday Book of the conquest of Kentucky," a volume in the possession of the clerk of the Fayette County Court. It is usually referred to as the "Certificate Book" and is the official record kept by the clerk of the Commission which heard proof of claims to settlements and preemption rights by early settlers in Kentucky, and issued certificates to the claimants which answered in lieu of deeds.

The existence of this rare old record having been called to the Editor's attention by the article referred to he made an examination of the volume and was at once impressed with the fact that here was no doubt the most valuable fund of source material concerning the early history of Kentucky settlers anywhere obtainable. The very large number of entries in this old record indicates that perhaps every pioneer who had made actual settlement in Kentucky prior to October 13th, 1779, the date when the Commission began its hearings, proved his claim and secured his certificate. This conclusion is all the more probable for the reason that the Commission, which held its first sittings at St. Asaphs (Stanford), also made the round more than once of the various stations and settlements, holding sessions at Harrodsburg, Bryant's Station, Boonesborough and Falls of the Ohio, thus affording every settler opportunity to establish his claim.

It is of course possible that there may have been bona fide settlers who did not prove their claims before this Commission, but it is very improbable. It is not our purpose to read out of the honor roll of pioneer settlers the names of any not mentioned in this "Doomsday Book," but rather to emphasize the fact that the book "reads the title clear" for every one mentioned in it.

As the data in this old record is of such very great value and as the Historical Society has not been able to secure possession of the book, we have decided to publish it in full, running through the three issues of 1923. Just here we wish to acknowledge our indebtedness to the County Court Clerk of Fayette County, Mr. Faust Foushee, for his kindness in allowing us to copy the record and for his courtesies in connection therewith.

The Commission.

Many things contributed to the confusion as to title to the Kentucky settlements. A settler would build a cabin, perhaps raise a crop of corn and then return to Virginia for his family; another pioneer, with the home building instinct, coming in later and knowing neither the intentions of the other settler nor the extent of his possible claim or survey, would build his cabin somewhere in the same neighborhood. Naturally there was much eagerness also to secure the sites where fine springs were found and along the water courses. As settlements multiplied the situation became more and more complicated. These pioneers were extending Virginia's power and adding to her glory and it was imperative that action be taken to adjust their conflicting claims, so the Legislature of Virginia, in 1779, passed an Act authorizing the Governor to appoint a Commission to come to Kentucky and sit as a Court, to hear proof and quiet the titles by issuing certificates to rightful claimants.

The Act is found in Henning's Statutes, Volume 10, pages 35 to 50. As the Act is very long we can give only the substance of it here. It provided for the appointment of four Commissioners, who should not be residents of Kentucky County, to sit as a court and hear proof of claims as above stated. They were given authority to issue a certificate for a 400 acre settlement when claimant's right was established, and the certificate might also cover a preemption right of 1000 acres additional and adjoining. The claimant was required to pay a fee of ten shillings for each 100 acres covered by his certificate, this being the "state price," and also an additional ten shillings as a fee for the clerk who issued the certificate.

In the majority of cases the claimant secured both a certificate of settlement and a preemption right, but in a few instances the settler exercised rare modesty and declined to accept his preemption right contenting himself with his four hundred acre settlement. In many cases it is apparent that the claimant was only entitled to his preemption right and not to an actual settlement right and in these cases the certificate issued to him gave him a preemption right only.

Personnel of the Commission.

As the responsibility resting on this Commission was very great it was important that the Governor exercise care in the selection of its members. That the Governor acquitted himself well in the premises is evidenced by the very high character of the men selected. The first entry in the record named only William Fleming, Edmund Lyne and James Barbour (by evident mistake shown as John Barber in first line of the record) as the Commissioners. Under date of October 28th, 1779, fifteen days after the organization of the Court, however, this entry appears: "Stephen Trigg—Gent'n this day produced his Commission appointing him a Commissioner in the room of James Steptoe for the purpose of executing, in conjunction with William Fleming, Edmund Lyne and James Barbour, in Kentucky district the act for adjusting disputed Titles or Claims to Land and was qualified accordingly and took his seat." From this entry it is evident that Steptoe had been appointed originally and for some reason had not accepted, so the Commission was composed of Fleming, Lyne, Barbour and Trigg.

As the members of this Commission played such a conspicuous part in the early history of Kentucky settlements we are publishing herewith a brief sketch of each of them.

William Fleming. Colonel William Fleming was born in Jedborough, Scotland, February 18th, 1729. He came to Virginia July 9th, 1755, and settled in Augusta County. He was an active participant in the early warfare against the Indians and was at first a lieutenant and surgeon and later was appointed captain. After the organization of Botetourt County he was Justice of the Peace for that county.

He was seriously wounded in the battle with the Indians at Point Pleasant and never fully recovered from his wounds. Due to this fact he was not able to participate in the military activities of the Revolution but gave distinguished service to his country in a civil capacity, especially as a member of the Commission for the settlement of the disputed land titles in Kentucky. As has been above stated this Commission met at St. Asaphs (Stanford) October 13th, 1779. The Commission sat through the winter of 1779-80. When these duties were finished and the Commission dissolved he returned to Virginia and was later on elected by the Legislature of Virginia as a member of the Council of State under Governor Jefferson. At the conclusion of Governor Jefferson's term he served for a time as Acting Governor of Virginia.

The Land Office at Frankfort shows that at various times Colonel Fleming secured as many as sixteen separate land grants in Kentucky aggregating about 30,000 acres, some of it being in Jefferson, some in Fayette and some in Lincoln County. At least one of Colonel Fleming's sons, Leonard Israel Fleming, settled in Kentucky and died near Midway October 27th, 1845. One of his sons was Colonel William B. Fleming of Louisville, Kentucky, a distinguished lawyer.*

Stephen Trigg. Colonel Stephen Trigg, the only son of Abraham Trigg, the Cornish emigrant, came to Augusta County, Virginia, about the year 1768 or 1769. He was present at the organization of Botetourt County on the 15th of February, 1770, and was appointed a Justice of the Peace of that county and later on was a member of the Convention which met at Richmond July 17th, 1775. In this Convention he was the representative of Fincastle County that had been organized from Botetourt in the year 1772, Fincastle including at the time the whole of Southwestern Virginia and Kentucky.

When he came to Kentucky as a member of the Commission to adjust the disputed land titles he settled at Trigg's

*Life and Times of Judge Caleb Wallace, Whitsett, Filson Club publication No. 4, page 80.

Station, otherwise known as Viney Grove, four miles from Harrodsburg on Cane Run. In 1780, in conjunction with John Todd he represented the county of Kentucky in the Legislature of Virginia. These two representatives during this session secured the passage of an Act for "establishing the town of Louisville at the Falls of Ohio."

After Kentucky County was subdivided into Lincoln, Jefferson and Fayette counties he was one of the Justices of the Peace and assisted in holding the first county court in Lincoln County. This first session was held at Harrodsburg January 16th, 1781.

Colonel Trigg was the father of five children. His oldest son, William, married Miss Susan Smith and lived in Frankfort, where he died without issue. Another son, Stephen Trigg, settled in Botetourt County, Virginia, married Miss Mary Harvie, and died without issue. Fleming Trigg, the youngest son, married Miss Susan Ditty of Southwestern Virginia. They had one daughter. Elizabeth Trigg became the wife of Preston Breckinridge. With her husband they removed to Fayette County, Kentucky and their decendants have been among the distinguished sons and daughters of the Commonwealth. Mary Trigg, the youngest child, married John David Logan. They left one son, Judge Stephen Trigg Logan of Illinois, who at one time was the law partner of Abraham Lincoln.

Colonel Trigg was killed at the disastrous battle of the Blue Licks, August 19th, 1782.*

*Life and Times of Judge Caleb Wallace, Whitsett, Filson Club publication No. 4, page 87.

EDMUND LYNE. Edmund Lyne was the fourth son of William Lyne, the first known of the family in Virginia. After coming to Kentucky he settled on a farm on Cane Ridge, in Bourbon County, where he died unmarried in 1791. In addition to his service on the Commission to settle the disputed land titles he was later on appointed, in 1786, together with Isaac Shelby and Richard Taylor as a Commission to adjust claims arising out of the expedition of General George Rogers Clark and Colonel Ben Logan against the Shawnee and Wabash Indians. He was also a Commissioner with Benjamin Logan, Green Clay, Isaac Shelby, and John Marshall, Jr., to receive subscriptions to open and establish a road from the falls of the Great Kanawha to Lexington, Ky., and also was one of the trustees with Daniel Boone and others to lay out the town of Washington in Bourbon County, now Washington in Mason County.**

JAMES BARBOUR. James Barbour was a member of the House of Burgesses from Culpepper County, Virginia, in 1764, County Lieutenant of the Militia of Culpepper in 1775, an officer in the Revolutionary War, and later a member of the Commission to settle the disputed land titles in Kentucky.

He married Frances Throckmorton and their son, James Barbour (who married Mary Taylor, daughter of James Taylor and Ann Pendleton of Orange County, Virginia, 1787) removed to Kentucky and became the an-

**Sullivant Family Memorial, page 283.

cestor of the large family of Barbours of Jefferson and Oldham Counties.*

These Commissioners rendered very great service not only to the Kentucky settlers but to the Commonwealth of Virginia. It was by no means a pleasant task that had been assigned them. Where there were rival claimants the loser might feel unkindly toward the Court. The country was still infested with Indians, and in traveling from one settlement to another to hold sessions of the Court they were exposed to great danger. They were asked to discharge this important duty in the midst of the Revolution, and at least three of them had had previous military experience, and one, James Barbour, was an officer in the Revolutionary War. It was but natural that personal and patriotic motives should have drawn them to the more stirring scenes of the conflict for their country's freedom, but because of their high standing and unimpeachable character Virginia had drafted them for this important civic duty, and they responded.

The Pioneer Settlers

The list of land claimants contains the name of practically every man who played a part in the stirring drama of Kentucky's early settlement. It is an Honor Roll of pioneer heroes who took their lives in their hands as they moved the outposts of civilization hundreds of miles into a savage-infested wilderness.

As we write the names of Boone, Kenton, Calloway, Harrod, Todd, Shelby, McGary, Logan, McAfee, Whitley, Meriweather, Clark, Combs, Davis, Harlin, Howard, Craig, Scott, Smith, Fields, Slaughter, Crockett, Floyd, and scores of others of equal fame, there is a strong temptation to write at least a brief sketch of each. Space will not permit this indulgence, however, and so we are using foot-note references only to a few of the most outstanding items of interest. Foot-note references are also made indicating where brief sketches may be found in Collins' History. As we have been pressed for time in preparing the copy for this first installment we are indexing only the names of persons appearing in the volume.

The majority of the entries in the record have a marginal notation showing the number of acres claimed, the fact of the payment of the fees, issuance of certificate, and in most cases the name of the person to whom the certificate was delivered. As it is not convenient to run these marginal notes as such in our style of make-up we are running them in parentheses at the beginning of the entries to which they apply.

The edge of the back of the book has a slip pasted on it with the word "Pre-emptions" written on the slip. It is rather apparent from the appearance of this writing that it was done at a later date and perhaps not a part of the original record. There is no title at the top of the first page of the record other than the date line. The first installment of the record follows herewith.

*Culpepper County History, R. T. Green, page 136.

St. Asaphs or Logans Fort* October ye 13th, 1779 William Fleming Edmond Lyne and John Barber Esquires, this day produced a Commission from under the hand of his Excellency the Governor, sealed with the Seal of the Commonwealth of Virginia, bearing date the 26th day of June 1779, Constituting and appointing them Commissioners for the purpose of carrying into execution the act of Assembly entitled an Act, for adjusting and settling the titles of Claimers, under the present and former Government, previous to the establishment of the Commonwealths land office.

James Barbour Esq—this day administered the Oath of a Commissioner to William Fleming, and he the said William Fleming Esq. to Edmond Lyne & James Barbour Esquires according to Law. After which they made choice of John Williams Junior Clerk who was sworn accordingly, the Court being Attended by the Sheriff of do adjourn untill to morrow 10 oclock

William Fleming

At a Court Continued & held for adjusting disputed Titles to the Kentucky Land, at St Asaphs' or Logans Fort. Oct 14th 1779

Present

William Fleming, Edmund Lyne
James Barbour Esquires

(Isued for 1400 Acres & D. D.** to Colonel Lyne fees paid)

Captain John Logan for and in behalf of Isaac Shelby this day produced a claim, and making a Crop of Corn on the same in the year 1776 Lying on a branch that heads at the Knob Lick, & about a mile and a half or two miles from the said Lick a southeastwardly course proof being made satisfactorily to the Court they are of Opinion that the said Shelby has a right to a settlement & Preemption according to Law and that Certificates issue for the same.

(Certificate issued for 1000 Acres fees paid Cash D. D.)

John Wilson this day appeared & claimed a Tract of Land lying on Harrods Run about miles from this place by building a Cabin on the same in the year 1774 And it Appearing that Colonel Boon claimed the same, the said Wilson withdraws the said claim and claims a preemption on Shawnees Run, joining James Carrs Land to the Westward, by virtue of his building a Cabin on the Land in the year 1774 And proof being made satisfactory to the Court they are of Opinion that the said Wilson has a right to a preemption of 1000 Acres of Land according to Law and that Certificate issue for the same including the said settlement.

Robert Espey this day claimed an improvement lying on a branch of Salt River on the North side of said River about 4 miles from floyds Fork between Brackens Creek & the said Fork with a at the head of a Spring by purchase from William Poage as appears by an Instrument of writing date the eighth day of July 1778. Continued at the request of the said Claimant.

William Jennings this day Appeared & claimed a Certain Tract of Land lying on the waters of Shawnee Run joining John Gordens Land by purchase from Jonathan Ingream as Appears by an

**Deed delivered.

instrument of writing bearing date the 9th day of September 1779 Continued for a hearing at Harrodsburg.

(Certificate issued for 400 Acres D. D. to himself fees paid).

Robert Esspie this day Appeared and claimed a preemption of 400 acres of Land being Settled in this Country & made Corn in the year 1778 as Appears by Testimony lying on the Waters of Paint Lick near the land of McKinnedy at a Spring with the letters R A cut on an Oak Tree the Court are of Opinion that the said Esspie has a right to the preemption of 400 Acres of Land according to Law and that a certificate issue for the same.—

(Isued for 400 for settlement & 200 for preemption fees paid & Cer. D. D.)

William Manifee this day Appeared and claimed a settlement and preemption for a Tract of Land lying on both sides of Dicks River and on a branch of Cedar Creek by a settlement on said Land and making Corn on the same in the year 1776 Sufficient proof being made, the Court are of Opinion that the said Manifee has a right to the Land for the Settlement & preemption of two hundred Acres Adjoining being his own choice & that a Certificate issue &c.—

(Certificate issued for 400 Acres and preemption granted the day following fees paid D. D.)

Gerrard Manifee this day Appeared & claimed a right to a settlement for a Tract of Land lying on the waters of Cedar Creek joining the Land of William Whitley by making Corn on the said Land in the year 1776 on Sufficient proof being made to the Court they are of Opinion that the said Manifee has a right to a settlement of 400 Acres according to Law, and that a certificate issue for the same, he claiming no preemption.—

(Cer. issued for 1400 Acres fees paid & Delivered)

Bartholomew Fenton this day Appeared & claimed a right to a settlement & preemption for a Tract of Land lying on Dicks River three miles below the mouth of Hawkins branch, by raising a Crop or Corn in the year 1777 and Clearing Land on the same place, on sufficient proof being made the Court are of Opinion that the said Fenton has a right to a settlement of 400 Acres a preemption of 1000 Acres of Land According to law and that A Certificate issue accordingly.

(Certificate issue for 1400 Acres D. D. himself.)

William Moore Appeared this day and claimed a right to a settlement & preemption to a Tract of Land known by the name of Crab Orchard Tract of Dicks River by making Corn in this County in the year 1775 And improving the said Land by clearing and building a Cabin on the same in the year 1776 on sufficient proof being made to the Court they are of Opinion that the said Moore has a right to a settlement of 400 Acres & a preemption of 1000 Acres according to Law, and that a Certificate issue for the same.

(Cert. issued for 1400 Acres D. D. himself)

Thomas Barton this day Appeared and claimed a right to a settlement and preemption as Heir at Law to William Barton deceased.

(Cert. issued for 1400 Acres D. D. himself & money paid.—)

Daniel Hawkings

At a Court continued and held for Adjusting disputed Titles to the Kentucky Lands at St. Asaphs or Logan Fort the 15th day of October 1779.

Present

William Fleming Edmund Lyne & James Barbour Esqrs.

William Pettitt.[2]

Gerard Manifee[2]

(Certificate issued for 1400 Acres fees paid. Cert. D. D.)

Hugh Leaper

(Certificate issued for 1400 Acres fees paid and D. D.)

Joseph Kennady

Michael Stoner[2]

Benjamin Logan[2]

Philip Tramell this day Appeared and claimed a right to of preemption for 400 Acres of Land lying on the Waters of Paint Lick Creek on the South of said Creek at the head of a branch about 5 M from Harmons Lick a North Course from the same, on account of a Settlement made in this County since the first of June 1778 and before the passing of the Act of Assembly for Opening the Land Office and raising Corn in this County satisfactory proof being made to the Court they are of Opinion that the said Tramell has a right to a preemption of 400 Acres including the said Settlement and that a Certificate issue for the same.

Then the Court Adjourned until to morrow morning ten oclock.

William Fleming

At a Court Continued & held for adjusting disputed titles to the Kentucky Lands at St. Asaphs or Logans fort Oct 10th 1779 Present

Wm. Fleming. Edmund Lyne & James Barbour Esqrs—

(Certificates issued for 400 Acres fees &c pd & D. D.)

Thomas Lovell this day Appeared & claimed a right to a preemption of 400 Acres of Land lying on a small Creek that runs into the Hanging fork of Dicks River, about 6½ M from this place he having made an Actual Settlement on the said place since the first of January 1778 And before the passing the Act of Assembly for Opening the Land Office—Satisfactory proof being made to the Court they are of Opinion that the said Lovell has a right to a preemption to the said Land, and that a Certificate issue for the same.

On a motion of Walter Overton by Nicholas Merriwether his Attorney to have the deposition of Captn Robert

---

[2]Name only appears.

Todd concerning a claim for Land in this County by the said Overton, It Appearing to the Court that the said Todd will leave this County before the said Overton can lay in his Claim, The Court are of Opinion that a dedimus issue for that purpose

On A Motion of Richard Thomas to have the deposition of Captn Robt Todd taken concerning a Claim to Lands in this County on Elkhorn by the s'd Thomas, It Appearing to the Court that the said Robert Todd will leave this County before the said Claim can be heard the Court are of Opinion that a dedimus issue for that purpose

And then the Court Adjourned untill Monday morning Next at 10 oclock

William Fleming

At a Court continued & held for Adjusting Titles to the Kentucky Lands at St. Asaphs or Logans fort on Monday 10th of Oct 1779—

Present

William Fleming Edmund Lyne & James Barbour Esqrs.

(Certificate issued for 1400 Acres fees &c pd D. D.)

Robcrt Todd this day Appeared & claimed a right to a settlement & preemption to a Tract of Land lying on Hickmans Creek adjoining the Lands claimed by Colo John Todd which lies up above the said Land, on the said Creek, & the Lands of Lieut Collins on the West & North West, and the Lands claimed by Walter Overton, on the East & North East by improving the said Land, in the year 1776 and resided in the Country twelve Months After making the said improvement on satisfactory proof being made to the Court they are of Opinion that the said Todd has a right to a settlement of 400 acres to include the said improvement & a preemption of 1000 Acres adjoining & that a Certificate issue for the same & then the Court adjourned untill Tomorrow Morning 10 oclock

William Fleming

At a Court continued & held for adjusting disputed Titles to the Kentucky Lands at St. Asaphs or Logans Fort Oct 19th 1779.

Present

William Fleming Edmund Lyne & James Barbour Esquires

(Certificate issued for 1400 Acres fees paid. D. D. Captn Harrod)

James Harrod[3] this day appeared & claimed a right to a settlement & preemption as Guardian to James McDonald an infant, to a Tract of Land settled by Patrick McDonald deceased who the said James McDonald is Heir at Law to, by the said Patrick McDonalds in his life time improving the said Tract of Land and making Corn in this Country in the year 1776 lying on Gilberts Creek a branch of Dicks River it being proved to the Court by the oath of Mr James Harrod that the Claimant is heir at law to the said Decedent James Coburn a Covenanter having declared it in solemn form according to the formality observed in similar Cases by those of that Church declares that Patrick McDonald

[3]Collins, Vol. 1, pp. 17-253.

took sick at his house & died intestate. The Court are of opinion that McDonald Heir at Law to the Decedent has a right to a settlement of 400 Acres of Land including the improvement and a preemption of 1000 acres of Land Adjoining and that a Certificate issue for the same.

(Certificate issued for 1400 Acres fees paid D. D.)

Charles Cameron this day claimed a right to a Settlement and preemption as Assignee of Henry Pawling who was Assignee of James Dorchester to a Tract of Land lying on the Waters of Dicks River Known by the name of Dorchesters improvement made by the said Dorchester in the year 1775. Benja'n Logan Appeared and contested the said Claim by virtue of a purchase from the Heir at Law to the said Dorchester the 23rd day of March 1779. Witnesses being sworn & examined and it appearing to the Court that the said James Dorchester sold his improvement to the Said Land to Henry Pawling in his life time in the year 1777. The Court are of Opinion that the said Cameron has a right to a settlement of 400 Acres of Land including the said improvement & the preemption of 1000 acres adjoining and that a Certificate issue for the same. And that the said Cameron have a Judgment against Logan for Costs &c.

(Certificate issued for 1400 Acres. D. D. to Cap'n Harrod fees &c paid.—)

James Corbun Heir at Law to Samuel Coburn deceased this day claimed a right to a Settlement & preemption to a Tract of Land lying on Mulberry Creek a branch of Bracheirs's Creek, a branch of Salt River, joining the Land claimed by Squire Boone by marking the said place in the year 1775 and making Corn in this County in the same year, Satisfactory proof being made to the Court they are of Opinion that the said Coburn has a right to a settlement of 400 Acres of Land including the said Marked place & the preemption of 1000 Acres adjoining & that a Certificate issue for the same.

(Certificate issued for 400 fees &c paid D. D. Benj. Pettitt)

William Phelp this day claimed a right of preemption of four hundred Acres of Land lying on the North of the Main North branch of Green River about fifty M. above the mouth of Barren River he having made an Actual Settlement on the said place in February 1779, Satisfactory proof being made to the Court they are of Opinion that the said Phelp has a right to the preemption of 400 Acres of land at the State price including the said Settlement & that a Certificate issue for the same.

Hugh McGary[4] Assignee of Ralph Williams this day claimed a right to a settlement & preemption to a tract of Land lying on Paint Lick Creek at a large spring lying North Course from the Land claimed by John Kenady and about two miles from the same by the said Williams having Made Corn in this Country in the year 1775 'And Mark'd out the said place. Satisfactory proof being made to the Court. they are

[4]Collins, Vol. 1, pp. 256-257.

of Opinion that the said McGary has a right to a settlement of 400 Acres including the said place & the preemption of 1000 Acres adjoining and that a Certificate issue for the same, not till the last day of this Court sitting.—

(Certificate issued for 400 Acres fees &c pd Cert. D. D. Benj Pettitt)

William Phelps Junior this day claimed the right to a preemption of 400 Acres lying on the North side of the Main North branch of Green River about fifty miles above the mouth of Barren River about two or three miles above Bryant's Lick he having made an Actual Settlement on the said place in February 1779 Satisfactory proof being made to the Court they are of Opinion that the said Phelps has a right to a preemption of 400 Acres of land at the State price including the said settlement and that a Certificate issue for the same.

(Cert issd for 400 acres fees &c paid D. D. Benj'n Pettitt)

Nicholas Phelps this day claimed a right of preemption of 400 acres of land lying on the North side of the Main North branch Green River about fifty two M above the Mouth of Barren River & about 2 miles below the land claimed by Wm. Phelps Jun he having made an Actual settlement on the sàid place ir Feby 1779 satisfactory proof being made to the Court they are of Opinion that the said Phelps has a right to a preemption of 400 Acres of Land at the State price including the said settlement and that a Certificate issue for the same.

(Cert. issd for 400 Acres fees &c paid Cert D. D. to Benj'n Pettitt)

Saml Phelps this day claimed a right to a preemption of 400 Acres of Land lying on the North side of the Main North branch of Green River about three miles before the lands claimed by Nich's Phelps he having made an Actual Settlement on the said Land in Feby 1779 satisfactory proof being made to the Court they are of Opinion that the said Phelps has a right to a preemption of 400 Acres of Land at the State price including said settlement & that a Certificate issue for the same

(Cert. - issd - for 1400 acres fees &c paid D. D.—)

Julius Sanders this day Appeared and claimed a right to a settlement & preemption to a small Tract of Land lying on the head of a Creek called Boons Mill Creek about four M from Dicks River about twelve M from this place by making Corn on the said land improving the same in the year 1776 satisfactory proof being made to the Court they are of Opinion that the said Sanders has a right to a Settlement of 400 Acres of Land including the said settlement & a preemption of 1000 Acres Adjoining and that a Certificate issue for the same.

Then the Court adjourned untill to Morrow 10 oclock

William Fleming

At a Court Continued & held for Adjusting disputed Titles to the Kentucky

Lands at St. Asaphs or Logans Fort†
Oct 20. 1779.
Present
William Fleming Edmund Lyne
& James Barbour Esquires—

(Cert issued for 1000 Acres fees &c. pd. Cert. D. D.)

Joseph Combs this day claimed a right to a preemption One Thousand Acres of Land lying on Comb's since called Howard's Creek about eight M above Boonesborough on both sides of the Creek and about three or four M from the Mouth of it by improving the said Land by building a Cabbin on the premises in the month of May 1775 Satisfactory proof being made to the Court they are of Opinion that the said Combs has a right to the preemption of One Thousand Acres including the said improvement and that a Certificate issue for the same.

(Cert issued for 1400 Acres fees &c paid Cert. D. D.)

Cuthburt Combs this day claimed a right to a settlement & preemption to a Tract of Land lying at an Indian Town on the North side of Kentucky between Lulbegrud Creek & Howards Creek to include both side of the said Howards Creek for quantity by making Corn in the Country in the year 1775 & Marking out the said place Satisfactory proof being made to the Court they are of Opinion that the said Combs has a right to a settlement of 400 Acres Land including the above mentioned place and the preemption of 1000 Acres and that a Certificate issue for the same.

(Cert iss'd for 1400 acres fees &c., paid D. D. to his wife—)

Benj Pettitt this day claimed a right of settlement & preemption to a Tract of Land lying on the dividing ridge of the Waters of the Hanging Fork a branch of Dicks River & Green River about 7 M from this place by making Corn in this Country in the year 1775 and residing in the Country 12 Months, On satisfactory proof being made to the Court they are of Opinion that the said Pettitt has a right to a settlement of 400 Acres of land including the place above mentioned 1000 Acres of Land Adjoining Cert'e issue for the same.

(Certificate issued for 1400 Acres fees &c paid cert. D. D.)

John Logan this day claimed a right to a settlement & preemption to a Tract of Land lying at the Mouth of St Asaphs Spring branch including both forks of the said branch by raising Corn in this Country on the said place in the year 1776 Satisfactory proof being made to the Court they are of Opinion that the said Logan has a right to a settlement of 400 Acres of Land including the said settlement and a preemption of 1000 Acres Adjoining, & that a Certificate issue for the same.

(Certificate issued for 1400 Acres fees &c paid & Cert. D. D. to Capt John Logan)

Capt John Logan for and in behalf of Nath'l Logan this day claimed a right to a settlement & preemption to a Tract of Land lying below the Mouth of St Asaphs Spring branch about 2 or 2½ M on both sides of a Creek by settling the

†This fort was about one mile west of the present town of Stanford. See Collins, Vol. 2, p. 469.

same & raising a Crop of Corn in the year 1776 Satisfactory proof being made to the Court, they are of Opinion that the said Nath'l Logan has a right to a settlement of 400 Acres including the said improvement and a preemption of 1000 Acres Adjoining & that a Certificate issue for the same.

William Logan this day claimed a right to a settlement preemption to land in this Country on satisfactory proof being made to the Court that the said Logan raise a Crop of Corn in this country in the year 1776 Residing in this Country twelve Months before the passing of the Act of Assembly for Opening the Land Office they are of Opinion that the said Logan has a right to the settlement of 400 Acres of Land with the preemption of 1000 Acres Adjoining or convenient to St Asaph

(Cert. issued for 1400 fees &c pd. Cert. D. D.)

Benj. Logan[5] this day claimed a right to a settlement preemption to a Tract of Land Known by the name of St Asaphs Lying on the Waters of Dicks River by raising Corn & settling the said Land in the year 1775 Satisfactory proof being made to the Court they are of Opinion that the said Logan has a right to a settlement of 400 Acres including the said settlement & a preemption of 1000 Acres Adjoining & that a Certificate issue for the same

Page Ass'ee of Logan

Then the Court Adjourned to Harrodsburg on Monday the 25 Inst.

William Fleming

At a Court Continued and Held for adjusting Disputed Titles to the Kentucky Lands at Harrodsburg Oct 26. 1779—

Present

Wm Fleming Edmund Lyne & James Barbour Esqs

David Barton Heir at Law to Joshua Barton deceased this day Claimed a right to a settlement & preemption to a tract of Land refered till the Coming meet at Boones borrough.

(Certificate issued for 1400 fees &c pd. & D. D.)

Azariah Davis this day claimed a right to a settlement & preemption to a Tract of Land Lying on the Waters of Salt River about one M from Harrodsburg Near a Southwest course to include Spring at which there is a large House built by the said Davis & his making Corn in this Country in the year 1775 George Mcafee Also appearing and contesting the said Claim* on which witnesses were sworn & examined in Consideration of the Testimony the Court are of Opinion that the said Davis has a right to a settlement of 400 Acres of Land including the said improvement & a preemption of 1000 Acres Adjoining the said settlement and that a Certificate issue for the same.

(Certificate issued for 1400, fees &c pd. cert. D. D.)

Thos. Baston (Barton?) this day claimed a right to a settlement &

[5]Collins, Vol. 1, pp. 20, 21, 22, 249, and index.

*See McAfee Papers.

preemption of a tract of Land lying on Dowlans or Bartons Creek a branch of Salt River about 2 M from Davis Spring & a South Course from the same in the fork of Salt River he having improved the said Land and raising a Crop of Corn in the year 1776 Satisfactory proof being made to the Court they are of Opinion that the said Baston is entitled to a settlement of 400 Acres of Land to include the said improvements to extend a 1/4 Mile toward McAfee Station from the Cabin & a preemption of 1000 Acres Adjoining the said settlement and that a Certificate issue for the same.

(Cert. issued for 1000, fees &c pd. Cert D. D. Henry Wilson)

Robt. McAfee[6] this day claimed a right to a settlement & preemption to a Tract of Land lying on the Town Fork of Salt River including McAfee's upper Station by raising Corn in the Country at Boons borough and improving the said Land in the year 1775 Henry Wilson Appeared & Contested the said claim & claimed the said Land by virtue of building a Cabin on the same in the year 1775 prior to the said McAfees improvement sundry witnesses being sworn & examined in consideration of which the Court are of Opinion that the said Henry Wilson is entitled to the preemption of 1000 Acres of Land including said improvement and that a Certificate issue for the same—Henry Wilson agrees that the inhabitants of McAfees Station shall have peaceable possession of one hundred Acres of Land to reside on for the term of Seven years and that the said inhabitants shall have leave to make use of Timber for Building Cabin &c & enclosing the said land & water for the use of the Garrison.—

(Cert. issued fees &c pd. Cert. D. D.)

Wm McAfee† this day claimed a right to a settlement & preemption to a tract of Land lying on Salt River adjoining the land whereon Harrodsburg is built a North Westerly course from the same by including the same & raising a Crop of Corn in the year 1776 Azariah Davis also Appeared & contested the said Claim on behalf of Anariah Davis sundry witnesses being sworn & examined in consideration of which the Court are of Opinion that the said Wm McAfee has a right to a settlement of 400 Acres including said improvement & a preemption of 1000 Acres Adjoining the said settlement & that a Certificate issue for the same.

(Cert. issued for 1400 fees &c pd. Cert. D. D. to John McGee)

James McCown‡ this day claimed a right to a settlement & preemption to a tract of Land lying on Salt River between the lands claimed by George & James McAfee by improving the said land & raising a Crop of Corn in the year 1776 satisfactory proof being made to the Court they are of Opinion that s'd McCown has a right to a settlement of 400 Acres of land including the said improvement & the preemption of 1000 Acres Adjoining & that a certificate issue for the same.—

[6]Collins, Vol. 1, p. 17. See McAfee Papers.

†See McAfee Papers.

‡See McAfee Papers.

(Cert. issued for 400 fees &c pd. & Cert. D. D. to George McAfee).

Rob. McAfee this day claimed a right to a settlement to a Tract of Land lying on Salt River on both sides about ¾ of a M below McAfee Station called Fort Liberty by improving the said Land and in making Corn in the year 1775 satisfactory proof being made to the Court they are of Opinion that the said McAfee has a right to a settlement of 400 Acres & that a Certificate issue for the same. He declining to claim his preemption

Vide p

(Cert. issued for 1400 fees &c pd Cert D. D.)

William McBrayers this day claimed a right to a settlement & preemption to a Tract of Land lying on the Waters of Salt River on the West side of Chaplins Fork on a small branch About ½ Miles from the head of said branch by improving the said land and raising of corn in the year 1776 satisfactory proof being made to the Court they are of Opinion that the said McBrayer has a right to a settlement of 400 Acres of Land including the said improvement & the preemption of 1000 Acres Adjoining and that a Certificate issue for the same/

(Cert issued for 1400 fees &c pd D. D. to Capt Levi Todd)

James McAfee this day claimed a right to a settlement & preemption to a Tract of Land lying on both sides of Salt River joining James McCowns on the North side & Sam'l McAfees on the South by improving the said land in the year 1775 and raising a Crop of Corn in the year 1776 satisfactory proof being made to the Court they are of opinion that the said James McAfee has a right to a settlement of 400 Acres of Land including the said improvement and the preemption of 1000 Acres Adjoining & that a Certificate issue for the same

(Cert D. D. Fees &c pd & cert. D. D.)

George McAfee this day claimed a right to a settlement & preemption to a Tract of Land lying on both sides of Salt River joining the lower side of James McCowns land by improving the same & raising a Crop of Corn in the year 1775 Satisfactory proof being made to the Court they are of Opinion that the s'd McAfee has a right to a settlement of 400 Acres of land including said improvement & a preemption of 1000 Acres Adjoining and that a Cert'e issue for the same

(Cert issued for 1400 fees &c pd & D. D.)

William Adams this day claimed a right to a settlement & preemption to a Tract of Land lying on both sides of Salt River joining the North Side of George McAfee's Land by improving the said land & raising a Crop of Corn at Boons borough in the year 1775 satisfactory proof being made to the Court they are of Opinion that the said Adams has a right to a settlement of 400 Acres including the said improvement & a preemption of 1000 Acres Adjoining and that a Certificate issue for the same

(Cert D. D. to George McAfee for 1400 fees &c pd.)

Sam'l McAfee this day claimed the right to a settlement and preemption to a tract of Land lying on both sides of Salt River joining James McAfees Land by improving the said land & raising a Crop of Corn at Boonsborough in the year 1775 Satisfactory proof being made to the Court they are of Opinion that the said Samuel McAfee has a right to a settlement of 400 Acres of Land including the said improvement & the preemption of 1000 Acres Adjoining & that a Certificate issue for the same.

(Cert issued for 1,000 fees &c pd cert D. D.)

John McGee this day claimed the right to a preemption of 1000 Acres of Land at the State price lying on both sides of Salt River joining the Land of claimed by Sam'l McAfee & Sam'l Adams by improving the said Land in the year 1775 satisfactory proof being made to the Court they are of Opinion that the said John McGee is entitled to a preemption of 1000 Acres of Land including the said improvement and that a certificate issue for the same.—

(Cert issued for 1400. fees &c pd D. D. to Geo'e McAfee)

James Curry this day claimed the right to a settlement & preemption to a Tract of Land lying on both sides of Salt River adjoining the lands of Robt. & Wm McAfee by improving the said land in the year 1775 and raising a crop of corn in the year 1776 satisfactory proof being made to the Court they are of Opinion that the said Curry has a right to a settlement of 400 Acres of land including the said improvement and a preemption of 1000 Acres Adjoining and that a Certificate issue for the same.—

(Cert. issued fees &c pd Cert D. D. to William Adams 1400 Acres).

David Adams this day claimed the right to a settlement and preemption to a tract of land by Virtue of an improvement made on a Tract of Land about ¼ a Mile above Fort Liberty on Salt River & raising Corn in the Country in the year 1776 Satisfactory proof being made to the Court, they are of opinion that the said Adams is intitled to a settlement of 400 Acres of land including said improvement & the preemption of 1000 Acres Adjoining and that a Certificate issue for the same.

(Cert issued for 1400 fees &c pd & D. D. to Colo. Barbour—)

Joseph Early Ass'ee of George Moss this day claimed a right to a settlement & preemption to a Tract of Land lying near the head of Bartons Fork on both sides of the said Moss' improving the said Land & raising a Crop of Corn in the year 1776 satisfactory proof being made to the Court they are of Opinion that the said Early is intituled to a settlement of 400 Acres of Land including the said improvement and a preemption of 1000 Acres Adjoining and that a Certificate issue for the same.

(Cert issued fees &c pd Cert D. D. Wm McAfee 1000)

Sam'l Adams this day claimed a right to a preemption to a Tract of

Land lying on both sides of Salt River joining John McGees Land above by improving the same in the year 1776 satisfactory proof being made to the Court they are of opinion that the said Adams is entitled to the preemption of 1000 Acres including the said improvement at the State price and that a Certificate issue for the same.—

It Appearing to the Court that Wm Jennings as Ass'ee of John Ingram is not entitled to any Land in this Country as the said Ingram was under age at the time of making improvement on the said Land

Then the Court Adjourned untill to Morrow Morning 10 oclock

Wm Fleming—

At a Court Continued & held at Harrodsburg for Adjusting disputed titles to the Kentucky Lands Oct 27th 1779.—

Present

William Fleming Edmund Lyne & James Barbour Esqurs

(Cert. issued for 1400, Fees &c pd Cert D. D.)

Hugh McGary this day claimed a right to a settlement and preemption to a Tract of Land lying about 6 miles from Harrodsburg known by the name of the Shawnee Spring by settling the said Land & raising a Crop of Corn in the year 1776 Benj'n Davis contested the claim by James Harrod & alledged that he the said Davis has a prior Improvement to the said Land Sundry Witnesses were Sworn and examined in the consideration of which the Court are of Opinion that the said McGary has a right to a settlement of 400 Acres of Land, including the said settlement & a preemption of 1000 Acres of Land Adjoining & that a Certificate issue for the same, And that the said McGary have a judgment against the said Davis for Costs.

(Cert issued for 1400. For Abra'm Chaplin fees &c pd D. D. Capt. Harrod—)

Ann Poag & Levi Todd Administrators of the Estate of Wm Poag dec'd this day claimed a right to a settlement and preemption to a tract of Land lying about 4 Miles nearly N. E. from Harrodsburg on the Waters of Shawnee Run including a Sinking Spring by the said Decedent improving the same in the year 1776 Abraham Chaplin contested the Claim by James Harrod & Alledging that He the said Chaplin has a prior improvement on the said Land in the year 1774 Sundry Witnesses were sworn and Examined in consideration of which the Court are of Opinion that the said Chaplin has a right to a settlement of 400 Acres of Land including said settlement and the preemption of 1000 Acres Adjoining and that a Certificate issue for the same and that the said Chaplin recover of the said Adm'nstrs his Costs

(Cert issued for 1400 fees &c pd D. D.)

James Harrod this day claimed a right to a settlement and preemption to a Tract of Land lying on Harrod's Run at a place known by the name of the Boiling Spring by improving the said Land in the year 1774 & raising a Crop of Corn in the Country in the year 1775

& 1776 and has been a resident in the country every since satisfactory proof being made to the Court they are of Opinion that said Harrod has a right to a settlement of 400 Acres of Land including the said improvement & the preemption of 1000 Acres Adjoining & that a Certificate issue for the same.—

(Cert. iss'd for 1400 fees &c pd D. D. to Capt'n Harrod.)

James Harrod this day appeared and claimed a right to a settlement and preemption as Guardian to James McDonald an infant heir at law to James McDonald deceased to a Tract of Land lying at the mouth of Gilberts Creek a branch of Dicks River by the s'd decedent improving the said land in his life time and raising a Crop of Corn in the year 1776 satisfactory proof being made to the Court they are of Opinion that the said James McDonald as Heir at Law to the s'd decedent has a right to a settlement of 400 Acres of Land including the said improvement and the preemption of 1000 Acres Adjoining & that a Certificate issue for the same.—

(Cert issued for 1400 fees &c pd D. D.)

James Berry this day claimed a right to a settlement and preemption to a Tract of Land lying on a Creek called Gilbert's Creek about 1 Mile & a half or two Miles above the fork of the Creek on Dicks River by raising Corn in the Country in the year 1775 whereon there is a Cabbin built and residing here ever since, satisfactory proof being made to the Court they are of Opinion that the said Berry has a right to a settlement of 400 Acres of Land at the above place & a preemption of 1000 Acres Adjoining & that a Certificate issue for the same.

(Cert issued 1000 D. D. George May)

David Finley this day appeared and claimed a right of settlement and preemption to a Tract of Land lying on the N. E. side of Dicks River about 3 or 4 Miles below the mouth of Falling Creek including two small Springs by building a Hut & raising a crop of Corn on the premises in the year 1776. Wm Frazer contested the claim by Joseph Frazer and alledged that the said Frazer has a prior improvement to the said land, sundry Witnesses were sworn & examined in consideration of which the Court are of Opinion that the said Finley has a right only to a preemption of 1000 Acres of Land including said improvement and that a Certificate issue for same and that the said Finley recover of the said Frazer his Costs.—

John Dougherty this day claimed a right to a settlement & preemption to a Tract of Land, the Court being informed that the claim of the Land will be disputed they are of Opinion that the Matter be postponed untill Wm Garrett appears

(Cert issued for 1400 fees &c D. D.)

Richard Hogan this day Appeared & claimed a right to a settlement & preemption to a Tract of Land lying on Cane run about 40? Miles from Harrodsburg by improving the said Land and raising Corn in this Country in the year 1775 satisfactory proof being made to the Court they are of Opinion that the s'd Rich'd Hogan is entitled to a settlement of 400 Acres of Land including s'd settlement & the preemption of 1000 Acres Adjoining & and that a Certificate issue for the same,—

(Cert issued for 1400 fees &c pd D. D.)

Thomas Denton this day Appeared and claimed a right to a settlement and preemption to a tract of Land lying on both sides of Salt River above the Land Claimed by Wm Stewart Known by the name of Rock spring, he having settled in this country and raised Corn in the year 1775 satisfactory proof being made to the Court they are of Opinion that the said Denton has a right to a settlement of 400 Acres including the above mentioned spring & a preemption of 1000 Acres adjoining & that a certificate issued for the same.

(Cert issued for 1400 fees &c pd D. D.)

John Bentley this day appeared and claimed a settlement and preemption to a Tract of Land lying on a branch of the Hanging Fork of Dicks River and joining the land said to be Edward Bulgers on the south side & Stephen Fisher on the North by improving the same and raising a Crop of Corn in the year 1776 satisfactory proof being made to the Court they are of Opinion that the said Bentley has a right to the said 400 Acres of Land including the said improvement & a preemption of 1000 Acres Adjoining & that a Certificate issue for the same.—

(Cert issued for 1400 fees &c pd D. D.)

James Whitley this day claimed a right to a settlement and preemption to a Tract of Land lying at a Sinking Spring about 3 Miles from this place nearly an East course joining Jacob Thomas' land to the South by improving the same in the year 1774 & raising a Crop of Corn in this Country in the year 1776 satisfactory proof being made to the Court they arė of Opinion that the said Whitley is entitled to a settlement of 400 Acres including the said improvement & the preemption of 1000 acres adjoining & that a Certificate issue for the same.—

Mathias Yocum this day claimed a right to a settlement and preemption to a tract of Land about 4 Miles from Harrodsburg lying between John Gordens claim to land & William Poag's former claim by raising Corn in this Country in the year 1776 and improving the same, satisfactory proof being made to the Court they are of Opinion that the said Yocum has a right to settlement of 400 Acres of Land including the above mentioned place & the preemption of 1000 Acres of Land adjoinging said settlement and that a Certificate issue for the same.

Then the Court adjourned untill to Morrow Morning 10 oclock—

William Fleming—

At a Court Continued & held for adjusting disputed titles of the Kentucky Lands at Harrodsburg Oct 28th 1779.—

Present

Wm. Fleming Edm'd Lyne

& Ja's Barbour—Gent-

(Cert issued 400 Acres fees &c pd D. D.

Nich's Merriwether)

Clough Overton this day day claimed a preemption of 400 Acres of Land by

Actual settlement made in the month of May 1779 raising Corn since this time lying on a branch of Salt River about 25 Miles from this place nearly a West Course adjoining the lands said to be claimed by John Glover & Capt Davis satisfactory proof being made to the Court they are of Opinion that said Overton has a right to a settlement of 400 Acres at the state price including the said improvement and that a certificate issue for the same.

(Cert issued for 1400 fees &c pd D. D.)

Williams Combs this day claimed the right to a settlement and preemption to a Tract of Land lying on the waters of Beach Fork of Salt River known by the name of the Cave Spring by residing in this Country for 12 Months before the year 1778, satisfactory proof being made to the Court they are of Opinion that the said Combs has a right to a settlement for 400 Acres of Land including said Spring & a preemption of 1000 Acres Adjoining & that a certificate issue for the same accordingly.

On the motion of Mary Hendericks for a Deddimus' to take the depos'n of Simon Butler† concerning her claim for land in this country Ordered the clerk to issue the same accordingly.—

(Cert issued 1000 fees &c pd Cert D. D. to Geor'e May)

Asael Davis this day claimed a right to a settlement and preemption of a tract of land lying on a Creek which enters into Falling Creek a branch of Dicks River by Virtue of clearing ground and planting Corn on the said place in the year 1776. Witnesses being sworn & examined the Court are of Opinion that the said Davis is only entitled to a preemption of 1000 Acres including the said improvement and that a Certificate issue for the same—

On the motion of Patrick Jordan Ord'd that a Ded's issue to take the deposition of Wm Lane concerning the claim to land in this country by the said Jordan.—

On the motion of Patrick Jorden Heir at Law to Garret Jorden dec'd Ordered that a Ded's issue to take the deposition of Wm Lane Concerning the claim to Land in this Country by the said Patrick Jordan as Heir to the said decedent.—

(Cert Issued for 1400 fees &c pd D. D.)

John Clark this day claimed a right to a settlement and preemption to a tract of land lying on Clarks Run on the road leading from the Boiling Spring to the Knob Lick by improving the same in the year 1774 and residing in the country 12 Months since making the said improvement. Satisfactory proof being made to the Court they are of Opinion that the said Clark has a right to a settlement of 400 acres including the said improvement, & a preemption of 1000 Acres adjoining and that a certificate issue for the same.

(Cert issued for 1400 fees &c pd D. D. to John Cowan)

John Cowan in behalf of James Brown this day claimed a right to a settlement and preemption to a tract of

†Simon Kenton.

land lying on Clarks Run about 1 Mile or 1 and a half Miles above Clarks Station by improving the same in the year 1774 and raising a Crop of Corn on the premises in the year 1776 satisfactory proof being made to the Court they are of Opinion that the said Brown is entitled to a settlement of 400 Acres of land including said improvement & the preemption of 1000 Acres Adjoining and that a Certificate issue for the same.—

(Cert issued for 600 fees &c pd D. D. to Capt. Harrod.)

Thomas Harrod by James Harrod this day claimed a right to a settlement and preemption to a tract of land lying on sinking spring joining the North West side of James Browns land by improving the same & raising a Crop of Corn in the year 1776 satisfactory proof being made to the Court they are of Opinion that the said Thos. Harrod has a right to a settlement of 400 Acres of Land including the said Improvement & a preemption of 200 Acres of Land Adjoining and that a Certificate issue for the same, he declining to take the remainder of his preemption.—

(Cert issued for 1000 fees &c pd Cert. D. D. Silas Harlin)

Elijah Harlin by Silas Harlin this day claimed a right to a preemption of 1000 Acres of land at the State price lying on the Waters of Harrods Run joining on the South side of James Harrods land by building a Cabbin on the same in the year 1774 satisfactory proof being made to the Court they are of Opinion that the said Elijah Harlin has a right to a preemption of 1000 Acres including the said improvement and that a Certificate issue for the same.

(Cert issued for 1400 Cert. D. D. fees &c paid)

Edward Worthington this day claimed a right to a settlement and preemption to a tract of land lying about 6 Miles from this place and nearly a West Course from the same on the dividing ridge of Shawnee Run & Salt River joining the Land of Peter Casey by having the same improved in the year 1774 and residing in the country 12 Month since the said improvement satisfactory proof being made to the Court they are of Opinion that the said Worthington has a right to a settlement of 400 Acres of land including said improvement & the preemption of 1000 Acres Adjoining and that a Certificate issue for the same.

(Cert issued for 1400 fees &c pd D. D.)

Silas Harlen this day claimed a right to a settlement and preemption to a tract of land lying on both sides of Salt River about 3 Miles from the Boiling Spring nearly a West course by improving the same in the year 1774 & raising a Crop of Corn in the year 1775 & residing in the Country ever since satisfactory proof being made to the Court they are of Opinion that the said Harlen has a right to the settlement of 400 Acres of land including the said improvement & the preemption of 1000 acres Adjoining & that a Certificate issue for the same.—

Stephen Trigg - Gent'n this day produced Commission appointing him a

Commissioner in the room of James Steptoe for the purpose of Executing in Conjunction with Wm Fleming Edmund Lyne & James Barbour in Kentucky District the Act for adjusting disputed Titles or Claims of land & was qualified accordingly and took his seat.—

Then the Court Adjourned untill tomorrow 10 oclock

Wm Fleming

At a Court Continued and Held for adjusting Disputed Titles to Lands of Kentucky at Harrodsburg Oct 29th 1779—

Present

Wm Fleming Edmund Lyne James Barbour & Stephen Trigg,

Absent Stephen Trigg, Gen'n.

The Court being informed by James Harrod that the claim laid before this Court by Matthias Yocum the 27th instant was located on a tract of Land which is claimed by John or Parmenus Briscoe prior to the said Yocum for which there was a Cert. ordered to be issued in favor of the said Yocum tho not delivered for the reason above mentioned the Court are of Opinion that the matter be reheard whereupon sundry witnesses were sworn and examined and it Appearing to the Court that the claim to the particular location cannot be Ascertained at this time as Doran agent for the said Briscoe Assee. of Davis Assee. of James Harrod Assee. of Davis who was Assee of John Smith the Original Cabin builder (is not present) it is the Opinion of the Court that the Certificate of Matthias Yocum for this Land in contest should not issue untill a further order of this Court.

(Cert. issued for 1400 fees &c pd. cert. D. D.)

Present

Stephen Trigg, Absent, James Barbour.

John Floyd[7] this day appeared and claimed a right to a settlement and preemption to a Tract of Land lying on 4 Miles Creek 8 Miles North West from Boonesborough including a plantation cleared by the said Floyd called Woodstock & raising Corn on the premises in the year 1776 satisfactory proof being made to the Court they are of Opinion that the said Floyd has a right to a settlement of 400 Acres including the said improvement & the preemption of 1000 Adjoining and that a Cert. issue for the same.—

Present James Barbour, Gen'n.—

(Certificate issue for 1400 fees &c pd Cert D. D.)

George Clarke this day claimed a right to a settlement & preemption to a Tract of Land lying on the waters of Clarks Run it being the same Land where the said Clarke now lives by improving the same in the year 1776 and raising Corn in the Country in the year 1777. satisfactory proof being made to the Court they are of Opinion that the said Clark has a right to a settlement of 400 Acres including the said improvement and the preemption of 1000 Acres Adjoining & that a Certificate issue for the same.—

Edward Worthington Assee of John Brown this day claimed a right to a settlement & preemption to a tract of Land lying on Dyx River—about 2 Miles

[7]Collins, Vol. 1, pp. 249, 250, 258.

from Harmons Lick partly a South West course joining the land said to be claimed by Lewis Holms by the said John Brown improving it in the year 1776 and raising a crop of Corn in the Country satisfactory proof being made to the Court they are of Opinion that the said Worthington Assee &c has a right to a settlement of 400 Acres including the said improvement & the preemption of 1000 Adjoining and that the Certificate should not issue untill further Orders of this Court.—

John Merts Ass'ee of Swethen Polson this day claimed a right to a settlement & preemption to a tract of Land by raising a crop of Corn in the year 1776 It appearing to the Court that it being necessary that the Matter may be fully investigated, the Court are of Opinion that this claim be postponed untill Tuesday the 4th of Nov Next &c, that James McAfee be summoned to Appear before this Court at the time above mentioned.—

V page

Richard Thomas in behalf of the Heirs of John Gabriel Jones dec'd this day claimed a right to a settlement & preemption by raising a crop of Corn in the year 1776 Improving & residence sundry witnesses be sworn & Examined the Court are of Opinion that the Heirs of the said Decedent is entitled to a settlement of 400 Acres of Land & a preemption of 1000 Acres Adjoining The location as Appears to the Court may be contested by Hogan, no Certificate issue untill further Order of this Court

V page

(Cert issued for 1400 fees &c pd D. D. to Capt. McGary)

James Ray this day Claimed a right to a settlement and preemption to a Tract of Land lying on the head of Salt River Known by the name of the big Boiling Spring by improvement made on the premises & raising a Crop of Corn at Harrodsburg in the year 1776 & residing in the country ever since satisfactory proof being made to the Court they are of Opinion that the said Ray is entitled to a settlement of 400 Acres including the said improvement & the preemption of 1000 Acres of Land Adjoining and that a Certificate issue for the same.

(Cert issued for 1000 fees &c pd. Cert D. D. to Silas Harlen)

Isaac Taylor by Silas Harlen this day claimed a right of preemption to a Tract of Land lying on both sides of Salt River joining on the North side of said Silas Harlens Land by building a Cabin on the said Land in the year 1774 satisfactory proof being made to the Court they are of Opinion that the said Isaac Taylor is entitled to a preemption of 1000 Acres of Land including the said improvement & that a Certificate issue for the same.

(Cert issued for 1400 fees &c p'd D. D.)

James Leaper this day claimed a right to a settlement and preemption to a tract of Land lying on the Waters of Wheatleys Creek about Six Miles from St. Asaphs and near Wheatleys Station by improving the same and raising a Crop of Corn in the year 1775 & 1776 satisfactory proof being made to the

Court they are of Opinion that the said Leaper has a right to a settlement of 400 Acres of Land including the said improvement & the preemption of 1000 Acres Adjoining & that a Certificate issue for the same.

Then the Court adjourned untill to Morrow Morning 10 oclock

William Fleming—

At a Court Continued & held for Adjusting disputed Titles to the Kentucky Lands at Harrodsburg the 30th of Oct. 1779

Present

William Fleming Edmund Lyne James Barbour & Stephen Trigg Gent'en

(Cert issued for 1400 fees &c pd D. D.)

Samuel Pickens this day claimed a settlement & preemption to A Tract of Land lying on the East Side of Mill Creek a branch of Salt River whereon there is a Cabbin built, by residing in this Country Twelve Months before the year 1778 and continuing in the Country ever since satisfactory proof being made to the Court they are of Opinion that the said Pickens has a right to a settlement of 400 Acres including the said improvement & the preemption of 1000 Acres Adjoining & that a Certificate issue for the same.—

William McBride this day claimed a right to a settlement and preemption to a Tract of Land lying on a large Spring that empties into Harrods Run on the North side of the said Run about 5 Miles from Harrodsburg by improving the same &c raising a Crop of Corn in the year 1776 satisfactory proof being made to the Court they are of Opinion that the said McBrid has a right to a settlement of 400 Acres including the said improvement & the preemption of 1000 Acres adjoining and that a Certificate issue accordingly.

Absent, Will'm Fleming—Gent'n

(Cert. for 400 fees &c pd D. D. to Silas Harlin)

James Harlin this day claimed a right to a preemption of 400 Acres of Land at the State price to a tract of Land lying on the Waters of Cane Run joining the Lands of James Wily to the East including a large Spring by improving the same and raising a Crop of Corn in the Country this present year satisfactory proof being made to the Court they are of Opinion that the said Harlen has a right to a preemption of 400 Acres including the said spring & and that a Certificate accordingly

(Cert issued for 1000)

John Howard this day claimed a right to a preemption of 1000 Acres of Land at the State price lying on the North side of Kentucky including his improvement at the mouth of Harrods Creek to extend up the Creek and Westward for quantity by improving the same in the year 1775 satisfactory proof being made to the Court they are of Opinion that the said Harrod has a right to a preemption of 1000 Acres of Land including the said improvement and that a Certificate issue accordingly.

Present William Fleming Gentl'n

(Cert issued for 1400 fees &c pd to Wm Triggs)

William Glasby by John Floyd this day claimed a right to a settlement & preemption to tract of Land lying on the West Branch of Boons Creek about 3 or 4 Miles and due South of the said John Floyds tract called Woodstock joining two hundred Acre Tract of Colo. Logans and on the West side of the tract of 1000 Acres of William Madisons by improving the same & raising a Crop of Corn in the County in the year 1775 satisfactory proof being made to the Court they are of Opinion that the said Glassby is entitled to a Settlement of 400 Acres of Land including the said improvement & the preemption of 1000 Acres adjoining & that a Certificate issue accordingly.—

(Cert issued for 1400 fees &c pd)

James Knox this day claimed a right to a settlement & preemption to a tract of Land lying on the Waters of Beargrass Creek to include a large Spring joining the Lands of South hall & Charlton about 254 poles from the South East Corner of their Land by marking the said Land & raising a Crop of Corn in the year 1775 in this country satisfactory proof being made to the Court they are of Opinion that the said Knox is intitled to a Settlement of 400 Acres of Land including the said Spring & the preemption of 1400 Adjoining & that a Certificate issue accordingly.

(Cert for 1400 iss'd by Order of Court at Bryants Station fees &c pd D. D.)

James Parbery Ass'ee of Elijah Este this day claimed a right to a settlement & preemption to a tract of Land lying on Green Creek a branch of Licking joining the Land claimed by John Gordon & John Grayson by improving the same & raising a Crop of Corn in the Country in the year 1775 satisfactory proof being made to the Court they are of Opinion that the said Parbery is entitled to a settlement of 400 Acres of Land including the said improvement & the preemption of 1000 Acres adjoining & that a Certificate shall not be issued untill a further Order of this Court

(Cert iss'd for 1400 by Order of Court at Bryants fees &c pd D. D.)

James Parbery Ass'ee of Bottom Estis this day claimed a right to a settlement & preemption to a tract of Land lying on Green Creek a branch of Licking joining the land granted to the said Parbery this day by improving the same and raising a Crop of Corn in the year 1775. in this Country satisfactory proof being made to the Court they are of Opinion that the said Parbery has a right to a settlement of 400 Acres of Land including said improvement and the preemption of 1000 Acres adjoining & that a Cert. do not issue untill further Order of the Court—

(Cert Iss'd for 1000 fees &c pd D. D. to Lewis Craig)

William Lane this day claimed a right to a preemption of 1000 Acres of Land at the State price lying on the North Fork of Elkhorn about 1 or two Miles above the Fork below the Survey of Land made for Patrick Henry on the

West side thereof by Building a Cabbin & clearing 3 Acres of Land on the premises in the year 1775 satisfactory proof being made to the Court they are of Opinion that the said Lane has a right to a preemption of 1000 Acres of Land including the said improvement & that a Cert issue accordingly.

John Boyd the surveyor was present and declared that he believed that the said Land was not surveyed by virtue of a Warrant to his Knowledge

(Cert iss'd for 1000 fees &c pd D. D. to Lewis Craig)

Patrick Jordon this day claimed a right to a preemption to a tract of Land at the State price lying on the North side of the North Fork of Elkhorn on the waters of the first branch along the Large Buffaloe road that goes through Patrick Henrys first survey, by building a Cabbin & improving the said Land by deadening Timber &c in the year 1775 satisfactory proof being made to the Court & the surveyor being present they are of Opinion that the said Jorden has a right to a preemption of 1000 Acres including the said improvement & that a Cert. issue accordingly.—

(Cert Issued for 1000 fees &c pd D. D. to Lewis Craig)

Garrott Jorden by Patrick Jorden this day claimed a right to a preemption to a tract of Land lying on the North side of the North Fork of Elkhorn on the waters of the first branch along the large Buffaloe road that goes thro'h Patrick Henrys first survey above the said Patrick Jordens claim by building a Cabbin and making other improvements by deadening &c in the year 1775 Satisfactory proof being made to the Court & the surveyor present they are of Opinion that the said Garrott Jorden has a right to a preemption of 1000 Acres including the said improvement & that a Cert issue accordingly

James McCown Jun'r this day claimed a right to a settlement & preemption lying on both sides of Salt River about 8 Miles below his Fathers Land and about 4 Miles below William Adams Land by improving & raising a Crop of Corn in the year 1776 Satisfactory proof being made to the Court they are of Opinion that the said McCown Jun'r has a right to a Settlement of 400 Acres including the above mentioned Land & the preemption of 1000 Acres Adjoining & that a Cert. issue accordingly

Absent Wm Fleming Gen'n

Daniel Higgins heir at Law to John Higins deceased this day claimed a right to a settlement & preemption to a tract of Land lying on chaplins Fork by the said decedents improving the same & raising a Crop of Corn in the year 1776 satisfactory proof being made to the Court they are of Opinion that the said Dan'l Hogans has a right to a settlement of 400 Acres of Land including the said improvement & the preemption of 1000 Acres of Land Adjoining No Cert to issue untill the further Order of this Court.—

(Cert iss'd for 1400 fees &c pd Cert D. D.)

Ben'j Linn this day claimed a right to a settlement & preemption to a tract of Land lying on the North side of

Green River in the Fork of a Creek about 40 Miles from this place and 12 from Pottengers Cabbin on the Roling fork near 35 Miles South of Bulletts Salt Lick by improving the same and residing in this Country ever since the year 1776 satisfactory proof being made to the Court they are of Opinion that said Lin has a right to a settlement of 400 Acres of Land including the said improvement & the preemption of 1000 Acres Adjoining & that a Cert issue accordingly

Present Wm Fleming Gent'n

(Cert iss'd for 400 fees &c pd D. D. to Pal M Lee)

John McCoun this day claimed a right to a settlement to a tract of Land on the East side of George McAfees land on a branch of Salt River joining the said McAfees Land by improving the same & raising a Crop of Corn in the year 1775 Satisfactory proof being made to the Court they are of Opinion that the said McCoun has a right to a settlement of 400 Acres of Land including the said improvement & that a Cert issue accordingly he declining to claim his preemption.—

Then the Court Adjourned untill to Morrow Morning 10 oclock

William Fleming—

At a Court held & Continued for Adjusting disputed Titles to the Kentucky Lands at Harrodsburg this First day of Nov'r 1779

Present

Stephen Trigg Edmund Lyne & James Barbour Gent'n

(Cert Iss'd for 1400)

John Cowan this day claimed a right to a settlement & preemption to a tract of Land lying on the Ohio Opposite the first Island above Harrods Creek by raising Corn in the Country in the year 1774[8] & 1776 & Marking out the said place satisfactory proof being made to the Court they are of Opinion that the said Cowan has a right to a settlement of 400 Acres including the above mentioned Land & the preemption of 1000 Acres adjoining and that a Certificate issue accordingly.

(Cert iss'd for 1400 fees &c pd Cert D. D.)

John Hawkins Ass'ee of Dan'l Turner this day claimed a right to a tract of Land lying on the East branch of Hickmans Creek joining the Land said to be claimed by Walter Overton & about 2½ Miles from John Todds improvment by the said Turner marking the said Land & building a Cabbin in the year 1776 & residing in the Country ever since. Satisfactory proof being made to the Court they are of Opinion that the said Hawkins has a right to a settlement of 400 Acres of Land including the said above mentioned Cabbin & the preemption of 1000 Acres adjoining & that a Cert'e issue accordingly.

(Cert. Iss'd for 1400 fees &c pd D. D. to Capt. Harlen)

Silas Harlen attorney for Hamond Consillia this day claimed a right to a settlement & preemption to a tract of Land lying on the Waters of Salt River on the East Fork by improving the same

[8]First claim of corn being raised as early as 1774.

Land in the year 1775 & residing in the Country twelve Months since satisfactory proof being made to the Court they are of Opinion that the said Consilia has a right to a settlement of 400 Acres of Land including the said improvement & the preemption of 1000 Acres Adjoining & that a Cert issue accordingly.—

(Cert Iss'd for 1000 fees &c pd. cert D. D.)

John Larue this day claimed a right to a preemption to a tract of Land lying in the fork of Barsheirs's Creek about 10 Miles from the Mouth the two first letters of the said Larues name cut on the log of the house above the door, and all the rest of his Company in the year 1776 Satisfactory proof being made to the Court they are of Opinion that the said LaRue has a right to a preemption of 1000 Acres to include the said Cabbin and that a Certificate issue accordingly—

(Cert iss'd for 1000 fees &c pd Cert D. D.)

John Larue Guardian to Phebe Larue the Heir of Sam'l Larue dec'd. this day claimed a right of preemption to a tract of Land of 1000 Acres lying on a branch of a small Creek that runs into the Kentucky withe the first letters of Natha'l Randles name cut on a Tree at a spring near a Cabbin built by the said Decedent in the year 1776 satisfactory proof being made to the Court they are of Opinion that the said Phebe Larue has a right to the preemption of 1000 Acres including the said Cabbin & that a Cert. issue accordingly.

(Cert iss'd for 1400 fees &c pd D. D.)

James Willy Exec'r of the last Will & testament of Richard Castleman dec'd this day claimed a settlement & preemption in behalf of William Castleman Jun'r an infant to a tract of Land devised to the said infant by the said Decedent lying on Brashier's Creek a branch of Salt River joining the Lands of Sam'l Pottenger by improving the said Land and raising a Crop of Corn in this Country in the year 1776 Satisfactory proof being made to the Court they are of Opinion that the said William Castleman has a right to a settlement of 400 Acres of Land including the said improvement & the preemption of 1000 Acres adjoining & that a Cert. issue accordingly.—

(Cert iss'd for 1400 fees pd D. D.)

Jacob Coffman this day claimed a settlement & preemption to a tract of Land lying on Hammons Creek joining the Lands said to be claimed by one bailly (?) on the South West by Settling the said Land & raising a Crop of Corn in the year 1776 satisfactory proof being made to the Court they are of Opinion that the said Coffman has a right to a settlement of 400 Acres including the said settlement & the preemption of 1000 Acres Adjoining & that a Cert issue accordingly.—

(Cert Iss'd for 1400 fees &c pd D. D.)

James Parberry this day claimed a settlement & preemption to a tract of Land lying on a branch of the North Fork of Elkhorn about 4 or 5 Miles from Bryants Station with the two first letters of the said Parberrys name cut on a Tree at a Spring by making an improvement & raising a Crop of Corn in the Country in the year 1776 Satisfactory proof being made to the Court they are of Opinion that the said Parberry has a right to a settlement of 400 Acres of Land including the said improvement & the preemption of 1000 Acres Adjoining & that a Cert issue accordingly.—

(Cert Iss'd for 1400)

Jonathan Martin this day claimed a settlement & preemption to a tract of Land lying on a branch of 4 Mile Creek South course from Mr Floyds tract called Woodstock by marking the said Land & raising a Crop of Corn in the year 1776 Satisfactory proof being made to the Court they are of Opinion that the said Martin has a right to a settlement of 400 Acres of Land including the above mentioned Land & the preemption of 1000 Acres adjoining & that a Cert issue accordingly.—

Elizabeth Johnson for and in behalf of Wm White an infant Heir at Law to Charles White dec'd this day made it Appear by Testimony that the said Wm White is entitled to a settlement & preemption in this Country by the said decedents raising a Crop of Corn in the year 1776.

Then the Court adjourned untill to Morrow Morning 10 oclock.

William Fleming.

At A Court continued & held for adjusting disputed Titles to the Kentucky Lands at Harrodsburg the 2nd day of Nov 1779.—

Present

Stephen Trigg Edmund Lyne & James Barbour Gen'n

(Cert iss'd for 1400 fees &c pd D. D. to Colo. James Barbour)

Lewis Craig[9] Attorney for John King this day claimed a right to a settlement & preemption to a tract of Land lying on Muddy Creek about 12 Miles from Boonesborough near a South East course where there is the two first letters of the said Kings name cut on a tree by marking the same in the year 1778 & residing in the Country ever since the year 1775 Satisfactory proof being made to the Court they are of Opinion that the said King has a right to a settlement of 400 Acres including the Land above mentioned & the preemption of 1000 Adjoining and that a Cert issue accordingly.

(Cert iss'd for 1400 fees &c pd D. D.)

Edward Hammond this day claimed a right to a settlement and preemption to a tract of Land lying on the Waters of the Rolling Fork below the South Fork about 3 quarters of A Mile by settling in the year 1777 & residing in the Country ever since Satisfactory proof being made to the Court they are of Opinion that the said Hammond has a right to 400 Acres of Land including his settlement & the preemption of 1000 Acres Adjoining & that a Cert issue accordingly.—

(Cert iss'd for 1400 fees &c pd D. D.)

James Hays this day claimed a settlement & preemption to a tract of Land lying on both sides of Salt River joining the lower side of James Rays Land by settling & raising a Crop of Corn in the year 1776 Satisfactory proof being made to the Court they are of Opinion

[9] Collins, Vol. 1, pp. 416, 420, 515.

that the said James Hays has a right to a settlement of 400 Acres including the said improvement and the preemption of 1000 Adjoining & that a Cert'e issue accordingly.—

Then the Court adjourned untill to morrow Morning 10 oclock

Stephen Trigg

At a Court held & Continued for adjusting disputed titles to the Kentucky Lands at Harrodsburg this 3d day of November 1779

Present

Stephen Trigg. Edmund Lyne & James Barbour Esq'r Gent

(Assigned to Craig &c cert issued for 1400 by order of Court)

John Evans this day claimed a settlement & preemption to a tract of Land lying on the South fork of Elkhorn joining Mary Frazers Land on the South side by settling in this Country in the year 1777 and residing in the Country ever since satisfactory proof being made to the Court they are of Opinion that the said Evans has a right to a settlement of 400 Acres of Land including the above mentioned Land & the preemption of 1000 Acres adjoining no Cert'e issue until further Order of this Court.

(Cert iss'd for 1400 by Order of Court at Bryants)—

John Shelp this day claimed a settlement & preemption to a Tract of Land lying on the Middle Fork of Licking about 3 Miles East of Harrods Lick joining above the Lands said to be claimed by James Sadusky by improving the same & raising a Crop of Corn in this Country in the year 1775 Satisfactory proof being made to the Court they are of Opinion that the said Shelps has a right to a Settlement of 400 Acres of Land including the said improvement & the preemption of 1000 Adjoining No Cert. to issue untill further Order of this Court.—

Roger Top Ass'ee of Thomas Gibson this day claimed a settlement & preemption to a tract of Land Lying on the Waters of Hickman Creek a branch of the Kentucky River 7 or 8 Miles from John Todd settlement on a branch of the said Creek known by the Name of Plumb Run about 9 Miles below the head Spring of the said Run by the said Gibsons improving the Land in the year 1776 & residing in the Country 12 Months since Satisfactory proof being made to the Court they are of Opinion that the said Top as Ass'ee has a right to a settlement of 400 Acres including the said improvement & the preemption of 1000 Acres of Land Adjoining No Cert to issue untill further Order of this Court.—

(Cert Issued for 1400 fees &c pd D. D. to L. Craig)

Elijah Craig[10] Ass'ee of John Marts who was Ass'ee of Swethen Paulson this day claimed a settlement & preemption to a tract of Land lying on the Dry Fork of Salt River above the Lands claimed by Thomas Barton by the said Paulson improving the same & raising a crop of Corn in the year 1776 satis-

[10]Collins, Vol. 1, pp. 407, 417, 516, 542.

factory proof being made to the Court, they are of opinion that the said Craig Ass'ee &c has a right to a settlement of 400 Acres of Land including the said improvement & the preemption of 1000 Acres adjoining & that a Certificate issue accordingly.— The claim of Land by John Marts before this Court is on the 29 Inst is dismissed.—

(Cert iss'd for 1400 fees &c pd D. D. to Capt. Wathington)

Edward Wathington Exo'r of Arch'd McNeil Deceased this day claimed a settlement & preemption to a tract of Land in behalf of Peggy McNeil which was devised to her by the last Will & Testament of the decedent lying on the Waters of Clarks Run joining the Land of James Brown, James Blair & Samuel Gibbons by the said decedents improving the same in the year 1775 & residing in the Country 12 Months before the year 1778 satisfactory proof being made to the Court they are of Opinion that the said Peggy McNeil has a right to a settlement of 400 Acres including the said improvement & the preemption of 1000 Acres Adjoining & that a Certificate issue accordingly.—

Edw'd Wathington, in behalf of Dan'l Wealen & James Finn motioned to the Court to examine Witnesses touching the claim of the said Whealens & Finn in consideration of which the Court are of Opinion that the said Whealen and Finn has each of them a right to a settlement & preemption.

(Cert iss'd for 1400 fees &c pd D. D. to Captn. Wathington)

Edward Wathington in behalf of Andrew Coil this day claimed a settlement & preemption to a tract of Land lying on the Waters of Dicks River about 4 Miles from where the trace crosses, a Cabbin stands, on the East side of a branch to include the said Cabbin by Settling in the Country in the year 1777 & residing in the Country 12 Months since, satisfactory proof being made to the Court they are of Opinion that the said Coil has a right to a settlement of 400 Acres & the preemption of 1000 Adjoining & that a Cert. issue accordingly

(Cert iss'd for 1400 by Order of Court at Bryants—)

George Timmerman this day claimed a right to a settlement & preemption to a tract of Land lying on Licking Creek on the south side of Hinsons Fork about 1½ Miles from a Lick on the said Hinsons Fork by improveing the same and settling in the year 1777 and residing in the Country ever since, satisfactory proof being made to the Court they are of Opinion that the said Timmerman has a right to a settlement of 400 Acres of Land including the said improvement & the preemption of 1000 Adjoining no Certificate to issue untill further Order of this Court.

Then the Court adjourned untill tomorrow Morning 10 oclock

Stephen Trigg

At a Court Continued & held for adjusting disputed titles to the Kentucky Lands at Harrodsburg the 4th November 1779—

Present

Will'm Fleming, Stephen Trigg, Edmund Lyne—Gent'n

(Cert iss'd for 400 fees & pd D. D. to Colo. Smith)

George Scott this day claimed a preemption of 400 Acres of Land at the State price lying on clear Creek a branch of Dicks River below Esael Davis's improvement about 1 Mile down the Creek by settling in March 1779 and improving the said Land, satisfactory proof being made to the Court they are of Opinion that the said Scott has a right to a preemption of 400 including the said improvement and that a Certificate issue Accordingly—

(Cert iss'd for 1400 fees &c pd Cert D. D.)

John Bunton this day claimed a settlement & preemption to a tract of Land lying on Cane between the waters of the said Run & Harrods Creek joining on the South East side by Rich'd Hogan's Land at a Sinking Spring by the said Bunton's settling in the year 1777 & residing in the Country 12 Months since satisfactory proof being made to the Court they are of Opinion that the said Bunton has a right to 400 Acres including said settlement & the preemption of 1000 Acres adjoining & that a Certificate issue accordingly.—

(Cert iss'd for 400—)

Henry Boughmen Heir at Law to Jacob Boughman dec'd this day claimed a settlement & preemption to a Tract of Land lying on Dicks River on the North side about 2 Miles above the Mouth of Gilberts Creek by the said Decedents settling on the premises & raising a crop of Corn in the year 1775 satisfactory proof being made to the Court they are of Opinion that the said Henry Boughman has a right to a settlement of 400 Acres including the said settlement & that a Cert'e issue accordingly—he refusing to Claim the preemption. page.

Henry Boughman this day claimed a right to a settlement & preemption to a tract of Land. Posponed to be heard at Boonesborough.—

Uriel Mallery & Lewis Craig Ass'ee of Bartlett Searcy this day claimed a settlement & preemption to a tract of Land lying on the Waters of Kentucky on a small branch on the North side the River about 1 Miles from the said River at a Spring called Rock House by the said Searcy marking the same, settling at Boonesborough the first day of August 1777 & residing in the Country ever since, his claim

Bartlett Searcy in behalf of Rich'd Searcy this day claimed a settlement & preemption to a tract of Land, the claimant withdraws his claim.—

(Cert iss'd for 1400 fees &c pd D. D.)

Lewis Craig Ass'ee of Jonathan Jennings this day claimed a right to a settlement & preemption to a tract of Land lying on the East side of Silver Creek beg'ng 1/ a mile above the Land said to be claimed by Harts running up the said Creek for quantity by the said Jennings settling at Boonesborough & raising a crop of Corn in the year 1775 satisfactory proof being made to the Court they are of Opinion that the said Craig has a right to a settlement of 400 Acres including the above mentioned Location & the preemption of 1000 Acres adjoining & that a Certificate issue accordingly

Rueben Searcy this day claimed a right to a preemption of 400 Acres of Land at the State price lying on &c the claimant withdraws his claim

(Cert iss'd for 1400 fees &c pd D. D.)

Henry Field Ass'ee of Ambrose Coffer this day claimed a settlement & preemption to a tract of Land lying on the Waters of Licking on the road from Boonesborough to the Salt Spring by residing in the Country ever since the year 1775 and improving the said land in the year 1777 satisfactory proof being made to the Court they are of Opinion that the said Field has a right to a settlement of 400 Acres including the said improvement & the preemption of 1000 Acres adjoining & that a Cert issue accordingly.—

(Cert iss'd for 1400 fees &c pd D. D.)

Henry Field Ass'ee of Lawrence Smith this day claimed a settlement & preemption to a tract of Land lying on Deals Run a branch of Licking about 6 or 7 Miles West of Stones's Settlement by the said Smiths raising a crop of Corn in the Country in the year 1776 satisfactory proof being made to the Court they are of Opinion that the said Fields has a right to a settlement of 400 Acres including the above mentioned Land & the preemption of 1000 Acres adjoining & that a Certificate issue accordingly.

Present

James Barbour Gen'n

(Cert iss'd for 400 fees &c pd D. D.)

Henry Fields Ass'ee of Charles Lockharts this day claimed a preemption of 400 Acres of Land at the State price lying on the Western branch of Otter Creek about eight miles from Boonesborough by the said Lockharts settling the same in the year 1779 in the month of January—Satisfactory proof being made to the Court they are of Opinion that the said Fields has a right to a preemption of 400 Acres to include the said settlement and that Certificate issue accordingly.

(Cert iss'd for 1400 fees &c pd cert D. D.)

John Doughardy this day claimed a settlement & preemption to a tract of Land lying on the Waters of Dicks River known by the name of The Locust Thickett by settling on the said place & raising a crop of corn in the year 1776 John Cowan in behalf of David Cowan Heir at Law to James Cowan Deceased came into Court & Alledged that the said Decedent made a prior improvement on the Land & that he raised a crop of Corn in this Country in the year 1774 Whereupon sundry Witnesses were sworn & Examined of which the Court are of Opinion that the said Dowardy has a right to a settlement of 400 Acres of Land including the said improvement & the preemption of 1000 Acres adjoining & that a Certificate issue accordingly.

John Cowan in behalf of David Cowan Heir at Law to James Cowan

Deceased this day made it Appear to the Court that the said David Cowan is entitled to a settlement & preemption by the said Decedents raising a crop of Corn in this Country in the year 1774—

(Cert iss'd for 1000 fees &c pd D. D.)

Andrew Woods Jun'r this day claimed a preemption to a 1000 Acres of Land at the State price lying at the mouth of Hawkins's branch on the South West side of Dicks River by improvement made on the said Land in the year 1775 satisfactory proof being made to the Court they are of Opinion that the said Woods has a right to a preemption of 1000 Acres of Land including the said improvement & that a Certificate issue Accordingly.—

Absent
Stephen Trigg Gen'n

(D. D. to Stephen Trigg)

John Gorden this day claimed a right to a settlement & preemption to a tract of Land lying on the Waters of Shawnee Run, Known by the Name of pleasant Fields it being Land that was settled by the said Gorden who raised Corn on the premises in the year 1776 Satisfactory proof being made to the Court, they are of Opinion that the said Gorden has a right to a settlement of 400 Acres including the said settlement & the preemption of 1000 Adjoining & that a Certificate issue accordingly.—

(Cert iss'd for 1400 fees &c pd D. D. Stephen Trigg)

John Grayson this day claimed a right to a settlement & preemption to a tract of Land lying on the waters of Cain Run joining the Lands of James Willys by improving the same & raising a Crop of Corn in this Country in the year 1775 satisfactory proof being made to the Court they are of Opinion that the said Grayson has a right to a settlement of 400 Acres including said improvement & the preemption of 1000 Acres adjoining & that a Certificate issue for the same accordingly.—

Then the Court adjourned untill to Morrow Morning 10 oclock.

William Fleming

At a Court continued & held for adjusting disputed titles to the Kentucky Lands at Harrodsburg the 5th of Nov 1779—

Present
William Fleming—Stephen Trigg—
& Edmund Lyne Gent'n

Walter Overton this day claimed by Clough Overton a settlement & preemption to a tract of Land on the East Fork of Hickmans Creek, John Todd Attorney for Martin Hawkins contested the matter whereon sundry Witnesses were sworn & Examined in consideration of which the Court are of Opinion that the said Overtons claim be rejected.—

Mary Hendricks this day claimed a right to a settlement and preemption to a tract of Land lying in the district by settling in the Country in May 1776 and residing in the Country ever since, Satisfactory proof being made to the Court they are of Opinion that the said Mary Hendricks has a right to a settlement of 400 Acres of Land adjoining this place or as convenient upon waste or unappropriated Lands & the preemption of 1000 Acres of Land Adjoining her said settlement, the Court has thought proper to reconsider the above judgment.—

(Cert iss'd for 1400 fees &c pd D. D. to Capt.'n Fields)

Robert Slaughter Jun'r Heir at Law to Thomas Slaughter Dec'd this day claimed a right to a settlement & preemption to a tract of Land lying on the Shawnee Run about a Mile North East of chaplains Cabbin by the said Decedents settling & raising a Crop of Corn on the premises in the year 1776 satisfactory proof being made to the Court they are of Opinion that the said Slaughter Jun'r has a right to a settlement of 400 Acres including the said improvement & the preemption of 1000 Acres Adjoining & that Cert issue accordingly

(Cert iss'd for 1000 fees &c pd D. D. to Cap't Mallery)

John Fields this day claimed a preemption of 1000 Acres of Land at the state price lying on the West side of the south Fork of Licking above the Mouth of Stoners Fork by the said Fields building a Cabbin on the said Land in the year 1776 satisfactory proof being made to the Court they are of Opinion that the said Fields has a right to a preemption of 1000 Acres including the said Cabbin & that a Certificate issue accordingly.—

(Cert iss'd for 1400 fees &c pd D. D.)

Elizabeth Stevens[11] this day claimed a right to a settlement and preemption to a tract of Land lying on a branch of the East Fork of Licking on the head of a Run called Summers Run by residing in the Country ever since the year 1776 satisfactory proof being made to the Court they are of Opinion that the said Elizabeth Steavens has a right to a settlement of 400 Acres of Land including the above location & the preemption of 1000 adjoining & that a Certificate issue accordingly.—

(Cert iss'd for 1400 fees &c pd D. D. to Sam'l Davis)

Samuel Scotts this day claimed a right to a settlement & preemption to a tract of Land lying on the North side of Dicks River on a dry branch by the said Scotts raising a Crop of Corn in the Country in the year 1775 satisfactory proof being made to the Court they are of Opinion that the said Scotts has a right to a settlement of 400 Acres of Land including the said location & the preemption of 1000 Acres adjoining & that a Certificate issue accordingly

(Cert iss'd for 400 fees &c pd D. D. to Capt Hugh McGary)

James Smith this day claimed the right to a preemption of 400 Acres of Land at the State price lying on the East side of Dicks River on a branch near a Sinking Spring by the said Smiths making an actual settlement on the premises the first of March 1779 satisfactory proof being made to the

---

[11]First certificate issued to a woman on her own claim of settlement.

Court they are of Opinion that the said Smith has a right to a preemption of 400 Acres including the above settlement & that a Certificate issue accordingly.

(Cert iss'd for 1400 fees &c pd D. D. to Hugh McGary)

Henry Dougherty this day claimed a right to a preemption of 400 Acres of Land lying on a branch White Oak North East of James Smiths claim a branch of Dicks River by the said Dougherty making an actual settlement in the Month of April 1779 satisfactory proof being made to the Court they are of Opinion that the said Dougherty has a right to the preemption of 1000 Acres including the s'd settlement & that a Certificate issue accordingly.

(Cert iss'd for 400 fees &c pd Cert D. D.)

James Patton this day claimed a right to 400 Acres of Land at the State price lying on Slate Creek a branch of Licking at an Old Indian Town by the said Pattons marking an actual settlement in the year 1778 satisfactory proof being made to the Court they are of Opinion that the said Patton has a right to a preemption of 400 Acres of Land including the said settlement & that a Certificate issue accordingly.—

Then the Court adjourned untill tomorrow Morning 10 oclock

William Fleming

At a Court Continued & held for the County of Kentucky adjusting disputed titles to the Kentucky Lands at Harrodsburg 6th of November 1779

Present

Stephen Trigg Edmund Lyne
& James Barbour Gent'n

John Evans came into Court and acknowledged that the Certificate granted him the 3d Inst should issue in the name of Lewis Craig & that Uriel Mallory as Ass'ee of him.—

(Cert iss for 1000 fees &c paid D. D.)

Thomas Grant this day claimed a preemption to 1000 Acres of Land at the State price lying on Salt River about 2 Miles above Fort Liberty & likewise above Dentons Land by the said grants improving the same in the year 1775 Satisfactory proof being made to the Court they are of Opinion that s'd Grant has a right to a preemp'n of 1000 Acres of Land to include the above improvement. & that a Certificate issue accordingly.—

(Cert iss'd for 1000 fees &c pd D. D.)

John Patterson this day claimed a right to a preemption of 1000 Acres of Land at the State price lying on the Hanging Fork of Dicks River including a Field cleared by Mr. Clark by the said Pattersons building a Cabbin on the premises in the year 1775 satisfactory proof being made to the Court they are of Opinion that the said Patterson has a right to a preemption of 1000 Acres including the said improvement & that Certificate issue accordingly.

(Cert iss'd for 1400 fees &c pd D. D. to Hugh McGary)

John Reed this day claimed a right to a settlement & preemption to a tract of Land lying on a branch of Dicks River about 2 Miles from the Knob Lick lying on the road from this to Logans by raising a Crop of Corn on the premises in the year 1776 satisfactory proof being made to the Court they are of Opinion that the s'd Reed has a right to a settlement of 400 Acres including the said improvement & the preemption of 1000 Acres adjoining & that a Certificate issue accordingly

(Cert iss'd for 1000 fees &c pd D. D. Hugh McGary)

William Warrand this day claimed a right to a settlement & preemption to a tract of Land lying on a branch of Dicks River about a mile from the Knob Lick by improving the same in the year 1776 Whereupon Witnesses were sworn & examined in consideration of which the Court are of Opinion that the said Warrand has a right to a preemption only of 1000 Acres including the said improvement & that a Certificate issue accordingly.—

(Cert iss'd for 400 fees &c pd D. D. to Hugh McGary)

James Davis this day claimed a preemption of 400 Acres of Land at the State price lying on wheatlys Creek on the West side of said Wheatleys by settling in March 1779 satisfactory proof being made to the Court they are of Opinion that the said Davis has a right to a preemption of 400 Acres of Land including the s'd settlement & that a Cert issue accordingly.—

On the motion of Ezeriah Davis to put a stop to the survey of Land which Robert McAfee made for it Appearing to the Court that the survey about to be made is contested & the s'd McAfee being summonsed & failing to Appear & there being no Sheriff present to enforce the Order of this Court, therefore ordered that the surveyor do not survey the same untill a further Order of this Court & that a copy of this Order be immediately sent to the surveyor—

Thomas Rowland Ass'ee to Mordeci Reed who was Ass'ee to John Love this day claimed a right to a settlement & preemption to a tract of Land by the said Love raising a Crop of Corn in this Country in the year 1776 satisfactory proof being made to the Court they are of Opinion of that the said Rowland has a right to a settlement & preemption.—

The judgment of this Court yesterday concerning the claim of M Hendricks was reheard today the Court are of Opinion that the judgment be confirmed.

(Cert iss'd for 1400 fees &c pd D. D. to D. Brown)

Dan'l Brown this day claimed a settlement & preemption to a tract of Land lying on Cartrights Creek a branch of Salt River about 4 or 5 Miles above the Mouth of said Creek by settling in the Country in the year 1776 and continuing there 12 Months since satisfactory proof being made to the Court they are of Opinion that the said Brown has a right to a settlement of 400 Acres of Land the preemption of 1000 adjoining & that a Certificate issue accordingly.

(Cert iss'd for 1400 fees &c pd D. D. to D. Brown)

Dan'l Brown this day claimed a settlement & preemption to a tract of Land in behalf of the Heirs of Burr Harrison Deceased lying at a sinking spring about 2 Miles South of the Knob Lick on the path that leads to Gordens Lick by the said Decedents improving the same & raising a Crop of Corn in the Country in the year 1776 satisfactory proof being made to the Court they are of Opinion that the Heirs of the said Decedent have a right to a settlement of 400 Acres of land including the said improvement & the preemption of 1000 Adjoining & that a Certificate issue accordingly.—

(Cert iss'd for 1400 fees &c pd D. D. to R. Thomas)

Richard Thomas this day claimed a settlement & preemption to a tract of Land lying on a branch of the South Fork of Elkhorn whereon the said Thomas built a good Cabbin & made other improvements & raising a crop of Corn in the year 1776 satisfactory proof being made to the Court they are of opinion that the s'd Thomas has a right to a settlement of 400 Acres including the said improvement & the preemption of 1000 Acres adjoining & that a Certificate issue accordingly.

(Cert issued for 1400 fees &c pd D. D. to R. Thomas)

It being proved to the Court the 29th Oct. that the Heirs of John Gab'l Jones dec'd has a right to a settlement & preemption to a tract of Land (tho not located) lying on the Waters of Dicks River about 3½ Miles East of Boiling Spring where Major Harrods has laid his settlement joining Clarks Land ordered that a Certificate issue accordingly.

(Cert iss'd for 1400 fees &c pd D. D. to Hugh McGary)

It being proved to this Court that Mary Hendricks has a right to a settlement & preemption to a tract of Land (tho did not locate it) now comes into Court & lays it on the Town Fork of Salt River about twenty Miles above Bullitts Lick joining the Lands said to be claimed by Dan'l Wheallen & Ordered that a Cert. issued.

(Cert iss'd for 400 fees &c pd D. D. to Hugh McGary)

Joseph Davis this day claimed a right to a preemption of 400 Acres of Land at the State price lying on the Waters of Paint Lick known by the name of the Walnut Meadow by a settlement made in March 1779 satisfactory proof being made to the Court they are of Opinion that the said Davis has a right to a preemption of 400 Acres including the said settlement & that a Certificate issue accordingly.

(Cert iss'd for 400 fees &c pd D. D. to Hugh McGary)

Samuel Davis this day claimed a right to a preemption to a tract of Land at the state price lying on the south side Wheatleys fort joining a place called Gilmore's Lick by making an actual settlement in March the year 1779, satisfactory proof being made to the Court they are of Opinion that the said

Davis has a right to a preemption of 400 Acres including the said improvement & that a Certificate issue accordingly.

(Cert iss'd for 400 Fees &c pd D. D. to Hugh McGary)

George Givens this day claimed a preemption of 400 Acres of Land at the State price lying & being on the West side of Knobs Lick fork adjoining the lands of Isaac Shelby on the West & James Brown on the North East by mak'g and Actual settlement in March 1779 satisfactory proof being made to the Court they are of Opinion. that the said Givens has a right to a preemption of 400 Acres of Land including the said settlement & that a Certificate issue accordingly.

(Cert iss'd for 1400 fees &c pd D. D. to Hugh McGary)

William Wheatley this day claimed a settlement & preemption to a tract of Land lying on Cedar Creek west of the Crab Orchard about 3 Miles from the said Wheathley Station by improving the same & raising a Crop of Corn in the year 1776 satisfactory proof being made to the Court they are of Opinion that the said Wheathley has a right to a settlement of 400 Acres of Land including the said improvement & the preemption of 1000 Acres adjoining & that a Certificate issue accordingly.—

(Cert iss'd for 1400 fees &s pd D. D. to M. McAfee)

David Robinson this day claimed a settlement & preemption to a tract of Land lying on Boons Creek adjoining a Survey of the said Robinsons by raising Corn in the Country in the year 1776 satisfactory proof being made to the Court they are of Opinion that the said Robinson has a right to a settlement of 400 Acres of Land & the preemption of 1000 Acres & that a Certificate issue accordingly.

(Cert iss'd for 1400 fees &s pd D. D. to Capt'n Levi Todd)

David Bell Ass'ee of Levi Todd this day claimed a settlement & preemption to a tract of Land lying on the East branch of Hickmans Creek joining the lands said to be claimed by John Todd, satisfactory proof being made to the Court they are of Opinion that the said Bell has a right to a settlement of 400 Acres including his improvement & the preemption of 1000 Acres by improving the same & by raising a Crop of Corn in the year 1776 & that a Certificate issue accordingly.

(D D to Captn Levi Todd)

John Todd Jun'r by Levi Todd this day claimed a settlement & preemption to a tract of Land lying on the head of the West branch of Hickmans Creek by the name of Mansfield by improving the same & raising a Crop of Corn in the year 1776 satisfactory proof being made to the Court they are of Opinion that the said John Todd Jun'r has a right to a settlement of 400 Acres of Land including the said improvement & the preemption of 1000 Adjoining, & that a Certificate issue accordingly.

(Cert iss'd for 1400 fees &c pd D. D. to Capt'n Levi Todd)

Levi Todd Adm'r of Elijah Beathy dec'd this day claimed a settlement &

preemption to a tract of Land lying on the South Fork of Elkhorn joining Rich'd Thomas on the South West by the said decedents settling in the Country in the year 1776 and residing in the Country twelve Months since satisfactory proof being made to the Court they are of Opinion that the Heirs of the said Beathy have a right to a settlement of 400 Acres of Land & the preemption of 1000 Acres adjoining & that a Certificate issue accordingly.

(Cert iss'd for 1000 fees &c pd D. D. to Capt. Levi Todd)

John Todd Sen'r[12] this day claimed a settlement & preemption to a tract of Land lying on the West branch of Hickmans Creek Joining the Lands claimed by Rob't Todd on the North East by the said Todds improving the same & building a Cabbin on the premises in the year 1776 satisfactory proof being made to the Court they are of Opinior that the said Todd has a right to a pre emption of 1000 Acres only, at the State price and to include the said improvement & that a certificate issue accordingly.

(Cert iss'd for 1400 fees &c pd D. D.)

Enoch Smith this day claimed a settlement & a preemption to a tract of Land lying near the head of Hinkstons Fork of Licking Creek on the West side of a Creek called small mountain Creek by improving the same & raising a Crop of Corn in the year 1775 & 1776 satisfactory proof being made to the Court they are of Opinion that the said Smith has a right to a settlement of 400 Acres including the said improvement & the preemption of 1000 acres adjoining & that a Certificate issue accordingly.—

(Cert iss'd for 1400 fees &c pd D. D. to E. Smith)

John Lane this day claimed a right to a settlement & preemption to a tract of Land lying on the dividing ridge between the head of the North Fork Lulbel Grood & the head of Hickstons Fork to include the Waters of Lulbul Grood & Hinkstons fork by the said Lanes raising a Crop of Corn in the Country in the year 1776 satisfactory proof being made to the Court they are of Opinion that the said Lane has a right to a settlement of 400 Acres of Land & the preemption of 1000 Acres & and that a Certificate issue accordingly.

(Cert iss'd for 1000 fees &c pd D. D. M. McGee)

William Robinson this day claimed a right to a small tract of Land lying on both side of Boons Creek joining the lands of David Robinson including a tract marked for the said Wm Robinson in the year 1775 by improving the said Land in the year 1775 satisfactory proof being made to the Court they are of Opinion that the said Robinson has a right to a preemption of 1000 Acres including the above improvement & that a Certificate issue accordingly.—

(Cert iss'd for 1400 fees pd D. D. to Hugh McGary)

Andrew Johnson this day claimed a right to a settlement & preemption to a tract of Land lying on Cartrights Creek

---

[12]Collins, Vol. 1, pp. 19, 20, 250, 256 and index.

on the South East side of said Creek by the said Johnsons improving the same & raising a Crop of Corn in the year 1776 satisfactory proof being made to the Court they are of Opinion that the said Johnson has a right to a settlement of 400 Acres of Land including the said improving & the preemption of 1000 Adjoining & that a Certificate issue accordingly.

(Cert iss'd by order of Court for 1400 fees &c pd D. D. to James Crockett)

Andrew Crockett Ass'ee of James Patrick this day claimed a settlement & preemption to a tract of Land lying on the mouth of Drake Camp Creek where it empties into Dicks River by the said Patricks improving the same & raising a Crop of Corn in the year 1776 satisfactory proof being made to the Court they are of Opinion that the said Crockett has right to a settlement of 400 Acres of Land including the said settlement & the preemption of 1000 Acres Adjoining & that no Certificate issue untill further Order of this Court.

(Cert iss'd for 1000 fees &c pd D. D. to Geo May)

Benj'n Blackburn this day claimed a preemption of 1000 Acres of Land at the State price lying on Cannons Run a branch of the South Fork of Elkhorn by the said Blackburn building a Cabbin on the premises in the year 1776 satisfactory proof being made to the Court they are of Opinion that the said Blackburn has a right to a preemption of 1000 Acres of Land including the s'd Cabbin not to interfere with Shannons improvement & that a Certificate issue accordingly.—

(Cert, iss'd for 1400 fees &c pd D. D.)

It was proved to this Court at Asaphs that Wm Logan was entitled to a settlement & preemption in this district came into Court and located the said Land lying on clarks Run joining John Doughertys to the West whereon there is a Cabbin built to include the said Cabbin & that a Certificate issue accordingly.

(Cert iss'd for 1000 fees &c pd D. D.)

Hugh Logan this day claimed a preemption to 1000 Acres of Land at the State price lying West from the little Flat lick on the Waters of Hanging Fork about 3½ Miles So. of St. Asaphs by improving the same in the year 1776 satisfactory proof being made to the Court they are of Opinion that the said Logan has a right to a preemption of 1000 Acres to include such improvement & and that a Certificate issue accordingly.

Ordered that the former order of this Court with regard to the dispute between Robt. McAfee & Ezeriah Davis be set aside the said McAfee agreeing that his land should not go near the said Davises Cabbin than 400 yds and that the surveyor be acquainted therewith.—

On the Motion of Benj. Logan Ass'ee of Robert & Thompson Sayers who was Ass'ee of Fred'k Off (?) to have ded's granted to have depos taken concerning a claim of the said Logan Ass'ee &c ordered that dede's issue accordingly.

Then the Court adjourned to the Falls of Ohio untill the 15th Inst.

At a Court held at the falls of Ohio for adjusting disputed titles to the Kentucky Lands on tuesday the 16th of Nov'r 1779.—

Present

William Fleming Stephen Trigg

Edmund Lyne & Jas Barbour Gent

(Cert iss'd for 1400 fees &c pd D. D.)

Edward Murray this day claimed a settlement & preemption to a tract of Land lying at the Mouth of Murrays Run a branch of the Town Fork of Salt River on both sides of the said Run & up the same for quantity by improving the same in the year 1776 & residing in the Country 12 Months since the year 1778 satisfactory proof being made to the Court they are of Opinion that the said Murray has a right to a settlement of 400 Acres of Land including the said improvement & the preemption of 1000 Acres adjoining & that a Certificate issue accordingly.—

(Cert iss'd for 1400 fees &c pd D. D.)

William Berchiers Heir at law to Joseph Berchiers deceased this day claimed a right to a settlement & preemption to a tract of Land lying in the Fork of Floyds Fork & the Town Fork of Salt River about 3½ Miles above the Mouth of Floyds Fork by the said decedents improving the same & raising a Crop of Corn in the year 1776, satisfactory proof being made to the Court they are of Opinion that the said Wm Berchiers has a right to a settlement of 400 Acres of Land including the said improvement & the preemption of 1000 adjoining & that a Certificate issue accordingly.—

(Cert iss'd for 1400 fees &c pd D. D.)

Marsham Brashear this day claimed a settlement & preemption to a tract of Land lying on the waters of Salt River joining the Land of Wm Brashear as Heir at Law to Joseph Brashear dec'd by improving the same in the year 1776 & raising Corn satisfactory proof being made to the Court they are of Opinion that the said Brashear has a right to a settlement of the said 400 Acres of Land & the preemption of 1000 Adjoining & that a Certificate issue accordingly.—

Absent William Fleming Gent'n

(Cert iss'd for 1400 fees &c pd D. D.)

Evan Hinton this day claimed a right to a settlement & preemption to a tract of Land lying on Brashears Creek on a Run Called Fox Run by improving the same & raising a Crop of Corn in the Country in the year 1776 satisfactory proof being made to the Court they are of Opinion that the said Hinton has a right to settlement of 400 Acres of Land including the said improvement & the preemption of 1000 adjoining & that a Certificate issue accordingly.—

Sam'l Moore this day claimed a settlement & preemption to a tract of Land lying on the North side of the Knob Lick including Half the said Lick by improving the same in the year 1776 & residing in the Country 12 Months before the year 1778 satisfactory proof being made to the Court they are of Opinion that the said Moore has a right to a settlement of 400 Acres of Land including the said improvement & the preemption of 1000 Acres adjoining & that a Certificate issue accordingly.—

Present Wm Fleming Gentleman
(Cert iss'd for 400 fees &c pd D. D.)
William pope this day claimed a right to a preemption of 400 Acres of Land at the State price lying on the lower end of the Brushy pond including part of the said pond upon an actual settlement since the year 1778 satisfactory proof being made to the Court they are of opinion that the said Pope has a right to a preemption of 400 Acres including the said improvement & that a certificate issue accordingly.

(Cert iss'd for 400 Acres fees &c pd D. D.)
William Pope Ass'ee of John Sanders this day claimed a preemption of 400 Acres of Land at the State price lying on brushy pond Creek by the said sanders making an actual Settlement since the 1st day of Jan'y 1778 satisfactory proof being made to the Court they are of Opinion that the said pope has a right to a preemption of 400 Acres of Land including the said settlement & that the certificate issue accordingly.

(Cert iss'd for 400 fees &c pd D. D.)
William Pope Ass'ee of Mathew Jones this day claimed a preemption to 400 Acres of Land lying on Brush pond Creek joining the said popes claim as Ass'ee of John Sanders by the said Jones making an actual settlement since the 1st day of Jan'y 1778 satisfactory proof being made to the Court they are of Opinion that the said Pope has a right to a preemption of 400 Acres of Land including the said settlement and that Certificate issue accordingly.

(Cert iss'd for 400 fees &c pd D. D.)
William Pope Ass'ee of Nich's Smith this day claimed a preemption of 400 Acres of Land at the State price lying the Brush pond joining above the claim of the said Smiths by making an actual settlement since the 1st day of Jan'y 1778 satisfactory proof being made to the Court they are of Opinion that the said pope has a right to a preemption of 400 Acres of Land including the said settlement & that a Certificate issue accordingly.

Then the Court adjourned untill tomorrow Morning 10 oclock
William Fleming

At a Court continu'd & held at the Falls of Ohio for adjusting disputed titles to the Kentucky Lands the 17th day of Nov'r 1779
Present
Stephen Trigg Edmund Lyne & James Barbour Gent'n

(Cert iss'd for 1400 fees &c pd D. D.)
Margarett Pendegrass this day claimed a right to a settlement & preemption to a tract of Land lying on Bresheirs Creek about 8 Miles below the head of said Creek on the South side by improving the same in the year 1777 and residing 12 Months since her Settlement satisfactory proof being made to the Court they are of Opinion that the said Margarett Pendegrass has a right to a settlement of 400 Acres including the s'd improv't & the preemption of 1000 Adjoining & that a Certificate issue accordingly.

(Cert iss'd for 1400 fees &c pd D. D. to Colo. Clark)

Robt Elliott by Colo. George Rogers Clark this day claimed a settlement & preemption to a tract of Land lying on the North side Brashiers's Creek about 3 Miles below the head of the said Creek by settling in the year 1775 & continuing in the Country 12 Months since the said settlement satisfactory proof being made to the Court they are of Opinion that the said Alliott has a right to a settlement of 400 Acres of Land to include the said settlement & the preemption of 1000 Adjoining & that a Certificate issue accordingly.

(Cert iss'd for 1400 fees &c pd D. D.)

Edward Holdman this day claimed a settlement & preemption to a tract of Land lying on the head Spring of Bucks Run the next branch below Grears Creek by improving the same in the year 1775 & raising Corn in the Country in the year 1776 satisfactory proof being made to the Court they are of Opinion that the said Holdman has a right to a settlement of 400 Acres including the said improvement & the preemption of 1000 Acres adjoining & that a Certificate issue accordingly.

(Cert iss'd for 400 fees pd D. D. to Peter Sturgus)

James Asturgus this day claimed a preemption to a tract of Land of 400 Acres at the State price lying on the first Waters of Floyds Fork on the old trace that leads from this to Harrodsburg by making an actual settlement in April in the year 1779—satisfactory proof being made to the Court they are of Opinion that the said Asturgus has a right to a preemption of 400 Acres of Land including the said settlement & that a Certificate issue accordingly.

(Cert iss'd for 400)

Archebald Lockhard this day claimed a preemption of 400 Acres of Land at the State price lying near the head of Hardens Creek joining a tract claimed by Wm Harden by making an actual settlem't in the Month of April 1779 satisfactory proof being made to the Court they are of Opinion that the said Lockhard has a right to a preemption of 400 Acres of Land including the s'd settlement & that a Certificate issue accordingly.

(Cert iss'd for 1000 fees & pd D. D. made out a copy)

Simpson Moore this day claimed a preemption of 1000 Acres of Land at the State price lying on the Waters of Shawnee Run about 2 Miles North of the Shawnee spring on the road that leads to Harrods Landing by building a Cabbin on the premises in the year 1776 satisfactory proof being made to the Court they are of Opinion that the said Moore is entitled to a preemption of 1000 Acres to include said improvement & that a Certificate issue accordingly.

(Cert iss'd for 400 fees &c pd D. D. R. Pope)

Jacob Shilling this day claimed a preemption of 400 Acres of Land at the State price lying near Clarks Station Known by the name of the round spring by making an actual settlement in the Month of may 1779 satisfactory proof being made to the Court they are of Opinion that the said Shilling has a right to a preemption of 400 Acres of Land to include the said settlement & that a Certificate issue accordingly.

On Motion of Wm. Swan ordered that a Ded's issue to take the deposi'ns of Margaret Pendegrass & John Porter touching his Claim to Lands in this Country.

(Cert iss'd for 1400 fees &c pd)

George Clear this day claimed the right to a settlement & preemption to a tract of Land lying on Floyds Fork of Salt River known by the name of Mulberry Spring by settling in the Country in the year 1776 & residing ever since satisfactory proof being made to the Court they are of Opinion that the said Clear has a right to a settlement of 400 Acres of Land including the above mentioned spring & the preemption of 1000 Acres adjoining & that a Certificate issue accordingly.

(Cert iss'd for 1400 fees &c pd)

Jesse Pendergrass Heir at Law to Garrett Pendergrass deceased this day claimed a settlement & preemption to a tract of Land lying on the Kentucky River about 5 Miles from the Mouth on the North side thereof where there is a large Hickory Bottom by the said Decedents improving the same & raising a Crop of Corn in the year 1776 satisfactory proof being made to the Court they are Opinion that the said Pendergrass has a right to a settlement of 400 Acres including the said improvement & the preemption of 1000 Adjoining & that a Certificate issue accordingly.

Thomas Hughs this day claimed a preemption of 400 Acres of Land at the State price lying: the Claimant withdraws his claim.

(Cert iss'd for 400 fees &c pd D. D.)

Daniel Meredith this day claimed a preemption to a tract of Land of 400 Acres at the State price lying on the Waters of Hardens Creek joining the lands of Wm Harden and Joseph Toby by making an Actual settlement in the month of May 1779 satisfactory proof being made to the Court they are of Opinion that the said Meredith has a right to 400 Acres of Land including such settm't & that a Certificate issue accordingly.

Then the Court adjourn'd untill untill to Morrow Morning 10 oclock.

Stephen Trigg

At a Court Continued & held for adjusting disputed Titles to the Kentucky Lands at the Falls of Ohio this 18th of Nov.'n 1779.

Present

Stephen Trigg, Edmund Lyne & James Barbour Gen't

(Cert iss'd for 1400 fees &c pd D. D. to J. Douglas)

Benj. Logan & James Douglass Ass'ee of Robt. & John Thompson Sayers who was ass'ee of Fred'k Off this day claimed a settlement & preemption to a tract of Land lying on Beargrass joining on the Upper Corner of James Knoxes Land by raising a Crop in the Country in the year 1776 satisfactory proof being made to the Court they are of Opinion that the said Logan &c is entitled to a settlement of 400 Acres of Land to include the above location & the preemption of 1000 Acres of Land Adjoining & that a Certificate issue accordingly.

(Cert iss'd for 400 fees &c pd D. D.)

John Faith Heir at Law to Wm Faith dec'd by Eliza Faith this day claimed a preemption of 400 Acres of Land at the State price lying at Sinking spring on the South side of the south Fork of Beargrass About 13 Miles from this place by the said decd' making an actual settlement in the year 1778 satisfactory proof being made to the Court they are of Opinion that the said John Faith has a right to a preemption of 400 Acres of Land to include the said settlement & that a Certificate issue accordingly.

(Cert iss'd for 1400 fees &c pd D. D. to Geo. R. Clark)

Leonard Helm[13] by Colo. George Rogers Clark this day claimed a settlement & preemption to a tract of Land lying on a branch of Jessemine Creek a branch of Kentucky about 3 Miles from the Mouth of the said Creek, by the said Helms improving the same in the year 1776 and residing in this Country 12 Months since, satisfactory proof being made to the Court they are of Opinion that the said Helms has a right to a settlement of 400 Acres of Land including the said improvement & the preemption of 1000 Acres adjoining & that a Certicate issue accordingly.

(Cert iss'd for 1400 fees &c pd D. D. to Mr. Randolph)

Richard Rue by Colo. George Rogers Clark this day claimed a right to a settlement & preemption to a tract of Land lying on the head Waters of Drenings Lick Creek by the said Rue's improving the same & building a Cabbin &c in the year 1776 and residing in the Country ever since satisfactory proof being made to the Court they are of Opinion that the said Rue has a right to a settlement of 200 Acres of Land including the said improvement & the preemption of 1000 Acres adjoining & that a Certificate issue accordingly.

(Cert iss'd for 400 fees &c pd D. D.)

Thomas Carter this day claimed a preemption of 400 Acres of Land at the State price lying on the Waters of Rolling Fork of Salt River joining the Land of John Beausarus by an actual settlement made in the month of May 1779. Satisfactory proof being made to the Court they are of Opinion that the said Carter has a right to a preemption of 400 Acres of Land including the said settlement & that a Certificate issue accordingly.—

(Cert iss'd for 1400 fees &c pd D. D.)

Peter Sturgus this day claimed a settlement & preemption to a tract of Land lying on hammons Creek the waters of Salt River joining the Lands of Jacob Coughman on the South East by improving the same in the year 1776 & raising a Crop of Corn in the Country in the year 1776 satisfactory proof being made to the Court they are of Opinion that the said Sturgus is entitled to a settlement of 400 Acres of Land including the said improvement & the preemption of 1000 Acres adjoining & that a certificate issue accordingly.

[13] Collins, Vol. 1, p. 19.

(Cert. iss'd for 400 fees &c pd D. D.)

John McManess this day claimed a preemption of 400 acres of land at the State price lying on the North branch of the South Fork of Beargrass about 3 Miles above the Sinking Spring where Faiths claim is made by actual settlement made in the year 1778 satisfactory proof being made to the Court they are of Opinion that the s'd McManess has a right to 400 Acres of Land to include s'd settlem't & that a Cert'e issued accordingly.—

(Cert Iss'd for 1400 fees &c pd D. D. to Mr. Pendergrass)

William Woodard this day claimed a Settlement & preemption to a tract of Land lying on the waters of Breasheirs's Creek about 4 or 5 Miles below the 3 Forks of the s'd Creek a branch of Salt River, by improving the same in the year 1776 & residing in the Country 12 Months before the year 1778 satisfactory proof being made to the Court they are of Opinion that the said Woodard has a right to a settlement of 400 Acres of Land to include said improvement & the preemption of 1000 Adj'og & that a Certi issue accordingly.

(Cert iss'd for 1000 fees &c pd D. D. to Wm Bard)

James Carroll by Wm Bard this day claimed a preemption of 1000 Acres of Land at the State price lying on the head of Benson Creek a branch of Kentucky by improving the same & building a Cabbin in the year 1775 satisfactory proof being made to the Court they are of Opinion that the said Carroll has a right to a preemption of 1000 Acres to include the said improvement & that a Certificate issue accordingly.

(Cert iss'd for 1000 fees &c pd D. D. to Wm Bard)

James Hall by Willi'm Bard this day claimed a preemption of 1000 Acres of Land at the State price lying on the head of Fox Run a branch of Breasheirs Creek a branch of Salt River by the s'd Halls improving the same by building a Cabbin in the year 1776 satisfactory proof being made to the Court they are of Opinion that the said Hall has a right to a preemption of 1000 Acres to include the s'd improvement & that a Certificate issue accordingly.

(Cert iss'd for 1400 fees &c pd D. D.)

George Smith claimed a right to a settlement & preemption of a tract of Land lying on the Waters of Harrods Run joining to Capt. Harrod on the North West by improving the same & raising a Crop of Corn in the year 1776 satisfactory proof being made to the Court they are of Opinion that the said Smith has a right to a settlement of 400 Acres of Land including the s'd improvement & a preemption of 1000 Acres adjoining & that a Certificate issue accordingly.

(Cert iss'd for 1400 fees &c pd D. D. to Mr. Randolph)

Jonathan Keekam by Nath'l Randolph this day claimed a settlement & preemption to tract of Land lying on the South Side of the Town Fork of Salt River about 2 Miles above Floyds Fork by improving the same in the year 1776 & residing in the Country ever since satisfactory proof being made to the

Court they are of Opinion that the said Keeham has a right to a settlement of 400 Acres of Land to include the said improvement & the preemption of 1000 Acres adjoining & that a Certificate issue accordingly.

(Cert iss'd for 1400 fees &c pd D. D.)
James McCauley this day claimed a settlement & preemption to a tract of Land lying on Fish pool Creek about 2 Miles West of the Fish pools by improving the same & residing in the country ever since the year 1776 satisfactory proof being made to the Court they are of Opinion that the said McCowley has a right to a settlement of 400 Acres of Land including the said improvement & the preemption of 1000 Acres adjoining & that a Certificate issue accordingly.

(Cert iss'd for 1000 fees etc. pd D. D. to Mr Bulger)
Isaac Keller this day claimed a preemption of 1000 Acres of Land at the State price about 12 Miles up Elkhorn above the Mouth on the South side thereof by improving the same & building a Cabbin in the year 1776 satisfactory proof being made to the Court they are of Opinion that the said Keller has a right to a preemption of 1000 Acres including the said improvement & that a Certificate issue accordingly.

Joseph Waller this day claimed a preemption to 400 Acres of Land at the State price.—withdrawn—

(Cert iss'd for 1400 fees &c pd D. D.)
John Porter this day claimed a settlement and preemption to a tract of Land lying on Brasheirs Creek about 6 Miles from the head thereof joining the land claimed by Squire Boone below by improving the same in the year 1776 and residing in the Country ever since satisfactory proof being made to the Court they are of Opinion that the said Porter has a right to a settlement of 400 Acres of Land to include the said settlement & the preemption of 1000 Acres adjoining & that a certificate issue accordingly.

Then the Court adjourned until to Morrow Morning 10 oclock

Stephen Trigg.—

At a Court Continued and held for adjusting disputed Titles to the Kentucky Lands at the Falls of Ohio this 20th of Nov'r 1779—

Present

Stephen Trigg, Edmund Lyne & James Barbour Gent'n

(Cert issd for 400 fees &c pd D. D. to B. Pope)
John Tuel by James Patoone this day claimed a preemption of 400 Acres of Land at the State price lying on the head of a branch of Green River on the North side thereof about 4 Miles East of the head of Hardens Creek a branch of the Ohio by making an actual settlement in the year 1778 satisfactory proof being made to the Court they are of Opinion that the said Tuel has a right to a preemption of 400 Acres of Land including the said improvement & that a Certificate issue accordingly.—

Benj' Pope this day proved to the Court that he is entitled to a preemption of 400 Acres at the State price.—

(Cert issd for 1400 fees &c pd by order of Court at Bryants)
Christopher Clark Assee of

John Soverns this day claimed a settlement & preemption to a tract of Land lying on a branch of the East Fork of licking Creek about 4 Miles from the head about 5 or 6 Miles from the head of Gists Creek to include a small Deer lick by improving the same in the year 1775 and residing in the Country ever since the year 1776 Satisfactory proof being made to the Court they are of Opinion that the said Soverns has a right to a settlement of 400 Acres to include the said settlement and preemption of 1000 Acres of Land Adjoining No Certificate issue untill the further Order of this Court.—

(Cert issd for 1000 fees &c pd D. D.)

John Townsend this day claimed a settlement and preemption to a tract of Land lying on a branch of Licking Creek known by the name of Townsends fork about 3 Miles from Redills (Riddles?) Fort by making an actual settlement in the year 1775 & raising a Crop of Corn on the premises satisfactory proof being made to the Court they are of Opinion that the said Townsend has a right to a settlement of 400 Acres of Land to include the said settlement & the preemption of 1000 Acres adjoining & that a Cert. issue accordingly.

(Cert issd for 400 fees &c pd D. D. to J. Pattoone)

Neal Dougharty this day claimed a preemption of 400 Acres of Land at the State price lying on the drain 2 Miles above the flat lick about 11 Miles from this place by making an actual settlement in the year 1778 satisfactory proof being made to the Court they are of Opinion that the said Dougharty has a right to a preemption of 400 Acres to include such settlement and that a Certificate issue accordingly.—

(Cert issd for 1400 fees &c pd D. D.)

John Martin this day claimed a settlement & preemption to a tract of Land lying on the south fork of Licking Creek on the South side thereof about 5 Miles from Riddes Station with the letters IM on a Tree at a small spring by improving the same and raising a Crop of Corn in the year 1775 and residing in the Country ever since satisfactory proof being made to the Court they are of Opinion that the said Martin has a right to a settlement of 400 Acres of Land—including the said improvement & the preemption of 1000 Acres adjoining and that a Certificate issue accordingly—

(Cert issd for 400 fees &c pd D. D.)

Henry French this day claimed a preemption of 400 Acres of Land at the State price lying on the head of a small branch of Brasheirs's Creek a branch of Salt River about ½ Mile below the Trace from this to Harrodsburg by making an actual settlement in the year 1778 satisfactory proof being made to the Court they are of Opinion that the said French has a right to preemption of 400 Acres to include such settlement and that a Certificate issue accordingly

Present Wm Fleming Gent'n

(Cert issd for 1400 fees &c pd D. D.)

George Rogers Clark[14] this day claimed a settlement & preemption to a tract of Land lying at Drenings Lick to include the said Lick by improving the same and raising a Crop of Corn on the premises in the year 1776 & residing in the Country 12 Months satisfactory proof being made to the Court they are of Opinion that the said Clark has a right to a settlement of 400 Acres of land including the said improvement & the preemption of 1000 Acres adjoining & that a Certificate issue accordingly.—

Abs't J. Barbour Gent

(Cert issd for 1400 fees &c pd D. D.)

Edward Wathington for and in behalf of Patrick Callagham this day claimed a settlement & preemption to a Tract of Land lying on the North side of the South Fork of Licking about 2 Miles below Riddles Station by the said Callagham improving the same in the year 1775 & raising a Crop of Corn in the same year satisfactory proof being made to the Court they are of Opinion that the said Callagham has a right to a settlement of 400 Acres including including the said improvement & the preemption of 1000 Acres Adjoining and that a Cert. issue accordingly.

Present James Barbour Gent.—

(Cert issd for 1400 fees &c pd D. D. to M. Pendergrass)

Margret Pendergrass for an in behalf of James Elliott this day claimed a settlement & preemption to a tract of Land lying on the first large Run that empties into Kentucky above Cedar Creek on the Opposite side by the said Elliotts improving the same & residing in the Country 12 Months before the year 1778 satisfactory proof being made to the Court they are of Opinion that the said Elliott has a right to a settlement of 400 Acres of Land to include the said improvement & the preemption of 1000 Acres adjoining and that a Certificate issue accordingly—

(Cert iss for 1000 fees &c pd D. D.)

Edward Wathington for & in behalf of Dan'l Callagham this day claimed a settlement & preemption to a tract of Land lying on the North side of the South Fork of Licking about One Mile below Riddles Station by actual settlement made and raising a Crop of Corn on the premises in the year 1775 satisfactory proof being made to the Court they are of Opinion that the said Callagham has a right to a settlement of 400 Acres of Land to include such settlement & the preemption of 1000 Adjoining & that a Certificate issue accordingly.—

(Cert iss for 400 fees &c pd D. D.)

John Dorme this day claimed a preemption of 400 Acres of Land at the State price lying on a branch of Kentucky near Drenings lick & near a place called New Market by making an actual settlement in the Month of May 1779 satisfactory proof being made to the Court they are of Opinion that the s'd Dorme has a right to a preemption of 400 Acres of Land to include the said settlement and that a Certificate issue accordingly.—

[14]Collins, Vol. 1, p. 18 and index.

(Cert iss for 1000 fees &c pd D. D.)
William Lynn this day claimed a preemption of 1000 Acres of land at the State price lying on the South side of licking Creek known by the name of the Big Blue Lick to include the said Lick lying in a short bend of the said Creek by improving the same in the year 1775 by building a Cabbin on the premises satisfactory proof being made to the Court they are of Opinion that the said Lynn has a right to a preemption of 1000 Acres of land to include to said improvement & that a Certificate issue accordingly.—

(Cert issd for 1000 fees &c pd D. D.)
Andrew Lynn by Wm Lynn this day claimed a preemption of 1000 Acres of land at the State price lying on the Most North Easterly branch of Hinktons Fork of Licking about 5 or 6 Miles above the Mouth of said branch where there is a remarkable large Bend at the Mouth by improving the same & building a Cabbin on the premises in the year 1775 satisfactory proof being made to the Court they are of Opinion that the said Lynn has a right to a preemption of 1000 Acres to include the said improvement and that a Certificate issue accordingly.—

(Cert iss for 1000 fees &c pd D. D.)
Thomas Clark this day claimed a preemption to 1000 Acres of Land at the State price lying about 5 Miles North of And'w Lynn's claim on the head of a branch of Licking Creek by the said Clarks improving the same & building a Cabbin on the premises in the year 1775 satisfactory proof being made to the Court they are of Opinion that the said Clark has a right to a preemption of 1000 Acres to include the said improvements and that a Certificate issue accordingly.—

(Cert issd for 400 fees &c pd D. D.)
William Chineath this day claimed a preemption of 400 Acres of land at the State price lying on the South fork of Pottengers Creek a branch of the Rolling Fork of Salt River about 4 Miles above Pottengers Cabbin by making a actual settlement in the Month of May 1779—satisfactory proof being made to the Court they are of Opinion that the s'd Chineath has a right to a preemption of 400 Acres of Land to include such settlement & that a Certificate issue accordingly.—

(Cert issd for 400 fees &c pd D. D.)
Thomas Philips this day claimed a preemption of 400 Acres of Land at the State price lying on the Waters of Floyd Fork of Salt River on the Trace from this to Babbetts Salt Lick about 8 Miles from the said Lick by actual settlement made in May 1779 satisfactory proof being made to the Court they are of Opinion that the said Philips has a right to a preemption of 400 Acres of Land to include the said Settlement and that a Certificate issue accordingly.—

(Cert issd for 400 fees &c pd D. D.)
Andrew Hines this day claimed a preemption of 400 Acres of Land at the State price lying on the Waters of Green River about 12 Miles from Benj'n Lynn's land partly a North West

Course by making an actual settlement in the Month of May 1779 Satisfactory proof being made to the Court they are of Opinion that the said Hines has a right to a preemption of 400 Acres of Land including the said settlement & that a Certificate issue accordingly.—

(Cert iss for 400 fees &c pd D. D. Capt'n pope)

Henry Floyd this day claimed a preemption to 400 Acres of land at the State price lying on the South side of the Brushy pond about 13½ Miles from this place joining the upper side of Capt' Pope's Land by making an actual settlement in the Month of May 1779 satisfactory proof being made to the Court they are of Opinion that the said Floyd has a right to a preemption of 400 Acres of Land to include such settlement & that a certificate issue accordingly.—

(Cert issd for 400 fees &c pd D. D.)

James Delany this day claimed a preemption of 400 A's of Land at the State price lying on the Waters of Floyds Fork about 3 Miles East from a big Flat lick at the head of Beargrass by making an Actual settlement in the Month of May 1779 satisfactory proof being made to the Court they are of Opinion that the said Delany has a right to a preemption of 400 Acres of land to inclcde the said Settlement & that a Certificate issue accordingly.—

(Cert iss for 400 Acres fees &c pd D. D.)

Jacob Vanmeters this day claimed a preemption of 400 Acres of land at the State price lying on the upper Fork of the North branch of the rolling fork of Salt River about 1½ Miles South of a big Lick by making a settlement in the Month of April 1779 satisfactory proof being made to the Court they are of Opinion that the said Vanmeters has a right to a preemption of 400 Acres to include the said Settlement & that a Certificate issue accordingly

(Cert iss for 400 fees &c pd D. D.)

Then the Court adjourned untill Monday Morning 10 oclock

William Fleming—

At a Court Continued and held at the falls of Ohio for Adjusting disputed Titles to the Kentucky Lands.—Nov. 22st 1779.—

Present

William Fleming Stephen Trigg & James Barbour Gent's

(Cert issd for 1400 fees &c pd D. D.)

John Bailey this day claimed a settlement & preemption to a Tract of Land lying on clear creek near the head thereof a branch of Bearsheir's Creek that runs into Salt River by improving the same and raising a Crop of Corn in the year 1776 satisfactory proof being made to the Court they are of Opinion that the said Bailey has a right to a settlement of 400 Acres of Land to include the said improvement & the preemption of 1000 Acres adjoining & that a Certificate issue accordingly.—

(Cert iss for 400 fees and 'c pd D. D.)

Benj'n Pope proved to the Court he was entitled to a preemption of 400 Acres of land at the State price the

20th instant by making an Actual Settlement in May 1779 lying on Clear Creek Opposite to Squire Boons improvement a branch of Bearsheir's Creek that runs into Salt River to include the s'd settlement & that a Certificate issue accordingly.—

(Cert issd for 1000 fees &c pd D. D.)

William Spangler this day claimed a preemption of 1000 Acres of Land at the State price lying on the head of the South Fork of Goose creek joining the lands of Colo. Christian & Capt'n Floyds on Beargrass on the North side to extend down the said Creek for quantity by improving the same and building a Cabbin on the premises in the year 1776 satisfactory proof being made to the Court they are of Opinion that the said Spangler has a right to a preemption of 1000 Acres to include the said improvement & that a Certificate issue accordingly.—

(Cert issd for 1400 fees &c pd D. D. to Colo. Clark)

Squire Boone[15] this day claimed a settlement & preemption to a tract of Land lying on Silver Creek known by the name of the Stockfields a branch of the Kentucky by improving the same & raising a crop of Corn in the year 1776 and residing in the Country ever since, satisfactory proof being made to the Court they are of Opinion that the said Boone has a right to a settlement of 400 Acres of Land to include the said improvement & the preemption of 1000 adjoining and that a cert'e issue accordingly.—

[15]Brother of Daniel Boone. See Collins, Vol. 1, pp. 13, 16, 355, 511.

David Barton Heir at Law to Joshua Barton decd this day claimed a settlement & preemption to a tract of Land lying on Silver Creek a branch of the Kentucky joining the Land of Squire Boone by the said decedents raising a Crop of Corn in the Country in the year 1777 & residing in the Country 12 Months before the year 1778 satisfactory proof being made to the Court they are of Opinion that the said Barton has a right to a settlement of 400 Acres of land to include the above location & the preemption of 1000 Acres adjoining & that a certificate issue accordingly.—

Absent William Fleming, Gent'en

William Moore Assee of Wm Moore this day claimed a settlement and preemption It appearing to the Court by the Oath of Squire Boone that the said Moore was a servant to Adam Fisher while in this Country therefore they are of Opinion that the s'd Moores claim is rejected.—

(Cert. iss'd for 1400 fees &c pd D. D.)

Peter Asturgus for and In behalf of John Asturgus this day claimed a settlement & preemption to a tract of Land lying on Hammonds Creek the Waters of Salt River joining on the North side of Peter Argustus Land by improving the same & raising a Crop of Corn in the year 1776 satisfactory proof being made to the Court they are of Opinion that the said Argustus has a right to a settlement of 400 Acres of Land to include the said improvement and the preemption of 1000 Acres of Land joining and that a Certificate Issue accordingly.—

(Cert issd for 400 fees &c pd D. D.)

John Alvy this day claimed a preemption to 400 Acres of Land at the State price lying on the head of a branch running South into pond Creek about 3 Miles from the Flat lick and about 12 Miles from this place by actual settlement made in the Month of May 1779 satisfactory proof being made to the Court they are of Opinion that the said Alvy has a right to a preemption of 400 Acres of Land including the said settlement & that a Cert issue accordingly.

(Cert issd for 1400 fees &c pd D. D. to Colo. Clark)

Squire Boone for and in behalf of Benj. Vancleve this day claimed a settlement & preemption to a tract of Land lying on Clear Creek known by the name of the painted Stone a branch of Brasheirs Creek a branch of Salt River by the said Vancleve's Improving the same & raising a Crop of Corn in the year 1776 satisfactory proof being made to the Court they are of Opinion that the said Vancleve has a right to a settlement of 400 Acres of Land including the said Improvement & the preemption of 1000 Acres of Land adjoining and that a Certificate issue accordingly.

(Cert issd for 1400 fees &c pd D. D. to Colo. Clark)

Squire Boone for and in behalf of Thomas Dagerly this day claimed a settlement & preemption to a tract of Land lying on the head of Gists on No E Fork of Bresheirs's Creek a branch of Salt River to include a small Deer lick by improving the same & raising a Crop of Corn in the year 1776 satisfactory proof being made to the Court they are of Opinion that the said Dagerly has a right to a settlement of 400 Acres of Land to include the said Improvement & the preemption of 1000 Acres Adj'g & that a Cert'e issue accordingly.

(Cert issd for 1400 fees &c pd D. D. to Colo Clark).

Squire Boone for & in behalf of James Lee this day claimed a settlement & preemption to a tract of Land lying on Bresheirs's Creek a branch of Salt River about 2 Miles above the painted Stone by improving the same & raising a Crop of Corn in the year 1776 & residing 12 Months in the Country before the year 1778 satisfactory proof being made to the Court they are of Opinion that the said Lee has a right to a settlement of 400 Acres of Land to include the said Improvement & the preemption of 1000 Acres adj'g & that a Cert'e issue accordingly.

(Cert issd for 1400 fees pd D. D. to M. Brashears)

Marsham Brasheir for and in behalf of Rich'd Brashears this day claimed a settlement and preemption to a tract of Land lying on Fox Run a branch of Brashears Creek a branch of Salt River about 3 Miles West of the painted Stone by the said Brashears raising a crop of Corn in the year 1775 & 1776 satisfactory proof being made they are of Opinion that the s'd Breashears has a right to a settlement of 400 Acres to include the above location and the preemption of 1000 Acres adjoining and that a Certificate issue accordingly.—

(Cert issd for 1000 fees &c pd D. D. to Mr. Pope)

Richard Chenoch this day claimed a preemption to 1000 Acres of Land at the State price lying on the head of Caney Fork a branch of Clear Creek a branch of Brashears's Creek which runs into Salt River by improving the same & building a Cabbin in the year 1776 satisfactory proof being made they are of Opinion that the said Chenoch has a right to a preemption of 1000 Acres of Land to include the said Improvement and that a Certificate issue accordingly.

Present Wm Fleming Gent'n.

(Cert iss 1400 fees &c pd D. D. to Mr. Pope)

Jacob Grotts this day claimed a settlement & preemption to a tract of Land lying on Coopers Run a branch of Licking Creek about 6 Miles south Eastward of Riddles Station satisfactory proof being made that the said Grootts improved the same and raised a Crop of Corn in the year 1776 the Court are of Opinion that the said Grotts has a right to a settlement of 400 Acres of Land to include the said Improvement and the preemption of 1000 Acres of Land adjoining & that a Certificate Issue accordingly.

Then the Court adjourned untill to Morrow Morning 10 oclock

Wm Fleming

At a Court continued & held for adjusting disputed titles to the Kentucky Lands at the falls of Ohio this 23d of Nov. 1779—

Present

Stephen Trigg Edm'd Lyne James Barbour Gent'n

(Cert issd for 400 fees &c pd D. D.)

Thomas McCarty this day claimed a preemption of 400 Acres of Land at the State price lying on the head of a branch the North Branch of Soverns Creek a branch of Green River in Soverns Valley by making an actual settlement in April 1779 satisfactory proof being made to the Court they are of Opinion that the said McCarty is entitled to a preemption of 400 Acres including the s'd Settlm't & that a Cert'e issue accordingly.

(Cert issd for 400 fees &c pd D. D.)

Elisha Freeman this day claimed a preemption of 400 Acres of Land at the State price lying on the first right hand Fork of the Creek that Soverns Cabbins is built upon, in Soverns Valley a branch of Green River satisfactory proof being made to the Court that the s'd Freeman made an actual settlement in May 1779 they are of Opinion that the said Freeman has a right to a preemption of 400 Acres of Land includ-ing s'd Settlem't & that a Cert'e iss'e Accordingly.

(Cert iss for 1400 fees & pd D. D.)

George Holeman this day claimed a settlement & preemption to a tract of Land lying on the East Fork of Brashears Creek a branch of Salt River joining the Lands said to be claimed by George M Clure on the one side & Wm Steal on the other by improving the same & residing in the Country ever since the year 1776 satisfactory proof being made to the Court they are of Opinion that the said Holeman has a right to a settlement of 400 Acres of Land to include the s'd improvement & the preemption of 1000 Adj'g & that a Cert'e issue accordingly.

(Cert issd for 400 fee &c pd D. D.)

Thos Bull this day claimed a preemption to 400 Acres of Land at the State price lying on the East Fork of Clear Creek about 2 Miles above the Mouth joining the lands said to be claimed by Wickerham a branch of Brashears's Creek the Waters of Salt River by actual Settlement made in 1778 satisfactory proof being made to the Court they are of Opinion that the said Bull has a right to a preemption of 400 Acres of land to include the said settlement & that a Certificate issue accordingly.

(Cert iss for 400 fees &c pd D. D.)

Joseph Irwin this day claimed a preemption to 400 Acres of Land at the State price lying on a branch of Salt River & lying East of the Knob Licks about 13 Miles from Bullitts Salt Lick including a sinking Spring by actual Settlement made in May. 1779 satisfactory proof being made to the Court they are of Opinion that the said Irwin has a right to a preemption of 400 Acres of Land including the said Improvement & that a Certificate issue accordingly.

(Cert issd for 400 fees &c pd D. D.)

Sam'l Brown this day claimed a preemption to 400 Acres of land at the State price lying about 4 Miles North East of James Pattoons land at an Old Indian Town on a large Buffaloe road between the said Town & a large Mud lick on a branch of licking by actual Settlement made in April 1779 satisfactory proof being made to the Court they are of Opinion that the said Brown has a right to a preemption of 400 Acres including the said Settlement & that a Certificate issue accordingly.

(Cert issd for 1400 fees pd D. D. to B. Pope)

Squire Boone Assee of Geo'e Paff this day claimed a settlement & preemption to a tract of Land lying on Mulberry Creek a branch of Brashears Creek the Waters of Salt River by the said Paff improving the same in the year 1775 & residing in the Country ever since, satisfactory proof being made to the Court they are of Opinion that the s'd Boone has a right to a settlement of 400 Acres of Land including the said improvement & the preemption of 1000 Acres adjoining & that a Certificate issue accordingly

(Cert issd for 400 fees &c pd D. D. to I. Barnett)

Jesse Rude this day claimed a preemption to 400 Acres of land at the State price lying on the South side of Salt River about five Miles from Bulletts Salt Lick and about 1/2 Mile from the long Lick by making an Actual settlement in May 1779 satisfactory proof being made to the Court they are of Opinion that the said Rude has a right, to a preemption of 400 Acres of Land to include the said Settlm't & that cert'e issue accordingly.

(Cert issd for 1400 fees &c pd D. D. to J. Soverins)

Ebenezer Soverins by John Soverins this day claimed a settlement & preemption to a tract of Land lying on one of the South branch of Hingstons Fork of licking called Soverins Creek about 4 Miles from the head of said Creek where a large Buffaloe road Crosses by the said Soverins improving the same & raising a Crop of Corn in the Country in the year 1776 satisfactory proof being made to the Court they are of Opinion that the s'd Soverins has a right to a settlement of 400 Acres of Land including the s'd improvement & the preemption of 1000 Acres adjoining & that a Cert. issue accordingly.

Present Wm Fleming. Abs. Edmund Lyne. Gent'n

(Cert issd for 400 fees &c pd D. D.)

Asham Barnett this day claimed a preemption to 400 Acres of Land at the State price lying Hammonds Creek a branch of the Town Fork of Salt River joining Peter Argustus Land by making an Actual settlement in May 1779 satisfactory proof being made to the Court they are of Opinion that the said Barnett has a right to a preemption of 400 Acres including the said Settlement & that a Certificate issue accordingly.

Present Ed'd Lyne, Abs. Wm Fleming Gent'n

Martin Fowler by Nath'l Randolph this day claimed a settlement & preemption to a tract of Land which he proved to the Court he was entitled to by residing in the Country 12 Months before the year 1778.

(Cert issd 1400 fees &c pd D. D. to Colo Clark)

Nathan'l Randolph this day claimed a settlement & preemption to a tract of Land lying on the North side of Kentucky River at a place known by the name of the Clay lick including a Salt Spring about 2 Miles from the said lick improvement by the said Randolph residing in the Country 12 Months before the year 1778 satisfactory proof being made to the Court they are of Opinion that the said Randolph has a right to a settlement of 400 Acres of Land including the said improvement & the preemption of 1000 Acres adjoining and that a Certificate Issue accordingly.

Then the Court adjourned to Harrodsburg on Monday the 29th Inst

Stephen Trigg

At a Court continued & held at Harrodsburg for adjusting disputed titles to the Kentucky lands this 2 'd Dec'r 1779.

Present

Wm Fleming Stephen Trigg & James Barbour—Gent

(Cert issd for 1000 fees &c pd D. D.)

Thomas Quirk this day claimed a preemption to a tract of land lying on the Waters of Dicks River joining the land of George Smith by building a Cabbin in the year 1774 John Bowman in behalf of the heirs of of Joseph Bowman Dec'd appeared & contested the said claim whereupon sundry Witnesses were sworn & examined in consideration of which the Court are of Opinion that the said Quirk has a right to a preemption of 1000 Acres of Land including the said Cabbin & that a Certificate issue accordingly.

John Bowman[16] for & in behalf of the Heirs of Joseph Bowman Dec'd this day claimed a settlement & preemption to a tract of Land satisfactory proof being made to the Court they are of Opinion that the Heirs of Joseph Bowman Dec'd has a right to a settlement & preemption, (Page)

(Cert issd for 1000 fees &c pd D. D. to Tho McGee)

William White this day claimed a preemption of 1000 Acres of Land lying on the head of a branch of Brasheirs Creek Opposite to the head of Dreenings lick Creek & about 12 Miles from the said by raising a Cabbin on the premises in the year 1775 Satisfactory proof being made to the Court they are of Opinion that the said White has a right to a preemption of 1000 Acres of Lands to include the said Cabbin & that a Certificate issue accordingly.—

(Cert iss for 1400 fees &c pd D. D.)

John & Edmund archer[17] Assees of the Heirs of James Archer dec'd this day claimed a settlement & preemption to a tract of land lying on the North side of Dicks River joining the Lands said to be claimed by Andrew Qumblin by the said decedents raising a Crop of Corn in the Country in the year 1776 satisfactory proof being made to the Court, they are of Opinion that the s'd John & Edmund Archer has a right to a settlem't of 400 Acres of Land to include the said location & the preemption of 1000 Acres adjoining & that a Certificate issue accordingly.—

Then the Court adjourned untill to Morrow Morning.—Wm Fleming

At a Court Continued & held at Harrodsburg for adjusting disputed Titles to the Kentucky Lands the 3 day of Dec'r 1779.

Present Stephen Trigg. Edmund Lyne & James Barbour.—Gent'n

(Cert issd for 1400 fees &c pd D. D.)

Henry Prather[18] this day claimed a settlement & preemption to a tract of land lying on Shawnee Run joining the land of Patrick Dowling by improving the said land in the year 1776 and residing in the Country 12 Months before the year 1778. James Hays App'd & contested the s'd land as Heir at law to John Hays dec'd and alledged that the s'd Decedent had a prior right whereupon sundry Witnesses were sworn & examined in consideration of which the Court are of Opinion that the said Prather has a right to a settlement of 400 Acres of Land to include the s'd improvement & that the preemption of 1000 Acres of Land adjoining & that a Certificate issue accordingly.

(Cert iss for 400 Acres fees &c pd D. D. to Capt Quirk)

Sam'l Kirkhan[19] this day claimed a preemption of 400 Acres of Land at

[16]Collins, Vol. 1, pp. 19, 240, 250, 253.
[17]Collins, Vol. 1, p. 8.
[18]Collins, Vol. 1, p. 12.
[19]Collins, Vol. 1, p. 13.

the State price lying Quirks Creek a branch of Salt River about 1 Mile from the place where the Creek sinks by the said Kirkhams making an actual settlement since the year 1778 satisfactory proof being made to the Court they are of Opinion that the said Quirkman has a right to a preemption of 400 Acres of land to include said Settlement & that a Certe' issue accordingly.—

(Cert issd for 1400 D. D.)

It being prove to this Court that the Heirs of Joseph Bowman[20] dec'd was intitled to a settlement & preemption to a tract of land lying on cane Run on the South side thereof to include a spring the Waters of Which runs into Harrods Run to include a Cabbin built by the said decedent & that a Certificate issue accordingly.

(Cert iss for 400 fees &c pd Capt Quirk)

Edward Quirk this day claimed a Preemption of 400 Acres of land at the State price lying on Quirks Creeks joining the lands of Samuel Kirkham by making an Actual settlement in April 1779 satisfactory proof being made to the Court they are of Opinion that the said Quirk has a right to a preemption of 400 Acres of Land to include the said settlement & that a Certificate issue accordingly.—

Then the Court adjourned to Boonesborough the 8th Inst

Stephen Trigg.

At a Court continued & held at Boonesborough for adjusting disputed titles to the Kentucky Lands the 18th day of Dec'r 1779.

Present Wm Fleming, Stephen Trigg & Edmund Lyne—Gent'n

(Cert issd for 1400 fees &c pd D. D.)

James Harbeson this day claimed a settlement & Preemption to a tract of Land lying on both sides Chaplins Fork near the head thereof at a Cove Spring by improving the same in the year 1776 & raising a crop of Corn in the Country in the year 1776 satisfactory proof being made to the Court they are of Opinion that the said Harbeson has a right to a settlement of 400 Acres of Land iscluding the said improvement & the preemption of 1000 Acres Adjoining & that a certificate issue accordingly.—

Arther Harbeson this day claimed a settlement & preemption to a tract of land lying on both sides of Chaplins Fork near the head thereof the Court being informed that this claim is contested by William Stewart they are of Opinion that it be Cont'd for a further hearing.

(Cert issd for 1000—)

William Thompson this day claimed a preemption of 1000 Acres of Land at the State price lying on the south side of Kentucky River at a spring that comes out of a steep Bank about ½ Mile from the river between Harrods Landing and the Shawnee Run by marking & Improving the said land in the year 1775 satisfactory proof being made to the Court they are of Opinion that the said Thompson has a right to a preemption of 1000 Acres of Land to

[20] Collins, Vol. 1, pp. 19, 513.

include the said Improv't & that a Certificate issue accordingly.

(Cert iss for 1000)

William Murtry this day claimed a preemption to 1000 Acres of Land at the State price lying on a Dry Run a branch of Chaplin Fork on the Hunters Path that leads from Harrodsburg & bear a S. W. course & 3 Miles from Wm Stewarts claim on Chaplin Fork by marking & improving the same in the year 1775 satisfactory proof being made to the Court they are of Opinion that the said Mr. Murtry has a right to a preemption of 1000 Acres including the said improvm't & that a Cert. issue accordingly.

Then the Court adjourned untill Monday Morning 10 oclock—Wm Fleming.

At a Court continued & held at Boonesborough by the Commissioners for adjusting disputed Titles to the Kentucky lands the 20th day of Dec'r 1779

Present Wm Fleming Stephen Trigg & Edmund Lyne Gent—

(Cert iss for 1400 fees &c pd D. D. location altered)

Rebuen Guthrie who was Assee of Thos Hartgrove this day claimed a settlement & preemption to a tract of land lying on the Waters of Boons Creek joining below a survey made for the said Logan or 200 Acres in the year 1775 by the said Hart Groves residing at this place 12 Months before the year 1778 Satisfactory proof being made to the Court they are of Opinion that the said Guthrie has a right to a settlement of 400 Acres including the above location & the preemption of 1000 Acres Adjoining & that a certificate issue accordingly.

(Cert issd for 1400 fees &c pd to J. Shelby)

James Shelby this day claimed a settlem't & preemption to a tract of land in the District of Kentucky lying on the head of & Easterly branch of Hickmans Creek about 10 Miles or 12 North Westerly of Boonesborough to include three large springs to include the s'd improvement by improving the same in the year 1776 & raising a Crop of Corn in this Country the same year satisfactory proof being made to the Court they are of Opinion that the said Shelby has a right to a settlement of 400 Acres of land to include the said improvement & the preemption of 1000 Acres Adjoining & that a Certificate issue accordingly.—

(Cert issd for 1400 fees &c pd D. D.)

Diannah Denton Heir to John Denton Dec'd by Thomas Denton[21] this day claimed a settlement & preemption to a tract of land in the District of Kentucky lying on the Waters of Shawnee Run between the lands of Hugh McGary & Harrods landing joining the said McGarys land & on the road that leads from Harrodsburg to the said landing including a small spring on the said Road by the said decedents improving the said land in the year 1776 & raising a crop of Corn in this Country the same year satisfactory proof be-

[21]Collins, Vol. 1, pp. 510, 511.

ing made to the Court they are of Opinion that the said Diannah has a right to a settlement of 400 Acres of Land to include the said improvement & the preemption of 1000 Acres adjoining & that a Certificate issue accordingly.

(Cert issd for 1400 fees &c pd D. D.)

Joshua Pennick this day claimed a settlement & preemption to a tract of land in the District of Kentucky lying on the waters of Stoners Fork a branch of licking Creek on both sides of said Fork joining the lands by Stephen Handcock below by improving the same & settling in the year 1777 & residing ever since satisfactory proof being made to the Court they are of Opinion that the said Pennick has a right to a settlement of 400 Acres of Land including the said improvement & the preemption of 1000 Acres Adjoining & that a Certificate issue accordingly.

(Cert issd for 1400 Acres fees &c pd D. D. to Jas Harbeson)

Arther Harbeson claims being reheard and the parties present, It Appearing to the Court by Testimony that the s'd Harbeson raised a crop of Corn in the year 1776 & improving a tract lying on both sides Chapplins Fork near the head thereof the same year they are of Opinion that the said Harbeson has a right to a settlement of 400 Acres of Land to include the said improvement & the preemption of 1000 Acres adjoining & that a Certificate issue accordingly.—

(Cert issd for 1400 fees &c pd D. D.)

John Kenady Jun'r this day claimed a settlement & preemption to a tract of Land in the District of Kentucky lying on both sides of Kennady's fork of paint lick Creek by the said Kenedys improving the same & raising a Crop of Corn in the year 1775 satisfactory proof being made to the Court they are of Opinion that the said Kennedy has a right to a settlement of 400 Acres of land to include the said improvement & the preemption of 1000 Acres adjoining and that a Certificate issue accordingly

(Cert issd for 1400 fees &c pd D. D.)

John Kennady Jun'r Assee of Roger Hinde this day claimed a settlement & preemption to a tract of land lying in the District of Kentucky lying on both sides Kennedys Fork of Paint lick Creek adjoining the s'd Kenadys claim above on the said fork by the said Hindes improving the said lands and raising a Crop of Corn in the year 1776 satisfactory proof being made to the Court they are of Opinion that the said Kennady has a right to a settlement of 400 Acres of Land including the said improvement & the preemption of 1000 Acres adjoining & that a Certificate issue accordingly.

(Cert issd for 1400 fees &c pd Jno. Kennedy)

John Kennady Sen'r this day claimed a settlement & preemption to a tract of land in the District of Kentucky lying on both sides of Silver Creek known by the name of the locust bend by improving the same in the year 1775 & raising a Crop of corn in the year 1776 satisfactory proof being made to the Court they are of Opinion that the said

Kennady has a right to a settlement of 400 Acres of land to include the said improvement & the preemption of 1000 Acres adjoining & that a Certe—issue accordingly.

(Cert iss for 1400 fees &c pd Jno Kennady)

John Tate this day claimed a settlement & preemption to a tract of land in the District of Kentucky, lying on the head of an Eastern branch of paint lick Creek joining an improvement made by John Kennedy & other in the year 1776 including a sink hole Spring near an old Indian Town house by improving the same & raising a Crop of Corn in the year 1776 satisfactory proof being made to the Court they are of Opinion that the said Tate has a right to a settlement of 400 of land including the said improvement & the preemption of 1000 Acres Adjoining & that a certificate issue accordingly.

(Cert issd for 1400 fees &c pd Jno Kenady)

Simon Canton[22] this day claimed a Settlement & preemption to a tract of land in the District of Kentucky lying on Elkhorn joining Colo. Prestons Survey at the Cave Spring on the South West Side by improving the same and residing in the Country ever since the year 1775 satisfactory proof being made to the Court they are of Opinion that the said Butler, has a right to a settlement of 400 Acres of Land including the said improvement & the preemption of 1000 Acres adjoining and that a Certificate issue accordingly.

(Cert issd for 1400 fees &c pd D. D. John Kenady)

John Pophams by John Kennady this day claimed a settlement and preemption to a tract of Land in the District of Kentucky lying on Drakes Camp Creek about 2 Miles from Harmons lick at the head of the said Creek about a North West course from the said Harmons lick by the said Pophams raising a Crop of Corn in the Country in the year 1775 satisfactory proof being made to the Court they are of Opinion that the said Pophams has a right to a settlement of 400 Acres of land to include the above location and the preemption of 1000 Acres adjoining & that a Certificate issue accordingly.—

(Cert issd for 1400 fees &c pd D. D. Jno. Kenady)

Humphrey Best by John Kenady this day claimed a settlement & preemption to a tract of Land in the District of Kentucky lying on the head of paint lick Creek near the Knobs including Best Cane Brake by raising a Crop of Corn in this Country in the year 1775 Satisfactory proof being made to the Court they are of Opinion that the said Best has a right to a settlement of 400 Acres of Land to include the above location & the preemption of 1000 Acres adjoining & that a Certificate issue accordingly.

[22]Simon Kenton. Clerk evidently misunderstood name and wrote it "Canton." In another place in same entry the clerk had written the name 'Canton," and had then drawn lines through the word, striking it out, and writing "Butler." Kenton had fled from his Virginia home, at the age of 16, after a difficulty with a rival, William Veach. Thinking he had killed Veach he assumed the name of Butler, which explains the name in this entry. Learning in after years that Veach had recovered, Kenton resumed his name. See Collins, Vol. 1, p. 17 and index; also Biographical Encyclopedia of Kentucky, p. 781, and Index to Register Kentucky Historical Society, Sup. to No. 60.

(Cert issd for 1000 fees &c pd D. D.)

Henry Boffman this day claimed a settlement & preemption to a tract of land in the district of Kentucky lying on Dick River about 1½ Miles from Whitleys Station by improving the same and building a Cabbin & raising a Crop of Corn in the year 1776 Satisfactory proof being made to the Court they are of Opinion that the said Boffman has a right to a preemption of 1000 Acres only including the said improvement and that a Certificate issue accordingly

(Cert issd for 1000 fees &c pd D. D. to Henry Boffman)

Christean Boffman the Heir to John Boffman dec'd by Henry Boffman this day claimed a settlement & preemption to a tract of Land in the District of Kentucky lying on a branch of Boons Creek known by the name of Boffmans Fork by the said decedents improving the same & rasing a Crop of Corn in the year 1776 Satisfactory proof being made to the Court they are of Opinion that the s'd Heir has a right to a settlement of 400 Acres of Land including the said improvement & the preemption of 1000 Acres adjoining & that a Certificate issue accordingly.

(Cert issd for 1400 fees &c pd D. D.)

Richard Burk this day claimed a settlement & preemption to a tract of land lying in the District of Kentucky on Fox Run a branch of Brasheirs Creek the Waters of Salt River by improving the same in the year 1775 & raising a Crop of Corn in the Country in the year 1775 satisfactory proof being made to the Court they are of Opinion that the said Burk has a right to a settlement of 400 Acres of Land including s'd improvement & the preemption of 1000 Acres adjoining & that a Certificate issue accordingly.

(Cert issd for 400 fees &c pd D. D.)

William Pattoone this day claimed a preemption of 400 Acres of land in the District of Kentucky at the State price lying on the Eastern Branch of paint lick Creek including a deep Spring about 2 Miles above the paint lick by making an actual Settlement in the month of May 1779 Satisfactory proof being made to the Court they are of Opinion that the said Pattone has a right to a preemption of 400 Acres of Land including the said settlement & that a Certificate issue accordingly.

(Cert issd for 1400 fees &c pd D. D.)

Samuel Bell[23] this day claimed a settlement & preemption to a tract of land in the District of Kentucky lying at the mouth of Kennadys Fork on the East side of the White lick Creek including a small Spring joining the land of John Kenady by making an actual Settlement in 1777 and residing in the Country ever since satisfactory proof being made to the Court they are of Opinion that the said Bell has a right to a settlement of 400 Acres of land including the s'd location & the preemption of 1000 Acres adjoining & that a Certe issue accordingly—

(Cert issued for 1400 fees &c pd D. D.)

William Miller[24] Assee of Will'm Dorton this day claimed a settlement &

[23]Collins, Vol. 1, p. 12.
[24]Collins, Vol. 1, p. 12.

preemption to a tract of land in the district of Kentucky lying on Silver Creek at the mouth of the Creek where there is a small Sulphur lick in the bank of the Creek in among some rocks about 3 Miles from the locust bend by the said Dorton raising a Crop of Corn in the Country in the year 1775 Satisfactory proof being made to the Court they are of Opinion that the said Miller has a right to a settlement of 400 Acres of Land including the above location & the preemption of 1000 Acres adjoining & that a Certificate issue accordingly.

(Cert issd for 1400 fees &c pd D. D.)

William Miller.—Assee of, Thomas Lovelaty this day claimed a Settlement & preemption to a tract of land in the District of Kentucky lying on the head of a Branch of the Kentucky River on the South side of the River with the letters IK 1775 cut on an Ash Tree, by the said Lovelty raising a Crop of Corn in the year 1775 satisfactory proof being made to the Court they are of Opinion that the said Miller &c had a right to a settlement of 400 Acres of Land to include the above location & the preemption of 1000 Acres adjoining & that a Certificate issue accordingly.

(Cert issd for 1400 fees &c pd D. D.)

William Miller this day claimed a settlement & preemption to a tract of land in the District of Kentucky lying on the paint lick Creek at the paint lick by the said Miller raising a crop of corn in the year 1775 & improving the land in the year 1776 satisfactory proof being made to the Court they are of Opinion that the said Miller has a right to a settlement of 400 Acres of land including the said improvement & the preemption of 1000 Acres adjoining & that a Certificate issue accordingly.

(Cert issd for 1400 fees &c D. D. Jno. Kenedy)

Sam'l Barton by John Kennady this day claimed a settlement & preemption to a tract of Land in the District of Kentucky lying on Silver Creek at the Bull lick by the said Bartons raising a Crop of Corn the Country in the year 1775 Satisfactory proof being made to the Court they are of Opinion that the said Barton has a right to a settlement of 400 Acres of Land to include the above location & the preemption of 1000 Acres adjoining & that a Certificate issue accordingly.

(Cert issd for 1400 fees &c pd D. D.)

William Stewart this day claimed a settlement & preemption to a tract of Land in the District of Kentucky lying on both sides of Chaplins Fork of Salt River at Chaplins Spring to run ½ a Mile above the said Spring by improving the same & raising a Crop of Corn in the year 1775 Satisfactory proof being made to the Court they are of Opinion that the said Stewart has a right to a settlement of 400 Acres of Land to include the s'd improvement & the preemption of 1000 Acres adjoining & that a Certificate issue accordingly.

(Cert issd for 400 fees &c pd D. D. to Jas Harbeson)

John Harbeson this day claimed a preemption of 400 Acres of Land at the

State price in the District of Kentucky lying on the South Fork of licking Creek about 3 Miles South of Harrods lick by making an actual settlement on the Month of May 1779 Satisfactory proof being made to the Court they are of Opinion that the said Harbeson has a right to a preemption of 400 Acres of Land to include the said Settlement & that a Certificate issue accordingly.

(Cert issd for 400 fees &c pd D. D.)

David Cooke[25] this day claimed a preemption of 400 Acres of land at the State price in the District of Kentucky lying on the South side of Dicks River Opposite to Henry Boffmans land by making an actual settlement in the Month of March 1779 Satisfactory proof being made to the Court they are of Opinion that the said Cooke has a right to a preemption of 400 Acres of Land to include the said Settlement & that a Certificate issue accordingly.

Then the Court Adjourned untill to Morrow Morning 10 oclock Wm Fleming.

At a Court continued & held at Boonesborough for adjusting disputed titles to the Kentucky lands the 21st day of Dec'r 1779—

Present Will'm Fleming Stephen Trigg & Edmund Lyne—Gent'n

(Cert issd for 400 fees &c pd D. D. to Colo. Calloway[26])

Hugh Ross by John Kennady this day claimed a preemption to 400 Acres of land at the State price in the District of Kentucky lying on Elk Garden Creek a branch of Silver Creek joining Joseph Kennadys land on the West by making an Actual Settlement in the Month of October 1778 Satisfactory proof being made to the Court they are of Opinion that the said Ross has a right to the preemption of 400 Acres including the s'd land & that a Certificate issue accordingly

(Cert iss for 1000 D. D.)

Henry Boffman Heir at law to Jacob Boffman dec'd—having not claimed the right of preemption when he obtained a certificate for Settlement Now comes into Court & claims the preemption of 1000 Acres adjoining the Settlement which is granted accordingly & that a Certificate order to issue for the same.

(Cert iss for 1400 by order of Court at Bryants)

Moses Thomas Assee of William Cradlebaugh[27] this day claimed a settlement & preemption to a tract of Land in the district of Kentucky lying on Stoners fork at the Mouth of a Creek called Wolf Creek branch of Licking by the said Cradlebough improving the same and raising a Crop of Corn in the Country in the year 1776 satisfactory proof being made to the Court they are of Opinion that the said Thomas has a right to a settlem't of 400 Acres of land including the s'd improvement & the preemption of 1000 Acres adjoining —Cert— not to issue untill the further order of this Court.

[25]Collins, Vol. 1, p. 13.
[26]Collins, Vol. 1, pp. 18, 249, 355, 366, 542.

[27]Collins, Vol. 1, p. 13.

(Cert issd for 1400 fees &c pd D. D.)

David McGee this day claimed a settlement & preemption to a tract of land in the District of Kentucky lying on the head of Durets Creek a branch of Kentucky River joining the Surveys of James Hickman & Patrick Henry by a Settlement made in the year 1775 & raising a Crop of Corn in the year 1776 satisfactory proof being made to the Court they are of Opinion that the said McGee has a right to a settlement of 400 Acres including the said improvement & the preemption of 1000 adjo'g & that a Cert'e issue accordingly.—

(Cert issd for 1400 fees &c pd D. D.)

William McGee[28] this day claimed a settlement & preemption to a tract of land in the District of Kentucky lying on Coopers Run a branch of licking about 2 Miles above Jacob Grotts settlement by improving the same & raising a Crop of Corn in the year 1776 Satisfactory proof being made to the Court they are of Opinion that the said McGee has a right to a settlement of 400 Acres of Land including the s'd improvement & the preemption of 1000 Acres adjoining & that a Certificate issue accordingly

(Cert issd for 1400 fees &c pd to D. McGee)

Bryant McDonald by David McGee this day claimed a Settlement & preemption to a tract of land in the District of Kentucky lying on the West fork of Howards Creek a branch of Kentucky River running up the said fork for quantity. by improving the same & raising a Crop of Corn in the year 1776 Satisfactory proof being made to the Court they are of Opinion that the said McDonald has a right to a settlement of 400 Acres of Land including the said improvement & the preemption of 1000 Acres Adjoining & that a Certificate issue accordingly.

(Cert issd for 1400 fees &c pd D. D.)

Joseph Benning this day claimed a settlement & preemption to a tract of land in the district of Kentucky lying on Silver Creek including a Mill Seat known by the name of Boons Mills Seat about 2 Miles below the locust Bend by improving the same & raising a Crop of Corn in the year 1775 satisfactory proof being made to the Court they are of Opinion that the said Benning has a right to a settlement of 400 Acres of land including the said Improvements & the preemption of 1000 Adjoining & that a Cert. issue accordingly—

(Cert issd for 1000 fees &c pd D. D.)

James Estill[28½] Assee of Solomon Carpenter[29] this day claimed a settlm't & preemption to a tract of land in the District of Kentucky lying on the head branch of paint lick Creek about 1 Mile from the Beach Spring by the said Carpenters improving the same by building a Cabbin &c in the year 1776 satisfactory proof being made to the Court they are of Opinion that the said Estill has a right to a preemption of 1000 Acres only including the said improvement & that a Certificate issue accordingly.

[28]Collins, Vol. 1, p. 13, 433, 452, 457.

[28½]Collins, Vol. 1, pp. 13, 20, 254, 513, 514.

[29]Collins, Vol. 1, p. 12.

(Cert issd for 1400 fees &c pd D. D.)

Peter Wooly this day claimed a settlement & preemption to a tract of land in the District of Kentucky lying on the dividing ridge of Paint lick & Dicks River by improving the same & raising a Crop of Corn in the Country in the year 1776 Satisfactory proof being made to the Court they are of Opinion that the said Wooly has a right to a settlement of 400 Acres of land including the said improvement & that a preemption of 1000 Acres Adjoining & that a Certificate issue accordingly.

(Cert issd for 1400 fees &c pd D. D.)

Nathaniel Hart[30] this day claimed a settlement & preemption to a tract of land in the District of Kentucky lying on a branch of Silver Creek on Boons Old Trace joining Squire Boons Stockfield Track by improving the same & raising a Crop of Corn in the year 1775 Satisfactory proof being made to the Court they are of Opinion that the said Hart has a right to a settlement of 400 acres of land to include the s'd improvement & the preemption of 1000 Acres of Land adjoining & that a Certificate issue accordingly.

(Cert issd for 1000)

Joseph Hughes[31] by Dan'l Boone this day claimed a settlement & preemption to a tract of land of 1000 Acres at the State price in the District of Kentucky lying on the Waters of Silver Creek joining on the North side of Nath'l Harts land by improving the same & marking in the year 1776 Satisfactory proof being made to the Court they are of Opinion that the said Hughes has a right to a preemp't of 1000 Acres of land including the said improvement and that a Certificate issue Accordingly.—

(Cert issd for 1400 fees &c pd D. D. to Cap Hart)

Jesse Benton by Nath'l Hart this day claimed a settlement & preemption to a tract of land in the District of Kentucky lying on the waters of Silver Creek joining on the North East side of Nath'l Harts land by settling & raising a Crop of Corn in the year 1776 Satisfactory proof being made to the Court they are of Opinion that the said Benton has a right to a settlm't of 400 Acres of Land to include the said location & the preemption of 1000 Acres adjoining & that a Certificate issue accordingly.

(Cert issd for 1400 fees &c pd D. D. to Capt. Hart)

David Hart by Nath'l Hart this day claimed a settlement & preemption to a tract of land in the District of Kentucky lying on the Waters of Silver Creek joining on the North & North West side of Hughs land by raising a Crop of Corn in the Country in the year 1776 Satisfactory being made to the Court they are of Opinion that the said D. Hart has a right to a settlement of 400 Acres of land including the above location & the preemption of 1000 Acres adjoining & that a Cert. issue accordingly—

(Cert issd for 1400 fees &c pd D. D. to I. Shelby)

Jacob Wiestenhunt by Isaac Shelby this day claimed a settlement & pre-

[30] Collins, Vol. 1, pp. 512, 514, 518.
[31] Collins, Vol. 1, p. 12.

emption to a tract of land in the district of Kentucky by raising a Crop of Corn in the Country in the year 1776 Satisfactory proof being made to the Court they are of Opinion that the said Wiestenhunt has a right to a settlement of 400 Acres of Land & the preemption of 1000 Acres adjoining & locates the same on hickmans Creek on the E. & North side of James Shelbys land joining the same & that a Cert. issue accordingly.—

(Cert issd for 400 fees &c pd D. D.)

Edward Williams this day claimed a preemption of 400 Acres of land at the State price in the District of Kentucky lying on the dividing ridge of Small Mountain Creek a branch of licking Creek & Lulburd Grud by the said Williams making an actual settlement in the Month of June 1779 satisfactory proof being made to the Court they are of Opinion that the said William has a right to a preemption of 400 Acres of land including the said settlement & that a Certificate issue accordingly.

(Cert issd for 1400)

Stephen Handcock[32] this day claimed a settlem't & preemption to a tract of land in the District of Kentucky lying on Tates Creek joining the land of George Boone. on the So. line including a Spring known by the name of Dentons Spring by raising a Crop of Corn in the Country in the year 1776 Satisfactory proof being made to the Court they are of Opinion that the said Handcock has a right to a settlement of 400 Acres of Land including the above location & the preemption of 1000 Acres adjoining & that a Certificate issue accordingly.

[32]Collins, Vol. 1, p. 13.

(Cert issd for 400 Acres fees &c pd D. D.)

Nich's Anderson this day claimed a preemption of 400 Acres of land in the District of Kentucky at the State price lying at the head of a branch of licking called the little Mountain Creek by making an Actual settlement on the 1st of June 1779 Satisfactory proof being made to the Court they are of Opinion that the said Anderson has a right to a preemption of 400 Acres including including the said settlement & that a Certificate issue accordingly.

(Cert issd for 400 fees &c pd D. D.)

Jesse Peake this day claimed a preemption for 400 Acres of land at the State price in the District of Kentucky lying on little Mountain Creek about 3 Miles from the head thereof on the South side by making an actual settlement in 1st of June 1779 satisfactory proof being made to the Court they are of Opinion that the said Peake has a right to a preemption of 400 Acres of land including the said settlement & that a Certificate issue accordingly.—

(Cert issd for 400 fees &c pd D. D.)

John Harper this day claimed a preemption of 400 Acres of land at the State price in the district of Kentucky lying on So. side of Lulbre Grud Creek Opposite the land of Edward Williams by making an Actual settlement on 1st June 1779 satisfactory proof being made to the Court they are of Opinion that the said Harper has a right to a preemption of 400 Acres of land including the said settlement & that a Certificate issue accordingly.

Then the Court adjourned untill to Morrow morning 10 oclock Wm. Fleming

At a Court continued & held at Boonesborough for adjusting disputed titles to the Kentucky lands the 22 of December 1779—

Present William Fleming Stephen Trigg & Edmund Lyne Gent'n

(Cert issd for 1400 by order of Court At Bryants.—)

Dan'l Dumpard Heir to John Dumpard dec'd by John Holder came into Court & claimed a right to a settlement & preemption to a tract of land in the District of Kentucky lying on Hustons fork of licking Creek about 4 Miles below a Buffaloe road that Crosses the said Creek known by the name of the Poplar ridge by the s'd decedents settling in this Country in september 1777 untill he was killed in July 1779 Satisfactory proof being made to the Court they are of Opinion that the said Dumpard has a right to a settlement of 400 Acres of land to include the above location & the preemption of 1000 Acres Adjoining Cert not to issue untill the further order of this Court.—

(Cert issd for 1400 fees &c pd D. D.)

Chistopher Irvin Jr.[32½] this day claimed a settlement & preemption to a tract of land in the District of Kentucky lying on a small Fork of tates Creek waters of Kentucky River to include a lick known by the name of Irvines lick by raising a Crop of Corn in the Country in the year 1776 satisfactory proof being made to the Court they are of Opinion that the said Irvine has a right to a settlement of 400 Acres of land to include the above location & the preemption of 1000 Acres Adjoining & that a Certificate issue accordingly.—

(Cert issd for 1400 by order of Court at Bryants)

John Beasly this day claimed a settlement & preemption to a tract of land in the District of Kentucky lying on the dividing ridge of licking Creek & Elkhorne near the head of Coopers Fork Known by the Name of lidia Mount by the s'd decedent raising a Crop of Corn in the year 1775 & residing in the Country 12 Months before the year 1778 Satisfactory proof being made to the Court they are of Opinion that the said Beasly has a right to a settlement of 400 Acres of land to include the s'd Location & the preemption of 1000 Adjoining No Certificate to issue untill the further Order of this Court.—

(Cert iss for 1400 fees &c pd D. D. to Capt'n Holder)

Major Beasly by John Holder this day claimed a settlement & preemption to a tract of land in the District of Kentucky lying on the dividing ridge between the Waters of Salt River & the Ohio including a spring called Stewarts about 15 Miles from the falls by the said Major Beaslys raising a Crop of Corn in the year 1775 & residing in the

32½Collins, Vol. 1, p. 354.

Country 12 Months before the year 1778 satisfactory proof being made to the Court they are of Opinion that the said Beasly has a right to a settlement of 400 Acres of land to include the above location & the preemption of 1000 Acres adjoining & that a Certificate issue accordingly.

(Cert issd for 400 Acres fees &c pd D. D. to Colo Calloway)

Benj'n White this day claimed a preemption of 400 Acres of land at the State price in the district of Kentucky lying on the East side of a branch of licking about 3 Miles from Nich's Andersons land by making an Actual settlement 1st of June 1779 satisfactory proof being made to the Court they are of Opinion that the said White has a right to a preemption of 400 Acres of land to include the said settlement & that a Certificate issue accordingly.

(Cert issd for 400 fees &c pd D. D.)

Peter Harper this day claimed a preemption of 400 Acres of land at the State price in the District of Kentucky lying on the South side of a branch of licking joining Benj'n Whites land— by making an Actual Settlement on the 1st June 1779— satisfactory proof being made to the Court they are of Opinion that the said Harper has a right to a preemption of 400 Acres of Land including the said Settlement & that a Certificate issue accordingly.

(Cert issd for 400 fees &c pd D. D.)

John Kelly this day claimed 400 Acres of land at the State price in the district of Kentucky lying on the West side of a branch of licking including a Spring about 8 or 10 Miles Westerly of Peter Harpers claim by the said Kelly making an actual settlm't in the month of May 1779 satisfactory proof being made to the Court they are of Opinion that the said Kelly has a right to a preemption of 400 Acres of Land including the s'd settlement & that a Certicate issue accordingly.

(Cert issd for 400 fees &c pd D. D.)

Beale Kelly this day claimed a preemption of 400 Acres of land at the State price in the District of Kentucky lying on the East side of a small Branch of licking adjoining John Kellys improvement by the said Kelly's making an Actual settlement in the Month of May 1779 satisfactory proof being made to the Court they are of Opinion that the said Kelly has a right to a preemption of 400 Acres of Land including the s'd settlement & that a Certificate issue accordingly.

(Cert issd for 1000 fees &c pd D. D.)

David Crow this day claimed a preemption of 1000 Acres of land at the State price in the district of Kentucky lying on the West side of a branch of Muddy Creek above a claim said to be Eppersons about 3 Miles & about 15 Miles from Boonesborough by marking & improving the said land in the year 1776 satisfactory proof being made to the Court they are of Opinion that the said Crow is entitled to a preemption of 1000 Acres of land to include the s'd improvm't & that a Certificate issue accordingly.

(Cert iss for 400 by order of Court at Bryants)

Edward Hall Heir at law to Wm Hall this day claimed a preemption of 400 Acres of land at the State price in the district of Kentucky lying on the East side of a small branch of licking the head branch of Coopers Run about 10 or 12 Miles from Bryants Station North Easterly by the said decedents making an actual settlement 1st June 1779 Satisfactory proof being made to the Court they are of Opinion that the said Hall has a right to a preemption of 400 Acres of land to include the s'd settlement Cert'e not to issue untill the further order of the Court.

(Cert iss for 400 by order of Court at Bryants)

Thomas Hall this day claimed a settlement of 400 Acres of land at the State price in the District of Kentucky lying on the West side of a small branch of licking adjoining Edward Hall as Heir at law to William Hall Claim by the said Thomas Hall making an Actual settlement on the first of June 1779 satisfactory proof being made to the Court they are of Opinion that the said Hall has a right to a preemption of 400 Acres of land including the s'd settlement No Certificate to issue untill the further order of this Court.—

(Cert issd for 400 by Order of Court at Bryants)

Edward Hall this day claimed a preemption of 400 Acres of land at the State price in the district of Kentucky lying on a ridge about 4 Miles from the head of Hinkstons fork about South West Course from by making an Actual settlement in may 1779 Satisfactory proof being made to the Court they are of Opinion that the said Hall has a right to a preemption of 400 Acres of Land to include the said Settlement Certificate not to issue untill the further order of this Court.—

(Cert issd for 1400 fees &c pd to Jas. Estill)

William Handcock[33] this day claimed a settlement & preemption to a tract of Land in the District of Kentucky lying on the dividing ridge of the Waters of Otter Creek & the head of tates Creek at a tree marked WH running down a branch of tates Creek for quantity by settling & raising a Crop of Corn in the Country in the year 1776 satisfactory proof being made to the Court they are of Opinion that the said Handcock has a right to a settlement of 400 Acres to include the above location & the preemption of 1000 Acres adjoining & that a Certificate issue accordingly.

(Cert issd for 1400 fees &c pd D. D.)

Flanders Callaway this day claimed a settlement & preemption to a tract of land in the District of Kentucky lying on the head branches of the West Fork of Otter Creek at a Spring known by the name of the Sinking Spring by settling & raising a Crop of Corn in the Country in the year 1775 satisfactory proof being made to the Court they are of Opinion that the said Callaway has a right to a settlement of 400 Acres of land including the above location & the preemption of 1000 Acres adjoining & that a Certificate issue accordingly.—

[33]Collins, Vol. 1, p. 13.

(Cert 'issd for 400 fees &c pd D. D.)

Thomas Doyl this day claimed a preemption of 400 Acres of land at the State price in the district of Kentucky lying on the Paint Creek a branch of Kentucky River on the War road about 4 or 5 Miles from the mouth of the said Creek by actual settlement made the 1st Jan'y 1779 Satisfactory proof being made to the Court they are of Opinion that the said Doyl has a right to a preemption of 400 Acres to include the said settlement & that a Certificate issue accordingly.—

(Cert iss by Order of Court advised)

George Madden this day claimed a preemp'n of 400 Acres of land at State price in the District of Kentucky lying on the dividing ridge of the Waters of Elkhorn & licking on a small branch of licking about 8 Miles South or So. West from the Rocky Ford on licking by settlement made on 3d of June 1779 satisfactory proof being made to the Court they are of Opinion that the said Madden has a right to preemption of 400 Acres of land to include the said Settlement Certi'e not to issue untill the further Order of this Court.—

(Cert issd for 400 by Order of Court at Bryants)

Lewis Runoe by George Madden this day claimed a preemption of 400 Acres of land at the State price in the District of Kentucky lying on both sides of a Creek of Licking and about 2 or 3 Miles to the left of the Salt spring (or Hunters trace) and about 2 Miles to the South of George Maddens land by making an Actual settlement on the 3d of June 1779 satisfactory Proof being made to the Court they are of Opinion that the said Runoe has a right to a preemption of 400 Acres of land to include the said Settlement Cert. not to issue untill the further Order of this Court.

(Cert issd for 400 by Order of Court at Bryants)

Nicholas George by George Madden this day claimed a preemption of 400 Acres of land at the State price in the District of Kentucky lying on each side of a small branch of licking about 2 Miles West of Edward Halls land by making an Actual settlement in the Month of May 1779 satisfactory proof being made to the Court they are of Opinion that the said George has a right to a preemption of 400 Acres of land to include the said settlem't & Cert's not to issue untill the further order of this Court.—

(Cert issd for 1400 by Order of Court at Bryants)

Jesse Copher.—this day claimed a settlement & preemption to a tract of land in the district of Kentucky lying on Stoners fork a branch of licking about 7 or 8 Miles above the Salt Spring trace known by the name of Bramlets Station by making an actual settlement in the year 1777 & residing in the Country ever since satisfactory proof being made to the Court they are of Opinion that the said Copher has a right to a settlement of 400 Acres of land to include the above location & the preemption of 1000 Acres adjoining Cert'e not to issue untill the further order of this Court.—

(Cert iss for 1000 fees &c pd Maj. Shelby)

Anthony Bledsoe this day claimed a preemption to 1000 acres of land at the State price in the district of Kentucky lying on the head of a branch running on the North side of Dicks River about 3 or 4 Miles from the said River and Nearly Opposite the Paint lick Creek on paint lick Creek by marking and improving the same in the year 1776 satisfactory proof being made to the Court they are of Opinion that the said Bledsoe has a right to a preemption of 1000 Acres including the said Improvement & that a Certificate issue accordingly.—

(Cert issd for 1400 fees &c pd D. D. to Maj. Shelby)

Anthony Bledsoe Assee of Wm Cooke this day claimed a settlement & preempt'n to a tract of land in the district of Kentucky lying on the head of a so'th branch of Tates Creek about ½ a mile above Some Deaden'd Trees on the branch whereon is marked WO by the said Cookes raising a crop of corn in the Country in the year 1775 satisfactory proof being made to the Court, they are of Opinion that the said Bledsoe has a right to a settlement of 400 Acres of land including the said location & the preemption of 1000 Acres adjoining & that a Certificate issue accordingly.

(Cert issd for 1400 fees &c pd D. D. to Maj Shelby)

Anthony Bledsoe Assee of Page Portwood this day claimed a settlem't & preemption to a tract of land in the district of Kentucky lying on a branch of Silver Creek about 4 Miles from the little fort on Boones old trace including a tree marked D B by the said Portwood raising a Crop of Corn in the Country in the year 1776 Satisfactory proof being made to the Court they are of Opinion that the said Bledsoe has a right to a settlement of 400 Acres of land including the above location & the preemption of 1000 Acres adjoining & that a Certificate issue accordingly.—

(Cert issd for 1400 by Order of Court at Bryants)

Edward Nelson this day claimed a settlement & preemption to a tract of land in the district of Kentucky lying on licking Creek Opposite to the Mouth of the Rocky Ford fork on the north side of Stoners Fork joining Wm Cradlebough on the North side by raising a Crop of Corn in the Country in the year 1776 & residing ever since satisfactory proof being made to the Court they are of Opinion that the said Nelson has a right to a settlement of 400 Acres of land including the above location & the premp't of 1000 Acres adjoining Cert. not to issue untill the further order of this Court.

(Cert issd 1400 for Robert McMullen &c pd D. D.)

Robt. Preston this day claimed a premp'n of 1000 Acres of land at the State price in the district of Kentucky lying on the south fork of Howard Creek Rob. McMullen comes into Court and alledged that he had a prior right to the said land & claims a settlement & preemption on the said land whereupon Sever'l Wit'es were sworn & examined

& it Appeared to the Court that the said McMullen raised a crop of Corn in the year 1776 & had a prior improvement on the s'd land, are of Opinion that the said McMullen has a right to a settlement of 400 Acres of land including this improvement & the preemption of 1000 Acres adjoining & that a Certificate issue accordingly.

(Cert issd for 1000 fees &c pd D. D.)
James Estill this day claimed a preemption of 1000 Acres of land at the State price in the District of Kentucky lying on the waters of Muddy Creek & Otter Creek within one mile of the little fork known by the name of the locust thicksett by marking & improving the same in the year 1775 satisfactory proof being made to the Court they are of Opinion that the said Estill has a right to a preemption of 1000 Acres including the said improvement & that a Cert. issue accordingly.

Robt. Preston by David McGee this day claimed a preemption of 1000 Acres of land at the State price in the District of Kentucky lying on the West side of Hickman Creek about 2 Miles below John Todds land by improving & building a Cabbin in the year 1776 Satisfactory proof being made to the Court they are of Opinion that the said Preston has a right to a preemption of 1000 Acres including the said improvement Cert'e not to issue until the further order of this Court.—

Then the Court Adjourned untill tomorrow Morning 10 oclock Wm Fleming—

At a Court continued & held at Boonesborough for Adjusting disputed Titles to Unpatented lands in the district of Kentucky the 23d day of December 1779.—

Present Wm Fleming Stephen Trigg & Edmund Lyne—Gent'n

Ephraim Drake this day claimed a preemption to a tract of land in district of Kentucky at the State price the said Drake withdraws his claim.

(Cert issd for 400)
John Calloway[34] this day claimed a preemption of 400 Acres of land at the State price in the District of Kentucky lying on a branch of Stoners fork of licking Creek joining on the south side by Wm Cradleboughs land by making an Actual settlement in the country since the first of Jany 1778 & before the passing the land law satisfactory proof being made to the Court they are of Opinion that the said Calloway has a right to a preemption of 400 Acres of land including the said Settlem't & that a Certificate issue accordingly—

(Cert iss for 1400)
Rich'd Taylor[35] by Rich'd Calloway this day claimed a settlement & preemption to a tract of land in the district of Kentucky lying on three Fork of the right hand fork of Otter Beginning at the fork running up each Different Fork & down the Main Creek for quantity by raising a Crop of Corn in the Country in the year 1776 satisfactory proof being made to the Court they are of Opinion that the said Taylor has

[34]Collins, Vol. 1, p. 13.
[35]Collins, Vol. 1, p. 9 and index.

a right to a settlement of 400 Acres of land including the above location & the preemption of 1000 Acres adjoining & that a Cert. issue accordingly.

(Cert issd for 400 by Order of Court at Bryants)

The Heir of Hm. Bramblett decd by Rich'd Calloway this day claimed a preemption of 400 Acres of land at the State price in the district of Kentucky lying on a branch of Stoners fork of licking Creek joining Ben'j Duniways Claim to land by actual settlm't made in the month of April 1779. satisfactory proof being made to the Court they are of Opinion that the s'd Heir has a right to a preemption of 400 Acres of land including the said Settlement Cert —not to issue untill the further Order of this Court.

(Cert issd for 1400 by order of Court at Bryants fees &c pd D. D. to Mr. Hall)

Sam'l Henderson[36] this day claimed a settlement & preemption to a tract of land in the district of Kentucky lying on the trace from Boonesborough to the lower Salt spring on licking Creek called the Sycamore Forest running down to the Creek for quantity by Settling & residing in the Country one year before the year 1778 & marking said land in May 1776 satisfactory proof being made to the Court they are of Opinion that the said Henderson has a right to a settlm't of 400 Acres of Land including the above location & the preemption of 1000 Acres Adjoining Cert. not to issue untill the further Order of this Court—

[36]Collins, Vol. 1, pp. 511, 513.

(Cert issd for 1400 by order of Court at Bryant)

James Cannay by Rich'd Calloway this day claimed a settlm't & preemption to a tract of land in the District of Kentucky lying on the North side of Stoners fork of licking Creek Opposite to Stoners improvem't by improving & raising a Crop of Corn in the Country in the year 1776 satisfactory proof being made to the Court they are of Opinion that the said Canny has a right to a settlement of 400 Acres of land including the above location & the preemption of 1000 Acres adjoining & Cert not to issue untill the further order of this Court.

(Cert issd for 1400)

Robt Fleming Assee of Burnard Tatum by Richard Calloway this day claimed a Settlement & preemption to a tract of land in the district of Kentucky lying on a branch of Muddy Creek to include a lick Known by the name of the little Blue lick on the path from this place to the log lick by the said Tatums raising a Crop of Corn in the Country in the year 1776 Satisfactory proof being made to the court they are of Opinion that the said Fleming has a right to a settlement of 400 Acres of land including the above location & the preemption of 1000 Acres adjoining & that Cert. issue accordingly.

(Cert issd for 1400 by order of Court at Bryants)

John Hall Assee of Sam'l Tate by Rich'd Calloway this day claimed a settlem't & preemption to a tract of land in the district of Kentucky lying on the dividing ridge between the Waters leading to the Salt Spring Trace & the large Creek running into the Rocky ford fork of Stoners fork of licking Creek at a Buffaloe pond by the said Tates raising a Crop of Corn in the year 1775 & marking the said land in November 1779 satisfactory proof being made to the Court they are of Opinion that the said Hall has a right to a settm't of 400 Acres including the said location & the premp'n of 1000 Adjoining & that no Cert. issue untill the further order of this Court.

(Cert iss for 1400)

Robt. Tate this day claimed a settlem't & preemption to a tract of land in the district of Kentucky lying on the first branch of Silver Creek on the other side of the little fort on Calloways trace to the Red Lick thence down the branch for quantity by the said Tates raising a crop of corn in the country in the year 1775 satisfactory proof being made to the Court they are of Opinion that the said Tate has a right to a settlement of 400 Acres of land including the above location & the preemption of 1000 Acres adjoining & that that a Certificate issue accordingly.—

(Cert iss for 1400)

Callip Calloway this day claimed a settlem't & preemption to a tract of land in the District of Kentucky lying on the head of Calloway Creek the last fork of Otter Creek known by the name of Knocks Buckle by the s'd Calloways residing in the Country 12 Months before the 1 Jany 1778 satisfactory proof being made to the Court they are of Opinion that the said Calloway has a right to a settlement to 400 Acres of land including the above location & the preemption of 1000 Acres adjoining & that a Certificate issue accordingly.

(Cert iss for 1400)

Rich'd Calloway this day claimed a settlement & preemption to a tract of land in the district of Kentucky lying on a Dreaming Creek a branch of the Middle fork of Otter Creek by the said Calloways raising a Crop of Corn in the year 1775 & residing ever since satisfactory proof being made to the Court they are of Opinion that the said Calloway has a right to a settlement of 400 Acres of land including the said location & the preemption of 1000 Acres adjoining & that a Certificate issue accordingly.

Wm Bailey Smith by Rich'd Calloway this day claimed a settlement & preemption to a tract of land in the district of Kentucky lying on Jessamine Creek including Jessamine spring the Court being informed that there is other Claimants to that land have Referred it until further hearing—

(Cert issd for 1400)

The Heirs of Dan'l Goodman decd this day claimed a settlement & preemption to a tract of land in the district of Kentucky by Rich'd Calloway lying on one of the South Forks of Brasheirs Creek the waters of Salt River at a place called the Vineyard with the letters DG marked on a tree by the said decedents raising a Crop of Corn & marking the said land in the year 1776 satisfactory proof being made to the Court they are of Opinion that the s'd heirs has a right to a settlement of 400 Acres of land including the above location & the preemption of 1000 Acres adjoining & that a Certificate issue accordingly.

(Cert issd for 1400)

Rich'd Henderson[37] by Rich'd Callaway this day claimed a settlement & preemption to a tract of land in the district of Kentucky lying on Otter Creek above Thomas Bartons land then up the Creek on both sides for quantity by settling & raising a Crop of Corn in the years 1775, 1776, 1778 & 1779 satisfactory proof being made to the Court they are of Opinion that the said Henderson has a right to a settlement of 400 Acres Acres of land Including the above location & the preemption of 1000 Acres Adjoining & that a Certificate issue accordingly.—

(Ress'd)

Sam'l Estill this day claimed a preemption of 400 Acres of land at the State price in the District of Kentucky lying on a branch of licking below the rocky fort at a Lick on the North side of the said Creek to include his improvement by making an Actual Settlement in April 1779 satisfactory proof being made to the Court they are of Opinion that the said Estill has a right to a settlement of 400 Acres of land to include the improvement Cert'e not to issue until a further order of this Court.

(Cert iss for 1400 fees &c pd D. D.)

Pemberton Rowlings this day claimed a settlm't & preemption to a tract of land in the district of Kentucky lying on a branch of Boons Creek called Boggers fork adjoining Benj'n Logans survey above by settling in the Country in the year 1775 & residing ever since Satisfactory proof being made to the Court they are of Opinion that the said Rawlings has a right to a settlement of 400 Acres to include the above location & a preemption of 1000 Acres Adjoining & that a Certificate issue accordingly.

(Cert iss for 400 fees &c pd D. D. to Colo Calloway)

John Peter Bondurant Heir at law to David Bondurant decd this day claimed a preemption of 400 Acres of land at the State price in the District of Kentucky lying on Tates Creek about 3 Miles from the Mouth thereof including the Walnut Bottom by the decedent making an actual settlem't in Feb'y 1778 satisfactory proof being made to the Court they are of Opinion that the said John P. Bondurant has a right to a preemption of 400 Acres including the above location & that a Certificate issue accordingly.

John South Jun'r[38] this day claimed a settlement & preemption to a tract of land in the district of Kentucky lying on the North Fork of Elkhorn at the head thereof at a rock spring about 8 Miles from Floyds improvement by raising a crop of corn in the year 1776 & residing in the Country ever since satisfactory proof being made to the Court they are of Opinion that the said South Jun'r has a right to a settlement of 400

[37]Collins, Vol. 1, pp. 18, 248, 511, 518.

[38]Collins, Vol. 1, p. 13.

Acres of land to include the above location & the preemption of 1000 Acres adjoining & Certificate not to issue untill the further order of this Court—Page

(Cert issd for 400)

Edward Harrod this day claimed a preemption of 400 Acres of land at the State price in the district of Kentucky lying on a branch of Silver Creek about 3 Miles above the little fork by making an Actual settlement in the Month of Feb'y 1779 satisfactory proof being made to the Court they are of Opinion that the said Harrod has a right to a preemption to 400 Acres of land including the said settlement & that a Certificate issue accordingly.

(Cert issd for 1400 by order of Court at Bryants)

David Gass[39] this day claimed a settlement & preemption to a tract of Land in the district of Kentucky lying on the dividing ridge of the south fork of Elkhorn & Jassemon Creek including a sinking spring by raising a Crop of Corn in the year 1775 & 1776 satisfactory proof being made to the Court they are of Opinion that the said Gass has a right to a settlement of 400 Acres of land including the above location & the preemption of 1000 Acres adjoining Certificate not to issue untill the further order of this Court.

(Cert issd for 1400 fees &c pd D. D.)

Wm Bush this day claimed a settlement & preemption to a tract of land in the district of Kentucky lying between Harrods lower creek & the two Mile Creek by improving the same & raising a Crop of Corn in the year 1775 & 1776 satisfactory proof being made to the Court they are of Opinion that the said Bush has a right to a settlement of 400 Acres of land to include the said improvement & the prempt'n of 1000 Acres adjoining & that a Certificate issue accordingly.

Then the Court untill to Morrow Morning 8 oclock

Wm Fleming

At a Court continued & held at Boonesboro for adjusting titles of claimants to unpatented lands by the Commissioners of Kentucky district the 24th day of December 1779

Present Wm Fleming Stephen Trigg & Edmund Lyne—Gent'n

(Cert iss for 400)

Will'm Collingsworth by Ephraim Drake this day claimed a preemption of 400 Acres of land at the State price in the district of Kentucky lying on the North fork of Howards Creek where the trace of the Salt Spring crosses the said Creek after passing the indian Camp by making an actual Settlement in the Month of April 1778 satisfactory proof being made to the Court they are of Opinion that the said Collinsworth has a right to a preemption of 400 Acres of land to include the said settlement & that a Certificate issue accordingly.

(Cert issd for 1400 by order of Court at Bryants)

Rich'd Epperson by Rich'd Callaway this day claimed a settlement & preemption to a tract of land in the district of Kentucky lying at the mouth

[39] Collins, Vol. 1, p. 13.

of the Creek that runs into the Woolf Fork of licking run up each Fork and down the Main Creek for quantity by the said Epperson settling & raising a Crop of Corn in the Country in the year 1776 satisfactory proof being made to the Court they are of Opinion that the said Epperson has a right to a settlement of 400 Acres of land including the above location & the preemption of 1000 Acres adjoining. Cert not to issue untill the further order of this Court.

Wm Cowan by David Gass this day claimed a settlement & preemption to a tract of land in the district of Kentucky lying— To be heard at Elkhorn.

Sam'l Porter[40] By david Gass this day claimed a preemption of 400 Acres of land at the State price in the district of Kentucky lying dismissed—

(Cert issd for 1400 by order of Court at Bryant fees &c pd D. D. to Jos Martin)

David Wilcox this day claimed a settlement & preemption to a tract of land in the district of Kentucky lying on the south fork of Elkhorn Easterly from Moffats line including a spring by the said Wilcox including the same in May 1779 & raising a Crop of Corn the same year satisfactory proof being made to the Court they are of Opinion that the said Wilcox has a right to a settlement of 400 Acres of Land & a preemption to 1000 Acres adjoining Certificate not to issue untill the further order of this Court.

[40]Collins, Vol. 1, p. 13.

(Cert issd for 1400 fees &c pd D. D.)

James McMuling this day claimed a settlement & preemption to a tract of land in the district of Kentucky lying in the Forks of Howard Creek joining Wm. Bushes Land to include his improvement by settlement made & raising a Crop of Corn in the year 1776 satisfactory proof being made to the Court they are of Opinion that the said McMulin has a right to a settlement of 400 Acres of land including the said improvement & the preemption of 1000 Acres Adjoining & that a Certificate issue accordingly.

(Cert iss for 1400)

William Hoge (Hoye) Assee of Thomas Johnson[42] by Rich'd Callaway this day claimed a settlement & preemption to a tract of land in the district of Kentucky lying between the head of Otter Creek and branches of Silver Creek including a Buckeye marked TE 1775 by the said Johnson raising a Crop of Corn in the Country in the year 1775 satisfactory proof being made to the Court they are of Opinion that the said Hoge has a right to a settlement of 400 Acres of land to include the above location & the preemption of 1000 Acres adjoining & that a Certificate issue accordingly.

(This claim dismissed)

William Hoge (Hoye) Assee of Wm Deal by Rich'd Callaway this day claimed a settlement & preemption to a tract of land in the district of Kentucky on the West side of a branch of Wolfs Creek a branch of licking run-

[42]Collins, Vol. 1, p. 18.

ning up & down the creek for quantity including a large black walnut marked R.C. by the said Deals raising a Crop of Corn in the Country in the year 1775 satisfactory proof being made to the Court they are of Opinion that the said Hoge has a right to a settlement of 400 Acres of land to include the above location & the preemption of 1000 Acres Certificate not to issue untill the further order of this Court.

(Cert issd for 1400 fees &c pd D. D.)

John Holder[43] this day claimed a settlement & preemption to a tract of land in the district of Kentucky lying about $1\frac{1}{2}$ Miles from the Mouth of Boons Creek on the West side thereof to include Russells spring by the said Holder settling in the Country in the year 1777 & residing ever since satisfactory proof being made to the Court they are of Opinion that the said Holder has a right to a settlement of 400 Acres of land to include the above location & the preemption of 1000 Acres adjoining & that a Certificate issue accordingly.

(Cert issd for 1000)

George Boone by Dan'l Boone this day claimed a preemption of 1000 Acres of land at the State price lying in the district of Kentucky on Tates Creek including a lick called Tates lick lying on the path leading from this to St Asaphs by marking & improving the same in the year 1775 satisfactory proof being made to the Court they are of Opinion that the said Boone has a right to a preemption of 1000 Acres including the above location & that a Certificate issue accordingly.

(Cert issd for 1400)

Daniel Boone[44] this day claimed a settlement & preemption to a tract of land in the district of Kentucky lying on the Waters of licking including a small spring on the North East side of a small branch a Camp & some Bushes Cut down at the same about 20 Miles East from Boonesborough by the said Boons settling & raising a Crop of Corn in the Country in the year 1775 & 1776 satisfactory proof being made to the Court they are of Opinion that the said Boone has a right to a settlement of 400 Acres of land including the above location & the preemption of 1000 Acres adjoining Cert issue accordingly.

(To be continued)

[43]Collins, Vol. 1, pp. 13, 20, 255, 512.

[44]Collins, Vol. 1, p. 20 and index.

MARTINETTE VILEY WITHERSPOON
See Page 169

OFFICERS

of the

KENTUCKY STATE HISTORICAL SOCIETY

SUBSCRIPTIONS.

Subscription, Yearly, $2.00 Current Number, 75c Per Copy.
Back Numbers, $1.00 Per Copy.

Subscriptions must be sent by check, or money order. All communications for The Register should be addressed to H. V. McChesney, Editor, Frankfort, Kentucky.

H. V. McCHESNEY, Editor and Business Manager.
MRS. JOUETT TAYLOR CANNON, Associate Editor

TO SUBSCRIBERS.

If your copy of The Register is not received promptly please advise us. It is issued in January, May and September.

Entered as second class matter September 17, 1919, at the Post Office at Frankfort, Kentucky, under the Act of August 24, 1912.

THE STATE JOURNAL COMPANY
FRANKFORT, KY.

CONTENTS

MAY, 1923

REGISTER

Kentucky State Historical Society

Vol. 21 May, 1923 No. 62

CERTIFICATE BOOK OF THE VIRGINIA LAND COMMISSION 1779-80—Continued.

EDITOR'S NOTE.

We are publishing in this issue the second installment of the "Certificate Book."

On a re-examination of certain of the entries in the book which we carried in the January issue, using a strong reading glass on some that were more or less faded, we are convinced that a few errors crept in, and we are correcting them herewith:

On page 52, paragraph 6, the name John Dorme should have been John Donne.

On page 80, paragraph 5, the name Will'm Collingsworth appears, spelled also Collinsworth in same entry. The index to the old volume does not disclose this name; but the name William Collins in the index bears page number referring to the entry showing name "Collingsworth." We have no means of knowing which is correct, the index reference or the entry in the body of the text.

On page 33, paragraph 4, we have the name Timmerman. The first letter of the word appears to be a capital T, and it appears the same way in the index, but it is grouped under the letter Z heading in the index; so we think the name must have been intended for Zimmerman.

An interested subscriber has written us that he thinks "Durets Creek" which we have on page 68, paragraph 1, should have been "Jouetts Creek." He says that Matthew Jouett, uncle of the distinguished Kentucky artist by that name, laid his land entries on a creek which took his name, and that the location makes it clear that our "Durets Creek" is the same. This is perhaps true, but as the entry in the old volume was perfectly clear, and written "Durets," we printed it in that form. The Clerk of the Land Commission might very readily have misunderstood the pronunciation of the word as it was called out in Court.

Our correspondent referred to above also thinks the name John Boffman, page 65, paragraph 2, should have been Jacob Boffman, but again the name in the old record is perfectly clear, and reads "John." It may have been an error of the clerk.

(Cert. iss'd for 1400)

[45]Israel Boone by Dan'l Boone this day claimed a settlement & preemption to a tract of land in the district of Ken-

[45] Collins, vol. 2, pp. 563-663.

tucky lying on Boones Creek between & joining Hickmans two surveys on the said Creek by the said Boones raising a crop of Corn in the Country in the years of 1775 & 1776 satisfactory proof being made to the Court they are of Opinion that the said Boone has a right to a settlement of 400 Acres of land including the above location & the preemption of 1000 Acres adjoining & that a Certificate issue accordingly.

(Cert. iss'd for 1400)

James Briges by Dan'l Boone this day claimed a Settlement & preemption to a tract of land in the District of Kentucky lying on Muddy Creek a branch of Kentucky River to include his improvement by settling & raising a crop of Corn in the Country in the year 1775 Satisfactory proof being made to the Court they are of Opinion that the said Briges has a right to a settlement of 400 Acres of land including the above location & the preemption of 1000 Acres Adjoining & that a Certificate issue accordingly.

(Cert. iss'd for 1400)

[46]Wm. Hicks by Dan'l Boone this day claimed a settlement & preemption to a tract of land in the district of Kentucky lying on a branch of Silver Creek including [47]Hancock Taylors grave & running No. & North W for quantity by making a settlement & raising a Crop of Corn in the Country in the year 1775 satisfactory proof being made to the Court they are Of Opinion that the said Hicks has a right to a settlement of 400 Acres of land to include the above location & the preemption of 1000 Acres Adjoining & that a Certificate issue accordingly.

(Cert. iss'd for 1400)

[48]John Hart by Dan'l Boone this day claimed a settlement & preemption to a tract of land in the district of Kentucky lying on a branch of Silver Creek joining Wm. Hick land on the West by settling & raising a Crop of Corn in the year 1775 Satisfactory proof being made to the Court they are of Opinion that the s'd Hart has a right to a settlement of 400 Acres of land including the above location & the preemption of 1000 Acres adjoining & that a Certificate issue accordingly.

(Cert iss for 1000)

James Wharton by Dan'l Boone this day claimed a preemption of 1000 Acres at the State price in the District of Kentucky on the East fork of Muddy Creek including a tree marked IW about 5 Miles from the red lick & about a N. West course from the said lick by marking & improving the same in the year 1775 satisfactory proof being made to the Court they are of opinion that the said Wharton had a right to a preemption of 1000 Acres including the above location & that a Certificate issue accordingly.

(Cert Iss'd for 1000)

Thomas Sanders by Dan'l Boone this day claimed a preemption of 1000 Acres of land at the State price in the district of Kentucky lying on the Waters of licking Creek Adjoining Wm. Moores land on the North Side by marking & improving the same in the year 1775 Satisfac-

[46] Collins, vol. 1, pp. 11, 18.
[47] McAfee papers.
[48] Collins, vol. 1, pp. 6, 18, 45, 215.

tory proof being made to the Court they are of an Opinion that the said Sanders has a right to a preemption of 1000 Acres of land to include the above location & that a Certificate issue accordingly.

(Cert iss'd for 1000 fees &c pd. D. D. to E. Smith)

Isaac Davis by [49]Enoch Smith this day claimed a preemption of 1000 Acres of land at the State price in the District of Kentucky lying on the West side of a small Mountain Creek a branch of Hinkstons fork of licking joining the lands of Enoch Smith to the North by the said Davis building a Cabbin on the premises in the year 1775 satisfactory proof being made to the Court they are of Opinion that the said Davis has a right to a preemption of 1000 Acres of land to include his improvement & that a Certificate issue accordingly.

(Cert iss for 400)

John Huley (Haley?) this day claimed a preemption of 40 Acres of land at the State price in the district of Kentucky lying on a branch of the South Fork of licking East of the Salt spring trace from Boonsborough & about 2 mile East of Ambrose Coffers land by settlement made in the year 1776 satisfactory proof being made to the Court they are of Opinion that the said Huley (Haley?) has a right to a preemption of 400 Acres of land to include the above location & that a Cert. issue accordingly.

(Cert iss'd for 1400 fees &c pd D. D.)

Thomas Phelps this day claimed a settlement & preemp. to a tract of land in the district of Kentucky lying on the Western branch of Otter Creek a branch of Kentucky River at popes lick to include his improvement by Settling & raising a Crop of Corn in the Country in the year 1776 Satisfactory proof being made to the Court they are of opinion that the said Phelps has a right to a settlement of 400 Acres of land to include his improvement & the preemption of 1000 Acres adjoining & that a Certificate issue accordingly.

Nath'l Hart Assee of Lancelett Johnson who was Assee of Elijah Munn this day claimed a settlement & preemption to a tract of land in the District of Kentucky lying—

(Cert iss'd for 1400 by order of Court at Bryant, fees &c pd to Cap't Molden)

James Callaway by [50]Flanders Calloway this day claimed a settlement & preemption to a tract of land in the district of Kentucky lying on the south fork of the Waters of licking known by the name Hustons fork on the No. west side of the said branch about one mile from the head by settling in the Country in the year 1777 & residing in the Country ever since satisfactory proof being made to the Court they are of Opinion that the said Callaway has a right to a settlement of 400 Acres of land to include the above location & the preemption of 1000 Acres adjoining Certificate not to issue until the further order of this Court.

(Cert iss'd for 1400 by order of Court at Bryants fees &c pd D. D. to Capt. Holden (Wolden?) (Holder?)

Micajah Callaway this day by Flanders Callaway claimed a settlement and

[49] Calk's Journal.

[50] Collins, vol. 2, p. 526.

preemption to a tract of land in the District of Kentucky lying on the Waters of the South fork of licking Creek known by the Name of Hustons fork adjoining James Callaway land on the East side by settling in the Country in the year 1777 & residing ever since satisfactory proof being made to the Court they are of Opinion that the said Callaway has a right to a settlement of 400 Acres of land including the above location & the preemption of 1000 Acres adjoining Cert. not issue untill the further order of this Court—

(Cert. iss'd for 400 fees &c pd D. D.)

[51]Ralph Morgan assee of John Peake this day claimed a preemption of 400 Acres of land at the State price in the District of Kentucky lying on a branch of Wolfs Creek waters of licking Creek about 6 or 7 Miles from Strodes Station by actual Settlement in Sept. 1776 satisfactory proof being made to the Court they are of Opinion that the said Morgan has a right to a preempt. of 400 Acres of land to include the above location Cert to issue accordingly.

(Cert iss'd for 400)

Chelsey Woodard Assee of James Bryant this day claimed a settlem't & preemption to a tract of land in the District of Kentucky lying on the Waters of licking on the Salt Spring trace near Stoners path including a tree marked CW on the path It Appearing to the Court by testimony that the said Bryant was not a Settler in this Country till 1778 they are of Opinion that the said Woodard has a right to a preemption only of 400 Acres of land at the State price to include the above location Cert to issue accordingly.

(Cert iss'd for 1000)

William Bird this day claimed a preemption of 1000 Acres of land at the State price in the District of Kentucky lying on a branch of Chaplins Fork of Salt River between Howards Creek & Buffaloe Creek to include his Cabbin by improving the same & building on the premises in the year 1776. satisfactory proof being made to the Court they are of Opinion that the said Bird has a right to a preemption of 1000 Acres including the said improvement & that a Certificate issue accordingly.

(Cert iss'd for 1400 by order of Court at Bryants—)

Wm. Hoye Assee of John Moore by Rich'd Callaway[52] this day claimed a settlement & preemption to a tract of land in the District of Kentucky lying on the Waters of licking Creek beginning about ¾ Miles East of Eppersons Claim on a ridge & running East for quantity by the said Moore raising a Crop of Corn in the Country in the year 1775 Satisfactory proof being made to the Court they are of Opinion that the said Hoye has a right to a settlement of 400 Acres of land to include the above location & the preemption of 1000 Acres Adjoining & that a Certificate issue accordingly—

(Cert iss'd for 1000 fees &c pd D. D.)

John Bowles this day claimed a preemption of 1000 Acres of land at the state price in the district of Kentucky lying on a branch of Muddy Creek join-

[51] Collins, vol. 1, p. 13.

[52] Collins, vol. 2, p. 110.

ing James Estills on the East side by marking & improving the same in the year 1775 satisfactory proof being made to the Court they are of Opinion that the said Bowles has a right to a preemption of 1000 Acres of land including the said improvement & that a Certificate issue accordingly.

(Cert iss'd for 400 fees &c pd D. D.)

John Mounee this day claimed a preemption of 400 Acres of land at the State price in the District of Kentucky lying on a branch running into Silver Creek on the North side to include his improvement by actual settlement made in April 1779 satisfactory proof being made to the Court they are of Opinion that the said Mounee has a right to a preemption of 400 Acres of land including the said improvement & that a Certificate issue accordingly.

(Cert iss'd for 400 fees &c pd D. D.)

John Kincaid by John Boles this day claimed a preemption of 400 Acres of land at the State price in the District of Kentucky lying on a branch running into Silver Creek on the North side down the s'd branch from Mounee land to include his improvement by making an actual settlement in April 1779 satisfactory proof being made to the Court they are of Opinion that the said Kincaid has a right to a preempt. of 400 Acres of land to include the said improvement & that a Cert. issue accordingly.

(Cert iss for 400 by order of Court at Bryants)

[53]James Berry this day claimed a preemption of 400 Acres of land at the State price in the District of Kentucky lying on a branch of Stoners Fork of licking about 2 Miles South East of Harrods lick an actual settlement in April 1779 satisfactory proof being made to the Court they are of Opinion that the said Berry has a right to a preemption of 400 Acres of land including the Above location Cert not to issue untill the further Order of this Court.

(Cert issued for 1400 fees &c pd D. D.)

[54]William Hays by Dan'l Boone this day claimed a settlement & preemption to a tract of land in the district of Kentucky lying on a branch of Silver Creek 4 Miles this side of the Blue lick beginning at Colo Callaways trace running up both sides of the Creek for quantity by settlem't & raising a Crop of Corn in the Country in the year 1776 satisfactory proof being made to the Court they are of Opinion that the said Hays has a right to a settlement of 400 Acres of land including the above location & the preemption of 1000 Acres adjoining & that a Certificate issue accordingly.

(this Claim set aside)

Wm. Moore Assee of James Anthony this day claimed a preemption of 400 Acres of land at the State price in the district of Kentucky lying on the Kentucky River about 2 Miles above this place including Tates Bottom by the said Anthonys making an Actual settlement in the Month of March 1779 satisfactory proof being made to the Court they are of opinion that the said Moore has a right to a preemption of 400 Acres of land to include the above location & that a Certificate issue accordingly.

[53] Collins, vol. 1, p. 13.

[54] Collins, vol. 1, p. 13.

(Cert iss'd for 1000 fees &c pd D. D.)

William Fleming[55] this day claimed a preemption to a tract of land of 1000 Acres at the State price in the district of Kentucky lying on the Waters of the North fork of Beargrass joining Colo. Wm. Christians land to include survey made for the said Fleming by marking & improving the same in the year 1775 satisfactory proof being made to the Court they are of Opinion that the said Fleming has a right to a preemption of 1000 Acres of land including the above location & that a Certificate issue accordingly.

(Cert iss'd for 1400)

Joshua Barton this day claimed a settlement & preempt'n to A tract of land in the District of Kentucky lying on the head of the 4 Mile run Waters of Kentucky River on the North side thereof about 15 Miles North East from this place & raising a Crop of Corn in the year 1776 satisfactory proof being made to the Court they are of opinion that the said Barton has a right to a settlement of 400 Acres of land including the above location & a preempt'n of 1000 Acres of land adjoining & that a Cert'e issue accordingly.

John South, Younger, this day claimed a preempt'n of 1000 Acres of land at the State price in the district of Kentucky on the left Hand fork of Otter Creek including a Clover Bottom about one Mile from the Mouth at a lick in the Spring the claim withdrawn.

(Cert iss'd for 400)

Waller Welch this day claimed a preemption of 400 Acres of land at the State price in the district of Kentucky lying on the North side of Kentucky Opposite to the Mouth of Station Camp Creek by making Actual Settlement in April 1779—satisfactory proof being made to the Court they are of Opinion that the said Welch has a right to a preemption of 400 Acres of land including the above location & that a Cert. issue accordingly.

(Cert iss'd for 1400 fees &c pd D. D. L. Hall)

[56]Benj'n Martin this day claimed a settlem't & preemption to a tract of land in the District of Kentucky lying &c It appearing to the Court by Testimony that the said Barton raised a Crop of Corn in the Country in the year 1775 & that he is intitled to a settlement & preemption lying on the branch of licking Creek about 3 Miles North West of Dan'l Boons land & Isarel Grant including a fork of said Creek on a small Buffaloe road which makes to a Spring near the said fork & running East for quantity Ordered that a Cert. issue accordingly—

Then the Court adjourned untill tomorrow Morning 10 Oclock.

William Fleming.

At a Court Continued & held for Adjusting disputed Titles to unpatent'd Land in the District of Kentucky, at Boonsborough this 27th day of Dec'r 1779

Present

William Fleming Stephen Trigg & Edmund Lyne Gent'n

[55] Collins, vol. 1, p. 20.

[56] Name was apparently written Martin, with a B written over the M—appears as Barton in body of entry, but is Martin in index.

(Cert iss'd for 1400 by order of Court at Bryants.)

Barlett Searcy[57] this day claimed a settlement & preemption to a tract of land in the District of Kentucky lying on the North side of the Kentucky river on a small branch called Rockhouse about 4 Mile from the river by the said Searcy settling in the Country in the year 1777 & residing ever since satisfactory proof being made to the Court they are of Opinion that the said Searcy has a right to a settlement of 400 Acres of land to include the above location & the preemption of 1000 Acres adjoining Certificate not to issue untill the further Order of this Court.

(Cert iss for 1400)

Rich'd Searcy by Barlett Searcy this day claimed a Settlemen't & preemption to a tract of land in the district of Kentucky lying on the head of a branch of Howards creek joining the lands of William Cothenworth on the Western side thereof by making An Actual Settlement in 1779 & residing ever since satisfactory proof being made to the Court they are of Opinion that the said Searcy has a right to a settlement of 400 Acres of land including the above location & the preemption of 1000 Acres adjoining & that a Cert—issue accordingly.

(Cert iss for 1400 by ord'r of Court at Bryants)

Reuben Searcy[58] this day claimed a settlem't & preemption to a tract of land in the District of Kentucky lying on Stoners Fork of licking at Martins Cabbin by settling in the year 1777 & residing ever since satisfactory proof being made to the Court they are of Opinion that the said Searcy has a right to a settlement of 400 Acres of land including the above location & the preemption of 1000 Acres Adjoining Cert. not to issue untill the further order of this Court.

(Cert iss'd for 1400 by ord'r at Bryants)

Nathan'l Bullock this day claimed a settlement and preemption to a tract of land in the District of Kentucky lying on the Sourth fork of licking about 5 Miles below the Salt Spring Trace that leads from this place by settling in this Country in the year 1777 & Residing ever since & by improving the said land in April 1778 satisfactory proof being made to the Court they are of Opinion that the said Bullock has a right to a settlem't of 400 Acres of land to include his improvement & the preemption of 1000 Acres Adjoining Certificate not to issue untill a further Order of this Court.

(Cert iss'd for 1400 by order of Court at Bryants)

John Bullock this day claimed a settlem't & preemption to a tract of land in the District of Kentucky lying on Stoners fork of licking about a Mile above McMullins Spring by Settling in the Country in the 1777 & residing ever since satisfactory proof being made to the Court they are of Opinion that the said Bullock has a right to a settlement of 400 Acres of land including the above location & the preemption of 1000 Acres Adjoining Cert. not to issue untill the further Order of this Court.

[57] Collins, vol. 1, p. 13.
[58] Collins, vol. 1, p. 13.

(Cert iss'd for 1000 Acres fees pd D. D.)

John Strode this day claimed a preemption to 1000 Acres of land at the State price in the District of Kentucky lying on the So. fork of licking near the head thereof to include his Station on the premises and running up the said Creek for quantity by marking & improving the same in April 1776 satisfactory proof being made to the Court they are of Opinion that the said Strode has a right to a preemption of 1000 Acres of land including the above location Cert. to issue accordingly.

(Cert iss for 1000 fees &c pd D. D. to Jn Strode)

James Strode by John Strode this day claimed a preemption of 1000 Acres of land at the State price in the District of Kentucky lying on the head of Howards Creek joining on the East side of John Strodes land by marking & improving the same in the year 1776 satisfactory proof being made to the Court they are of Opinion that the said Strode has a right to a preemption of 1000 Acres of land to include the said improvement & that a Certificate issue accordingly.

(Cert iss'd for 1000 fees &c pd D. D.)

Edward Wilson[59] by Jno. Strode this day claimed a preemption to 1000 Acres of land at the State price in the district of Kentucky lying at the East side of James Strodes land including the Waters of 2 Mile creek of Howards Creek by marking & improving the same in the year 1776 satisfactory proof being made to the Court they are of Opinion that the said Wilson has a right to a preemption of 1000 acres of land including the said improvement & that a Certificate issue accordingly.

(Cert iss'd for 1000 fees &c pd to J. Strode)

Benedick Couchman by John Strode this day claimed a preemption of 1000 Acres of land in the district of Kentucky lying between the head of Howards Creek & two Mile Creek by improving & marking the same in the year 1776 Satisfactory proof being made to the Court they are of Opinion that the s'd Couchman has a right to a preemption of 1000 Acres of land to include his improvement and that a Certificate issue accordingly.

(Cert iss'd for 1000 fees &c pd D. D.)

John Taylor[60] this day claimed a preemption of 1000 Acres of land at the State price in the District of Kentucky lying on licking about 1 Mile below three Forks by marking & improving the same in the year 1776 satisfactory proof being made to the Court they are of Opinion that the said Taylor has a right to a preemption of 1000 Acres of land to include his improvement & that a Cert. issue accordingly.—

(Cert iss'd for 1400 by ord'r of Court at Bryants)

Jesse Hodges[61] this day claimed a settlem't & preemption to a tract of land in the District of Kentucky lying on Wolf Creek a branch of licking below Rich'd Eppersons land by Settling in the Country in the year 1777 & residing ever since satisfactory proof being

[59] Collins, vol. 1, p. 9.

[60] Collins, vol. 1, pp. 416, 421.

[61] Collins, vol. 1, p. 13.

made to the Court they are of Opinion that the said Hodges has a right to a settlement of 400 Acres of land including the above location & the preemption of 1000 Acres adjoining Certificate not to issue untill the further Order of this Court.

(Cert iss'd for 1000)

John Sterns Heir at law to Fred'k Sterns Dec'd this day claimed a preemption to a tract of 1000 Acres of land at the State price in the District of Kentucky lying at the Mouth of Strodes Fork of licking up & down the Creek for quantity by the decedents Marking & improving the same in the year 1775 satisfactory proof being made to the Court they are of Opinion that the said Sterns has a right to a preemption of 1000 Acres of land to include his improvements & that a Certificate issue accordingly.

(Cert iss'd for 1400 fees &c pd D. D.)

Thomas Kennedy[62] this day claimed a settlem't & preemption to a tract of land in the district of Kentucky lying on Strodes fork of licking about 2 Miles below John Taylors land by the s'd Kenedys Settling & raising a crop of Corn in the year 1776 satisfactory proof being made to the Court they are of Opinion that the s'd Kennedy has a right to a settlement of 400 Acres of land to include the above location & the preemption of 1000 Acres adjoining & that Certificate issue accordingly.

(Cert iss for 1400 fees &c pd D. D.)

William Bird this day came into Court & made it appear that the land granted him 24 ins't was rongly located by William Stewart & moves that he may locate the same on the Waters of Buffaloe Creek a branch of Chaplins Fork of Salt River to include his improvements & running up the branches towards the knobs for quantity and that Certificate issue accordingly.

(Cert iss for 1400)

Marquis Calmes Jun this day claimed a settlem't & preemption to a tract of land in the district of Kentucky lying on an Old Indian Town on Lulbers Grud Creek by Settling & raising a Crop of Corn in the year 1775 satisfactory proof being made to the Court they are of Opinion that the said Calmes has a right to a settlem't of 400 Acres of land including the s'd settlement & the preempt'n of 1000 Acres adjoining & that a Cert issue accordingly—

(Cert iss for 1000)

[63]Benj. Combs this day claimed a preemption of 1000 Acres of land at the State price in the district of Kentucky lying at the fork of lulbergrud Creek Crossing Howards Creek for quantity by marking & improving the same in the year 1775 satisfactory proof being made to the Court they are of Opinion that the said Combs has a right to a preemption of 1000 Acres of land including the above location and that a Certificate issue Accordingly.

Marquis Calmes this day claimed a preemption of 1000 Acres of land at the State price in the District of Kentucky lying on the levels of Elkhorn & Kentucky at the double spring about 20

[62] Collins, vol. 1, pp. 23, 355 and index.

[63] Biographical Enc. Ky., p. 75.

Miles South East of Lee's Town by marking & improving the same in the year 1775 satisfactory proof being made to the Court they are of Opinion that the said Calmes has a right to a preemption of 1000 Acres to include the above location Cert. not to issue untill the further Order of this Court.

Benj'n Berry this day claimed a preemption to 1000 Acres of land at the State price in the district of Kentucky lying between the Waters of lulbergrud & licking about 3 or 4 Miles North East from several Trees marked M C by marking & improving the same in the year 1775, satisfactory proof being made to the Court they are of Opinion that the said Berry has a right to a preemption of 1000 Acres to include the above location & that a Certificate issue accordingly.

(Cert iss'd for 1400 by Ord'r of Court at Bryants)

John Kennedy[64] son of John Assee of John Kenedy son of Dan'l this day claimed a settlem't & preemption of a tract of land in the District of Kentucky lying on a branch of Stoners fork of licking running on the South side of about 4 Miles South west of Michael Stoners improvement & Settling & raising a Crop of Corn in the year 1776 satisfactory proof being made to the Court they are of Opinion that the said John Kenady son of John has a right to a settlem't of 400 Acres of land to include the said location & the preempt of 1000 Acres adjoining Cert. not to issue untill the further order of this Court.—

(Cert iss'd for 1400 by ord'r of Court at Bryants)

John Kenedy son of John this day claimed preempt of 1000 Acres of land at the State price in the District of Kentucky lying on a branch of Stoners fork of licking running into the s'd Creek on the South side about 3 Miles from the Mouth of the said branch by marking & improving the same in the year 1776 and Building a Cabbin satisfactory proof being made to the Court they are of Opinion that the said Kennedy has a right to a preemption of 1000 Acres to include the said improvement. Cert not to issue untill the further order of this Court.

(Cert iss'd for 400 fees &c pd D. D.)

John Constant[65] this day claimed a preemption of 400 Acres of land in the District of Kentucky at the State price lying on a branch of Strodes fork a branch of licking about 2½ Mile East of Strodes Station by making an Actual Settlement Ap'l 1779 satisfactory proof being made to the Court they are of Opinion that the said Constant has a right to a preemption of 400 Acres of land to include the s'd Settlement & that a Cert issue accordingly.

(Cert. iss'd for 1400 fees &c pd D. D.)

Joseph Phelps[66] this day claimed a settlement & preemption to a tract of land in the District of Kentucky lying on a branch of the West Fork of the B Fork of Otter Creek about ½ Mile from Hammons lick beginning at a tree marked TP & running South by settling & raising a Crop of Corn in the year 1776 satisfactory proof being made to the

[64] Collins, vol. 1, pp. 12, 18 (may refer to the elder John).

[65] Collins, vol. 1, p. 13.

[66] Collins, vol. 1, p. 12.

Court they are of Opinion that the said Phelps has a right to a settlement of 400 Acres of land to include the above location & the preemption on 1000 Acres adjoining & that a certificate issue accordingly.

(Cert. iss for 1400 by order of Court at Bryants fees &c pd D. D. to L. Hall—)

Sam. Henderson Assee of Abraham Mitchell this day claimed a settlem't & preemption to a tract of land in the district of Kentucky lying at Harrods lick on the Hunters trace from this to the lower Salt Springs on the Waters of licking by the s'd Mitchell raising a Crop of Corn in the year 1775 satisfactory proof being made to the Court they are of Opinion that the said Henderson has a right to settlem't of 400 Acres of land to include the above location & the preemption of 1000 Acres Adjoining Certificate not to issue untill the further Order of this Court.

Then the Court adjourned untill tomorrow Morning 10 Oclock

William Fleming.

At a Court Continued & held for adjusting Titles to unpattented lands in the district of Kentucky by the Commissioners the 28th day of December 1779.—at Boonsborough

Present William Fleming Stephen Trigg & Edmund Lyne Gent

(Cert Iss'd for 400)

John South Younger[67] this day claimed a preemption of 400 Acres of land at the State price in the district of Kentucky lying on the left hand fork of Otter Creek about a Mile from the Mouth thereof including a lick in the Creek & Known by the name of the Clover Bottom by settlement in April 1779 satisfactory proof being made to the Court they are of Opinion that the said Younger has a right to a preemption of 400 Acres of land to include the above location & that a Cert. issue accordingly.

(Cert iss'd for 1400 fees &c pd D. D.)

Rob't Whiteledge this day claimed a settlem't & preemption (by Rich'd Henderson) to a tract of land in the District of Kentucky lying on Coopers run a branch of licking joining the land of Wm. McGee on the East side by improving the same & raising a Crop of Corn in the year 1776 satisfactory proof being made to the Court they are of Opinion that the said Whiteledge has a right to a settlem't of 400 Acres of land to include his improvement & the preemption of 1000 Acres Adjoining Cert to issue accordingly.

(Cert iss'd for 1400 fees &c pd D. D.)

Thos Whiteledge by Rich'd Henderson this day claimed a settlem't & preempt'n to a tract of land in the district of Kentucky lying on the Middle branch of Coopers run water of licking Creek at a small spring with the two first letters of John Tounsends name cut on a tree by the said Whiteledges Settling & raising a Crop of Corn in the year 1776 satisfactory proof being made to the Court they are of Opinion that the said Whiteledge has a right to a settlem't of 400 Acres of land to include the above location & the Preemption of 1000 Acres adjoining & that a Certificate issue accordingly.

---

[67] This is probably John South, younger, as Collins, vol. 1, p. 13 lists "John South, Sr.", "John South, Jr., and "John South, younger."

(Cert iss. for 400)

Overton Peyton by John Boles this day claimed a preempt'n of 400 Acres of land at the State price in the District of Kentucky lying on the Stone lick branch of Silver Creek including the Stone lick by making an Actual Settlement in the year 1779 satisfactory proof being made to the Court they are of Opinion that the said Peyton has a right to a preemption of 400 Acres of land to include the said settlement & that a Cert. issue accordingly.

(this entry set aside)

[68]John South Sen'r this day claimed a preemption of 400 Acres of land at the State price in the District of Kentucky lying on the dividing ridge between the Harrods lick branch & the Flat lick branch Water of licking Creek running Westward for quantity by making an Actual Settlement in the year of 1778 satisfactory proof being made to the Court they are of Opinion that the said South has a right to the preemption of 400 Acres of land to include the above location Cert. not to issue untill the further Order of this Court—

[69]William Kelly by John South Sen'r this day claimed a preemption to a tract of land at the State price in the District of Kentucky lying on a branch of Flat lick Creek the Waters of licking including the Flat lick on the salt Spring trace joining the lands of John South by making an Actual Settlem't in 1778 satisfactory proof being made to the Court they are of Opinion that the said Kelly has a right to a preemption of 400 Acres of land including the above location Cert. not to issue untill the further Order of this Court—

(Cert iss for 1400 fees &c pd D. D.)

William Deal came into Court & contested the Claim laid in by William Hoye as Assee of him Evidence being sworn it Appeared to the Court that the s'd claim is the property of the said William Deal therefore they are of Opinion that the former Order in favor of Hoye be set aside.—The said William Deal proved to the Court that he raised a crop of Corn in the Country in the year 1775 & that he is intitled to a settlem't of 400 Acres & the preemption of 1000 Acres adjoining & locates the same line on an East branch of Stoners fork at a spring where there is an Elm Tree at the head thereof marked TB about 6 Miles above the Mouth of Wolf Creek & that a Certificate issue accordingly.

(Cert iss'd for 400)

Charles Tate this day claimed a preemption of 400 Acres of land at the State price in the District of Kentucky lying on Strodes fork of licking Creek about One Mile below Strodes Station by Making an Actual Settlement in April 1779. satisfactory proof being made to the Court they are of Opinion that the said Tate has a right to a preemption to a tract of land of 400 Acres to include the above location & that a Cert'e Accordingly—.

(Cert iss for 1400 by Order of Court at Bryants—)

Thos. Brooks this day claimed a settlem't & preemption to a tract of land in the District of Kentucky lying on the

[68] Collins, vol. 1, p. 13.
[69] Collins, vol. 1, p. 8.

East side of the Rocky ford fork of licking Creek joining Jesse Hodges land by raising Corn in the Country in the year 1776 Satisfactory proof being made to the Court they are of Opinion that the s'd Brooks has a right to a settlem't of 400 Acres of land to include the above location & the preemption of 1000 Acres adjoining Certificate not to issue untill the further Order of this Court.—

(Cert iss'd for 400)

Sam'l Brooks by Thos. Brooks this day claimed a Settlement & preemption to a tract of land in the district of Kentucky lying on the Waters of Silver Creek at an Old Indian Town about 2 Miles from the Stone lick by the said Sam'l Brooks settling in the Country in the year 1777 & residing ever since satisfactory proof being made to the Court they are of Opinion that the said Brooks has a right to a settlem't of 400 Acres of land to include the above location & the preemption of 1000 Acres adjoining & that a Certificate issue accordingly.

(Cert iss for 1400)

William Brooks by Thos. Brooks this day claimed a settlem't & preemption to a tract of land in the District of Kentucky lying the big Bent of Kentucky, below the Mouth of Boons Creek on the Waters of Marble above the Marble lick by settling in the Country in the year 1777 and residing the Country ever since satisfactory proof being made to the Court they are of Opinion that the said Brooks has a right to a Settlement of 400 Acres to include the above location & the preemption of 1000 Acres adjoining & that a Cert. issue accordingly.

(Cert iss'd for 400)

Jeremiah Barnett this day claimed a preemption of 400 Acres of land at the State price in the District of Kentucky lying on the South Fork of licking Creek about 3 Miles to the West of Ambrose Coffers Land by making an Actual Settlement in 1778 satisfactory proof being made to the Court they are of opinion that the said Barnett had a right to a preemption of 400 Acres to include the above location & that a Certificate issue accordingly.

(Cert iss for 1000 by Ord. of Court at Bryants)

John South Younger Heir at law to Thos. South Dec'd this day claimed a preemption of 1000 Acres at the State price in the district of Kentucky lying on Stoner fork of licking Creek about 2 or 3 Miles from Harrods lick & about 2 Miles above the Salt Spring trace including a Spring the bank of the Creek by the s'd Decedents building a Cabbin in the year 1775 satisfactory proof being made to the Court they are of Opinion that the s'd John South has a right to a preemption of 1000 Acres to include the above location Certificate not to issue untill the further Order of this Court.

(Cert iss'd for 400)

Eliza'th Horn this day claimed a preemption to a tract of 400 Acres at the State price in the District of Kentucky lying on the North side of the Kentucky River above the Coperas lick including Bottom by Actual Settlem't made in 1778 satisfactory proof being made to the Court they are of Opinion that the Horn has a right to a preemption of 400

Acres of Land to include the above location & that a Certificate issue accordingly.

(Cert iss'd for 400)

Mathew Horn this day claimed a preemption of 400 Acres of land at the State price in the district of Kentucky lying on the South side of the Kentucky river at the Mouth of Station Camp Creek by making an Actual Settlement in 1778 Satisfactory proof being made to the Court they are of Opinion that the Said Horn has a right to a preemption of 400 Acres of land to include the above location & a Certificate issue accordingly.

(Cert. iss'd for 1400 fees &c pd D. D.)

William Bailey Smith came into Court & withdraws his claim laid in by Colo. Callaway 23d Inst. & now claims a settlem't & preemption to a tract of land in the District of Kentucky lying on a large Creek on the North side of Green River about 7 Miles above the Mouth of Panther Creek on the said Creek on the North said Creek including three springs a small distance from above a Spring on the Creek under a very high bank marked on a Beech Tree EHLH by the said Smith settling in the Country in the year 1775 & residing ever since Satisfactory proof being made to the Court they are of Opinion that the said Smith has a right to a settlem't of 400 Acres of land including the above location & the preemption of 1000 Adjoining & that a Cert issue Accordingly.—

Then the Court Adjourned untill to Morrow Morning 10 Oclock—

William Fleming—

At a Court Continued & held at Boonsborough by the Commissioners for Adjusting the disputed titles to the Kentucky lands the 29 day of December 1779.

Present

Wm. Fleming Stephen Trigg & Edmund Lyne—Gent'n—

(Cert iss'd for 1000)

Valentine Sterns this day claimed a preemption of 1000 Acres of land at the State price in the district of Kentucky lying about one Mile above John Taylors land on Strodes fork of licking Creek at the Mouth of a branch to include his improvement by mark'g & improving the same in the year 1775 Satisfactory proof being made to the Court they are of Opinion that the said Sterns has a right to a preemption of 1000 Acres to include the s'd improvement and that a Certificate issue accordingly.

[70]John Convey (Conway) Jun'r this day claimed a settlem't & preemption to a tract of land in the district of Kentucky by settling in the Country in the year 1777 & residing in the Country ever since satisfactory proof being made to the Court they are of Opinion that the said Conway has a right to a settlement & preemption.

(Cert iss for 400)

Sam'l Deryea by Sam'l Westewall this day claimed a preemption of 400 Acres of land at the State price in the District of Kentucky lying on Muddy Creek including a Mill Seat & the said Deryeas improvement by making an Actual Settlement in April 1779 satis-

[70] Collins, vol. 1, p. 12.

factory proof being made to the Court they are of Opinion that the said Deryea has a right to a preemption of 400 Acres of land to include the said improvements & that a Certificate issue Accordingly.

(Cert iss for 400 by ord'r of Court at Bryants. fees pd)

Ben'j Duniway this day claimed a preemption of 400 Acres of land at the State price in the District of Kentucky lying on a Small branch of Stoners Fork a branch of licking Creek on the East side of the said Fork including his improvement by making an Actual settlement April 1779 satisfactory proof being made to the Court they are of Opinion that the said Duniway has a right to a preemption of 400 Acres of land to include the said settlement Cert not to issue untill the further Order of this Court.

(Cert iss for 1400 by Ord'r of Court at Bryants)

Robert McMullin Heir at law to John McMullin deceased this day claimed a settlement & preemption to a tract of land in the District of Kentucky lying on licking Creek joining Micheal Stoners land above the South Side of the said Creek including McMullins spring by the said Decedents raising a Crop of Corn in the year 1775 & 1776 satisfactory proof being made to the Court they are of Opinion that the said McMullin has a right to settlement of 400 Acres to including the above location & the preemption of 1000 Acres adjoining Cert. not to issue untill the further order of this Court.

(Cert iss'd for 1400 fees &c pd D. D. by Order of Court at Bryants Station)

Edward Bradley this day claimed a settlement & preemption to a Tract of land in the district of Kentucky by raising a Crop of Corn in the Country year of 1775 satisfactory proof being made to the Court they are of Opinion that the said Bradley has a right to a settlement of 400 Acres of land & the preemption of 1000 Acres adjoining lying on Jessemen Creek on the North side of the Kentucky River About 8 Miles below the head Springs Cert. not to issue untill the further Order of this Court.

(Cert—for 1400)

William Cooper by Colo. Will'm Henderson this day claimed a settlem't & preemption to a tract of land in the district of Kentucky lying on the left hand fork of Otter Creek above the Clover Bottom including a Spring by the said Coopers raising a Crop of Corn in the year 1775 & 1776 satisfactory proof being made to the Court they are of opinion that the Said Cooper has a right to the settlem't of 400 Acres of land to include the above location & the preemption of 1000 Acres adjoining & that a Certificate issue accordingly.

(Cert iss for 1400)

John Farrow by [71]Colo Rich'd Henderson this day claimed a Settlement & preemption to a tract of land in the district of Kentucky lying on the South Fork of the left hand fork of Otter Creek near the head thereof known by the Name of Farrows land by raising a crop of Corn in the year 1775 Satisfactory proof being made to the Court they are of Opinion that the said Farrow has a

[71] Revolution on the Upper Ohio, pp. 1, 4, 16.

right to a settlement of 400 Acres of land & the preemption of 1000 Acres adjoining & that a Certificate issue accordingly.

(Cert iss for 1000)

Rich'd Morrison by Colo Rich'd Henderson this day claimed a preemption to a tract of 1000 Acres at a State price in the district of Kentucky lying on the ridge between Otter Creek & Kentucky River including some of the heads of branches of Muddy Creek & about five miles from this place by marking & improving the same in the year 1775 satisfactory proofs being made to the Court they are of Opinion that the said Morrison has a right to a preemption of 1000 Acres of land to include the above location & that a Certificate issue accordingly.

(Cert iss'd for 1400)

[72]John Lutrell by Colo Rich'd Henderson this day claimed a settlem't & preemption to a tract of land in the District of Kentucky lying on the West & South'ry lines of the bounds of the land belonging to the town of Boonsborough by raising a Crop of Corn in the year 1775 Satisfactory proofs being made to the Court they are of Opinion that the said Lutrell has a right to a settlem't of 400 Acres of land to include the above location & the preemption of 1000 Acres of land adjoining & that a Certificate issue accordingly.

(Cert iss'd for 1400 fees &c pd D. D. to Capt. Henderson)

John Lutrell Heir at law to Thos. Lutrell Dec'd by Colo. Rich'd Henderson this day claimed a settlem't & preemption to a tract of land in the district of Kentucky lying on Boons fork of Silver Creek adjoining the lands of Wm. Hays above on both sides for quantity by the said decedents Settling in the Country in the year of 1775 and residing 12 months before the year 1778 satisfactory proofs being made to the Court they are of Opinion that the said Lutrell has a right to a settlem't of 400 Acres of land to include the above location and the preemption of 1000 Acres adjoining & that a Cert. issue accordingly.

(Cert iss for 1000 fees &c pd D. D. Capt. Henderson)

John Henderson by Colo Richard Henderson this day claimed a preemption of 1000 Acres of land at the State price in the district of Kentucky lying on the Kentucky River including the Mouths of Muddy & Indian Camp Creek by marking and improving the same in the year 1775 Satisfactory proof being made to the Court they are of Opinion that the said Henderson has a right to a preemption of 1000 Acres of land to include the above location & that a Certificate issue accordingly.

(Cert iss for 1400 fees &c pd D. D. to Benj'm Searcy)

Aswell Towns this day claimed a settlement & preempt to a tract of land in the District of Kentucky lying on an East branch of Hustons fork beginning at the Mouth of the branch and extending up for quantity by raising a crop of Corn in the Country in the Year 1776 Satisfactory proof being made to the court they are of Opinion that the said Towns has a right to a settlem't of 400 Acres of land to include the above loca-

[72] Collins, vol. 1, p. 18; vol. 2, p. 326.

tion & the preemption of 1000 Acres Adjoining And that a Cert. issue accordingly.

(Cert iss'd for 1400)

James Gales by Sam'l Henderson this day claimed a settlem't & preemption to a tract of land in the district of Kentucky lying on Muddy Creek about 2 Miles above the long lick including his improvement by Settling & raising a Crop of Corn in the Country in the year 1776 Satisfactory proofs being made to the Court they are of Opinion that the said Gales has a right to a settlement of 400 Acres of land to include improvement & the preemption of 1000 Acres adjoining & and that a Certificate issue accordingly.

(Cert iss for 1400)

Joel Walker by Sam'l Henderson this day claimed a settlement & preemption to a tract of land in the district of Kentucky lying in the big bent of Muddy Creek about 1 mile above Gales land by Settling & raising a Crop of Corn in the year 1775 satisfactory proof being made to the Court they are of Opinion that the said Walker has a right to a settlement of 400 Acres of land to include the above location & the preemption of 1000 Acres adjoining & that a Cert. issue Accordingly.

(Cert iss'd for 1400)

The Heirs of William Walker Dec'd by Sam'l Henderson this day claimed a settlement & preemption to a tract of land in the district of Kentucky lying on the South side of the Kentucky River opposite to the Mouth of Red River by the said decedents raising Corn in the Country in the year 1776 Satisfactory proofs being made to the Court they are of Opinion that the said Heirs of Will'm Walker dec'd has a right to a settlement of 400 Acres of land to include the above location & the preemption of 1000 Acres adjoining & that a Cert. issue accordingly.

(Cert iss'd for 1400 fees &c pd D. D. to L Hall)

Rob't Rolestone Jun'r by Sam'l Henderson this day claimed a settlement & preemption to a tract of land in the district of Kentucky lying joining Sam'l Henderson land at Harrods lick on the East side by raising a Crop of Corn in the Country in the year 1775 satisfactory proof being made to the Court they are of Opinion that the said Rolestone has a right to a settlement of 400 Acres of land to include the above location & the preemption of 1000 Acres Adjoining & that a Certificate issue accordingly.

(Cert iss for 1400 fees &c pd D. D. to L Hall)

Isaac Rolestone by Sam'l Henderson this day claimed a settlement & preemption to a tract of land the district of Kentucky lying on the leading road from Boonsborough to the lower Salt Spring on licking Creek on the North side of Hinkstons Fork including a tree marked NH on the said road by raising a Crop of Corn in the Country in the year 1775 satisfactory proof being made to the Court they are of opinion that the said Rolestone has a right to a settleme't of 400 Acres of land to include the above location & the preemption of 1000 Acres adjoining & that a Certificate issue Accordingly.

(Cert iss for 1400 fees &c pd D. D. to Capt. Hart)

David Johnston by Nath'l Hart this day claimed a settle't & preemption to a tract of land in the district of Kentucky lying on the West side of Panther Creek about 4 Miles from the Creek and about 15 Miles from the Mouth thereof including a Sugar Tree marked LH by raising a Crop of Corn in the Country in the year 1775 satisfactory proof being made to the Court they are of Opinion that the said Johnstone has a right to a settlement of 400 Acres to include the above location & the preemption of 1000 Acres Adjoining & that a cert. issue accordingly.

(Cert iss for 400 fees &c pd D. D. to Jos Phelps)

[73]George Phelps this day claimed a preemption of 400 Acres of land at the State price in the district of Kentucky lying on a branch of Gap fork of Brasheirs Creek to include his improvement by making an Actual Settlement in 1778 satisfactory proof being made to the Court they are of Opinion that the said Phelps has a right to a preemption of 400 Acres of land to include the said improvement Cert. to issue accordingly.

(Cert issd for 1400)

Jacob Stains Assee of Rich'd Hines (Wines?) this day claimed a settlement & preemption to a tract of land in the district of Kentucky lying on the South side of Kentucky River about 6 Miles below this place known by the name of Hines Bend to include the said Hines improvem't.

[74]David Gass Adm'or to Rich'd Hines Dec'd came into Court & Alleged that the said decedent did not sell his right to a settleme't & preemption to land in the district of Kentucky Allow'd him by An Act of Assembly whereupon witness were sworn & examined in Consideration of which the Court are of Opinion that the said Hines was Intitled to a settleme't & preemption by raising Corn in the Country in the year 1775 & that he sold the same to the said Starns therefore the Court are of Opinion that the said Starns had a right to a settlement of 400 Acres of land to include the above location & the preemption of 1000 Acres adjoining & that a Certificate issue accordingly.

(Cert iss for 1400 fees &c pd D. D.)

[75]Nath'l Henderson this day claimed a settlem't & preempt. to a tract of land in the district of Kentucky lying on the North side of the Middle fork of Hingston fork of licking Creek adjoining the lands of John Calloway below by raising a Crop of Corn in the year 1775 & 1776 satisfactory proofs being made to the court they are of Opinion that the said Henderson has a right to a settlem't of 400 Acres of land to include the above location & the preemption of 1000 Acres adjoining & that a Certificate issue accordingly.

(Cert iss'd for 1000)

Sam'l Drake by Ephaim Drake this day claimed a preemption of 1000 Acres of land at the State price in the district of Kentucky lying on the North side of Kentucky on the first branch above the Mouth of Jessemine Creek on the West

[73] Collins, vol. 1, p. 12.

[74] Collins, vol. 2, p. 514.
[75] Collins, vol. 1, p. 366.

side thereof by marking & improving the same in the year 1775 satisfactory proof being made to the Court they are of Opinion that the said Drake has a right to a preemption of 1000 Acres of land to include the above location and that a Certificate issue accordingly.

(Cert iss for 400)
Margret Drake this day claimed a preemption to a tract of land of 400 Acres at the State price in the district of Kentucky lying on the Waters of Downing Creek Waters of Kentucky River about 1½ Miles above the Mulberry lick by making an Actual Settlement in March 1779 satisfactory proof being made to the Court they are of Opinion that the said Drake has a right to a preemption of 400 Acres of land to include the above location & that a Certificate issue accordingly.

(Cert iss'd for 1400 by Ord'r of Court at Bryants)
John South Sen'r came into Court & moved for leave to withdraw his claim entered the 28th Inst which is granted & now claims a settlem't & preemption to a tract of land in the district of Kentucky lying on the dividing ridge of the Waters Harrods lick & the flat lick branch the Waters of licking Creek to include Irvins Cabbin & to run Westwardly for quantity by the said South raising a Crop of Corn on Cumberland River at prices settlem't in the year 1776 & moved up to Boonsborough on the Kentucky the 1 of April 1778 Satisfactory proofs being made to the Court they are of Opinion that the said South Sen'r has a right to a settlem't of 400 Acres of land to include the above location and the preemption of 1000 acres Adjoining & that a Certificate issue not untill the further Order of this Court.

John Callaway came into Court & moved to withdraw his claim intered the 23d inst which is granted him & now comes into Court & claims a settlem't & preemption to a tract of land in the District of Kentucky lying on Stoners fork of licking Creek joining on the South side by William Cradleboughs land by settling in the Country in the year 1777 & residing ever since satisfactory proofs being made to the Court they are of Opinion that the said Callaway has a right to a settlem't of 400 Acres of land to include the above location & preemption of 1000 Acres Adjoining Cert not to issue untill the further Order of the Court.

Then the Court Adjourned to Bryants Station on Elkhorn 31st Inst.
William Fleming.

At a court held by the Commissioners of the Kentucky district for adjusting Title to unpatented lands at Bryants Station on Elkhorn. Jan'y 3d 1780.
Present
William Fleming Stephen Trigg Edmund Lyne Gent'n.

(Cert iss'd for 400 fees &c pd D. D.)
Samuel Dennis this day claimed a preemption to a tract of land of 400 Acres at the State price in the district of Kentucky lying on the South West side of licking Creek below George Grays claim about 8 Miles below Riddles Station including a remarkable Spring on the bank of the Creek by making an Actual

Settlement in 1778.—satisfactory proof being made to the Court they are of Opinion that the said Dennis has a right to a preemption of 400 Acres of land to include the above location & that a Certificate issue accordingly.

(Cert iss'd for 1400 fees &c pd D. D.)

Isaac Riddle this day claimed a settlem't and preemption to a tract of land in the District of Kentucky lying on flat run a branch of licking Creek that runs into the said Creek about 3 Miles above the forks & about 1¼ Miles above the Mouth of the said run to include his improvement by Settling in the Country in the year 1777 & residing ever since satisfactory proof being made to the Court they are of Opinion that the s'd Riddle has a right to a settlem't of 400 Acres of land to include his improvement & the preemption of 1000 Acres adjoining & that a Cert. issue accordingly.

(Cert iss'd for 1400)

Thos. Shores by Levi Todd[77] this day claimed a settlem't & preemption to a tract of land in the District of Kentucky lying on Haskins run about 5 Miles from Riddles Station including an improvement by making a settlement in the Country in the year 1775 & residing untill the year 1777 when he was taken prisoner satisfactory proof being made to the Court they are of Opinion that the said Shores has a right to a settlem't of 400 Acres of land to include the said improvement & the preemption of 1000 Acres adjoining & that a certificate issue accordingly.

[77] Collins, vol. 1, p. 250 and index.

(Cert iss for 1400 fees &c pd D. D.)

George Riddle by Isaac Riddle this day claimed a settlement & preemption to a tract of land in the district of Kentucky lying on the South West side of licking & in the forks of the Creek for quantity about 3 Miles above Riddles Station by settling in the Country in the year 1777 & residing ever since satisfactory proof being made to the Court they are of Opinion that the said Riddle has a right to the settlem't of 400 Acres to include the above location & the preemption of 1000 Acres adjoining & that a Certificate issue accordingly.

(Cert iss for 400 fees &c pd D. D.)

Cornelious Riddle by Isaac Riddle this day claimed a preemption of 400 Acres of land at the State price in the district of Kentucky lying on flat run joining above Isaac Riddles lands by making a settlement in the Country in the year 1778 Satisfactory proof being made to the Court they are of Opinion that the said Cornelias Riddle has a right to a preemption of 400 Acres of land to include the above location & that a Cert issue accordingly.—

(Cert. Issd for 1400)

[78]James Sadowski this day claimed a settlem't & preemption to a tract of land in the district of Kentucky lying on a branch of Coopers Run a branch of licking Creek on the West side of the road leading from Boonsborough to the Blue licks and ½ a mile from Randolphs lick to include his improvement by raising a Crop of Corn in the Country in the year 1775 satisfactory proof being made to the Court they are of Opinion that

[78] Collins, vol. 1, p. 17 ("Sandusky or Sodowsky.")

the S'd Sadowski has a right to a settlem't of 400 Acres of land to include the said improvement & the preemption of 1000 Acres adjoining and that a Certificate issue accordingly.

(Cert iss for 1400)

Jonathan Sadowski this day claimed a settlem't & preemption to a tract of land in the district of Kentucky lying on the East Fork of Jassamine Creek a branch of Kentucky about ½ Miles above Douglass's lower line where it Crosses to include his Cabbin by raising a Crop of Corn in the year 1776 satisfactory proof being made to the Court they are of Opinion that the said Sadowski has a right to a settlem't of 400 Acres of land to include the said Cabbin & the preemption of 1000 Adjoining & that a Certificate issue accordingly.

(Cert iss for 1000)

[79]James Douglass this day claimed a preemption of 1000 Acres of land at the State price in the District of Kentucky lying on Jasemine 5 or 6 Miles below Hickmans Creek a branch of Kentucky on the head of the s'd Jasemine Creek at a remarkable Camping place by the said Douglass's marking & improving the same in the year 1774 & 1775 satisfactory proof being made to the Court they are of Opinion that the said Douglass has a right to a preemption of 1000 Acres of land to include the s'd improvem't & that A Cert issue accordingly—

(Cert issd for 400)

John Jameson this day claimed a preemption of 400 Acres of land at the State price in the District of Kentucky lying on the Waters of the South fork of Elkhorn Joining on the South West side of a Survey supposed to be General Lewis's & about 3 Miles from Capt'n Todds Station by making a settlem't in March 1779 satisfactory proof being made to the Court they are of Opinion that the said Jameison has a right to a preemption of 400 Acres to include the above location & that a Certificate issue accordingly.

(Cert. issd for 1400 fees &c pd. D. D.)

John Spurger for William Spurger this day claimed a settlem't & preemption to a tract in the District of Kentucky lying on the West branch of Hickmans Creek about 4 Miles from levi Todds Settlem't & about an East Course from the same by the said Spurgers raising a Crop of Corn in the Country in the year 1776 satisfactory proof being made to the Court they of an Opinion that the said Spurger has a right to a settlem't of 400 Acres to include the above location & the preemption of 1000 Acres Adjoining and that a Certificate issue Accordingly.

(Cert issd for 1400 fees &c pd. D. D.)

John Spurger this day claimed a settlem't & preemption to a tract of land in the District of Kentucky lying on a fork of Hinkstons Fork known by the name of Deals run of the Waters of licking Creek to include a Spring about 2 Miles from the head of the said Creek on the North Side by the said Spurger raising a Crop of Corn in the County in the year 1776 satisfactory proof being made to the Court they are of Opinion that the said Spurger has a right to a

[79] Collins, vol. 1, p. 17.

settlem't of 400 Acres of land to include the above location & the preemption of 1000 Acres Adjoining & that a Certificate issue accordingly.

(Cert issd for 1400 fees &c pd. D. D.)
Saml Spurger by John Spurger this day claimed a settlement & preemption to a Tract of land in the district of Kentucky lying on a North Branch of the North Fork of Elkhorn water of Kentucky River about 3 Miles North East from this place including a Spring at an improvement made by Saml Bryant by the said Spurger raising a Crop of Corn in the Country in the year 1776 satisfactory proof being made to the Court they are of Opinion that the said Spurger has a right to a settlem't of 400 Acres of land to include the above location & the preemption of 1000 Acres adjoining & that a Certificate issue accordingly.

(Cert iss for 1400)
[80]William McConnell this day claimed a settlement and preemption to a tract of land in the district of Kentucky lying on the Waters of the South fork of Elkhorn joining on the East side of Colo. Shelbys land & Colo Prestons on the South West including a Sinking Spring & joining the claims of Rob't Patterson and Fran's McConnell to include the s'd McConnells improvement by raising a Crop of Corn on the premises in the year 1776 satisfactory proof being made to the Court they are of Opinion that the said McConnell has a right to a settlem't of 400 Acres to include the said improvement & the preemption of 1000 Acres adjoining & that a Certificate issue accordingly.

(Cert issd for 1400)
[81]Alexander McConnell Heir at law to Frances McConnell Dec'd this day claimed a settleme't & preemption to a tract of land in the District of Kentucky lying on the Waters of the South fork of Elkhorn waters of Kentucky to include the said decedents improvement by the s'd Decedents raising a Crop of Corn in the country in the Year 1776 Satisfactory proof being made to the Court they are of Opinion that the said McConnell has a right to a settlem't of 400 Acres of land to include the s'd improvem't & the preemption of 1000 Acres adjoining & that a Cert. issue accordingly.

(Cert issd for 400)
Alexander McConnell this day claimed a preemption of 400 Acres of land at the State price in the District of Kentucky lying on the South fork of Elkhorn about 2 Miles below John Martins land at the Mouth of a branch to include his improvement by making a Settlem't in 1778—satisfactory proof being made to the Court they are of Opinion that the said McConnell has a right to a preemption of 400 Acres of land to include the said improvement & that a Certificate issue accordingly.

(Cert issd for 400 fees &c pd D. D.)
John Riddle by Isaac Riddle this day claimed a preemption of 400 Acres of land at the State price in the District of Kentucky lying on licking Creek adjoining the lands belonging to Riddles

[80] Revolution on the Upper Ohio, pp. 176, 189.

[81] Collins, vol. 2, p. 172.

Station above by the s'd Riddles settling in the Country in the year 1779 in the Month of April satisfactory proof being made to the Court they are of Opinion that the said Riddle has a right to a preemption of 400 Acres of land to include the above location & that a Cert. issue accordingly.

(Cert issd for 400 fees &c pd D. D.)

James Riddle this day claimed a preemption of 400 Acres of land at the State price in the district of Kentucky lying on licking Creek joining John Riddles claim of land above by making a Settlement in Apr in 1779 satisfactory proof being made to the Court they are of Opinion that the said Riddle has a right to a preemption of 400 Acres of land to include the above location & that a Certificate issue accordingly.

(Cert iss for 1400 fees &c pd D. D.)

[82]Robert Patterson this day claimed a settlem't & preemption to a tract of land in the district of Kentucky lying on the Waters of the South fork of Elkhorn about ½ Mile from Lexington to include his improvement by raising a Crop of Corn on the premises in the year 1776 satisfactory proof being made to the Court they are of Opinion that the said Patterson has a right to a settlem't of 400 Acres of land to include his improvement & preemption of 1000 Acres Adjoining & that a Cert iss Accordingly.

(Cert issd for 1400)

[83]John Haggin this day claimed a settlem't and preemption to a tract of land in the district of Kentucky lying on the Waters of Coopers run on the North side thereof & about 1½ Miles No. of Grotts land to include a spring & his improvement by raising a Crop of Corn in the year 1775 satisfactory proof being made to the Court they are of Opinion that the said Haggon has a right to a settlem't of 400 Acres of land to include the above location & the preemption of 1000 Acres adjoining & that a Certificate issue accordingly.

(Cert issd for 1000 pd D. D.)

[84]William Haydon this day claimed a settlem't & preemption to a tract of land in the district of Kentucky lying on Kentucky River about two Miles above Lees Town by improving the same in the year 1776 Witness being sworn and examined the Court are of Opinion that the said Haydon/has a right to a preemption of 1000 Acres only to include his Cabbin & that a Cert. issue accordingly.

(Cert issd for 400 fees &c pd)

Benj'n Haydon this day claimed a preemption of 400 Acres of land at the State price in the District of Kentucky lying on the Kentucky River joining the lands of Wm Haydon above on the said river by making a settlem't in April 1779 Satisfactory proof being made to the Court they are of Opinion that the said Haydon has a right to a preemption of 400 Acres of land to include the above location & that a Cert. issue accordingly.

Then the Court Adjourned untill tomorrow Morning 10 OClock

William Fleming.

[82] Collins, vol. 1, pp. 18, 22 and index; vol. 2, p. 178.

[83] Collins, vol. 1, pp. 13, 19.

[84] Collins, vol. 2, p. 172.

At a Court Continued & held at Bryants Station on Elkhorn Creek for Adjusting disputed Title to the Kentucky lands by the Commissioners for the Kentucky District this 4 day of Jan'y 1780—

Present William Fleming Stephen Trigg Edmund Lyne Gent'n

(Cert iss for 400 fees &c Pd D. D.)

Levi Todd Assee of Benj. Berry this day claimed a prempt. of 400 Acres of land at the State price in the district of Kentucky lying on the South fork of Elkhorn on the E. side of Harrodsburg road to include the s'd Todds Station by the said Berrys making an Actual Setteme't in the spring 1779 satisfactory proof being made to the Court they are of Opinion that the said Todds has a right to a preemption of 400 Acres of land to include the above location & that a Certificate issue accordingly.

(Cert issd for 400 fees &c pd D. D.)

John Jackson this day claimed a preemption to 400 Acres of land at the State price in the district of Kentucky lying on the North Fork of the Forks of South fork of licking Creek 7 Miles above Riddle Station by making a Settlem't in April 1779 satisfactory proof being made to the Court they are of Opinion that the said Jackson has a right to a preemption to a tract of land of 400 Acres to include the above location & that a Certificate issue accordingly.

(Cert iss for 400 fees &c pd)

John Jackson Assee of David McKinzer this day claimed a preemption of 400 Acres of land at the State price in the District of Kentucky lying on the North fork of licking about 6 Miles above Riddles Station by making an Actual Settlement in Ap'r 1779 satisfactory proof being made to the Court they are of Opinion that the said Jackson has a right to a preemption of 400 Acres of land to include the above location & that a Certificate issue accordingly.

(Cert iss for 1400 fees &c Pd D. D.)

William May by George May[85] this day claimed a settlem't & preemption to a tract of land in the district of Kentucky lying on the East side of licking on both sides of the road leading from the Lower Blue licks to Limestone run & about 10 Miles from the said lick beginning at the head on the upper side of the said road & to include & extend down the same taking in Haydons big spring & two other improvements made by Wm Haydon for quantity by Settling in the Country in the year 1777 & residing ever since Satisfactory proof being made to the Court they are of Opinion that the said May has a right to a settlem't of 400 Acres to include the above location & the preemption of 1000 Acres adjoining & that a Certificate issue accordingly.—

(Cert iss for 1400 fees &c pd D. D. to Levi Todd.)

John Maxwell this day claimed a settlement & preemption to a tract of land in the district of Kentucky lying on the North fork of Cane run about One Mile below the Licking creek road including an improvem't made by Rob't Patterson by Settling in the Country in the

[85] Collins, vol. 1, p. 20.

year 1776 & residing 12 Month before the year 1778 Satisfactory proof being made to the Court they are of Opinion that the said Maxwell has a right to a settlem't of 400 Acres of land to include the above location & the preemption of 1000 Acres adjoining & that a cert. issue accordingly.

(Cert issd for 400 fees &c pd D. D.)

James Parberry this day claimed a preemption of 400 Acres of land as Assee of Andrew Hampton at the State price in the District of Kentucky lying adjoining around a fifty Acre Warrant of John Floyds laid on the lower Blue licks on licking by the said Hamptons making an Actual settlement in the April 1779 satisfactory proof being made to the Court they are of Opinion that the said Parberry has a right to a preemption of 400 Acres of land to include the above location & that a Certificate issue accordingly.

(Cert issd for 1400)

Sam'l McMullen this day claimed a settlem't & preemption to a tract of land in the district of Kentucky lying on the South Fork of licking Creek below Stoners Settlement adjoining Rueben Searcy land above & running up to the Mouth of Coopers run for quantity including his improve't by raising a Crop of Corn in the year 1776 satisfactory proof being made to the Court they are of Opinion that the said McMullen has a right to a settlem't of 400 Acres of land to include the said improvement & the preemption of 1000 Acres adjoining & that Cert'e issue accordingly.

(Cert issd for 1400 fees &c pd D. D. to P. Rizer.)

[86]John Crittenden by Anthony Buckner this day claimed a settlem't and preemption to a tract of land in the District of Kentucky lying on a sinking Creek about 2 Miles South of Crittendons Camp to include his improve't by raising a Crop of Corn in the Country in the year 1776 satisfactory proof being made to the Court they are of Opinion that the said Crittenden has a right to a settlement of 400 Acres of land to include the above mentioned improveme't and the preemption of 1000 Acres Adjoining & that a Certificate issue accordingly.

(Cert issd for 1400 fees &c pd to P. Pinger)

Anthony Buckner, this day claimed a settleme't & preempti'n to a tract of land in the District of Kentucky lying on the North fork of the South fork of licking to include his improveme't of about 25 Miles from the Mouth of s'd No. fork by raising a crop of Corn in the year 1776 Satisfactory proof being made to the Court they are of Opinion that the S'd Buckner has a right to a settleme't of 400 Acres of land to include the said improveme't & the preemption of 1000 Acres adjoining & that a Cert. iss'e accordingly.

(Cert iss for 1400 fees &c pd to P. Ringer)

[87]James French by Anthony Buckner this day claimed a settleme't & preemption to a tract of land in the district of Kentucky lying on the North fork of the

[86] Collins, vol. 1, pp. 9, 366.
[87] Collins, vol. 1, p. 355.

South fork of licking Creek on the South side thereof Opposite to Anthony Buckners land by raising a crop of Corn in the Country in the year 1776 satisfactory proof being made to the Court they are of Opinion that the said French has a right to a settleme't of 400 Acres of land to include the above location & the preemption of 1000 Acres Adjoining & that a Cert. issue Accordingly.

(Cert issd for 1400 fees &c pd D. D.)

Peter Ringoe this day claimed a settleme't & preemption to a tract of land in the District of Kentucky lying on the head of a branch of the South fork of Elkhorne Creek and Empties in below Shannons run about 2½ Miles East of Crittenden Camp to include his improveme't by raising a Crop of Corn in the Country in the year 1776 Satisfactory proof being made to the Court they are of opinion that the said Ringoe has a right to a settleme't of 400 Acres of land to include the s'd improvement & the preemption of 1000 Acres adjoining & that a Certificate issue accordingly.

(Cert issd for 1000)

Will'm Elliott this day claimed a preemption to 1000 Acres of land at the State price in the District of Kentucky lying on the Waters of Shannons run about 13 Miles from the Mouth & West course from the same Waters of Elkhorne Creek to include his improvement by building a Cabbin on the premises in the year 1776 satisfactory proof being made to the Court they are of Opinion that the said Elliott has a right to a preemption of 1000 Acres to include the said improvemen't & that a Certificate issue accordingly.

(Cert issd for 1000 fees &c Pd D. D.)

John Vance this day claimed a preemption to a tract of land in the district of Kentucky of 1000 Acres at the State price lying on the head Spring of Steels run, a branch of the South Fork of Elkhorn and about 3 Miles from the fork of the South Fork to include his improvem't by building a Cabbin on the premises in the year 1776 in the Month of Jan'y satisfactory proof being made to the Court they are of Opinion that the said Vance has a right to a preemption of 1000 Acres to include the s'd improvement & that a Certificate issue accordingly.

(Cert iss for 400)

[88]James Guthrie this day claimed a preemption to 400 Acres of land at the State price in the District of Kentucky lying on a small branch of Floyds fork of Salt River about five or six Miles East from Bullets lick to include his improvem't by Settling in the Country in the year 1779.—in the Month of April Satisfactory proof being made to the Court they are of Opinion that the said Guthrie has a right to a preemption of 400 Acres of land to include the S'd improvement & that a Cert. issue accordingly.—

(Cert issd for 1000)

Sam'l Stevenson this day claimed a preemption to a tract of land of 1000 Acres at the State price in the District of Kentucky lying on Shannons run about 1½ Miles from the Mouth of the said run Waters of Elkhorn to include his Cabbin built in the year 1776 Satisfactory proof being made to the Court

[88] Collins, vol. 1, p. 12.

they are of Opinion that the said Stevenson has a right to a preemption of 1000 Acres to include the said Cabbin & that a Certificate issue accordingly.

It was proved to the Court that Thomas Rowlin Assee of Mordecai Reed who was Assee of John Love (Who was entitled to a Settlement & preemption) the 6th day of November 1779 Geo'e May in behalf of the said Rowlan now comes into Court & moves to locate the same lying withdraws.

(Cert issd for 1400)

The Heir of Wm. Hudson[88*] Dec'd by Benj Logan this day came into Court & claimed a settlem't & preemption to a tract of land in the District of Kentucky lying on paint lick Creek including a Cabbin Known by the name of Hudson Cabbin adjoining Estiles Assee of Carpenters Land by the Said Decedents raising a Crop of Corn in the Country in the year 1776 satisfactory proof being made to the Court they are of Opinion that the said Heir of Wm. Hudson Dec'd has a right to a settlement of 400 Acres of land to include his improvem't & the preemption of 1000 Acres adjoining & that a Cert. issue accordingly.

Will'm Beckley this day claimed a settlem't & preemption to a tract of land in the District of Kentucky lying on the head Waters of Coopers run waters of licking Creek, withdraws his location But prove to the court that he settled in the Country in the year 1777 and that he resided in the Country ever since and that he is Intitled to a settlement & preemption.

(Cert issd for 1400)

John McCracking by Rob't Patterson this day claimed a settlem't & preemption to a tract of land in the District of Kentucky lying on the South fork of Elkhorn joining Shelbys land on the West & about 3 Miles No. West of Simon Cantons land including the Mouth of Starrats branch & his improvment by raising a Crop of Corn in the year 1776 satisfactory proof being made to the Court they are of Opinion that the said McCracking has a right to a settlem't of 400 Acres of land to include the said improvem't & the preemption of 1000 Acres adjoining & that a Certificate issue accordingly.

(Cert issd for 400)

James McCracking by John Morrison[89] this day claimed a preempt'n of 400 Acres of land at the State price in the District of Kentucky lying at a sinking Spring in some Cain about 1½ Miles East of Lexington by the s'd McCracking Settling in the Country in the year 1779 in April satisfactory proof being made to the Court they are of Opinion that the said McCracking has a right to a preemption of 400 Acres of land to include the above location & that a Certificate issue accordingly.

Ordered that several Certificates which were detained at Boonsborough except Bradleys Gass to issue like Wise it is ordered that John Shelps[90] Geo'e Timmermans (Zimmermans?) & James Parberry Assee of Bottom Estis & Elisha Estis & John Soverins Certificates be issued.

[88*] See Clark's Diary Conquest of the N. W. by English, p. 580.

[89] Collins, vol. 1, p. 356.
[90] Collins, vol. 1, p. 513.

Then the Court adjourned till 9 Oclock tomorrow Morning

William Fleming.

At a Court continued & held at Bryants Station on Elkhorn Creek for Adjusting titles to unpattented lands in the District of Kentucky the 5th day of Jan'y 1780 Present Wm Fleming Stephen Trigg Edmund Lyne Gent'n

(Cert issd for 1400)

Francis Hobson by Jacob Grotts this day claimed a settlem't & preemption to a tract of land in the District of Kentucky lying on the West side of the South Fork licking Creek at the Mouth of Mill Creek to include his improvement. by raising a Crop of Corn in the year 1776 satisfactory proof being made to the Court they are of Opinion that the said Hobson has a right to a settlem't of 400 Acres to include his improvement & the preemption of 1000 Acres adjoining & that a certificate issue accordingly.

(Certificate iss for 400)

James Bracking heir at law to Jas. Bracking, Dec'd by Jacob Grotts this day claimed a preemption of 1000 Acres of land at the State price in the District of Kentucky lying on the West side of the South fork of licking Creek about 2 Miles below the Mouth of Mill Creek by marking & improving the same in the year 1776 satisfactory proof being made to the Court they are of Opinion that the said James Bracking &c has a right to a preemption of 1000 Acres of land to include his said improvement & that a certificate issue accordingly.

(Cert iss for 400)

Joseph Waller this day claimed a preemption of 400 Acres of land at the State price in the District of Kentucky lying on a North branch of the North fork of Elkhorn known by the name of Leconts run & at a Spring called Lecounts Spring by making a Actual Settleme't in May 1779 satisfactory proof being made to the Court they are of Opinion that the s'd Waller has a right to a preemption of 400 Acres of land to include the above location & that a Certificate issue accordingly.

(Cert issd for 1400)

Jacob Sodusky this day claimed a settleme't & preemption to a tract of land in the district of Kentucky lying on the head Spring of Clear Creek joining Douglass Survey on the West side not to extend from his Spring 1¼ Miles towards David Gass claim of land by the s'd Sodowski improving the same & raising a Crop of Corn in the year 1776 satisfactory proof being made to the Court they are of Opinion that the Said Sodowski has a right to a settlem't of 400 Acres of land to include his improvement & the preemption to a tract of 1000 Acres Adjoining & that a Certificate issue accordingly.

It appearing to the Court that there was no reasonable cause for detaining David Gass Certificate ordered that it be issued.

(Cert issd for 1000)

Andrew Warnock Heir at Law to James Warnock Dec'd this day claimed a preemption of 1000 Acres of land at the State price in the District of Kentucky lying one mile West of Gras big spring including an improvement made by the s'd Decedent marked JW on the the West branch of clear creek near the heads by building a Cabbin & improving the same in the year 1776 satisfactory proof being made to the Court they are of Opinion that the said Warnock has a right to a preemption of 1000 Acres to include the said improvement & that a Certificate issue accordingly.—

(Cert issd for 400)

It Appearing to the Court that Wm Kellys location was laid on Sadowski Settlement & preemption John South moved to the Court to move the preemption & locate the same lying on the North East line of John Souths land on the Waters of licking Creek & that a Certificate issue accordingly on the Waters of licking.

(Cert issd for 1400)

Edward Loc (Loe?) by Colo. Logan this day claimed a settlement & preemption to a tract of land in the District of Kentucky lying where the Middle Fork of clear creek enterlocks with Elkhorn by settling in the Country in the year 1777 and residing ever since satisfactory proof being made to the Court they are of Opinion that the said Loc has a right to a settlem't of 400 Acres of land to include the above location & the preemption of 1000 Acres adjoining & that a Certificate issue accordingly.

(Cert issd for 1400)

It appearing to the Court that John Smith Jun. laid his claim on lands survey by a Military Warrant & now moves to alter his location & lays on Johnson fork of licking Creek on the No. side of the same about 1½ miles below the Sycamore Forrest ordered that the certificate issue accordingly.

(Cert issd for 1400)

It appearing to the Court that John Calloway laid his claim on lands supposed to be surveyed by a Military Warrant now moves to alter his location and lays it on the Middle Fork of licking Creek above Benj Johnson survey 1½ Miles including and old Camping place running up the creek for quantity & that a Certificate issue accordingly.

Then the Court adjourned untill tomorrow Morning 9 Oclock.

At a Court Cont and held at Bryant Station on Elkhorn Creek for adjusting Titles to unpattened lands by the Commissioners of Kentucky District the 6th of Jan'y. 1780—Present

Wm. Fleming Stephen Trigg Edmund Lyne Gent'n.

(Cert issd for 1400)

[91]Van Swearingen Assee of Edward Bradley who was Assee of John Campbell this day claimed a Settlement & preemption to a tract of land in the District of Kentucky lying on Johnson Fork of licking Creek some small distance above John South Jun'rs claim with the letters BA. cut on a Hickory Tree near a spring by the s'd Campbell raising a Crop of Corn in the Country in the year 1775 satisfactory proof being made to the Court they are of Opinion that the said Swearingan has a right to a settlem't of 400 Acres of land to include

[91] Collins, vol. 1, p. 12, also George Michael Bedinger, A Kentucky Pioneer, by Dankse Dandridge, p. 140.

the above location & the preemption of 1000 Acres adjoining & that a Cert issue accordingly

(Cert issd for 400)

Joseph Donathan by Colo. Swearingen this day claimed a preemption of 400 Acres of land at the State price in the district of Kentucky lying on the South Fork of Strodes fork of licking Creek about 6 Miles below Strodes Station & 1½ Mile from the Mouth of the said So. fork by making & actual settlement in the April 1779 satisfactory proof being made to the Court they are of Opinion that the said Donathan has a right to a preemption of 400 acres of land to include the Above location & that a Certificate issue accordingly.

(Cert issd for 400)

[92]Wm Morgan by Colo. Swearingen this day claimed a preemption of 400 Acres of land at the State price in the District of Kentucky lying on a fork of Glens Creek at a place improved by Ambrose Coffer to include the s'd improving by the said Morgan Settling in the Country in the Month of April 1779 satisfactory proof being made to the Court they are of Opinion that the said Morgan has a right to a preemption of 400 Acres of land to include the s'd improvement & that a Certificate issue accordingly.

(Cert iss for 400)

Thomas Swearingen by Colo. Swearingen this day claimed a preempt'n of 400 Acres of land at the State price in the district of Kentucky lying on Muddy Creek a small distance below the Mouth of s'd Creek that runs in from toward the red lick to include his improvement by settling in the Country in the Month of April 1779 Satisfactory proof being made to the Court they are of Opinion that the said Swearingen has a right to a preemption of 400 Acres of land to include improvement & that a Certificate issue accordingly.

(Cert issd for 400)

Benoni Swearingen by Colo. Swearingen this day claimed a preemption of 400 Acres of land at the State price in the district of Kentucky lying on muddy Creek about 11 Miles below Thos. Swearingens claim to include his improvm't by settling in the Country in the Month of April 1779 satisfactory proof being made to the Court they are of Opinion that the said Swearingen has a right to a preemption of 400 Acres of land to include his improvem't & that a Cert issue accordingly.

(Cert issd for 400)

Ralph Morgan by Colo. Swearingen this day claimed a preemptn of 400 Acres of land at the State price in the district of Kentucky lying on a South branch of licking Creek about 5½ Miles below Strodes Station with the letters WM. cut on a Tree at a Spring by settling in the Country in the Month of April 1779 satisfactory proof being made to the Court they are of Opinion that the s'd Morgan has a right to a preemption of 400 Acres of land to include the above location & that a Certificate issue accordingly.

(Cert issd for 400)

[93]Michael Bedinger by Colo Swearin-

[92] Collins, Vol. 1, p. 7.

[93] George Michael Bedinger, A Kentucky Pioneer, by Danske Dandridge, p. 47.

gen this day claimed a preemption of 400 Acres of land at the State price in the district of Kentucky lying on Muddy Creek on a west branch of the same below Benoni Swearingen about $\frac{3}{4}$ of a Mile from the main Creek to include his improvme't by settling in the Country in the Month of April 1779 satisfactory proof being made to the Court they are of Opinion that the said Bedinger has a right to a preemption of 400 Acres of land to include his improvement and that a Certificate issue accordingly.

(Cert issd for 1400)

Wm. Frazier by Joseph Frazier this day claimed a settlement & preemption to a Tract of land in the district of Kentucky lying on the North side of the North Fork of Elkhorn on a branch empting in Opposite to McClaluns Fork at the fork of the said branch joining Mr. McCracking on East & Mr. Stewart on the South by raising a Crop of Corn in the Country in the year 1776 satisfactory proof being made to the Court they are of Opinion that the said Frazier has a right to a settlem't of 400 Acres to include the above location & the preempt'n of 1000 Acres adjoining & that a Certificate issue accordingly.

(Cert issd for 1400)

Joseph Frazier this day claimed a settlem't & preempt'n to a tract of land in the District of Kentucky lying on the waters of licking Creek & on the Middle fork of lawrence Creek & about 4 Miles from the Mouth of limestone by raising a Crop of Corn in the Country in the year 1776 satisfactory proof being made to the Court they are of Opinion that the Said Frazier has a right to a settlem't of 400 Acres of land to include the above location & the preemption of 1000 Acres Adjoining & that a Certificate issue accordingly.

(Cert issd for 1400)

Wm. Cowan by David Gass this day claimed a settlemt & preemption to a track of land lying in the District of Kentucky lying on a small fork of Stoners fork of licking Creek on the South side of the s'd Stoners fork where a Buffaloe Road crosses the s'd small Fork running up the fork & Westwardly for Quantity by the s'd Cowan raising a a Crop of Corn in the year 1775 satisfactory proof being made to the Court they are of Opinion that the s'd Cowan has a right to a Settlem't of 400 Acres of land to include the above location & the preemption of 1000 Acres adjoining & that a Cert. issue accordingly.

(Cert issd for 1400)

John Gass by David Gass this day claimed a settlem't & preemption to a tract of land in the District of Kentucky lying on Johnson fork joining Colo. Swearingens land above by raising a Crop of Corn in the year 1775 & 1776 satisfactory proof being made to the Court they are of Opinion that the s'd Gass has a right to a settlem't of 400 Acres of land to include the above location & the preempt'n of 1000 Acres adjoining & that a Cert'e issue accordingly.

Then the Court Adjourned untill tomorrow Morning 10 Oclock

Wm. Fleming.

At a Court continued & held at Bryants Station on Elkhorn Creek by the

Commissioners of the District of Kentucky for adjusting disputed Titles to the Kentucky lands 7th day of Jan'y 1780. Present

Wm. Fleming Stephen Trogg & Edmund Lyne Gent'n

(Cert issd for 400 fees &c pd D. D. to Capt Holder)

[94]Nicholas Procter this day claimed a preemption of 400 Acres of land at the State price in the district of Kentucky lying at the Mouth of a branch that runs in to Silver Creek from towards the Blue lick about 2 Miles from the s'd lick by settling in the Country in the year 1778 satisfactory proof being made to the Court they are of Opinion that the said Proctor has a right to a preemption of 400 Acres of land to include the above location & that a Certificate issue accordingly.

(Cert issd for 400 fees &c pd D. D. to Colo. Logan)

George Sumwalt by Colo. Logan this day claimed a preemption of 400 Acres of land at the State price in the district of Kentucky lying on Green Creek joining James Parberrys Assee of Estis Land extending towards McMullens Spring for quantity by making a settlem't in April 1779 satisfactory proof being made to the Court they are of Opinion that the said Sumwalt has a right to a preemption of 400 Acres of land to include the above location & that a Certificate issue accordingly.

(Cert issd for 400 fees &c pd D. D. to colo Logan)

Stuffel Sumwalt by Colo Logan this day claimed a preemption of 400 Acres of land at the State price in the district of Kentucky lying on Green Creek a branch of licking Creek joining Geo'e Sumwalts land below by making a settlem't in April 1779 satisfactory proof being made to the Court they are of Opinion that the said Sumwalt has a right to a preempt. of 400 Acres of land to include the s'd location & that a Certificate issue accordingly.

(Cert issd for 1400)

[95]Anthony Bleadsoe Assee of Wm Pittman this day claimes a Settlem't & preemption to a tract of land in the District of Kentucky lying on the North side of the North fork of Elkhorn on a Creek running into the s'd Fork Called the Stamping ground on the right hand fork to include a Spring by the s'd Pittman raising a crop of Corn in the Country in the year 1775 Satisfactory proof being made to the Court they are of Opinion that the s'd Bleadsoe has a right to a settlem't of 400 Acres of land to include the above location & the preemption of 1000 Acres adjoining & that a Certificate issue accordingly.

(Cert issd for 1000)

It appearing to the Court that Robt. Prestons claim was laid on the land claimed by the Reverend John Todd moves to the Court that he may locate the same on the West side of the East branch of Hickmans Creek about 3 Miles below the land sold by Levi Todd who Dav'd Bell joining John Hawkins on N. E. by Shelby on the S. E. & that a Cert. issue accordingly.

[94] Collins, Vol. 1, p. 13.

[95] Historic Sumner Co., Tenn., p. 55 and Bulletin Va. St. Library, Vol. 14, p. 99.

(Cert issd for 400 fees &c pd D. D. to Capt Holder)

[96]Joseph Proctor this day claimed a preemption to 400 Acres of land at the State price in the District of Kentucky lying on Silver creek joining Nich's Proctors land below by settling in the Country in the year 1778 Satisfactory proof being made to the Court they are of Opinion that the said Proctor has a right to a preemption of 400 Acres to include the above location & that a Cert. iss'e accordingly.

(Cert issd for 400 fees &c pd. D. D. to Capt. Hunter)

Patrick Donielson Assee of Equilla White this day claimed a preemption of 400 Acres of land at the State price in the District of Kentucky lying on the No'th side of the So. fork of licking Creek 3 Miles N. W. of Stoners improvment by the s'd Whites Settling in the Country in the month of April 1779 satisfactory proof being made to the Court they are of Opinion that the s'd Donielson has right to a preemption of 400 Acres of land to include the above location & that a Certificate issue accordingly.

Aquilla White this day claimed a preempt'n of 400 Acres of land at the State price in the District of Kentucky Witnesses being sworn & examined the Court are of Opinion that the s'd claim be rejected as it Appeared to the Court that he had disposed of his claim to Patrick Donielson.

(Cert issd for 1400 fees &c pd D. D.)

Peter Johnson Heir at law to Jacob Johnson Dec'd this day claimed a settlement & preemption to a tract of land in the District of Kentucky lying on the East side of the Buffaloe road leading from the blue lick to limestone 9 Miles from the lick on the Upper road by the s'd decedents raising a Crop of Corn in the year 1776 satisfactory proof being made to the Court they are of Opinion that the s'd Peter Johnson &c has a right to a settlement of 400 Acres of land to include the above location & the preemption of 1000 Acres adjoining & that a Certificate issue accordingly.

(Cert issd for 1000 fees &c pd D. D. to Mr Hunter)

[97]Joseph Kennady this day claimed a preemption of 1000 Acres of land at the State price in the District of Kentucky lying on a branch of Stoners fork of licking Creek running on the So. side thereof about 1½ Miles above John Kennadys land by Marking & improving the same in the year 1776 satisfactory proof being made to the Court they are of Opinion that the Said Kennady has a right to a preemption of 1000 Acres of land to include the S'd improvements & that a Cert. issue accordingly.

(Cert issd for 400 fees &c pd D. D. to Mr Hunter)

James Key this day claimed a preemption to 400 Acres of land at the State price in the district of Kentucky lying on a So. fork of a branch of Stoners fork of licking Creek running in on the So. side thereof about 1 Miles below Joseph Kennadys land by making Actual settlement in April 1779 Satisfactory proof being made to the Court they are of Opinion that the s'd Key has a right to

[96] Collins, Vol. 1, p. 6.

[97] Collins, vol. 1, pp. 8, 355.

a preemption of 400 Acres of land to include the above location & that a Certificate issue accordingly.

(Cert issd for 400 fees &c pd D. D. to Mr Hunter)

John Keyth this day claimed a preemption of 400 Acres of land at the State price in the District of Kentucky lying on one of the West branches of licking Creek includeing an improvm't above John Soverins claim about 6 Miles East from this place by making an Actual Settlem't in April 1779 Satisfactory proof being made to the Court they are of Opinion that the s'd Keyth has a right to a preempt'n of 400 Acres to include the above location & that a Certificate issue Accordingly.

(Cert issd for 1000 fees &c pd D. D. to Mr. Hunter)

Jacob Starns this day claimed a preemption of 1000 Acres of land at the State price in the district of Kentucky lying on a branch that runs into Strodes fork of licking Creek on the No. side thereof near the Mouth of the s'd branch and running down the s'd Creek for quantity by marking and improving the same in the year 1775 Satisfactory proof being made to the Court they are of Opinion that the s'd Starns has a right to a preempt'n of 1000 Acres of land to include the above location and that a Certificate issue accordingly.

(Cert issd for 1400)

Ephraim Drake this day claimed a settlem't & preemption to a tract of land in the district of Kentucky lying on the Waters of Hinkstons fork on the East side thereof about 4 Miles from the same & where a Buffaloe road crosses by Settling in the Country in the year 1777 & residing ever since Satisfactory proof being made to the Court they are of Opinion that the said Drake has a right to a settlem't of 400 Acres of land to include the above location & the preemption of 1000 Acres adjoining & that a Cert issue accordingly.

(Cert issd for 1000)

James Newell this day claimed a preemption of 1000 Acres of land at the State price in the district of Kentucky lying near the head of a dry Creek a branch of Howards creek & about 5 Miles from the mouth thereof & Eastwardly for quantity by Marking & improving the same in the year 1775 Satisfactory proof being made to the Court they are of Opinion that the s'd Newell has a right to a preemption of 1000 Acres of land to include the above location & that Cert. issue accordingly.

(Cert issd for 1000)

Wm. Nowell this day claimed a preemption of 1000 Acres of land at the State price in the district of Kentucky lying adjoining James Nowell land to the Eastward by marking and improving the same in the year 1775 satisfactory proof being made to the Court they are of Opinion tha the s'd Wm Nowell has a right to a preemption of 1000 Acres of land to include the above location & that a Certificate issue accordingly.

(Cert issd for 1000)

Sam'l Nowell this day claimed a preempt'n of 1000 Acres of land in the District of Kentucky at the State price lying at a fork of a small branch of licking Creek near the dividing ridge between the s'd Creek & Howards where there is a number of Trees pealed running up the left hand of the said branch for quantity by Marking & improving the same in the year 1775 satisfactory proof being made to the Court they are of Opinion that the s'd Nowell has a right to a preemption of 1000 Acres to include the above location & that a Certificate issue accordingly.

(Cert issd for 1400 fees &c pd D. D. to Capt'n Holder)

Rich'd Weid by Judith Weid his wife this day claimed a settlem't & preemption to a tract of land in the District of Kentucky lying on a branch of Cees Creek on the West side thereof on a branch of the North fork of licking to include Simon Cantons Cabbin by Settling in the Country in the year 1777 & residing ever since satisfactory proof being made to the Court they are of Opinion that the s'd Weid has a right to a settlem't of 400 Acres of land to include the above location & the preempt'n of 1000 Acres adjoining & that a Certificate issue accordingly.

(Cert issd for 400 fees &c pd D. D. to Capt'n Holder)

[98]John Webber by James Estill this day claimed a preemption of 400 Acres of land at the State price in the district of Kentucky lying adjoining James Estills land at the Locust thickett on the South by settling in the Country in the Month of Jan'y 1779 satisfactory proof being made to the Court they are of Opinion that the s'd Webber has a right to a preemption of 400 Acres of land to include the above location & that a Certificate issue accordingly.

(Cert issd for 400 fees &c pd to Capt. Holder)

It Appearing to the Court that Sam'l Estills location is in or near a Military Claim & he moved to locate the same on a branch of Glens Creek on the South side thereof adjoining Glens Claim to include John Clarks Cabbin to join Patrick Doline on the South side & that a Certificate issue accordingly.

(Cert issd for 400 fees &c pd D. D. to Capt'n Holder)

James Doster this day claimed a preemption to a tract of land in the district of Kentucky of 400 Acres at the State price lying near the head of a North west Drean that leads to Stoner fork of licking at a place Marked by John Taylor by settling in the Month of March 1779 satisfactory proof being made to the Court they are of Opinion that the s'd Doster has right to a preemption of 400 Acres of land to include the above location & that a Certificate issue accordingly.

James Parbery Assee of Peter Williams this day claimed a preemption of 400 Acres of land at the State price in the District of Kentucky lying on the South side of the Kentucky River opposite to Lees Town[99] to include a Spring & running up towards the Mouth of Benson Creek to include a Cabbin the s'd Williams settling in the Country in the year 1779 in the Month of April satisfactory proof being made to the Court they are of Opinion that the said

[98] Collins, vol. 1, p. 13.

[99] Opposite Frankfort.

Parbery has a right to a preemption to 400 Acres of land to include the above location & that a Certificate issue accordingly.

(Cert issd for 1400)

John William this day claimed a settlement & preemption to a tract of land in the district of Kentucky lying on a sinking Creek the Mouth of which is Opposite the head of Greers Creek about 2 Miles So. of Crittendens Camp including his improvment on the So. side of the said Creek by settling in the Country in the year 1775 & residing 12 Months before the year 1778 Satisfactory proof being made to the Court they are of Opinion that the said Williams has a right to a settlemen't of 400 Acres of land to include the s'd improvement & the preemption of 1000 Acres adjoining & that a Cert. iss'e accordingly.

(Cert issd for 1000 fees &c pd D. D.)

It appearing to the Court that Benj Berrys claim was laid on lands which there is an Older Claim for & the s'd Berry moved to locate the same on the E. & N. E. side of the Old Indian Town on lilbergrud Creek & joining Cap'n Calmes Ordered that a Cert. issue Accordingly.

(Cert issd for 1000 fees &c pd D. D.)

It Appearing to the Court that Marquis Calmes claim was Located on land which there is an Older Claim for & the s'd Calmes moves to locate the same on the So. side of Cap'n Calmes land & joining the same on lelbergrud Creek ordered that a Certificate issue accordingly.

(Cert issd for 1400)

Bryus (Cyrus?) McCrackin this day claimed a settlem't & preemption to a tract of land in the District of Kentucky lying on a small branch on the North side of Glens creek about 1 Mile East of Glens Cabbin & adjoining Sam Estill on the South & Rob't McCoy on the East by settling in the Country in the year 1775 residing 12 Months before the year 1778 satisfactory being made to the Court they are of Opinion that the s'd McCrackin has a right to a settlem't of 400 Acres of land to include the above Location & the preemption of 1000 Acres adjoining & that a Certificate issue accordingly.

(Cert issd for 1000)

Ovid McCrackin this day claimed a preemption to 1000 Acres of Land at the State price in the district of Kentucky lying on the head of Willis Lees run at a pond including a Cabbin by marking & improving the same in the year 1776 satisfactory proof being made to the Court they are of Opinion that the said McCrackin has a right to a preemption of 1000 Acres of land to include the s'd improvement and that a Certificate issue accordingly.

(Cert issd for 1000)

Isaac McCrackin this day claimed a preemption of 1000 Acres of land at the State price in the District of Kentucky lying on Cartrights Creek branch of Salt river running down the s'd creek for quantity to include his Cabbin by Marking & improving the same in the year 1775 satisfactory proof being made to the Court they are of Opinion that the s'd McCrackin has a right to a preemption of 1000 Acres of land to include the said Improv't & that a Certificate issue accordingly.

(Cert issd for 1000)

Patrick Sheald this day claimed a preemption to a tract of land of 1000 Acres in the District of Kentucky at the State price lying on Sinking Creek joining John Williams below on the s'd Creek to include his Cabbin by marking and improving the same in the year 1776 satisfactory proof being made to the Court they are of Opinion that the s'd Sheald has a right to a preemption of 1000 Acres of land to include the said improvement & that a Certificate issue accordingly.

(Cert issd for 1000 fees &c pd D. D. to Colo Logan)

Thomas Stevenson by Colo Logan this day claimed a prempt of 1000 Acres of land in the District of Kentucky lying near the Mouth of the flat Lick branch a branch of Dicks river within 2½ Miles of flat lick by marking & improving the same in the year 1776 satisfactory proof being made to the Court they are of opinion that the s'd Stevenson has a right to a preemption of 1000 Acres of land to include the s'd improvement & that a Certificate issue accordingly.

Then the Court adjourned untill tomorrow Morning 9 Oclock

Wm. Fleming

At a Court Continued & held by the Commissioners for adjusting title to unpatented lands in the District of Kentucky at Bryants Station on Elkhorn Creek this 10 day of Jan'y 1780

Present

Wm. Fleming Stephen Trigg & Edmund Lyne—Gent'n.

It Appearing to the Court that Rich'd Waides Claim to land in this District was allowed him for w'h a Cert. was made out & signed & by some accident was lost Ord'd that another Cert. issue accordingly. Cert. recovered.

(Cert issd for 400 fees &c pd D. D.)

John Holder Assee of Moses Nelson this day claimed a preempt of 400 Acres of land at the State price in the District of Kentucky on Acc't of the s'd Nelsons making an actual Settlement in 1778 lying on Silver Creek about ½ Mile from the Mouth thereof to include a Spring Satisfactory proof being made to the Court they are of Opinion that the said Holder has a right to a preempt of 400 Acres of land to include the above location & that a Cert. issue accordingly.

(Cert issd for 1400 fees &c pd D. D.)

John Holder & John Martin[100] Assee of Edm'd Fear[101] this day claimed a settlem't & preempt'n to a tract of land in the District of Kentucky lying on Hustons fork of licking Creek about 4 Miles from the Mouth on the West side thereof abo't ½ a Mile from the Creek at a Spring by the s'd Fears Settling in the Country & residing 12 Months before the year 1778 satisfactory proof being made to the Court they are of Opinion that the s'd Holder has a right to a settlement of 400 Acres of land to include the above location & the preemption of 1000 Acres Adjoining and that a Certificate issue accordingly.

[100] Collins, vol. 1, pp. 7, 12, 354, 356.
[101] Collins, vol. 1, p. 13.

(Cert issd for 1400 fees &c pd D. D.)

Wm. Grant Sen'r this day claimed a settlement & preemption to a tract of Land in the district of Kentucky lying on the North fork of Elkhorn on both sides thereof adjoining Wm Ingles assee of Cools who was Assee of Thos. Booth 2000 Acres Survey on the No. side by raising a Crop of Corn in the Country in the year 1776 satisfactory proof being made to the Court they are of Opinion that the s'd Grant has a right to a settlem't of 400 Acres of land to include the above Location & the preemption of 1000 Acres adjoining & that a Certificate issue accordingly.

(Cert issd for 1400 fees &c pd. D. D.)

Isreal Grant this day claimed a Settlem't & preemption to a tract of land in the district of Kentucky lying on the Middle fork of licking Creek joining Dan'l Boons Settlem't & preempt'n on the North side by raising a Crop of Corn in the Country in the year 1776 satisfactory proof being made to the Court they are of Opinion that the s'd Grant has a right to a Settlement of 400 Acres to include the above location & the preemption of 1000 Acres Adjoining & that a certificate issue accordingly.

(Cert issd for 1400 fees &c pd D. D.)

Wm. Bryan Assee of Antho'y Havelow this day claimed a Settlem't & preemption to a tract of land in the District of Kentucky lying on the North side of the North fork of Elkhorn on both sides of the Shawnee Trace made by Capt Holdersmon[102] going to the Nation including a Spring on the East side of the said Trace & another on the West side by the said Havelow raising a crop of Corn in the Country in the year 1776 satisfactory proof being made to the Court they are of Opinion that the S'd Bryan has a right to a settlem't of 400 Acres of land to include the above Location & the preemption of 1000 Acres adjoining & that a Certificate issue accordingly.

(Cert issd for 1400 fees &c pd D. D.)

[103]Sarah Bryan this day claimed a settlem't & preempt'n to a tract of land in the district of Kentucky lying on the South side of the North fork of Elkhorn about 2 Miles from s'd Creek including a large Well Spring & Wm. Bryants former claimed spring by raising a crop of Corn in the Country in the year 1776 satisfactory proof being made to the Court they are of Opinion that the s'd Bryant has a right to a settlement of 400 Acres of land to include the above location & the preempt'n of 1000 Acres adjoining & that a Certificate issue accordingly.

(Cert issd for 1400 fees &c pd D. D.)

James Forbes this day claimed a settlem't and preempt'n to a tract of land in the district of Kentucky on Dav'd Jones fork a branch of Elkhorn 5 Miles So. E. of Bryants Station by raising a Crop of Corn in the Country in the year 1776 Satisfactory proof being made to the Court they are of Opinion that the s'd Forbes has a right to a settlement of 400 Acres of land to include the above location & the preemption of 1000 Acres adjoining & that a Certificate issued accordingly.

[102] Evidently means "Capt. Holders' men."

[103] Collins, vol. 1, p. 7.

(Cert issd for 1400 fees &c pd D. D.)

Wm Forbes this day claims a settlem't and preemption to a tract of land in the District of Kentucky lying on the head of Wolf Creek a branch of licking Creek adjoining the falling Timber by raising a Crop of Corn in the Country in the year 1776 satisfactory proof being made to the Court they are of Opinion that the s'd Forbes has a right to a Settlem't of 400 Acres of land to include the above location & the preemption of 1000 Acres of land adjoining & that Cert. Iss'e accordingly.

(Cert issd for 1400 fees &c pd D. D.)

Dav'd Jones this day claimed a settlem't & preemption to a tract of land in the District of Kentucky lying on Came (Carne?) river at the Mouth of a branch part of the s'd run runs one way & the other part the other way & raising a Crop of Corn in the Country in the year 1776 satisfactory proof being made to the Court they are of Opinion that the s'd Jones has a right to a settlem't of 400 Acres of land to include the above location & the preemption of 1000 Acres of land adjoining & that a Cert. iss accordingly.

(Cert issd for 1400 fees &c pd D. D.)

Allen Jones by Dav'd Jones this day claimed a settlem't and preemption to a tract of land in the District of Kentucky lying on the Middle fork of licking Creek adjoining Israel Grants land above by raising a Crop of Corn in the Country in the year 1776 satisfactory proof being made to the Court they are of Opinion that the s'd Jones has a right to a settlem't of 400 Acres of land to include the above location & the preempt'n of 1000 Acres adjoining & that a Cert. issue accordingly.

(Certificate issd for 1400 fees &c pd D. D.)

Telman Cradlebough by John Spurger this day claimed a settlement & preemption to a tract of land in the district of Kentucky lying on a West branch of Cane run near the head where there is 4 trees marked near together A Black Walnut a Honey Locust a Sugar Tree with FE & an Elm with 1776 in 2 Sink holes by raising a Crop of Corn in the Country in the year 1776 Satisfactory proof is being made to the Court they are of Opinion that the s'd Cradlebough has a right to a settlement of 400 Acres of land to include the above location and the preemption of 1000 Acres Adjoining & that a Certificate issue accordingly.

(Cert iss for 1000 fees &c pd D. D.)

Samuel Bryant this day claimed a preemption of 1000 Acres of land at the State price in the district of Kentucky lying on the North side of Elkhorn on Dav'd Jones Fork including a Small lick & Spring 4 Miles North East of Bryant Station by marking & improving the same in the year 1777 Satisfactory proof being made to the Court they are of Opinion that the said Bryant has a right to a preemption of 1000 acres of land to include the above location & that a Certificate issue accordingly.

(Cert issd for 400 fees &c pd D. D.)

Wm Grant Jun'r this day claimed a preemption of 400 Acres of land at the State price in the district of Kentucky lying between Hansons Dandridges & Ingles Assee of Cools who was Assee of

Thos Booth Surveys on a Small fork of Elkhorn empting in on the North Side by making Actual Settlement in April 1779 Satisfactory proof being made to the Court they are of Opinion that the said Grant has a right to a preemption of 400 Acres of land to include the above location and that a Certificate issue Accordingly.

(Cert issd for 1400 fees &c pd D. D.)
Jacob Johnson by Dan'l Wilcox[104] this day claimed a settlement & pre-empt'n to a tract of land in the District of Kentucky lying about 8 Miles from the lower blue licks at a Deer lick on Hinstons Buffaloe road on a branch running up & down for quantity by the s'd Johnston raising a Crop of Corn in the Country in the year 1776. Satisfactory proof being made to the Court they are of Opinion that the said Johnstone has a right to a settlement of 400 Acres of land to include the above Location & the preemption of 1000 Acres Adjoining & that a Certificate issue accordingly.

(Cert issd for 1400 fees &c pd D. D.)
Uriah Gaston this day claimed a preemption to 400 Acres of land at the State price in the District of Kentucky lying 3 Miles No. of the Kentucky River on Haggins Trace marked D R on a black Walnut Tree on a branch of Kentucky about 30 Yds S. E. of the said trace by making an Actual settlement in the month of April 1779 satisfactory proof being made to the Court they are of Opinion that the said Gaston has a right to a preempt. of 400 Acres of land to include the above location & that a Certificate issue accordingly.

(Cert issd for 1400 fees &c pd D. D.)
Wm Hays Assee of Sam'l Wilcoxon this day claimed a preempt. of 1000 Acres of land at the State price in the District of Kentucky lying on a branch of licking Creek joining the Lands s'd to be claimed by Wm. Moore on the South side by the Said Wilcoxons marking & improving the same in the year 1775 Satisfactory proof being made to the Court they are of Opinion that the s'd Hays has a right to a preemption of 1000 Acres of land to include the above location & that a Cert issue accordingly.

(Cert issd for 1000)
Wm Vancleave this day claimed a preemption of 1000 Acres of land in the District of Kentucky at the State price lying on the forks of paint lick Creek on the Trace from Boonsborough to St Asaphs to include a lick by marking & improving the same in the year 1777 satisfactory proof being made to the Court they are of Opinion that the s'd Vancleave has a right to a preempt'n of 1000 Acres of land to include the above location & that a Certificate issue accordingly.

Sam'l Bryan jun'r by Wm Hays this day claimed a preemption dismissed

(Cert issd for 1000 fees &c pd D. D.)
Levi Todd Assee of Israel Wilcox this day claimed a preemption to a tract of land of 400 Acres at the State price in the district of Kentucky lying between the Middle & upper roads leading from the lower blue Licks to Limestone run & Lawrence Creek about 10 Miles from the Licks & two Miles from Wm. McConels including a spring & improvm't by the s'd Wilcox making an Actual set-

[104] Collins, vol. 1, p. 13.

tlement in April 1779 satisfactory proof being made to the Court they are of Opinion that the said Todd has a right to a preempt'n of 400 Acres of land to include the above Location & that a Certificate issue accordingly.

(Cert issd for 400 fees &c pd D. D.)

Mijah Wood this day claimed a settlem't & preemption to a tract of Land in the district of Kentucky lying on the Water of Boones Creek adjoining Colo Robinsons Survey to the E. including a small sinking Spring that empties into a big pond by raising a Crop of Corn in the Country in the year 1776 satisfactory proof being made to the Court they are of Opinion that the s'd Wood has a right to a Settlem't of 400 Acres of land to include the above Location & the preemption of 1000 Acres Adjoining & that a Certificate issue accordingly.

(Cert issd for 1400 fees &c pd D. D. to Mr. Martin)

Wm Lee by John Martin this day claimed a settlement & preemption to a tract of Land in the District of Kentucky lying on Hustons fork of Licking Creek below Hoder & Martins Land on the bank of Creek 2 Miles to include an improvment by the said Lees raising a Crop of Corn in the Country in the year 1776 satisfactory proof being to the Court they are of Opinion that the s'd Lee has a right to a settlement of 400 Acres of land to include the s'd improvement & the preemption of 1000 acres adjoining & that a Certificate issue accordingly.

(Cert issd for 1400 fees &c pd D. D.)

James Forbes this day claimed a settlem't & preemption to a tract of land in the district of Kentucky lying on the Middle Fork of licking Creek adjoining Allen Jones land above by raising a Crop of Corn in the Country in the year 1776 satisfactory proof being made to the Court they are of Opinion that the said Forbes has a right to a settlem't of 400 Acres of land to include the above Location & the preemption of 1000 Acres adjoining and that a certificate issue accordingly.

(Cert issd for 1400 fees &c pd D. D.)

[105]George Bryan this day claimed a settlem't & preemption to a tract of land in the District of Kentucky on the head of Cane run including a Spring which sinks after running about 300 yds near a pond & about 5 Miles from Bryants Station by raising a Crop of Corn in the Country in the year 1776 satisfactory proof being made to the Court they are of Opinion that the s'd Bryan has a right to a settlem't of 400 Acres of land to include the above location & the preemption of 1000 Acres adjoining and that a Certificate issue accordingly.

(Cert issd for 1400 fees &c pd D. D.)

Thomas Thompson by Geo'e Bryant this day claimed a settlem't & preemption to a tract of Land in the District of Kentucky lying to the Eastward of Ingles Survey including a large boiling Spring about 3 Miles above the Licking Trace which sinks in a small distance by the s'd Thompson raising a Crop of Corn in the Country in the year 1776 Satisfactory proof being made to the Court they are of Opinion that the s'd Thompson has a right to a settlem't of

[105] Collins, Vol. 1, p. 6.

400 Acres of land to include the above location & the preemption of 1000 Acres adjoining & that a Certificate issue accordingly.

(Cert issd for 1400 fees &c pd D. D.)

Joseph Bryan Sen'r this day claimed a settlem't & preemption to a tract of Land in the District of Kentucky lying on the North fork of Elkhorn Creek joining Audleys Pauls & John Wares E line by raising a Crop of Corn in the Country in the year 1776 Satisfactory proof being made to the Court they are of Opinion that the s'd Bryan has a right to a settlem't of 400 Acres of land to include the above Location & the preemption of 1000 Acres Adjoining & that a Certificate issue accordingly.

(Cert issd for 1400 fees &c pd D. D.)

[106]Dan'l Bryan this day claimed a preempt of 400 Acres of Land in the District of Kentucky at the State price lying Adjoining Isreal Grants Land on the N. E. line by making an Actual settlem't in Apr 1779 satisfactory proof being made to the Court they are of Opinion that the s'd Bryan has a right to a preemption to a tract of land to include the above location & that a Certificate issue accordingly.

(Cert issd for 1400 fees &c pd D. D.)

Morgan Bryan Sen'r this day claimed a settlem't & preemption to a tract of land in the district of Kentucky lying on the Second small fork that comes in the North fork of Elkhorn adjoining Sam'l Meradiths west line by raising a crop of Corn in the Country in the year 1776 Satisfactory proof being made to the Court they are of Opinion that the s'd Bryan has a right to a settlem't of 400 Acres of Land to include the above Location & the preemption of 1000 Acre adjoining & that a Certificate issue accordingly.

(Cert issd for 1400 fees &c pd D. D.)

John Forbes this day claimed a settlem't and preemption to a tract of land in the district of Kentucky lying on the North west side of Smiths & South west of Philips survey by raising a crop of Corn in the Country in the year 1776 satisfactory proof being made to the Court they are of Opinion that the s'd Forbes has a right to a settlem't of 400 Acres of land to include the above Location & the preemption of 1000 Acres adjoining & that a Certificate issued accordingly.

(Cert iss for 1000 fees &c pd D. D.)

James Power this day claimed a preempt. of 1000 Acres of land at the State price in the District of Kentucky lying on the Second small fork that comes in the North fork of Elkhorn Creek on the West side thereof about 2½ miles from this place down the s'd Creek on the Hunters trace by Mark'g & improving the same in the year 1777 satisfactory proof being made to the Court they are of Opinion that the s'd power has a right to a preemption of 1000 Acres of land to Include the above Location & that a Cert iss accordingly.

(Cert iss for 1400 fees &c pd D. D.)

Daniel Wilcoxson this day claimed a settlem't and preemption to a tract of land in the district of Kentucky lying about 8 or 9 Miles from Bryants Station on the dividing ridge between the big

[106] Collins, Vol. 1, p. 7.

fork of Elkhorn & Coopers run a branch of licking Creek Including a sinking Spring by settling in the Country in the year 1777 and residing ever since satisfactory proof being made to the court they are of Opinion that the said Wilcoxson has a right to a settlem't of 400 Acres of land to include the above location & the preemption of 1000 Acres adjoining & that a Certificate issue accordingly.

(Cert issd for 1400 fees &c pd D. D.)

Wm Bryan this day claimed a settlem't & preempt'n to a tract of Land in the district of Kentucky lying Adjoining Adam Stephens on the East & Ward on the South lying between the head waters of Elkhorn & Hickmans to include a large Spring by raising a Crop of Corn in the Country in the year 1776 satisfactory proof being made to the Court they are of Opinion that the s'd Bryan has a right to a settlem't of 400 Acres of land to include the above location & the preemption of 1000 Acres adjoining & that a Certificate issue accordingly.

Then the Court Adjourned untill Tomorrow Morning 10 OClock

William Fleming

At a Court continued & held by the Commissioners for adjusting disputed Titles to unpatented Lands at Bryants Station on Elkhorn Creek this Eleventh day of Jan'y 1780.

Present

Wm. Fleming Stephen Trigg &
Edmund Lyne—Gent'n

(Cert issd for 1400)

James Peack by Dan'l Boone this day claimed a settlem't & preempt'n to a tract of land in the district of Kentucky lying about 7 or 8 Miles N. E. of the lower blue lick upon licking on a large Buffaloe Road includeing about 3 Or 4 Acres of clear & Open Land including three forks of branches of licking running East for quantity by raising a Crop of Corn in the Country in the year 1775 satisfactory proof being made to the Court they are of Opinion that the said Peack has a right to a settlement of 400 Acres of land to include the above location & the preemption of 1000 Acres adjoining and that a Certificate issue accordingly.—

(Cert issd for 1400)

Wm Moore Assee of Edmund Givins this day claimed a Settlement & preemption to a tract of land in the District of Kentucky lying on the waters of licking Creek adjoining James Peacks land on the E. side of the said Givins raising a Crop of Corn in the Country in the year 1775 satisfactory proof being made to the Court they are of Opinion that the s'd Moore has a right to a settlem't of 400 Acres of Land to include the above Location & the preempt. of 1000 Acres Adjoining & that a Certificate iss Accordingly.—

(Cert iss for 1400)

Dav'd Burney by Wm Hays this day claimed a settlem't & preemption to a tract of Land in the District of Kentucky lying on the waters of Licking Creek adjoining Jas. Peacks Land on the So. Side by raising a Crop of Corn in the Country in the year 1775 Satisfactory proof being made to the Court they are of Opinion the s'd Burney has a right to a settlem't of 400 Acres of

Land to include the above Location & the preemption of 1000 Acres Adjoining & that a Certificate issue accordingly.—

(Cert issd for 1400 fees &c pd D. D.)

The'e Boone this day claimed a settlem't & preempt'n to a tract of Land in the District of Kentucky lying on the Waters of licking Creek adjoining Jas. Peacks Land on the North Side by raising a Crop of Corn in the Country in the year 1776 Satisfactory proof being made to the Court they are of Opinion that the s'd Boone has a right to a settlement of 400 Acres of land to include the above location & the preempt'n of 1000 Acres adjoining & that a Cert. issue accordingly.—

(Cert issd for 1000)

Wm Henry by Dan'l Boone this day claimed a preemption of 1000 Acres of Land at the State price in the district of Kentucky lying on the Waters of licking Creek adjoining the Lands of Sam'l Thompson (?) on the East and by Mark'g & improving the same in the year 1775 satisfactory proof being made to the Court they are of Opinion that the s'd Henry has a right to a preemption of 1000 Acres of land to include the Location & that a Cert. issue accordingly.

(Cert iss for 1400 fees &c pd D. D. to Colo Fleming)

George Hendrix by Colo Fleming this day claimed a settlem't & preempt to a tract of Land in the District of Kentucky lying on an East branch of Hustons fork of Licking including two of Crittendons Cabbins also a Marked Tree with R. S. upon the West side of the s'd Branch by settling in the Country in the year 1777 and residing ever since satisfactory proof being made to the Court they are of Opinion that the s'd Hendrix has a right to a settlem't of 400 Acres of Land to include the above Location & the preempt of 1000 Acres adjoining & that a Cert issue accordingly.

(Cert iss for 1400)

It was proved to the Court the 4th Inst. that Wm. Beckley has a right to a settlem't & preemption tho did not at that time locate it Now comes into Court and Locates the same on the Waters of Licking Creek on the head of the first left hand fork of Lawrence Creek about 4 Miles from the Mouth of Limestone Ordered that a Cert issue accordingly.

(Cert iss for 1400)

John Ellis by Wm Bryan this day claimed a settlem't & preemption to a tract of Land in the District of Kentucky lying on the No. side of No. fork of Elkhorn creek joining the Lands of Wm Russell & Vaughan by raising a Crop of Corn in the Country in the year 1775. Satisfactory proof being made to the Court they are of Opinion that the s'd Ellis has a right to a settlement of 400 Acres of Land to include the above Location & the preemption of 1000 Acres Adjoining & that a Certificate issue accordingly.

(Cert issd for 1000 fees &c pd D. D. to Capt'n Smith)

John Dobbin by John Smith this day claimed a preemption of 1000 Acres of Land at the State price in the district of Kentucky lying on a Creek running into the N. fork of Elkhorn Creek about 5 or 6 Miles up the Creek including an old Camp made by Dan'l Boone & Wm Bryant by mark'g & improving the same in the year 1775 Satisfactory proof being made to the Court they are of Opinion that the s'd Dobbin has a right to a preemption of 1000 Acres of land to include the above Location & that a Cert. issue accordingly.

(Cert issd for 1000 fees &c pd D. D.)

John Smith this day Claimed a preemption to 1000 Acres of Land at the State price in the district of Kentucky lying about 3 Miles South of Deals lick on a branch of the South fork of Elkhorn by marking & improving the same in the year 1775 satisfactory proof being made to the Court they are of Opinion that the s'd Smith has a right to a preemption to 1000 Acres of Land to include the above Location and that a Cert. issue accordingly.

(Cert issd for 1000 fees &c pd D. D. to R. Guthrie)

Elias Harris by Rueben Guthrie this day claimed a preempt'n to a tract of 1000 Acres at the State price in the district of Kentucky lying on Stoners fork of Licking adjoining Dan'l Boones Land on the West by marking & improving the same in the year 1775 satisfactory proof being made to the Court they are of Opinion that the s'd Harris has a right to a preempt. of 1000 Acres of Land to include the above Location & that a Certificate issue accordingly.

(Cert issd for 1000)

John Snody by Dan'l Boone this day claimed a preemption to a tract of 1000 Acres of Land at the State price in the district of Kentucky lying on the Waters of Drowning Creek to include the Mulberry lick adjoining Margret Drakes land by marking & improving the same in the year 1775 satisfactory proof being made to the Court they are of Opinion that the s'd Snody has a right to a preemption of 1000 Acres of Land to include the above Location & that a Certificate issue accordingly.

(Cert issd for 1000)

Ebenezer Frost by D. Boone this day claimed a preemption of 1000 Acres of Land at the State price in the district of Kentucky lying on Boones Creek near the head thereof adjoining Dan'l Robinsons preemption on the North side by marking & improving the same in the year 1775 Satisfactory proof being made to the Court that the s'd Frost has a right to a preempt'n of 1000 Acres of Land to include the above Location & that a Certificate issue accordingly.

(Cert issd for 400 fees &c pd D. D. to Jno. Martin)

[107]John Burger this day claimed a preemption to 400 Acres of Land at the State price in the district of Kentucky lying about 6 Miles from Riddles Station a South course on the dividing ridge between hinkstones branch & coopers run Waters of licking Creek including a Sinking Spring by settling in the Country in the year 1778 satisfactory proof being made to the court they are of Opinion that the s'd Burger has a right to a preemption of 400 Acres of land to include the above location & that a Cert. issue accordingly.

[107] Collins, Vol. 1, p. 13.

(Cert issd for 400 fees &c pd D. D. Jno Martin)

[108]John Burger Jun'r this day claimed a preemption of 400 Acres of land at the State price in the district of Kentucky lying on Hingstons branch of Licking Creek about 8 Miles from Riddles Station lying on the Trace that leads from Licking to Lexington including a Spring by making an Actual settlement in March 1779 Satisfactory proof being made to the Court they are of Opinion that the S'd Burger Jun'r has a right to a preemption of 400 Acres of Land to include the above Location & that a Cert issue accordingly.—

(Cert issd for 400 fees &c pd D. D. to Jno Martin)

Christopher Spear this day claimed a preemption of 400 Acres of land at the State price in the district of Kentucky lying on Hingstons branch on Licking Creek adjoining John Burger Jun'r Land on the So. side by making an Actual Settlem't in the year 1778 satisfactory proof being made to the Court they are of Opinion that the s'd Spear has a right to a preemption of 400 Acres of Land to include the above location & that a Certificate issue accordingly.

(Cert issd for 400 fees &c pd D. D. to Jno Martin)

Casper Karsner this day claimed a preempt'n of 400 Acres of land at the State price in the District of Kentucky lying on the North branch of the North fork of Elkhorn Creek including a small sinking spring on the south side of the s'd branch and about two miles up the said branch from the licking Trace a North E. course by Making an actual Settlem't in the year 1778 Satisfactory proof being made to the Court they are of Opinion that the s'd Karsner has a right to a preempt of 400 Acres of Land to include the above Location & that a Cert. issue accordingly.

(Cert issd for 400 fees &c pd D. D.)

James Heath by James Forbes this day claimed a preemption of 400 Acres of Land at the State price in the district of Kentucky lying on a branch of licking Creek Known by the name of Coopers run about 1 Mile from the head thereof adjoining a large Cain brake including a Spring in the Edge of the Cain brake on the So. E. Side of the s'd branch by making an Actual Settlem't in April 1779 Satisfactory proof being made to the Court they are of Opinion that the s'd heath has a right to a preemption of 400 Acres of Land to include the Above Location & that a Cert. issue accordingly.

(Cert issd for 1000 fees &c pd D. D.)

Dav'd Vance this day claimed a preemption to 1000 Acres of land at the State price in the district of Kentucky lying on the town fork of Elkhorn Creek about 1½ Miles from the Mouth thereof by marking & improving the same in the year 1776. Satisfactory proof being made to the Court they are of Opinion that the s'd Vance has a right to a preempt of 1000 Acres of land to include the above location and that a Cert issue accordingly.

(Cert issd for 1000 fees &c pd D. D.)

[109]Jacob Hunter this day claimed a preemption of 1000 Acre of land at the

[108]Collins, Vol. 2, p. 13.

[109]Collins, Vol. 1, p. 8.

State price in the District of Kentucky lying 3 Miles below the Mouth of Linseys run on the North side of South fork of Elkhorn Creek by mark'g an improv't by Mark'g & improving the same in the year 1775 satisfactory proof being made to the Court they are of opinion that the s'd Hunter has a right to a preemption of 1000 Acres of Land to include the above Location & that a Certificate issue accordingly.

Then the Court adjourned untill Tomorrow Morning 9 Oclock

Wm Fleming.

At a Court Continued & held for adjusting Titles to Unpatented Lands by the Commissioners of Kentucky District at Bryants Station on Elkhorn Creek this 12th day of Jan'y 1780.

Present

Wm Fleming Stephen Trigg &
Edmund Lyne—Gent'n

(Cert issd for 400 fees &c pd D. D.)

The former order of this Court for granting Wm Moore Assee of James Anthony for a preempt. of 400 Acres of land at the State price is sett aside as it appeared to the Court that the s'd Anthony has sold the same to Wm Hays who comes into Court & claims the same by the s'd Anthony making an Actual Settlement in March 1779. Locates the same at Dan'l Boones old beginning on Otter Creek running up the s'd Creek for quantity ordered that a Certificate issue accordingly.

(Cert issd for 1000 fees &c pd D. D.)

Henry Field Jr Assee of George Boyde this day claimed a preemption of 1000 Acres of land at the State in the district of Kentucky lying between the Waters of Glens Creek and clear Creek including his Cabbin by the s'd Boyd marking & improving the same by building a Cabbin &c in the year 1776 satisfactory proof being made to the Court they are of Opinion that the s'd Field has a right to a preempt of 1000 Acres of land to include the above location & that a Certificate issue accordingly.

(Cert issd for 1400 fees &c pd D. D.)

Sam'l Bryant by Wm. Bryant this day claimed a settlement & preemption to a tract of Land in the district of Kentucky lying about a West course from [110]Spottswood Dandridges land about 2 Miles from the North fork of Elkhorn Creek by raising a Crop of Corn in the Country in the year 1776 satisfactory Proof being made to the Court they are of Opinion that the said Bryan has a right to a settlem't of 400 Acres of land to include the above Location & the preemption of 1000 Acres Adjoining & that A Certificate issue accordingly.

(Cert issd for 1000 fees &c pd D. D. to J. Bryan)

Dav'd Bryan by James Bryan this day claimed a preemption of 1000 Acres of Land at the State price in the district of Kentucky lying on the branch of Elkhorn Creek about 4½ Miles South West of this place by Marking & improving the same in the year 1776 Satisfactory proof being made to the Court they are of Opinion that the s'd Bryan has a right to a preemption of 1000 Acres of Land to include the above location & that a Cert. issue accordingly.

[110] Collins, Vol. 2, p. 337.

(Cert issd for 1400 fees &c pd D. D. to Steph Trigg)

John Bryan Sen'r this day claimed a settlement & preempt to a tract of land in the district of Kentucky lying on Hustons fork of Licking Creek at a buffaloe Crossing including a spring & an improvement on the bank of the Creek by raising a Crop of Corn in the Country in the year 1776 Satisfactory proof being made to the Court they are of Opinion that the s'd Bryan has a right to a settlem't of 400 Acres of Land to include the above location & the preemption of 1000 Acres of land Adjoining and that a Cert. issue accordingly.

(Cert issd for 1400 fees &c pd D. D. to Steph'n Trigg)

[111]James Bryan this day claimed a settlement & preemption to a tract of Land in the district of Kentucky lying on the head of the South fork of Elkhorn Creek where Mr. Douglass began a large Survey that includes a part of Hickmans Creek & running North and in Direction of that line and Southward for quantity by raising a Crop of Corn in the Country in the year 1776 Satisfactory proof being made to the Court they are of Opinion that the s'd Bryan has a right to a settlement of 400 Acres of land to include the above Location & the preemption of 1000 Acres of Land adjoining & that a Certificate issue accordingly.

(Cert issd for 1400 fees &c pd D. D.)

James Bryan Jr this day claimed a settlement & preemption to a tract of Land in the district of Kentucky lying on Cane run adjoining Maxwell on the South & McConnell on the East including a big Spring on the North side of Cane run & up the s'd run for quantity by raising a Crop of Corn in the Country in the year 1776 satisfactory proof being made to the Court they are of Opinion that the s'd Bryan has a right to a settlem't of 400 Acres of Land to include the above location & the preemption of 1000 Acres adjoining and that a Certificate issue accordingly.

(Cert issd for 1000 fees &c pd D. D.)

[112]James McBrid this day claimed a preemption of 1000 Acres of land at the State price in the district of Kentucky lying on the South fork of Elkhorn about 7 Miles above the Mouth of Shannons run by marking & improving the same and building &c in the year 1776 Satisfactory proof being made to the Court they are of Opinion that the s'd McBrid has a right to a preemption of 1000 Acres of land to include the above Location & that a certificate issue accordingly.

(Cert issd for 400 fees &c pd D. D. to Jas McBride)

[113]Isaac McBrid by James McBrid this day claimed a preemption of 400 Acres of land at the State price in the District of Kentucky lying on the South fork of Elkhorn adjoining Adams McConnells on the West & about 2½ Miles above the forks by making an Actual settlement in the year 1778 Satisfactory proof being made to the Court they are of Opinion that the s'd McBride has a right to a preempt of 400 Acres of land to include the above location and that a Certificate issue accordingly.

[111] Collins, Vol. 1, p. 13.

[112] (McBride) Collins, Vol. 1, pp. 16, 519.

[113] Collins, Vol. 1, p. 12.

(Cert issd for 1000 fees &c Pd. D. D.)

Wilson Hunt this day claimed a preemption of 1000 Acres of land at the State price lying in the district of Kentucky on the North side of the North fork Elkhorn at an Indian Ditch about six miles North of Bryants Station by Marking & improving the same in the year 1775 satisfactory proof being made to the Court they are of Opinion that the s'd Hunt has a right to a preemption of 1000 Acres of Land including the above location & that a Certificate issue Accordingly.

(Cert issd for 1000 fees &c pd D. D.)

Charles Hunter this day claimed a preemption of 1000 Acres of land at the State price in the district of Kentucky Lying on the Kentucky River at the Mouth of Elkhorn Creek by Marking & improving the same in the year 1777.—Satisfactory proof being made to the Court they are of Opinion that the s'd Hunter has a right to a preemption of 1000 Acres of land to include the above Location & that a Certificate issue accordingly.

(Cert issd for 1400 fes &c pd D. D.)

[114]Wm McConnell Assee of John Clarke[115] this day claimed a settlem't & preemption to a tract of land in the district of Kentucky lying about 1½ Miles North of Colo Shelbys Land & a West Course from the Land said to be claimed by David Pery including a Sinking Spring by residing in the Country 12 Month before the year 1778 satisfactory proof being made to the Court they are of Opinion that the s'd McConnell has a right to a settlem't of 400 Acres of Land to include the above Location & the preemption of 1000 Acres adjoining & that a Certificate issue accordingly.—

(Cert issd for 400 fees &c pd D. D. to J. Forbes)

John Hower this day claimed a preemption to 400 Acres of land in the district of Kentucky lying on a branch of North fork of Elkhorn that comes in on the North side above the Land claimed by Jno Dobbins on the North side by Making an Actual Settlement in April 1779 Satisfactory proof being made to the Court they are of Opinion that the s'd Hower has a right to a preempt of 400 Acres of Land to include the above location & that a Certificate issue accordingly.

(Cert issd for 400 fees &c pd D. D. to J. Forbes)

John Hover Jun this day claimed a preemption of 400 Acres of Land at the State price in the District of Kentucky lying about a Mile from the Lands claimed by John Dobbins a North West Course on a small Creek by making an actual settlem't in the Month of April 1779 Satisfactory proof being made to the Court they are of Opinion that the s'd Howver has a right to a preemption of 400 Acres of land to include the above location & that a Certificate issue accordingly.

(Cert issd for 400 fees &c pd D. D. to John Smith)

John Goodnight this day claimed a preemption of 400 Acres of Land at the State price in the district of Kentucky lying on Hingstons fork about 5 Miles

[114] Collins, vol. 1, p. 457.
[115] Collins, vol. 1, p. 6.

from the Mouth thereof and about 4 Miles from Riddles Station by making an Actual Settlement in April 1779 Satisfactory proof being made to the Court they are of Opinion that the s'd Goodnight has a right to a preemption of 400 Acres of Land to include the above location & that a Certificate issue accordingly.

(Cert issd for 400 fees &c pd D. D. to Jno Smith)

David Goodnight this day claimed a preemption of 400 Acres of land at the State price in the District of Kentucky lying on Johnson Creek about 3 Miles from the Mouth thereof upon the North East side of Licking Creek & six miles below the blue lick by making an Actual settlement April 1779. satisfactory proof proof being made to the Court they are of Opinion that the s'd Goodnight has a right to a preemption of 400 Acres of land to include the above location & that a Cert issue accordingly.

(Cert issd for 400 fees &c pd D. D.)

John Smith this day claimed a preemption of 400 Acres of Land at the State price in the District of Kentucky lying on broad run Waters of the South fork of licking Creek adjoining Sam'l McMullens below & Isaac Riddle above by making an Actual Settlement in 1778 satisfactory proof being made to the Court they are of Opinion that the s'd Smith has a right to a preemption of 400 Acres of land to include the above location & that a Cert. issue accordingly.

(Cert issd for 400 fees &c pd D. D.)

John Smith Assee of Frederick Tanner[116] this day claimed a preemption of 400 Acres of land at the State price in the district of Kentucky lying on the North fork of licking in the forks 3 Miles above the fork on a small run by the s'd Tanner making an Actual settlement in 1778 Satisfactory proof being made to the Court they are of Opinion that the s'd Smith has a right to a preemption of 400 Acres of land to include the above location & that a Certificate issue accordingly.

(Cert isd for 400 fees &c pd D. D.)

George Layall by John Smith this day claimed a preemption of 400 Acres of land in the district of Kentucky at the State price lying on a small run Waters of the North Fork of licking about 1 Mile below John Smiths Assee of F Tanner land on the s'd run by making an Actual settlement in the year 1778 Satisfactory proof being made to the Court they are of Opinion that the s'd Layall has a right to a preemption of 400 Acres of Land to include the above location & that a Certificate issue accordingly.

(Cert issd for 400 fees &c pd D. D. to Jno Smith)

Catherine Edleman by Jo'n Smith this day claimed a preemption of 400 Acres of Land at the State price in the District of Kentucky lying on the East side of the So. fork of licking Creek 1¼ Miles from John Martins land & running Eastwardy for quantity by Settling in the Country in the year 1778 Satisfactory proof being made to the Court they are of Opinion that the s'd Edleman has a right to a preempt of 400 Acres of land to include the above location and that a Certificate issue accordingly.

[116] Collins, vol. 1, p. 13.

(Cert issd for 400 fees &c pd D. D.)

[117]Paul Fisher this day claimed a preemption of 400 Acres of land at the State price in the district of Kentucky lying on a branch of the North fork of licking on the South side thereof & on the No. side of the s'd branch about 4 miles from the Forks by making an Actual Settlem't in 1778 Satisfactory proof being made to the Court they are of Opinion that the s'd Fisher has a right to a preemption of 400 Acres of land to include the above Location & that a Cert isse accordingly.

Then the Court adjourned untill To-morrow Morning 9 Oclock

Wm Fleming

At a Court Continued & held for adjusting Titles to the Kentucky land by the Commissioners of Kentucky District at Bryants Station on Elkhorn Creek this 13th day of Jan'y 1780.—

Present

Wm Fleming Stephen Trigg &
Edmund Lyne—Gent'n

(Cert iss for 400 fees &c pd D. D. to Sam'l McMullen)

Nichlas Bradstone this day claimed a preemption of 400 acres of land at the State price in the District of Kentucky lying on the forks of Elkhorn Creek on the head of Lindseys branch waters of the South fork of Elkhorn by making an Actual settlement in the Month of March 1778 satisfactory proof being made to the Court they are of Opinion that the s'd Bradstone has a right to a preemption of 400 Acres of land to include the above location & that a Cert. issue accordingly.

[117] Collins, vol. 1, p. 13.

(Cert issd for 1400 fees &c pd D. D. to Wm McConnell)

Francis McConnell this day claimed a settlement & preemption to a tract of land in the district of Kentucky lying on the head of the South fork of Elkhorn Creek adjoining the Lands of Wm. McConnell on the East by Settling & residing in the Country 12 Month before the year 1778 satisfactory proof being made to the Court they are of Opinion that the s'd McConnell has a right to a settlement of 400 Acres of Land to include the above Location and the preemption of 1000 Acres adjoining & that a Certificate issue accordingly.

(Cert issd for 400 fees &c pd D. D. Sam'l McMullen)

James Wason this day claimed a preemption of 400 Acres of land at the State price in the district of Kentucky lying on the North side of the North fork of Elkhorn Creek on a branch called Laines run by making an Actual settlement in March 177.9 Satisfactory proof being made to the Court they are of Opinion that the said Wason has a right to a preempt of 400 acres of land to include the above location & that a Cert. iss'e accordingly.

(Cert issd for 400)

Levi Todd Assee of Jonathan Bryan this day claimed a preemption of 400 Acres of land at the State price in the district of Kentucky lying on Mill Creek a branch of the E. fork of licking about 3 Miles from the mouth of the s'd Creek includ'g a Cabbin at a large Spring by the s'd bryants Making an Actual settlem't in Apr 1779 Satisfactory proof being made to the Court they are of

Opinion that the s'd Todd has a right to a preemption of 400 Acres to include the above location & that a Certificate issue accordingly.

Then the Court adjourned untill tomorrow Morning 9 Oclock

Wm Fleming

At a Court Continued & held for adjusting disputed Titles to unpatented land by Commissioners of Kentucky district this 14th day of Jan'y 1780 at Bryants Station on Elkhorn Creek

Present

Wm Fleming Stephen Trigg & Edmund Lyne—Gent'n

(Cert issd for 1400 fees &c pd D. D. to R. Patterson)

Abraham McClallen Heir at law to John McClelan[118] Dec'd by Rob't Patterson this day claimed a settlem't & preemption to a tract of land in the District of Kentucky lying on the North fork of Elkhorn Creek adjoining the lands of McClellen Johnson he has a Station by the s'd decedents raising a Crop of Corn in the Country in the year 1776 & residing 12 Month before the year 1778 satisfactory proof being made to the Court they are of Opinion that the s'd McClellen &c has a right to a settlem't of 400 Acres of land to include the above Location and the preempt of 1000 Acres Adjoining & that a Certificate issue accordingly.

(Cert issd for 1000 fees &c pd D. D. to R. Patterson)

Thos McMullen by Sam'l McMullen this day claimed a preemption to a tract of 1000 Acres of land in the district of Kentucky at the state price on the waters of the North fork of Elkhorn Creek on the West fork of Cane run & on the W. side thereof including an improvement by mark'g & improv'g the same in the year 1776 Satisfactory proof being made to the Court they are of Opinion that the s'd McMullen has a right to a preempt of 1000 Acres of land to include the said improvement & that a Cert. issue accordingly.

(Cert issd for 1000 fees &c pd D. D. to H Shannon)

John Shannon by Hugh Shannon this day claimed a preemption of 1000 Acres of land at the State price in the district of Kentucky lying on Shannons run Waters of the S. fork of Elkhorn Creek Adjoining John Blackburns land on the South side by Marking & improving by building a Cabbin & on the premises in the year 1776 satisfactory proof beng made to the Court they are of Opinion that the s'd Shannon has a right to a preemption of 1000 Acres of land to include the above Improvement & that a Cert. issue accordingly.

[119]Joseph Lindsey this day claimed a settlem't & preemption to a tract of land in the district of Kentucky Witnesses being sworn & examined in Consideration of which the Court are of Opinion that the s'd Lindsey has a right to a settlem't of 400 Acres of land & the preempt of 1000 Acres adjoining he offering to locate the same on a large spring three Miles below Lexington Joining Wm McConnells thence West for Quantity which Spring & land Ap-

[118] Collins, vol. 1, p. 18.

[119] Collins, vol. 2, p. 514.

pearing by Colo Prestons Books to have been Surveyed for Evan Shelby the 16 of July 1775 by Virtue of a Military Warent the s'd lindsey alledging that the said Survey was not legal he being Settled on the land before the s'd Shelby entered it with the Surveyer; several Witnesses were Sworn & examined the depositions of Patrick Jourden taken before John Cowan Gent a magestrate for Kentucky County was given into court in Evidence & showeth that Patrick Jourden was in company with the s'd Joseph Lindsey on or about the 1st day of May 1775 when the s'd Lindsey marked out & improved a certain tract of land at a large Spring near the head of the North fork of the South fork of Elkhorn & at the same time heard the s'd Lindsey declare that he intended that place for his settlement Wm McConnell Appeared in Court & being sworn declared he knew the s'd Lindsey about 1st day Jan'y 1776 & saw him on the above mentioned tract of land employ'd in building a Cabbin in company with 2 other men & that the s'd Lindsey shew'd the s'd McConnell his name marked on a tree & some trees deadned which has been done in 1775 He likewise saw where some Apple seed had been sowed by the s'd Lindsey & that some time after that he knew the s'd Lindsey & his brother to go & finish the said Cabbin by Covering & cutting a door in it It Appears to the Court by the Testimony of Hugh Shannon that the s'd Lindsey had planted a few hills of corn near the Cabbin in the year 1776 Wm McConnel being further Called upon declared that in May 1776 being at work on his own land John Floyd & Isaac Shelby & John Mills in Company with some others came to him when the Surveyor John Floyd informed him that the Land the witness was then at work on had been run out for John Maxwell the year before & that he would not Compound with Maxwell for the same that he would lay on a Military Warrant for Evan Shelby on which the s'd McConnell gave the s'd Maxwell seventy pounds for his claim to the s'd land the s'd McConnell further witnesseth that he heard the Surveyor John Floyd declare that he had run out a Survey for Wm. Garriott & that he understood by John Maxwell that Garriott was willing to give up his claim to the s'd Land & that he would lay even Shelbys Warrant on the same the s'd Floyd Declared he understood that Joseph Lindsey had improved the land in dispute & that Garriott could not get the s'd Survey after which Conversation they went from the s'd McConnells to Look at the s'd land & were gone about 2 hours when they returned the witness heard Isaac Shelby Say that he liked the Land & that he would lay his father Evan Shelbys warrant on it the above Evidence being taken at the request of the s'd Joseph Lindsey the s'd Shelby not being present & was at so great a distance that he possibly cannot attend this Court during its sitting to make his defense therefore this Court thinks they are not Authorized to give the s'd Lindsey a Certificate for the above Location.

(Cert issd for 1400 fees &c pd D. D.)

Hugh Shannon this day claimed a settlem't & preemption to a tract of land in the district of Kentucky lying on the Middle Road leading to Larence run & building a Cabbin in the fork of a run about 9 Miles from the lower Blue lick by raising a Crop of Corn in the Country in the year 1776 & residing 12 Months before the year 1778 satisfactory proof being made to the Court they are of Opinion that the s'd Shannon has a right to a settlement of 400 Acres of land to include the above Location & the preemption of 1000 Acres adjoining & that a Certificate issue accordingly.

(Cert issd for 1000 fees &c pd D. D. to Hugh Shannon)

[120]Wm Shannon this day claimed a preemption of 1000 Acres of land at the State price in the district of Kentucky lying on the South fork of Elkhorn Creek about 2 Miles below the Mouth of Lindsey run by Marking & improving the same in the year 1776 satisfactory proof being made to the Court they are of Opinion that the s'd Shannon has a right to a preemption of 1000 Acres of Land to include the above Location & that a Cert. issue accordingly.

(Cert issd for 400 fees &c pd D. D. to R. Patterson)

Sam'l Johnson this day claimed a preemption of 400 Acres of Land at the State price in the district of Kentucky lying on the Big Forks of Elkhorn Creek on the North side of Edmund Taylors Survey to include an improvment made on the same by Making an Actual Settlem't in Jany 1779 Satisfactory proof being made to the Court they are of Opinion that the s'd Johnson has a right to a preemption of 400 Acres of Land to include the above location & that a Cert. issue accordingly.

[120] Collins, vol. 1, p. 366.

(Cert issd for 400 fees &c pd D. D. to R. patterson)

Mathew Coldwell this day claimed a preemption of 400 Acres of land at the State price in the district of Kentucky lying on the North side of the North fork of Elkhorn lying on the Buffaloe road joining Wm McConnells west line to include a small spring about 10 Yds South of the s'd road by making an Actual Settlement in May 1779 Satisfactory proof being made to the Court they are of Opinion that the s'd Coldwell has a right to a preempt or 400 Acres of Land to include the above location & that a Cert. issue accordingly.

Wm. Davis this day claimed a preempt. of 400 Acres of land at the State price in the District of Kentucky lying on the North branch of Clear Creek including a Spring by Making an Actual settlement in the Month of April 1779 Satisfactory proof being made to the Court they are of Opinion that the s'd Davis has a right to a preemption of 400 Acres of land to include the above location & that a Certificate issue accordingly.

(Cert issd for 400 fees &c pd D. D. to R. Patterson)

James McNutt this day claimed a preemption of 400 Acres of land at the State price in the district of Kentucky lying on the waters of Elkhorn Creek about three Miles from Lees Town at a sinking spring about 1 Mile East of the Stamping Ground by Making an Actual Settlem't in 1778. Satisfactory proof being made to the Court they are of Opinion that the said McNutt has a right to a preemption of 400 Acres of Land to include the above location & that a Certificate issue accordingly.

(Cert issd for 400 fees &c pd D. D. to R. Patterson)

John Newell this day claimed a preempt of 400 Acres of land at the State price in the District of Kentucky lying on the South fork of Elkhorn Creek about ¾ of a Mile below the Mouth of Shannons run by Making an Actual settlem't the 1st day of June 1779 satisfactory proof being made to the Court they are of Opinion that the s'd Newell has a right to a preemption of 400 Acres of Land to include the above Location & that a Certificate issue accordingly.

(Cert issd for 400 fees &c pd D. D. to Robt. Patterson)

[121]Josiah Collins this day claimed a preempt of 400 Acres of Land in the District of Kentucky at the State price lying on the South Side of the South fork of Elkhorn Creek adjoining the lands of John William by making an Actual Settlement in 1778 satisfactory proof being made to the Court they are of Opinion that the s'd Collins has a right to a preemption of 400 Acres of land to include the above location & that a Cert issue accordingly—

(Cert issd for 1000 fees &c pd D. D.)

Robt. Thompson this day claimed a preemption of 1000 Acres of land at the State price in the district of Kentucky lying about 5 Miles below Lexington beginning about ½ Mile above a large Spring empting in on the North side of the South fork of Elkhorn Creek to include both sides of the Creek thence West for quantity by marking and improving the same in the year 1776 Satisfactory proof being made to the Court they are of Opinion that the s'd Thompson has a right to a preemption of 400 Acres of Land to include the above Location & that a Cert. issue accordingly.

(Cert issd for 400 fees &c pd D. D. to R. Thompson)

Hugh Thompson this day claimed a preemption of 400 Acres of Land at the State price in the District of Kentucky lying adjoining Robt Thompsons Land on the North side on the Waters of Elkhorn Creek by making an Actual Settlem't in the Month of May 1779. Satisfactory proof being made to the Court they are of Opinion that the s'd Thompson has a right to a preempt of 400 Acres of land to include s'd Improvement & that a Certificate issue accordingly.

(Cert issd for 1000 Acres fees &c pd. D. D. R. Patterson)

John Vance by Dav'd Vance this day claimed a preempt—of 1000 Acres of land at the State price in the District of Kentucky lying on a fork of the East branch of Licking Creek called Mill Creek to include his improvement by marking and improving the same in the year 1776 by building a Cabbin &c satisfactory proof being made to the Court they are of Opinion that the s'd Vance has a right to a preemption of 1000 Acres of land to include the above Location & that a Cert. issue accordingly.

[121] Collins, vol. 1, pp. 5, 13.

(Cert issd for 400 feet &c pd D. D. to R. Patterson)

David Hunter this day claimed a preemption of 400 Acres of land at the State price in the District of Kentucky lying on one of the North Westerly branches of Cane run to include his improvement by making an Actual Settlem't on the 1st June 1779 satisfactory proof being made to the Court they are of Opinion that the s'd Hunter has a right to a preemption of 400 Acres of Land to include the above Location & that a Cert. issue accordingly.—

(Cert issd for 1000 Fees &c pd D. D. to ———)

James Lindsey this day claimed a preemption of 1000 Acres of Land at the State price in the district of Kentucky lying at a large Spring near the Mouth of Lindseys run waters of the South fork of Elkhorn beginning about ½ a Mile below the s'd Spring thence Eastwardly for quantity by marking and improving the same in the year 1776 by building a Cabbin &c Satisfactory proof being made to the Court they are of Opinion that the s'd Lindsey has a right to a preempt of 1000 Acres of land to include the above location & that a Cert. issue accordingly.—

(Cert issd for 400 fees &c pd D. D. to Levi Todd)

Wm Anderson this day claimed a preemption of 400 Acres of land at the State price in the District of Kentucky lying on the waters of Hickmans Creek on the West side of the Creek about 7 Miles South from Colo. John Todds land by making & Actual Settlement in April 1779 satisfactory proof being made to the Court they are of Opinion that the s'd Anderson has a right to a preemption of 400 Acres of land to include the above Location & that a Cert. iss accordingly.

(Cert issd for 1000 fees &c pd D. D. to Jas. Lindsey)

Wm Lindsey by James Lindsey this day claimed a preempt. of 1000 Acres of land at the State price in the District of Kentucky lying on Lindseys run beg'g at the forks of a branch below his Cabbin to include both sides of the s'd Creek thence Eastwardly for quantity by marking & improving the same in the year 1776 by building a Cabbin &c on the premises satisfactory proof being made to the Court they are of Opinion that the s'd Lindsey has a right to a premption of 1000 Acres of land to include the above location & that a Certificate issue accordingly.)

(Cert issd for 1000 fees &c pd D. D. Jno Johnson)

Christopher Johnson this day claimed a preempt of 1000 Acres of land in the district of Kentucky at the State price lying on the North fork of licking on the South side thereof on Sinake run to include his improvement by marking & improving the same by building a Cabbin &c in the year 1775 satisfactory proof being made to the Court they are of Opinion that the s'd Johnston has a right to a preemption of 1000 Acres of Land to include the above location & that a Cert issue accordingly.

(Cert issd for 1000 fees &c pd D. D. to Jno Johnson)

Moses Kelpatrick by John Johnson this day claimed a preempt. of 1000

Acres of Land in the District of Kentucky at the State price lying on a small branch of Harrods Creek running in on the South Side thereof about 5 Miles above the Mouth by Mark'g & improving the same by building a Cabbin and etc In the year 1775 satisfactory proof being made to the Court they are of Opinion that the s'd Kelpatrick has a right to a preempt'n of 1000 Acres of Land to include the s'd improvement & that a Cert issue accordingly.

(Cert issd for 400 fees &c pd D. D. to Robt Thompson)

Arthur Lindsey this day claimed a prempt. of 400 Acres of land at the State price in the district of Kentucky lying on a run that empties into the South fork of Elkhorn about 1 Mile below Lindsey run by making an Actual Settlement in 1778 Satisfactory proof being made to the Court they are of Opinion that the s'd Lindsey has a right to a preemption of 400 Acres of land to include the above location & that a Cert issue accordingly.

(Cert issd for 1400 fees &c pd D. D. R. Patterson)

[122]Andrew McConnell by Rob't Patterson this day claimed a settlem't & preemption to a tract of land in the district of Kentucky lying about 2 Miles below the fork of Elkhorn Creek including his improv't by raising a Crop of Corn in the Country in the year 1776 Satisfactory proof being made to the Court they are of Opinion that the s'd McConnell has a right to a settlement of 400 Acres of land to include the s'd improvement & the preempt of 1000 Acres adjoining & that a Cert issue accordingly.

(Cert issd for 1000 fees &c pd D. D. to Jos Lindsey)

Fulton Linsey this day claimed a preemption of 1000 Acres of Land at the State price in the district of Kentucky lying adjoining Arthur Linseys land on the Waters of the South fork of Elkhorn Creek to include his improv't at the head of a Spring & running North Easterly for quantity by marking & improving the same in the year 1776 by building a Cabbin &c Satisfactory proof being made to the Court they are of Opinion that the s'd Lindsey has a right to a preempt of 1000 Acres of Land to include to s'd improv't and that a Cert isse accordingly.

Then the Court adjourned untill tomorrow Morning 9 Oclock

Wm Fleming

At a Court Cont'd & held at Bryants Station on Elkhorn Creek for adjusting Titles to unpatented Lands by the Commissioners of Kentucky District this 15th day of Jan'y 1780

Present

Wm Fleming Stephen Trigg &
Edmund Lyne—Gent'n

(Cert issd for 400 fees &c pd D. D.)

John Dunkin this day claimed a preemption of 400 Acres of land at the State price in the district of Kentucky lying on Hinkstons Mill run & about 1 Mile below a Covered Cabbin built by one townsend by making an Actual settlement in the year 1779 Satisfactory proof being made to the Court they are

[122] Revolution on the Upper Ohio, p. 175.

of Opinion that the s'd Dunkin has a right to a preempt of 400 Acres of land to include the above location & that a cert. iss'e accordingly.—

(Cert issd for 1000 fees &c pd D. D. to R. Patterson)

[123]James Duncan by Robert Patterson this day claimed a settlement & preemption to a tract of land in the district of Kentucky lying on the North fork of Lindseys ran the waters of the South fork of Elkhorn Creek by settling in the Country & residing 12 Months before the year 1778 Satisfactory proof being made to the Court they are of Opinion that the s'd Duncan has a right to a Settlem't of 400 Acres of land to include the above location & the preempt of 1000 acres adjoining & that a Cert issue accordingly.

(Cert issd for 400 fees &c pd D. D. to Jas Dunkin)

Francis Berry by John Haggen this day claimed a preemption of 400 Acres of Land at the State price in the district of Kentucky lying on the Middle fork of Cuppers (Coopers) run about 1 Miles up the s'd Fork by making an Actual settlem't in March 1779 Satisfactory proof being made to the Court they are of Opinion that the s'd Berry has a right to a preempt. of 400 Acres of Land to include the above location & that a cert. issue accordingly.

(Cert issd for 400 fees &c pd D. D.)

Solomon Letten this day claimed a preemption of 400 Acres of land at the State price in the district of Kentucky lying on the Middle fork of Coopers run above F. Berrys claim to lands by making an Actual settlem't in the Month of March 1779 Satisfactory proof being made to the Court they are of Opinion that the s'd Letten has a right to a preemption of 400 Acres of land to include the above location & that a Cert issue Accordingly.—

(Cert issd for 400 fees &c pd D. D. to Jas. Dunkin)

Joseph Lovlass by John Haggin this day claimed a preemption of 400 Acres of land at the State price in the district of Kentucky lying on the West fork of Coopers run adjoining William McGee on the s'd Fork by making an Actual settlement in the Month of March 1779 Satisfactory proof being made to the Court they are of Opinion that the s'd Lovelass has a right to a preemption of 400 Acres of land to include the above location & that a Cert issue accordingly.

(Cert issd for 400 fees &c pd D. D. to Jas. Dunkin)

Charles Gatliff by John Haggen this day claimed a preempt of 400 Acres of land at the State price in the district of Kentucky lying Hingstons Mill run about 3 Miles above John Dunkin claim by making an Actual settlement in the Month of March 1779 Satisfactory proof being made for the Court they are of Opinion that the s'd Gatliff has a right to a preemption of 400 Acres of land to include the above Location & that a Cert. issue accordingly,—

(Cert issd for 400 fees &c pd D. D.)

[124]Thomas MeHan this day claimed a preempt of 400 Acres at the State price

[123] Collins, vol. 1, p. 566.

[124] Index has it Mchan.

in the district of Kentucky lying on the Middle fork of Coopers run joining Solmon Littens up the s'd run above the s'd Littens Claim by making an Actual settlement in the Month of March 1779 Satisfactory proof being made to the Court they are of Opinion that the s'd Meehan has a right to a preempt. of 400 Acres of land to include the above location & that a Cert. issue accordingly.

(Cert issd for 400)

And'w Lear this day claimed a preemption of 400 Acres of land at the State price in the district of Kentucky lying on a small Creek running into Kentucky River about 13 Miles from the Mouth & on the South side thereof and about 5 Miles up the s'd Creek from the river by making an Actual settlement in the month of March 1779 Satisfactory proof being made to the Court they are of Opinion that the s'd Lear has a right to a preemption of 400 Acres of Land to include the above Location & that a Cert. issue accordingly.

(Cert iss for 400)

John Penter this day claimed a preempt of 400 Acres of land at the State price in the district of Kentucky lying on a small Creek running into Kentucky River about 6 Miles from the Mo. adjoining the lands of Andrew Lear by making and Actual settlement in the Month of March 1779 satisfactory proof being made to the Court they are of Opinion that the s'd Penter has a right to a preempt of 400 Acres of land to include the above Location & that a Cert issue accordingly.

(Cert issd for 400 fees &c pd D. D. to R. Patterson)

Elisha Collins this day claimed a preemption of 400 Acres of land at the State price in the District of Kentucky lying on a North side of Kentucky River about 3 Miles above the Mouth of Dicks river by making an Actual settlement in the Month of Feb'y 1779 satisfactory proof being made to the Court they are of Opinion that the s'd Collins has a right to a preemption of 400 Acres of Land to include the above location & that a Cert. issue accordingly.

(Cert issd for 400 fees &c pd D. D.)

George Carlisle Assee of John Morrison this day claimed a preempt of 400 Acres of land at the State price in the district of Kentucky lying on the south side of Kentucky opposite to the Mouth of Millers Creek above Boonsborough the s'd Morrison making an Actual settlement in the Month of April 1779 satisfactory proof being made to the Court they are of Opinion that the s'd Carlisle has a right to a preempt of 400 Acres of Land to include the above Location & that a Cert issue accordingly.

(Cert issd for 1000 fees &c pd D. D. to D. Hampton)

[125]James Wilson this day claimed a preempt of 1000 Acres of land at the State price in the district of Kentucky on Acc't of Marking & improving the same in the year 1775 lying on the two mile creek above Boonsborough on the East side of s'd Creek Adjoining Wm Bush on the East side satisfactory proof being made to the Court they are of Opinion that the s'd Wilson has a right

[125] Collins, vol. 1, p. 7.

to a preempt'n of 1000 Acres of Land to include the above & that a Cert. issue accordingly.

(Cert issd for 1400 fees &c pd D. D.)

Rich'd Lee by Hancock Lee[126] this day claimed a settlement & preemption to a tract of land in the district of Kentucky lying on the East branch of the North fork of Licking Creek beginning at the head of the Branch & running down the branch for quantity by raising a crop of Corn in the year 1775 & residing in the Country 12 Months before the year 1778 Satisfactory proof being made to the Court they are of Opinion that the s'd Lee has a right to a Settlement of 400 Acres of Land to include the above location & the preemption of 1000 Acres Adjoining & that a Cert. issue accordingly.

(Cert issd for 1400 fees &c pd D. D.)

Henry Lee by Hancock Lee this day claimed a settlement & preempt'n to a tract of Land in the district of Kentucky lying on the Waters of the North fork of licking Creek adjoining the Land of Richard Lee by raising a crop of Corn in the Country in the year 1775 & residing 12 Months before the year 1778 satisfactory proof being made to the Court they are of Opinion that the s'd lee has a right to a settlem't of 400 Acres of Land to include the above Location & the preempt of 1000 Acres adjoining & that a Cert issue accordingly.

(Cert issd for 1400 fees &c pd D. D.)

Hancock Lee this day claimed a settlement & preemption to a tract of land in the district of Kentucky lying on the Waters of the North fork of licking Creek joining the Land of Henry Lee by raising a Crop of Corn in the Country in the year 1775 satisfactory proof being made to the Court they are of Opinion that the s'd H. Lee has a right to a Settlement of 400 Acres to include the above Location & the preempt of 1000 Acres adjoining & that a Cert. issue accordingly.

(Cert isd for 1400 fees &c pd D. D.)

Hancock Lee Heir at Law to Willis Lee[126] dec'd this day claimed a Settlement & preemption to a tract of land in the district of Kentucky lying on the main fork of Elkhorn Creek on the Waters of the South fork beginning at Edmund Taylors upper line & to extend up the Creek North for quantity by the said decedents residing in the Country 12 Months before the year 1778 satisfactory proof being made to the Court they are of Opinion that the s'd Lee has a right to a settlem't of 400 Acres of land to include the above location the preempt of 1000 Acres adjoining & that a Cert. issue accordingly.

(Cert issd for 1000 fees &c pd D. D.)

[127]John Lee by Hancock Lee this day claimed a preemption of 1000 Acres of Land at the State price in the district of Kentucky lying in the Main forks of Elkhorn Creek adjoining the lands of Hancock Lee Heir at law to Willis Lee dec'd on the West side by marking & improving the same in the year 1775 Satisfactory proof being made to the Court they are of Opinion that the s'd J. Lee has a right to a preempt of 1000 Acres of Land to include the above Location & that a Cert. iss'e accordingly.

[126] Revolution on the Upper Ohio, pp. 153, 154.

[126] Revolution on the Upper Ohio, pp. 153, 154.

[127] Collins, vol. 1, p. 13.

(Cert issd for 400)

It appearing to the Court that James Bryants Location Ent'd the 12th Inst is on the Lands of Edward Ward he now comes into Court & Motions to have the s'd Location remov'd which being granted he locates the same near the head of Jassemine Creek & near where Mr Douglass Noted the first large survey he made (on the head of Elkhorn & Hickmans Creek) & running South and Eastwardly for quantity Ord'd that a Certificate issue accordingly.

Then the Court Adjourned untill tomorrow Morning 9 OClock

William Fleming

At a Court Continued & held at Bryants Station on Elkhorn Creek by the Commissioners for Adjusting Titles to the Kentucky Lands the 17th day of Jan'y 1780.

Present

Wm Fleming Stephen Trigg & Edmund Lyne—Gent'n

(Cert issd for 1400)

[128]David Perry by Rob't Patterson this day claimed a settlement & preempt to a tract of land in the district of Kentucky lying on the Waters of the south fork of Elkhorn creek adjoining Shelbys Survey on the North & Wm McConnel on the West to include a sinking Spring & his improvement by raising a Crop of Corn in the Country in the year 1776 satisfactory proof being made to the Court they are of Opinion that the s'd Perry has a right to a settlement of 400 Acres of land to include the above location & the preempt of 1000 Acres of land Adjoining & that a Cert. issue accordingly.—

(Cert issd for 1400)

Alexander McMullen by Rob't Patterson this day claimed a settlem't & preempt'n to a tract of land in the district of Kentucky lying on the Waters of the North fork of Elkhorn Creek on the North side thereof adjoining Patrick Henry on the North by settling in the Country & residing 12 Months before the year 1778 satisfactory proof being made to the Court they are of opinion that the s'd McMullen has a right to a right to a settlem't of 400 of land to include the above Location & preemption of 1000 Acres adjoining & that a Cert issue accordingly.

It appearing to the Court that Wm Grant Jun'r obtained a Certificate for a preempt of 400 Acres the 10th Instant & that it was located on Land that is taken by a settlem't & preemption Now moves to alter his Location which is granted him lying adjoining Ingless Assee of Cools who was Assee of Thos Boothes 200 Acres Survey on the East side on the Water of the North fork of Elkhorn on the North side thereof & that a Certificate issue accordingly.

(Cert issd for 1000)

Frances Patterson by Rob't Patterson this day claimed a preemption of 1000 Acres of land at the State price in the district of Kentucky lying on the North fork of Cane run to include his improv't & to extend Westwardly for quantity by marking & improving the same in the year 1776 Satisfactory proof being made to the Court they are of Opinion that the s'd Patterson has a

[128] Revolution on the Upper Ohio, p. 210 and Collins, vol. 2, p. 176.

right to a preempt of 1000 Acres of Land to include the above Improvement & that a Cert issue accordingly.

(Cert issd for 1400 fees &c pd D. D.)

It Appearing to the Court that John Conway Jun'r made it appear that he was intitled to a settlem't & preempt'n at Boonsborough the 29th day of Dec'r 1779 but did not locate the same Now comes into Court & locates the same on the Buffaloe road leading to the lower Salt Spring from Riddles Station including Tree Marked & running Eastwardly for Quantity—that a Cert issue accordingly.

(Cert issd for 1400 fees &c pd D. D.)

John Conway Sen'r this day claimed a settlem't & preemption to a tract of Land in the district of Kentucky lying on a branch of the Middle fork of licking Creek near a Buffaloe road that leads to the lower Blue licks joining Jacob Sadowski on the North Eastwardly including a lick & Cabbin by settling in the Country in the year 1777 & residing ever since Satisfactory proof being made to the Court they are of Opinion that the s'd Conway has a right to a settlem't of 400 Acres of land to include the above Location & the preempt of 1000 Acres adjoining & that a Cert issue accordingly.

(Cert issd for 400 fees &c pd D. D.)

Morgan Bryant Jr this day claimed a preemption of 400 Acres of land at the State price in the district of Kentucky lying on Boons creek waters of Kentucky River adjoining John Floyds on the North by making an Actual settlem't in the Month of April 1779 Satisfactory proof being made to the Court they are of Opinion that the s'd Bryant has a right to a preemption of 400 Acres to include the above location & that a Cert. issue accordingly.

(Cert issd for 400 fees &c pd D. D.)

Sam'l Vanhook this day claimed a preemption of 400 Acres of Land at the State price in the district of Kentucky lying on the South fork of licking Creek adjoining Sam'l Dennis's land below by making an actual settlem't in the Month of March 1779 Satisfactory proof being made to the Court they are of Opinion that the s'd Vanhook has a right to a preemption of 400 Acres of land to include the above location & that a Cert iss accordingly.

(Cert issd for 400 fees &c pd D. D.)

Sam'l Vanhook Jr this day claimed a preempt. of 400 Acres of land at the State price in the district of Kentucky lying about 1½ Miles N. E. of the buffaloe road leading from Riddles Station to the lower Blue licks & 5 Miles from the s'd Station by making an Actual Settlem'n in the Month of March 1779 Satisfactory proof being made to the Court they are of Opinion that the said Vanhook has a right to a preemption of 400 Acres of Land to include the above location & that a Cert iss'e accordingly.

(Cert issd for 400 fees &c pd D. D. to Jno Martin)

Thomas Foster this day claimed a preempt. of 400 Acres of land in the District of Kentucky at the State price lying about 1¼ Mile above John Martin Land on licking Creek by making an Actual Settlem't in the Month of March 1779 Satisfactory proof being made to the Court they are of Opinion that the s'd Foster has a right to a preemption of 400 Acres of land to include the above Location & that a Cert. issue accordingly.

(Cert iss for 400 fees &c pd D. D. to Jno Martin)

Joel Will this day claimed a preempt'n of 400 Acres of Land at the State price in the District of Kentucky lying adjoining Thos. Fosters land on licking Creek by making an Actual settlem't in the Month of April 1779 satisfactory proof being made to the Court they are of Opinion that the s'd Will has a right to a preempt'n of 400 Acres of land to include the above location & that a Cert. issue accordingly.

(Cert issd for 400 fees &c pd D. D. to Jno Martin)

Ica Rice this day claimed a preempt of 400 Acres of land at the State price in the district of Kentucky lying on licking Creek adjoining Joel Wills land by making an actual settlement in the Month of April 1779 Satisfactory proof being made to the Court they are of Opinion that the s'd Rice has a right to a preemption of 400 Acres of land to include the above location & that a Cert iss'e accordingly.

(Cert issd for 400 fees &c pd D. D.)

John Denton this day claimed a preempt'n of 400 Acres of land at the State price in the district of Kentucky lying on a North branch of the Middle fork of licking Creek adjoining the Lands s'd to be claimed by Alexander Poeg by making an actual settlem't in the Month of April 1779 Satisfactory proof being made to the Court they are of Opinion that the s'd Denton has a right to a preemption of 400 Acres of Land to include the above location & that a Cert. issue accordingly.

(Cert issd for 400 fees &c pd D. D.)

George Davis this day claimed a preemption of 400 Acres of land at the State price in the district of Kentucky lying on the waters of the Middle fork of licking Creek adjoining the lands of John Denton to the Westward by making an actual settlement in the Month of April 1779 Satisfactory proof being made to the Court they are of Opinion that the s'd Davis has a right to a preempt of 400 Acres of Land to include the above Location & that a Certificate issue accordingly.

(Cert issd for 400 fees &c pd D. D. to Geo. Davis)

[129]John Davis this day claimed a preempt. of 400 Acres of land at the State price in the district of Kentucky lying on the waters of Licks adjoining the Lands of charles Gatliff by making an actual settlement in the month of April 1779 satisfactory proof being made to the Court they are of Opinion that the s'd Davis has a right to a preemption of 400 Acres of land to include the above location & that a Cert isse accordingly.

(Cert issd for 400 fees &c pd D. D. to Geo. Davis)

Joseph Essex this day claimed a preempt'n of 400 Acres of land at the State price in the District of Kentucky lying on the Middle fork of Licking creek on the North side thereof Adjoining John Callaways by making an Actual set-

[129] Collins, vol. 1, p. 6 or 9 (Two men by same name).

tlem't in the year 1779 Satisfactory proof being made to the Court they are of Opinion that the s'd Essex has a right to a preëmpt. of 400 Acres of land to include the above location & that a Cert. issue accordingly.

(Cert iss for 400 fees &c pd D. D. to John Conway)

[130]Gasper Brown this day claimed a preempt'n of 400 Acres of land at the State price in the district of Kentucky lying on Woods Creek about 2 Miles from the Mouth waters of licking Creek by making an Actual settlement in the Month of October 1778 satisfactory proof being made to the Court they are of Opinion that the s'd Brown has a right to a preemption of 400 Acres of land to include the above location & that a Cert. issue accordingly.

(Cert issd for 400 fees &c pd D. D.)

[131]Wm. Morris this day claimed a preempt'n of 400 Acres of land at the State price in the district of Kentucky lying on the Water of licking Creek about 1 Mile E. of John Martins land by making an Actual settlement in the Month of October 1778 satisfactory proof being made to the Court they are of Opinion that the s'd Morris has a right to a preemption of 400 Acres of land to include the above Location & that a Cert issue accordingly.

(Cert issd for 1400 fees &c pd D. D. to Leonard Hall)

Isaac Frasher this day claimed a settlem't and Preemption to a tract of Land in the District of Kentucky lying 8 Miles North west from Bryants Station on a branch of Elkhorn Creek including a Spring & a Camp made by Dan'l Boone & Edward Bradley & running Eastwardly for quantity by raising a Crop of Corn in the Country in the year 1775 Satisfactory proof being made to the Court they are of Opinion that the s'd Frasher has a right to a settlem't of 400 Acres of Land to include the above Location & the preempt'n of 1000 Acres adjoining & that a Certificate issue accordingly.

(Cert issd for 400 fees &c pd D. D.)

[132]John Jones heir at law to Stephen Jones dec'd this day claimed a preemption of 400 Acres of Land at the State price in the district of Kentucky lying on the head of the right hand fork of the stamping Ground lick including a Cabbin by the s'd decedents making an Actual settlem't in the Month of April 1779 Satisfactory proof being made to the Court they are of Opinion that the s'd Jones has a right to a preemption of 400 Acres of land to include the above Location & that a Cert issue accordingly.

(Cert issd for 400)

Peter Fare this day claimed a preemption of 400 Acres of Land at the State price in the district of Kentucky lying in the forks of the North Fork of the South Fork of licking including his improvement, & by making an Actual settlement in the month of April 1779 Satisfactory proof being made to the Court they are of Opinion that the s'd Fare has a right to a preemption of 400 Acres of land to include the above Location & that a Cert issue accordingly.

---

[130] Probably Caspar Brown, Collins, vol. 1, p. 13.

[131] Collins, vol. 1, p. 12 or 13 (Two men by same name.)

[132] Collins, vol. 1, p. 12.

(Cert issd for 400 fees &c pd D. D. to E Smith)

John Henderson this day claimed a preempt. of 400 Acres of land at the State price in the district of Kentucky lying on Silver Creek below the Road from Boonsborough to Logans by making an Actual Settlem't in the Month of April 1779 satisfactory proof being made to the Court they are of Opinion that the said Henderson has a right to a preemption of 400 Acres of land to include the above Location & that a Cert issue accordingly.—

(Cert iss for 1400 fees &c pd D. D.)

James Haggin by John Haggin this day claimed a settlement & preemption to a tract of Land in the district of Kentucky lying on the South fork of licking Creek on the South side thereof about 3 Miles below Riddle Station by Having Wm Sheald to raise a crop of Corn in the Country for his use in the year 1775 Satisfactory proof being made to the Court they are of Opinion that the s'd Haggin has a right to a settlem't of 400 Acres of Land to include the above location & the preemption of 1000 Acres adjoining & that a Cert issue accordingly.—

(Cert issd for 400 fees &c pd D. D. to E. Smith)

[133]Reuben Procter this day claimed a preemption of 400 acres of land at the State price in the district of Kentucky lying on the E. Side of Stoners fork of licking Creek and about 2 Miles above Bramblets Lick by making an Actual settlem't in the year 1778 Satisfactory proof being made to the Court they are of Opinion that the s'd Procter has a right to a preemption of 400 Acres of land to include the above Location & that a Cert issue accordingly.

[133] Collins, vol. 1, p. 13.

(Cert issd for 400 fees &c pd D. D. to E. Smith)

[134]Nich's Procter Jun'r this day claimed a preemption of 400 Acres of land at the State price in the district of Kentucky lying on a small Branch of licking Creek Waters of the rocky ford fork & about 3 Miles from the Mouth of the s'd fork & on the N. side thereof by making an Actual settlem't in the year 1778 satisfactory proof being made to the Court they are of Opinion that the s'd Procter has a right to a preemption of 400 Acres of Land to include the above location & that a Cert. issue accordingly.

It appearing to the Court that there is no just cause for detaining Edward Bradley Cert ordered that it issue—

(Cert issd for 1400 fees &c pd D. D. to Len'd Hall)

John Booker by Pemberton Rowlins[135] this day claimed a settlement & preemption to a tract of Land in the district of Kentucky lying on 4 Mile Creek about 6 Miles from Boonsborough including a spring at a lick by residing in the Country 12 Months before the year 1778 Satisfactory proof being made to the Court they are of Opinion that the s'd Booker has a right to a settlem't of 400 Acres of land to include the above Location & the preemption of 1000 Acres adjoining & that a Cert. issue accordingly.

[134] Collins, vol. 1, p. 12.
[135] Collins, vol. 1, p. 13.

Then the Court adjourned untill to-morrow Morning 9 Oclock

Wm Fleming

At a Court continued & held at Bryants Station of Elkhorn Creek for adjusting titles to unpatented lands by the Commissioners of Kentucky District the 18th day of Jan'y 1780.

Present

Wm Fleming Stephen Trigg & Edmund Lyne—Gent'n

(Cert issd for 1000 Fees &c pd D. D. to E. Field)

[136]Lewis Lunsford by Ezecle Field this day claimed a preempt of 1000 Acres of land at the State price in the district of Kentucky on Acc't of Marking & improving the same in the year 1779 lying N. E. of the lands claimed by Wm Cradlebough between the Hunters road & Stoners fork & below the Land claimed by John Feild satisfactory proof being made to the Court they are of Opinion that the s'd Lunsford has a right to a preemption of 1000 Acres of Land to include the above Location & that a Certificate issue accordingly.—

(Cert issd for 1400 fees &c pd D. D.)

Wm Calk by Enoch Smith[137] this day claimed a settlement & preemption to a tract of land in the district of Kentucky on Acc't of raising a crop of Corn in the Country in the year 1775 lying on small Mountain Creek waters of licking Creek to include his improvement satisfactory proof being made to the Court they are of Opinion that the s'd Calk has a right to a settlement of 400 Acres of land & the preemption of 1000 Acres adjoining & that a Cert. issue accordingly.

(Cert issd for 1000 fees &c pd D. D.)

[138]Hugh Innes by Jas. Parberry this day claimed a preemption of 1000 Acres of land at the State price in the district of Kentucky on acc't of Mark'g and improving the same in the year 1776 building a Cabbin &c on the premises lying adjoining the Land of James Parberry Assee of Elisha Estis on the North side running down toward Hustons fork for quantity Satisfactory proof being made to the Court they are of Opinion that the s'd Innes has a right to a preemption of 1000 Acres of land to include the s'd improvement & that a Certificate issue accordingly.

James Seburn Assee of Edmon Douglass this day claimed a settlement & preemption to a tract of land in the district of Kentucky on acc't of the s'd Douglass raising a Crop of Corn in the Country on Pittman Creek branch of Cumberland River that runs on the North side in the year 1776 It appearing to the Court by the Evidence Offered that the s'd Douglass raised the Corn in that part of the Country reserved for the use of the Army & having made no Settlem't or improvement in any other part of the Country the Court are of Opinion that the Law has made no provisions for persons in that Situation that they are not Authorized to grant a Certificate for the same.

(Cert made out &c D. D.)

It Appearing to the Court that Wilson Hunt Obtained a Cert'e the 12 Inst for

[136] Collins, vol. 1, p. 416.
[137] Collins, vol. 2, pp. 47, 416, 633.
[138] Bulletin Va. State Library, vol. 14, p. 59.

a preemption 1000 Acres of land now comes into Court & moves to withdraw it appearing to the Court that there is a Sufficient reason for a removal it is granted him & he locates the s'd Land about 5 Miles a North westly Course from Wm Bryant Spring adjoining the falling Timber on the North side of Elkhorn Creek & that a Cert. issue accordingly.

(Cert issd for 400)
Wm Tomlinson this day claimed a preempt'n of 400 Acres of Land at the State price in the District of Kentucky on Account of Making an Actual settlement in April 1779 lying about 3 Miles from Bryants Station including a Well spring on the head of Cane run Satisfactory proof being made to the Court they are of Opinion that the s'd Tomlinson has a preemption of 400 Acres of land to include the above location & that a Certificate issue accordingly.

(Cert issd for 400)
Christopher Stokes this day claimed a preemption of 400 Acres of land at the State price in the District of Kentucky on Acct of making an Actual settlem't in the Month of April 1779 lying on the Middle fork of licking Creek adjoining the land said to be claimed by Alexander Poag above satisfactory proof being made to the Court they are of Opinion that the s'd Stoakes has a right to a preempt of 400 Acre of land to include the above Location & that a Cert. issue accordingly.

It appearing the Court that James McCracken obtained a Cert. the 4 Inst for a preempt of 400 Acres of Land Now comes into Court & Moves to withdraw his Location it appear that there is a sufficient reason for a removal it is granted him Locates the Land 2 Miles North below Lees Town on the Waters of Kentucky Ordered that a Cert issue accordingly.

(Cert issd for 1000)
George Frazer this day claimed a preempt of 1000 Acres of land at the State price in the district of Kentucky on Account of Mark'g and improving the same in the year 1776 in the forks of Harrod creek at a spring running into the North branch about 1 Mile from the fork & about 12 or 14 Miles from the Falls of Ohio satisfactory proof being made to the Court they are of Opinion that the s'd Frazier has a right to a preemption of 1000 Acres of Land to include his improvement & that a Cert. issue accordingly.

Then the Court adjourned to Harrodsburg the 21st Inst

Wm Fleming

At a Court held for adjusting Titles to unpatented Land by the Commissioners of Kentucky District at Harrodsburg this 28th day of Jan'y 1780
present
Wm Fleming Step'n Trigg & Edmund Lyne—Gent'n

(Cert issd for 1400 fees &c pd D. D.)
[139]James Hogan Sen'r by James Hogan Jun this day claimed a settlem't & preempt'n to a tract of Land in the District of Kentucky on acc't of raising

[139] Collins, vol. 1, p. 542.

a Crop of Corn in the year 1776 lying on the North side of Elkhorn Creek on the first Big fork below Dobbins claim including a Cabbins on the West side of the s'd fork at James Forbes Camp satisfactory proof being made to the Court they are of Opinion that the s'd Hogan has a right to a settlement of land to include the above location and preempt of 1000 Acres adjoining & that a Cert issue accordingly.

(Cert issd for 1400 fees &c pd D. D.)

James Hogan Jun'r this day claimed a settlement & preemption of a tract of Land in the district of Kentucky on account of raising a Crop of Corn in the Country in the year 1776 lying on the North fork of Elkhorn Creek on the North s'd thereof including a small lick on the s'd Creek & about 4 or 5 Miles South East from the White Oak Woods satisfactory proof being made to the Court they are of Opinion that the s'd Hogan has a right to a settlement of 400 Acres of Land to include the above Location & the preempt. of 1000 Acres adjoining & that a Cert. issue accordingly.

(Cert issd for 1400 fees &c pd D. D.)

Wm Hogan by James Hogan this day claimed a settle't & preempt. to a tract of Land in the district of Kentucky on Acc. of raising a Crop of Corn in the Country in the year 1776 lying adjoining on the lower side of the Land claimed by James Hogan Sen'r satisfactory proof being made to the Court they are of Opinion that the s'd Hogan has a right to a settlem't of 400 Acres of Land to include the above Location & the preempt of 1000 Acres Adjoining & that a Cert. issue accordingly.

(Cert issd for 1400 fees &c pd D. D.)

Stephen Fisher this day claimed a settlem't & preemption to a tract of land in the district of Kentucky on account of raising a Crop of Corn in the Country in the year 1776 lying about ¾ of a Mile East from Jones Settlement & adjoining the same to include his improvment Satisfactory proof being made to the Court they are of Opinion that the s'd Fisher has a right to a settlement of 400 Acres of land to include the above location and the preemption of 1000 Acres adjoining & that a Cert. do not issue untill the further order of this Court—

(Cert issd for 1400 fees &c pd D. D.)

Barnard Fisher by Stephen Fisher this day claimed a settlement & preemption to a tract of Land in the district of Kentucky on account of raising a Crop of Corn in the Country in the year 1776 lying on the Waters of Salt River to include a Cabbin built by John Cowan adjoining the Lands claimed by Isaac Hite on the East satisfactory proof being made to the Court they are of Opinion that the s'd Fisher has a right to a settlement of 400 Acres of lands to include the above Location & the preemption of 400 Acres adjoining & that a Cert issue accordingly.

(Cert issd for 1400 fees &c pd D. D.)

Adam Fisher this day claimed a settlement & preemption to a tract of land in the district of Kentucky on account of raising a Crop of Corn in the Country in the year 1776 lying on the Waters of

Dicks River near the Mouth of Howards run to include the improvm't Made by Dowgins & Glens satisfactory proof being made to the Court they are of Opinion that the s'd Fisher has a right to a settlement of 400 Acre of Land to include the s'd improvement & the preempt'n of 1000 Acres adjoining & that a Cert issue Accordingly.

(Cert issd for 1400 fees &c pd D. D.)

George Spear this day claimed a settlement & preempt'n of a tract of Land in the district of Kentucky on Acc't of raising a Crop of Corn in the Country in the year 1776 lying about 1 Mile East of Gorden lick on the North side of the hanging fork of Dick river to include his improv't satisfactory proof being made to the Court they are of Opinion that the s'd Spear has a right to a settlement of 400 Acres of land to include the s'd improvement & the preempt of 1000 Acres adjoining & that a Cert issue accordingly.

(Cert issd for 400 fees &c pd D. D.)

John Capenter this day claimed a settlem't & preempt'n to a tract of Land in the district of Kentucky on Acc't of raising a Crop of Corn in the Country in the year 1776 lying two Miles South of Gordens Lick on the dividing ridge of the Hanging fork of Dick river & Green river to include his improv't satisfactory proof being made to the Court they are of Opinion that the said Carpenter has a right to a settlem't of 400 Acres of Land to include the s'd improvment & the preempt'n of 1000 Acres adjoining & that a Cert. issue accordingly.

(Cert issd for 1400 fees &c pd D. D.)

Coonrod Carpenter this day claimed a settlem't & preemption to a tract of land in the district of Kentucky on acc't of raising a Crop of Corn in the Country in the year 1776 lying below Gordens lick & nearly an E. course adjoining the lands of John Carpenter & Geor'e Spear to include his improv't satisfactory proof being made to the Court they are of Opinion that the s'd Carpenter has a right to a settlem't of 400 Acres of Land to include the above improvement & the preemption of 1000 Acres adjoining & that a Cert. issue accordingly.

(Cert issd for 1000 fees &c pd D. D.)

Charles Morgan heir at law to John Morgan dec'd by Bradford this day claimed a preemption to 1000 Acres of land in the district of Kentucky on account of marking & improving the same in the year 1776 lying on the Most Easterly branch of Stoners fork of licking Creek near the head thereof including a Spring Known by the Name of John Morgans spring & a Cabbin Satisfactory proof being made to the Court they are of Opinion that the s'd Morgan has a right to a preemption of 1000 Acres to include the s'd Cabbin & that a Cert. issue accordingly.

(Cert issd for 1400 fees &c pd to Ad'm Fisher)

Andrew Gumlin this day claimed a settle't & preemption to a tract of Land in the District of Kentucky on acc't of raising a Crop of Corn in the Country in the year 1776 lying on the North side of Dicks river about 1 Mile E. of James & Edmund Archers land to include his improvement satisfactory proof being made to the Court they are of Opinion that the s'd Gimlin has a right to a settlem't of 400 Acres of land to include the s'd improvement & the preempt'n of 1000 Acres adjoining & that a Cert. issue accordingly.

(Cert issd for 1400 fees &c pd D. D.)

Cornelias Yager by Nich's Yager this day claimed a settlem't & preemption to a tract of land in the district of Kentucky on account of raising a crop of Corn in the Country in the year 1776 lying on the Waters of the Hanging fork of Dicks river about 4 Miles East of John Carpenters Land to include his improv't satisfactory proof being made to the Court they are of Opinion that the s'd Yager has a right to a settlem't of 400 Acres of land to include his improv't & the preempt'n of 1000 Acres adjoining & that a Certificate issue accordingly.

(Cert issd for 400 fees &c pd D. D.)

John Hawkins this day claimed a preempt'n of 400 Acres of Land at the State price in the district of Kentucky on Acc't of settlement made in March 1779 lying on the West fork Hickmans creek adjoining the Lands of Levi Todd on the West side to include his improvement satisfactory proof being made to the Court they are of Opinion that the s'd Hawkins has a right to a preempt'n of 400 Acres of land to include the above Location & that a Cert. issue accordingly.

(Cert issd for 400 fees &c pd D. D.)

John Spear this day claimed a preempt of 400 Acres of land at the State price in the District of Kentucky on account of Making an Actual settlem't in the year 1778 lying on Fun (?) Creek a branch of the Ohio about 10 Miles from the falls of Ohio to include his improvment Satisfactory proof being made to the Court they are of Opinion that the s'd Spear has a right to a preempt'n of 400 Acres of Land to include the s'd improvement & that a Cert issue accordingly.

(Cert issd for 1400 fees &c pd D. D.)

Zacheriah Smith by Peter Watts this day claimed a settlem't & preempt'n to a tract of Land in the district of Kentucky on Acc't of raising a Crop of Corn in the Country in the year 1776 lying on Harrods run known by the name of the Crow Mill Seat about 3 Miles from Maj'r Harrods & two Miles from Dicks river Satisfactory proof being made to the Court they are of Opinion that the s'd Smith has a right to a settlement of 400 Acres of land to include the above Location & the preempt of 1000 Acres adjoining & that a Cert. iss'e accordingly.

(Cert issd for 1400 fees &c pd D. D.)

Jacob Holtclaw by Peter Watts this day claimed a settlem't & preemption to a tract of Land in the district of Kentucky on Account of raising a crop of Corn in the Country in the year 1776 lying on the North side of Dicks river adjoining the land of James and Edmund Archer on the W. side to include his improvement Satisfactory proof being made to the Court they are of Opinion that the s'd Holtclaw has a right to a settlement of 400 Acres of land to include the s'd improvement & the preemption of 1000 Acres adjoining & that a Cert. issue accordingly.

(Cert issd for 1000 fees &c pd D. D.)

John Gar by Stephen Fisher this day claimed a preempt of 1000 Acres of Land at the State price in the District of Kentucky on Acc't of Marking & improving the same in the year 1776 lying about 3 or 4 Miles below Gordons lick on a branch of the Hanging fork of Dicks river on the North side thereof to include his cabbin Satisfactory proof being made to the Court they are of Opinion that the s'd Gar has a right to a preempt of 1000 Acres of land to include his s'd Cabbin & that a Cert. issue accordingly.

(Cert issd for 1400 fees &c pd D. D.)

Wm McCracken Assee of John Harmon this day claimed a Settlem't & premption to a tract of Land in the district of Kentucky on Acc't of raising a Crop of Corn in the Country in the year 1775 lying on the head of a Spring that empties in about 4 or 5 Miles below Lees Town on the North side of Kentucky on an improvement by Francis McConnell satisfactory proof being made to the Court they are of Opinion that the s'd McCracken &c has a right to a settlem't of 400 Acres of Land to include the above Location & the preempt'n of 1000 Acres adjoining & that a Cert. issue accordingly.

Then the Court Adjourned untill tomorrow Morning 9 Oclock

Wm Fleming—

At a Court continued & held at Harrodsburg for adjusting Titles to Kentucky Lands by the Commissioners of Kentucky District this 29th day of Jan'y 1780

Present

Wm Fleming Steph'n Trigg & Edmund Lyne

(Cert issd for 1400 fees &c pd D. D.)

Thomas Johnson Assee of James McCullock this day claimed a settlem't & preemption to a tract of land in the District of Kentucky on account of raising a Crop of Corn in the year 1775 Lying at the poplar Level about 8 Miles above the Mouth of Floyds fork of Salt River on a branch called McCollock run to include his improvment. satisfactory proof being made to the Court they are of Opinion that the s'd Johnson &c has a right to a settlem't of 400 Acres of land to include the above Location & the preemption of 1000 Acres adjoining & that a Cert issue accordingly.

(Cert issd for 400 fees &c pd D. D. to Wm. Williams)

Benj'n Cooper this day claimed a preemption of 400 Acres of Land at the State price in the District of Kentucky on Account of Making an Actual settlem't in the Month of April 1779 lying on the South fork of Coopers run Waters of licking Creek about 2 or 3 Miles above the forks of the s'd Coopers run Satisfactory proof being made to the Court they are of Opinion that the s'd Cooper has the right to a preemption of 400 Acres of land to include the above location & that a Cert issue accordingly.

(Cert issd for 1400 fees &c pd D. D. to Geo. May)

[140]George Adams by Wm Miller this day claimed a settlm't & preemption to

[140] Collins, vol. 1, p. 355.

a tract of land in the District of Kentucky on account of raising a Crop of Corn in the Country in the year 1776 lying on the E. Fork of Paint lick Creek including 2 improvements made for Wm McConnell & Thos Pattone adj'g the Lands of Wm Pattoone satisfactory proof being made to the Court they are of Opinion that the s'd Adams has a right to a settlem't of 400 Acres of land to include the s'd improvement & the preempt of 1000 Acres adjoining & that a Cert. issue accordingly.

(Cert issd for 1000 fees &c pd D. D.)

Senica McCracken by Isaac McCracken this day claimed a preempt'n of 1000 Acres of land at the State price in the district of Kentucky on Account of Marking & improving the same in the year 1776 lying on small run at a Spring Empting in on the West side of Drennens lick Creek about 5 Miles from the s'd lick to include his Cabbin Satisfactory proof being made to the Court they are of Opinion that the s'd McCracken has a right to a preempt of 1000 Acres of land to include s'd improvement & that a Cert. issue accordingly.

(Cert issd for 400 fees &c pd D. D.)

[141]Alexander Robertson Assee of Sam'l Woods this day claimed a settlem't & preemption to a tract of land in the district of Kentucky on Acc't of the s'd Woods raising a crop of Corn in the Country in the year 1775 lying between the Shawnee run & Cedar run including 2 Cabbins which was built by Martin Nalle Jun'r satisfactory proof being made to the Court they are of Opinion that the s'd Robertson has a right to a settlement of 400 Acres of land to include the above location & the preempt of 1000 Acres adjoining & that a Cert. iss'e accordingly.

(Cert issd for 1400 fees &c pd D. D.)

Adam Wallis by Sam'l Woods this day claimed a settlement & preemption to a tract of Land in the district of Kentucky on Account of raising a Crop of Corn in the Country in the year 1775 lying on the dividing ridge on the head Waters of Gilberts Creek & Dicks river Satisfactory proof being made to the Court they are of Opinion that the s'd Wallis has a right to a settlem't of 400 Acres of land to include the above location & the preempt'n of 1000 Acres of land adjoining & that a Cert. issue accordingly.

(Cert issd for 1400 fees &c pd D. D.)

Thos. Black this day claimed a settlement & preemption to a tract of land in the district of Kentucky on Account of raising a crop of Corn in the Country in the year 1775 lying on the waters of the Hanging fork of Dicks river at a large spring on the North side of the s'd fork 4 or 5 Miles from Logans Station Satisfactory proof being made to the Court they are of Opinion that the s'd Black has a right to a settlem't of 400 Acres of land to include the above location & the preempt of 1000 Acres adjoining & that a Certificate issue accordingly.

(Cert issd for 400 fees &c pd D. D.)

John Pearce this day claimed a preemption of 400 Acres of Land at the State price in the district of Kentucky

[141] Collins, vol. 1, p. 355 and index.

on Account of Making an Actual settlement in May 1779 lying on the North side of Dicks river a Mile No. course from Jas. Smiths Station & ¾ of a Mile N. W Coarse from Dougharty Station satisfactory proof being made to the Court they are of Opinion that the said Pearce has a right to a preemption of 400 Acres of land to include the s'd Settlem't & that a Cert. issue accordingly.

(Cert issd for 1400 fees &c pd D. D. to Colo. Logan)

Archibald McKeny this day claimed a settlem't & preempt'n to a tract of land in the District of Kentucky on Acc't of Settling in the Country in the year 1777 & residing ever since lying on a small branch of Green River on the North side thereof about 1½ Miles So. Westerly from Briggs Camp satisfactory proof being made to the Court they are of Opinion that the s'd McKenny has a right to a settlem't of 400 Acres of land to include the above location & the preemption of 1000 Acres adjoining & that a Certificate issue accordingly.

(Cert issd for 1000 fees &c pd D. D.)

Wm McCracken Jun'r this day claimed a preemption of 1000 Acres of Land at the State price in the District of Kentucky on Account of Marking and improving the same in the year 1775 lying at a Cave Spring on the North Side of the North fork of Elkhorn Creek joining a Survey of Patrick Henry on a run know by the Name of McCracken run to include his cabbin Satisfactory proof being made to the Court they are of Opinion that the s'd McCracken has a right to a preemption of 1000 Acres of Land to include the above location & that a Cert issue accordingly.

(Cert iss for 1400 fees &c pd D. D.)

John Mchan this day claimed a settlem't & preemption to a tract of Land in the district of Kentucky on Acc't of raising a crop of Corn in the year 1776 lying between the Land of John Dunkin & charles Gatliff on Hingstons Creek of licking Creek satisfactory proof being made to the Court they are of Opinion that the s'd Mchan has a right to a settlem't of 400 Acre of Land to include the above location & the preemption of 1000 Acres adjoining & that a Cert. issue accordingly.

(Cert iss for 400 fees &c pd D. D. to Colo Logan)

[142]John McKeny this day claimed a preempt'n of 400 Acres of land at the State price in the district of Kentucky on Acc't of making an Actual settlem'n in May 1779 lying on the So. fork of licking Creek on the South side thereof about 2 Miles above John Martins Land to include an improvement in a Bottom Satisfactory proof being made to the Court they are of Opinion that the s'd McKenny has a right to a preempt. of 400 Acres of land to include the s'd improvement & that a Certificate issue accordingly.

[143]Benj. Briggs by Benj. Logan this day claimed a settleme't & preemption to a tract of Land in the district of Kentucky on Acc't of Settling in the Country in the year 1777 & residing ever since lying on the Waters of the Hanging fork of about 1½ Miles No. West of

[142] (McKinney) Collins, vol. 1, pp. 355, 356.
[143] Collins, vol. 1, p. 12.

Briggs Camp Witnesses being Sworn & examined It is the Opinion that the s'd Claim is dismissed.

(Cert issd for 400 fees &c pd D. D. to Colo Logan)

[144]Robert Barnett by Colo Logan this day claimed a preemption of 400 Acres of land at the State price in the district of Kentucky on Acc't of Making an Actual settlement in the Month of April 1779 lying on the hanging fork of Dicks River about 6 Miles from St Asaphs know by the Name of the little Salt Spring Satisfactory proof being made to the Court they are of Opinion that the s'd barnett has a right to a preempt'n of 400 Acres of land to include the above Location & that a Cert. issue Accordingly.

(Cert issd for 1400 fees &c pd D. D. to Colo Logan)

[145]Wm. Montgomerie Jun'r this day claimed a settlem't & preempt to a tract of Land in the district of Kentucky on Acc't of raising a Crop of Corn in the Country in the year 1776 lying on the Waters of Green River Near the Pine lick about 1 Mile West of the same to include his improvement Satisfactory proof being made to the Court they are of Opinion that the s'd Montgomerie has a right to a settlem't of 400 Acres of land to include the s'd Improvement & the preemption of 1000 Acres adjo'g & that a Cert. issue accordingly.—

(Cert issd for 1400 fees &c pd D. D. to Wm Mongomerie)

[146]John Montgomery by Colo Logan this day claimed a settlem't & preempt to a tract of Land in the district of Kentucky on Acc't of Settling in the Country in the year 1777 & residing ever since lying on the Waters of flat lick branch of Dick river about 1½ Miles below the flat lick to include his improvment Satisfactory proof being made to the Court they are of Opinion that the s'd Mongomery has a right to a settlem't of 400 Acres Land to include the s'd improv'ment & the preempt of 1000 Acres Adjoining & that a Cert. issue accordingly.

(Cert issd for 1400 fees &c pd D. D. to Colo Logan)

[147]Sam'l Briggs this day claimed a settlem't & preempt'n to a tract of land in the District of Kentucky on Acc't of raising a Crop of Corn in the Country in the year 1776 Lying on the Waters of the hanging Fork of Dicks river at Briggs Camp to include his improvment satisfactory proof being made to the Court they are of Opinion that the s'd Briggs has a right to a settlem't of 400 Acres of land to include the s'd improvement & the preempt'n of 1000 Acres Adjoining & that a Cert issue accordingly.

(Cert issd for 1400 fees &c pd D. D.)

[148]Wm Montgomery heir at law to Alex'r Montgomery[159] dec'd this day claimed a settlem't & preemption to a tract of land in the district of Kentucky on Acc't of the s'd dec'd Settling in the Country in the year 1777 & residing untill he was kill'd by the Indians lying on a branch of Green River about 2

[144] Collins vol. 1, p. 12.
[145] Collins, vol. 2, p. 472.
[146] Collins, vol 1, p. 12.
[147] Collins, vol. 1, p. 12.
[148] Collins, vol. 1, p. 11; Collins, vol. 2, p. 664.
[149] Collins, vol. 1, p. 12.

Miles Westwardly of Archi'd McKenny Land Satisfactory proof being made to the Court they are of Opinion that the s'd Montgomery has a right to a settlem't of 400 Acres of land to include the above location & the preemption of 1000 Acres adjoining & that a Cert issue accordingly.

(Cert issd for 400 fees &c pd D. D.)

[150]Wm Montgomery Ju'n this day claimed a preempt of 400 Acres of Land at the State price in the district of Kentucky on Acc't of Making an Actual settlment in the Month of May 1779 lying on a branch of Carpenters Creek at the head thereof about 2½ Miles from a Small lick on the Said Creek satisfactory proof being made to the Court they are of Opinion that the s'd Mongomery has a right to a preemption of 400 Acres of land to include the above location & that a Cert issue accordingly.

(Cert issd for 1000 D. D.)

Ovid McCracken Moves to remove his location of a Cert. obtained the 7 Inst. at Bryants Station Sufficient Cause Appearing to the Court for removal it is granted him & Locates the same on the Main fork of Elkhorn Creek & running up the North Fork for quantity Ordered that a Cert. issue Accordingly.—

(Cert issd for 400 fees &c pd D. D. to Colo Logan)

James McKenny this day claimed a preemption of 400 Acres of land at the State price in the district of Kentucky on Acc't of making an Actual settlement in the Month of April 1779 lying about 2½ Miles above Briggs Camp of the Waters of the Hanging fork of Dicks river satisfactory proof being made to the Court they are of Opinion that the s'd McKeny has a right to a preempt'n of 400 Acres of land to include the above Location & that a Cert. issue accordingly.—

(Cert issd for 400 fees &c pd D. D. to Colo Logan)

[151]Joseph Martin by Colo Logan this day claimed a preemption of 400 Acres of land at the State price in the district of Kentucky on account of making an Actual settlme't in the Month of April 1779 lying on a branch called Briggs where the road cross from the little flat Lick to the little Salt Lick on the West side of s'd Creek satisfactory proof being made to the Court they are of Opinion that the s'd Martin has a right to a preemption of 400 Acres of land to include the above location & that a Certificate issue accordingly.--

(Cert issd for 400 fees &c pd D. D.)

Thos. Reeves this day claimed a preemption of 400 Acres of Land at the State price in the district of Kentucky on Acc't of making an Actual settlem't in the Month of April 1779 lying on a Creek emptying in on the South side of Kentucky about 5 Miles from the Mouth & about 5 Miles up the s'd Creek to include a Cabbin on the W. side of the s'd Creek satisfactory proof being made to the Court they are of Opinion that the s'd Reaves has a right to a preempt'n of 400 Acres of land to include the above location & that a Cert issue accordingly.

[150] Collins, vol. 1, p. 12 and index.

[151] Collins, vol. 1, pp. 12, 542.

Ordered that the Cert. Edward Wathington Assee of John Brown[152] issue—

Then the Court adjourned untill to Monday Morning 10 Oclock—
Wm Fleming

At a Court Continued & held at Harrodsburg for adjusting Titles to unpatented land by the Commissioners of Kentucky District this 31st day of Jan'y 1780

Present
Wm. Fleming Stephen Trigg & Edmund Lyne—Gent.

(Cert issd for 1000 D. D.)
Thomas Gant made it Appear to the Court that the Land he obtained a Cert. for the 6th of November 1779 was wrongly located now moves to the Court to have the same altered & locates the same lying on Salt River about 1 Mile above Fort liberty[153] between the Lands of David Adams & Thomas Denton Ordered that a Cert issue accordingly.—

(Cert issd for 1400 fees &c pd D. D.)
John Cameron by James Wiley this day claimed a settlme't & preempt'n to a tract of land in the district of Kentucky on Acc't of raising a Crop of Corn in the Country in the year 1776 lying on the North side of Kentucky about 1½ Miles from Harrods landing place on a branch of Clear Creek to include a Spring satisfactory proof being made to the Court they are of Opinion that the s'd Camren has a right to a settlement of 400 Acres of land to include the above Location & the preemption of 1000 Acres adjoining & that a Cert. iss'e accordingly.

[152] Collins, vol. 1, pp. 9, 641.
[153] Collins, vol. 2, p. 24.

(Cert issd for 1400 fees &c pd D. D. to Colo Fleming)
Thos. Edger this day claimed a settlem't & preemption to a tract of land in the district of Kentucky on Acc't of raising a crop of Corn in the Country in the year 1776 lying on Cedar Creek a branch of Dicks River near Gilmour Lick to include his improv't satisfactory proof being made to the Court they are of Opinion that the s'd Edgar has a right to a settlement of 400 Acres of land to include the said improv't & the preemption of 1000 Acres adjoining & that a Cert. iss'e accordingly.

(Cert issd for 1400 fees &c pd D. D.)
Thos. Denton Sen'r by Thos. Denton Jun'r this day claimed a settlme't & preemption to a tract of land in the district of Kentucky On Acc't of raising a Crop of Corn in the year 1776 lying about 3 or 4 Miles from the Mouth of Salt River on the South side of the s'd River adjoining the Barrens to include a Spring at his improvement with the letters T D Marked on a Tree Satisfactory proof being made to the Court they are of Opinion that the s'd Denton has a right to settlme't of 400 Acres of land to include the above Location & the preemption of 1000 Acres of Land adjoining & that a Cert issue accordingly.

(Cert issd for 400 fees &c pd D. D.)
Spencer Collins by James Pattone this day claimed a preemption to a tract of 400 Acres of land at the State price in the district of Kentucky on Acc't of making An Actual Settlement in the Month of May 1779 lying on licking

Creek about 2 Miles from James Pattones Land to include a Cabbin built by the s'd Pattone satisfactory proof being made to the Court they are of Opinion that the s'd Collins has a right to a preempt of 4000 Acres of Land to include the above location & that a Certificate issue accordingly.

(Cert issd for 1000 fees &c pd D. D.)

Aniah Davis by Jeriah Davis this day claimed a preempt of 1000 Acres of Land at the State price in the district of Kentucky on Acc't of Marking & improving the same in the year 1776 lying on Benson Creek on the North side thereof near the head of the s'd Creek to include his improvment satisfactory proof being made to the Court they are of Opinion that the s'd Davis has a right to a preemption of 1000 Acres of land to include the above location & that a Cert iss'e accordingly.—

(Cert issd for 400 fees &c pd D. D. to Thos. Reeves)

[154]Rob't Deshay this day claimed a preemption of 400 Acres of land at the State price in the District of Kentucky on Acc't of Making an Actual settlem't in the Month of April 1779 lying on the South fork of Elkhorn about 2 Miles South of the stamping ground to include a Cabbin built at a Spring joining Crittendons Camp Satisfactory proof being made to the Court they are of Opinion that the s'd Deshay has a right to a preemption of 400 Acres of Land to include the above Location & that a Certificate issue accordingly.

(Cert issd for 400 fees &c pd D. D. Location Altered)

Jacob Coblin this day claimed a prempt'n of 400 Acre of Land at the State price in the district of Kentucky on Account of making an Actual settlement in the Month of April 1779 lying on Clarks run adjoining the land of Jas. Brown on the Upper side to include his improvment satisfactory proof being made to the Court they are of Opinion that the s'd Coblin Has a right to a preemption of 400 Acres of land to include the above Location & that a Cert issue accordingly.

(Cert issd for 1400 fees &c pd D. D. to James Samuel)

John Lynch by James Samuel this day claimed a right to a settlement & preemption to a tract of Land in the district of Kentucky on Acct of raising a Crop of Corn in the Country in the year 1775 lying on Mill Creek Waters of the Ohio Emptying below salt river joining the Lands claimed by Capt. Hines including a large Spring & improvement satisfactory proof being made to the Court they are of Opinion that the s'd Lynch has a right to a settlem't of 400 Acres of land to include the s'd improvement & the preemption of 1000 Acres adjoining & that a Cert iss'e accordingly.—

(Cert issd for 400 fees &c pd D. D.)

James Samuel this day claimed a preemption of 400 Acres of land at the State price in the district of Kentucky on Acc't of Making an Actual settlement in the Month of May 1779 lying on Wilson Creek a branch of the Rowling forks of Salt River joining the Bald

[154] Desha, Collins, vol. 1, p. 11.

Ridge & include the forks & both sides of s'd Creek Satisfactory proof being made to the Court they are of Opinion that the s'd Samuel has a right to a preempt of 400 Acres of land to include the above location & that a Cert issue accordingly.

(Cert issd for 400 fees &c pd D. D. to Thos Denton)

John Holloway by John Dunken (Denton?) this day claimed a preemption of 400 Acres of land at the State price in the District of Kentucky on Account of Making an Actual settlem't in the year 1778 lying on the Doctors Fork of Salt river to include an improvement made by James Ray satisfactory proof being made to the Court they are of Opinion that the s'd Holloway has a right to a preempt'n of 400 Acres of land to include the above location & that a Cert. issue accordingly.

(Cert issd for 400 fees &c pd D. D.)

Henry Spillman this day claimed a preemption of 400 Acres of Land at the State price in the District of Kentucky On Acc't of Making and Actual settlement in the Month of May 1779 lying on a large run that empties into Salt river against Bulletts Lick about 6 Miles up the s'd run to include his improvement satisfactory proof being made to the Court they are of Opinion that the s'd Spillman has a right to a preemption of 400 Acres of land to include the s'd improvement & that a Cert issue accordingly.

(Cert issd for 1000 fees &c pd D. D.)

John McFall this day claimed a preempt of 1000 Acres of land at the State price in the district of Kentucky On Acc of Marking & improving the same in the year 1776 lying on Mill Creek Waters of licking about 6 Miles from Riddles Station to include a Small Deer lick & his Cabbin Satisfactory proof being made to the Court they are of Opinion that the said Mcfall has a right to a preempt'n of 1000 Acres of land to include the s'd improvement & that a Cert. issue accordingly.

(Cert issd for 1000 fees &c pd D. D.)

Wm. Eastace (Eustace?) by Hancock Lee this day claimed a preempt of 1000 Acres of Land at the State price in the district of Kentucky On Acc't of Marking & improving the same in the year 1775 lying on the South side of Higstons fork of licking Creek on a small branch running into the s'd Creek just above a small lick on the Bank of the s'd creek to include his improvement satisfactory proof being made to the Court they are of Opinion that the s'd Eastace has a right to a preemption of 1000 Acres of land to include the s'd improvment & that a Cert issue accordingly.

(Cert issd for 1000 fees &c pd D. D.)

Dan'l Leet by Hancock Lee this day claimed a preemption of 1000 Acres of land at the State price in the district of Kentucky on Acct of Mark'g & improving the same in the year 1775 lying on the North fork of Elkhorn Creek about 8 to 10 Miles above the fork to include a Spring about 40 Yds from the s'd Creek & his improvment Satisfactory proof being made to the Court they are of Opinion that the Leet has a right to a preemption of 1000 Acres of land to include s'd improvement & that a Cert issue accordingly.

(Cert issd for 1000 fees &c pd D. D.)

[155]Abraham Hamptonstall this day claimed a preempt of 1000 Acres of land at the State price in the district of Kentucky On Acc't of Marking & improving the same in the year 1774 lying on the South fork of Elkhorn Creek on the South side thereof adjoining the Lands of Charles Lewis on the North side Satisfactory proof being made to the Court they are of Opinion that the s'd Hamptonstall has a right to a preemption of 1000 Acres of land to include the above Location & that a Cert issue accordingly.—

(Cert issd for 400 fees &c pd D. D.)

[156]James Brown by James Pattone this day claimed a preempt'n of 400 Acres of land at the State price in the district of Kentucky on Acc't of Making an Actual settlem't in the Month of May 1779 Lying adjoining the lands of James Pattone State (Slate?) Creek a branch of licking to include a large Spring Satisfactory proof being made to the Court they are of Opinion that the s'd Brown has a right to a preemption of 400 Acres of land to include the above Location & that a Cert issue accordingly.

(Cert issd for 400 fees &c pd D. D.)

Edward Cather this day claimed a preempt'n of 400 Acres of land at the State price in the district of Kentucky on Acc't of Making an Actual settlem't in the Month of April 1779 lying on a small branch of Kentucky on the North side thereof about 2 Miles from the fording North of the river including a Sinking Spring satisfactory proof being made to the Court they are of Opinion that the s'd Cather has a right to a preemption of 400 Acres of land to include the above Location & that a Cert issue accordingly.

(Cert issd for 1000 fees &c pd D. D.)

The Heir of Reuben Waits Dec'd by Eliza'th Waits this day claimed a preemption of 1000 Acres of land at the State price in the district of Kentucky on Acc't of the s'd decedents Marking & improving the same in the year 1776 lying on Coopers run a branch of licking Creek about 2 Miles from the head thereof to include the s'd Decedents Cabbin Satisfactory proof being made to the Court they are of Opinion that the s'd Heir &c has a right to a preemption of 1000 Acres of land to include the s'd Cabbin & that a Certificate issue accordingly.

(Cert issd for 400 fees &c pd D. D.)

Nathan Linn this day claimed a preemption of 400 Acres of land at the State price in the District of Kentucky On Acc't of Making an Actual settlement in the Month of May 1779 lying on the Waters of Hingston fork of licking Creek about 5 Miles below Andrew Guns (linns?) land Satisfactory proof being made to the Court they are of Opinion that the said Linn has a right to a preemption of 400 Acres of Land to include the above Location & that a Cert. iss'e accordingly.

(Cert issd for 400 fees &c pd D. D.)

Joseph Carswiler this day claimed a preempt of 400 Acres of land at the State price in the district of Kentucky

[155] Collins, vol. 2, p. 367, and McAfee papers.
[156] Collins, vol. 1, pp. 12, 641.

on Acc't of Making an Actual settlement in the month of March 1779 lying in the forks of Cedar Creek about 1 Mile South E. of the Cedar Spring on the South side of the Beech fork of Salt River satisfactory proof being made to the Court they are of Opinion that the s'd Carswiler has a right to a preemption of 400 Acres of Land to include the above location & that a Cert. issue accordingly.

(Cert issd for 400 fees &c pd D. D.)

[157]Ann Poag this day claimed a preempt of 400 Acres of land at the State price in the district of Kentucky On Acc't of Making an Actual settlement in 1776 lying on the road leading from Harrodsburg to the falls of Ohio about 7 Miles from McAfees Lower station Known by the Name of McGrays Spring beginning East of the said Spring thence for quantity & including the Spring Satisfactory proof being made to the Court they are of Opinion that the s'd Poagg has a right to a preempt of 400 Acres of Land to include the above location & that a Certificate issue accordingly.

Then the Court adjourned untill tomorrow Morning 9 Oclock

Wm Fleming

At a Court Continued & held at Harrodsburg for Adjusting Titles to unpatented Lands by the Commissioners of the Kentucky District the 1 day of February 1780.

Present

Wm Fleming Stephen Trigg &
Edmund Lyne—Gent'n

(Cert issd for 1400 fees &c pd D. D.)

Stephen Trigg Assee of Edward Loe petitions the Court to have Loes location Altered it being on land belonging to Gen'l Lewis (?) which being Granted he locates on Harrods Creek a branch of the Ohio about 1½ or 2 Miles above the 2d fork of the Creek on the South branch of the fork to include a Spring that empties into the Creek on the So. side near which there is the Appearance of An Old Camp Ord'd that a Cert issued accordingly.

(Cert issd for 400 fees &c pd D. D.)

Dan'l Hogan by Edward Hammon this day claimed a preemption of 400 Acres of land at the State price in the district of Kentucky on Acct of making an Actual settlement in the Month of May 1779 lying on the Rowling fork of Salt River about 17 Miles from Harrodsburg to include his improvement Satisfactory proof being made to the Court they are of Opinion that the s'd Hogan has a right to a preemption of 400 Acres of land to include the s'd improvement & that a Cert. issue accordingly.—

(Cert issd for 1000 fees &c pd D. D.)

[158]David Bard by Wm Bard this day claimed a preempt of 1000 Acres of land at the State price in the district of Kentucky on Acc't of Marking & improving the same in the year 1775 lying on the Waters of Stewarts fork of Salt River to include a Cabbin known by the Name of Bards Ceder Cabbin satisfactory proof being made to the Court they are of Opinion that the s'd Bard has a right to a preempt of 1000 Acres to include the

[157] Collins, vol. 2, p. 301.

[158] Collins, vol. 2, p. 644.

s'd Cabbin & that a Certificate issue accordingly.

(Cert issd for 1000 fees &c pd D. D.)

Sam'l Wethrow by Wm Bard this day claimed a preemption of 1000 Acres of land at the State price in the district of Kentucky on Acc't of Marking & improving the same in the year 1775 lying a branch between the Buffaloe Creek and Stewart Waters of Chaplins of Salt River to include his Cabbin Satisfactory proof being made to the Court they are of Opinion that the s'd Wethrow has a right to a preemption of 1000 Acres of Land to include the s'd Cabbin that a Cert issue accordingly.

(Cert issd for 1400 fees &c pd D. D.)

Nath'l Hart Assee of Lanclett Johnson who was Assee of Elijah Nunn this day claimed a settlement & preemption to a Tract of land in the district of Kentucky on Acc't of the s'd Nunns raising a Crop of Corn in the Country in the year 1775 lying on the banks of the Ohio at the end of a long reach about 4 Miles above the first Isla'd in the low Country opposite a large rock on the Indian Shore Known by the Name of Rock dunda & to include a poplar Marked LH & an Ash marked EH Satisfactory proof being made to the Court they are of Opinion that the s'd Hart &c has a right to a settlement of 400 Acres of land to include the above location & the preempt'n of 1000 Acres adjoining & that a Cert issue accordingly.

(Cert issd for 400 fees &c pd D. D.)

[159]James Stewart this day claimed a preemption of 400 Acres of land at the State price in the district of Kentucky on Acc't of Making an Actual settlement in the Month of May 1779 lying on the Waters of Salt River about 1 Mile from a large Buffaloe road leading to a Long Lick to include his improvement satisfactory proof being made to the Court they are of Opinion that the s'd Stewart has a right to a preemption of 400 Acres of land to include the s'd improvement & that a Certificate issue accordingly.

(Cert issd for 400 fees &c pd D. D. to —— David)

Wm Robinson this day claimed a preemption of 400 Acres of land at the State price in the District of Kentucky on Acc't of Making a Actual settlement in the Month of April 1779 lying on the North side of Dick River on a branch of the Kentucky to include his improvement Satisfactory proof being made to the Court they are of Opinion that the s'd Robinson has a right to a preemption of 400 Acres of land to include the s'd Improvement & that a Cert iss'e Accordingly.

(Cert issd for 400 Fees &c pd D. D.)

Wm Marshall this day claimed a preempt of 400 Acres of land at the State price in the district of Kentucky on Acc't of Making an Actual settlement in the year 1778 lying on the Waters of licking Creek within about 7 Miles of Riddles Station Satisfactory proof being made to the Court they are of Opinion that the s'd Marshall has a right to a preemption of 400 Acres of land to include the above location & that a Cert issue accordingly.

[159] Collins, vol. 1, p. 12.

Edw'd Camp by Patrick Jordon this day claimed a preempt of 400 Acres of land at the State price in the district of Kentucky On Acct of Making an Actual settlement in the Month of May 1779 Satisfactory proof being made by the Court they are of Opinion that the s'd Camp has a right to a preemption of 400 Acres of Land to include the above location.

(Cert issd for 400 fees &c pd D. D.)

Rueben Camp this day claimed a preempt'n of 400 Acres of land at the State price in the District of Kentucky on Acc't of making an Actual settlement in the Month of May 1779 lying on the North fork of Mill Creek Waters of the Ohio about 1½ Miles from the mouth of the s'd Fork to include his improvment satisfactory proof being made to the Court they are of Opinion that the s'd Camp has a right to a preemption of 400 Acres of land to include the above location & that a Cert issue accordingly.

(Cert issd for 1400 fees &c pd D. D.)

Wm Grayson this day claimed a settlement & preemption to a tract of land in the district of Kentucky on Acc't of raising a crop of Corn in the Country in the year 1776 lying on the Beech fork of Salt River near the Indian Lick to include his improvement satisfactory proof being made to the Court they are of Opinion that the s'd Grayson has a right to a settlement of 400 Acres of land to include s'd improvement & the preemption of 1000 Acres Adjoining & that a Certificate issue accordingly.

(Cert issd for 1400 fees &c pd D. D.)

Jonathan Ingrum by John Gordon this day claimed a settlement & preemption to a tract of land in the district of Kentucky on Acc't of raising a crop of Corn in the Country in the year 1776 lying on the Rowling Fork of Salt River near the Indian Lick on the North side thereof to include his improvement. Satisfactory proof being made to the Court they are of Opinion that the s'd Ingrum has a right to a settlement of 400 Acres of land to include the s'd improvement & the preemption of 1000 Acres adjoining & that a Cert issue accordingly.

(Cert iss for 400 fees &c pd D. D. to E. Hammond)

John Divine this day claimed a preemption of 400 Acres of Land at the State price in the district of Kentucky on Acc't of making an Actual settlement in the Month of March 1779 lying on the Pleasant run near the head thereof Waters of the Beech Fork of Salt River on the Hunters road to include his improvment satisfactory proof being made to the Court they are of Opinion that the s'd Divine has a right to a preempt'n of 400, Acres of land to include the above improv'ment & that a Cert issue accordingly.

(Cert issd for 1000 fees &c pd D. D.)

John Brexdel Heir at law to John Brexdel dec'd this day claimed a preemption of 1000 Acres of land at the State price in the district of Kentucky on Acc't of the s'd dec'd Mark'g & improving the same in the year 1775 lying 2 Miles South of Maj'r Harrods land to include his Cabbin satisfactory proof being made to the Court they are of Opinion that the s'd Brexel has a right to a preempt'n of 1000 Acres of land to include the s'd Cabbin & that a Cert issue accordingly.

(Cert issd for 1000 fees &c pd D. D.)

Dan'l McCormack this day claimed a preempt of 1000 Acres of Land at the State price in the district of Kentucky on Acc't of Marking & improving the same in the year 1775 lying on the Hanging fork of Dick River where the old path crosses between the knobb Lick & the flat lick to include both sides of the Creek & his improvment satisfactory proof being made to the Court they are of Opinion that the s'd McCormack has a right to a preemption of 1000 Acres of land to include the above Location & that a Certificate issue accordingly.—

(Cert iss for 400 fees &c pd D. D.)

Elisha Allen this day claimed a preemption of 400 Acres of land at the State price in the district of Kentucky on Acc't of making an actual Settlement in the Month of march 1779 lying on the dividing ridge between Cedar run & Dicks river including an Improvment 1½ Miles above the Mouth of Dicks river Satisfactory proof being made to the Court they are of Opinion that the s'd Allen has a right to a preemption of 400 Acres of land to include the above location & that a Certificate issue accordingly.

Then the Court adjourned untill tomorrow Morning 9 Oclock

Wm Fleming

At a Court continued & held at Harrodsburg for adjusting Titles to unpatented lands by the Commissioners for Kentucky District this 2d day of Jan'y 1780.—

Present

Wm Fleming Stephen Trigg &
Edmund Lyne—Gent

(Cert issd for 1000 Acres fees &c pd D. D.)

Charles Stewart by Will'm Stewart this day claimed a preemption of 1000 Acres of land at the State price in the district of Kentucky on Acc't of marking & improving the same in the year 1775 lying on both sides of Dowlin run a branch of Glens Creek to extend up the s'd Run for quantity & adjoining the Lands of Cerus (Cyrus?) McCracken to include his improvement satisfactory proof being made to the Court they are of Opinion that the s'd Stewart has a right to a preemption of 1000 Acres of land to include the above location & that a Cert. issue accordingly.

(Cert issd for 1400 fees &c pd D. D. to Wm Craig)

Wm Craig this day claimed a settlement & preemption to a tract of land in the district of Kentucky on Acc't of raising a crop of Corn in the Country in the year 1776 lying on the hanging fork of Dick River on the E. side of the said branch 3 miles from Colo. Logan station to include his improvement Satisfactory proof being made to the Court they are of Opinion that the s'd Craig has a right to a settlement of 400 Acres of land to include the s'd improvement & the preempt of 1000 Acres adjoining & that a Cert issue accordingly.

(Cert issd for 400 fees &c pd D. D. to W. Wheatly) (Whitley?)

Alex'r Buckhannon this day claimed a preemption of 400 Acres of land at the State price in the district of Kentucky on account of making an Actual settlem't in the Month of Nov'r 1778 lying Gasts (Gests?) Creek a fork of licking Creek to include an improv't made by Joseph Robertson. Satisfactory proof being made to the Court they are of Opinion that the s'd Buckhannon has a right to a preemption of 400 Acres to include the s'd improvement & that a Certificate issue accordingly.

(Cert issd for 1400 fees &c pd D. D. to W. Craig)

[160]John Craig by Wm Craig this day claimed a settlem't & preemption to a tract of land in the district of Kentucky on Account of raising a Crop of Corn in the Country in the year 1776 lying on a branch of the Hanging fork of Dicks river about ¾ of a Mile from the s'd Fork on the E. side 2 Miles from Colo Logans Station to include his improvment Satisfactory proof being made to the Court they are of Opinion that the s'd Craig has a right to a settlem't of 400 Acres of land to include the s'd improvement & the preemption of 1000 Acres adjoining & that a Cert. issue accordingly.—

(Cert issd for 400 fees &c pd D. D. to Wm Craig)

James Craig this day claimed a settlem't & preempt'n to a tract of land in the District of Kentucky on Acc't of raising a Crop of Corn in the year 1776 lying on a branch of the hanging Fork of Dicks river on the E. side of the East fork 2 Miles from Colo Logans Fort to include his improvment Satisfactory proof being made to the Court they are of Opinion that the s'd Craig has a right to a settlement of 400 Acres of land to include the s'd improvement & the preempt'n of 1000 Acres adjoining & that a Cert issue accordingly.—

(Cert issd for 1000 fees &c pd D. D. to Wm Craig)

John Craig Sen'r by Wm Craig this day claimed a preemption of 1000 Acres of land at the State price in the district of Kentucky on Acc't of Marking & improving the same in the year 1776 lying on a branch of the hanging Fork of Dicks river on the East side of the s'd fork ¾ of a Mile from the mouth of the branch known by the little Flat lick Creek to include his improvement satisfactory proof being made to the Court they are of Opinion that the s'd Craig has a right to a preemption of 1000 Acres of Land to include the s'd improv't & that a Cert. issue accordingly.—

(Cert issd for 1000 fees &c pd to Wm Craig)

Sam'l Craig this day claimed a preemption of 1000 Acres of land at the State price in the district of Kentucky on Acc't of Marking & improving the same in the year 1776 Lying on the Hanging fork of Dicks River on the West side thereof adjoining the lands of John Craig to include his improvment Satisfactory proof being made to the Court they are of Opinion that the s'd Craig has a right to a preempt of

[160] Collins, vol. 1, p. 354.

1000 Acres of land to include the said improvement & that a Cert issue accordingly.

(Cert issd for 1400 fees &c pd D. D. to Wm Weathing)

James Gilmore this day claimed a settlement & preemption to a tract of Land in the district of Kentucky on Acc't of raising a Crop of Corn in the Country in the year 1775 & 1776 lying on both sides of the Hanging fork of Dicks river joining the lands of John Daugherty including a Small improvment of Walter Stewarts & his own improvement satisfactory proof being made to the Court they are of Opinion that the s'd Gilmore has a right to a settlement of 400 Acres of land to include the above location & the preemption of 1000 Acres Adjoining & that a Certificate issue accordingly.

(Cert issd for 400 fees &c pd D. D.)

[161]Nehemiah Poor this day claimed a preempt'n of 400 Acres of land at the State price in the district of Kentucky on acc't of Making an actual settlement in the year 1778 lying on the head of a branch of Gilberts Creek that heads towards Hammons lick satisfactory proof being made to the Court they are of Opinion that the said Nehemiah Poor has a right to a preempt'n of 400 Acres of land to include the s'd location & that a Cert. issue accordingly.

(Cert issd for 1000 Acres fees &c pd D. D. to Carlswiler (?)

George Helms Assee of Constant Cade this day claimed a preempt'n of 1000 Acres of land at the State price in the district of Kentucky on Acc't of the s'd Cade marking & improving the same in the year 1776 lying on the North branch of the hanging fork of Dicks river Near the knobb lick adjoining the land said to be claimed by Edw'd Bulger & Burr harris (Harrison?) satisfactory proof being made to the Court they are of Opinion that the s'd Helms has a right to a preempt'n of 1000 Acres of land to include the s'd improvm't & that a Cert iss'e accordingly.

(Cert issd for 1000 fees &c pd D. D.)

Edw'd Johnson by John Johnson this day claimed a preemp't of 1000 Acres of Land at the State price in the district of Kentucky on Account of Marking & improving the same in the year 1775—lying on a small branch of Harrods Creek running in on the South side thereof adjoining the Lands of Moses Kilpatrick to include his improvment satisfactory proof being made to the Court they are of Opinion that the s'd Johnston has a right to a preempt'n of 1000 Acres of land to include the s'd improvement & that a Cert. issue accordingly.

(Cert issd for 400 fees &c pd D. D.)

[162]Wm Young this day claimed a preempt'n of 400 Acres of land at the State price in the district of Kentucky on Acc't of making an Actual settlem't in the Month of March 1779 lying on the Waters of Gilberts Creek adjoining the lands of Nehemiah Poor on the West satisfactory proof being made to the Court they are of Opinion that the said Young has a right to a preemption of 400 Acres of land to include the above location & that a Cert issue accordingly.

[161] Collins, vol. 1, p. 11.

[162] Collins, vol. 1, p. 11.

(Cert issd for 400 fees &c pd to W. Craig)

James Craig by Sam'l Craig this day claimed a preemption of 400 Acres of Land at the State price in the district of Kentucky on Acc't of Making an Actual settlem't in Novemb'r 1778 lying on the hanging fork of Dicks River about 2 Miles above Dan'l McCarmacks land to include his improvement; Satisfactory proof being made to the Court they are of Opinion that the s'd Craig has a right to a preemption of 400 Acres of land to include the above location & that a Cert. issue accordingly.

(Cert issd for 1000 fees &c pd D. D.)

Stephen Trigg this day claimed a preempt'n of 1000 Acres of Land at the State price in the district of Kentuck on account of Marking & improving the same in the year 1775 lying on the head of the North branch of beargrass about 2 or 3 Miles from Colo Wm Flemings land Near a North East fork; Satisfactory proof being made to the Court they are of Opinion that the s'd Trigg has a right to a preempt'n of 1000 Acres of land to include the above location & that a Cert. issue accordingly.

(Cert issd for 1000 fees &c pd D. D.)

Martin Armstrong by Thos. Denton this day claimed a preempt'n of 1000 Acres of land at the State price in the district of Kentucky on Acc't of Marking & improving the same in the year 1775 lying on the Ohio River below the Mouth of Mill Creek a branch of the Ohio emptying in below the Mouth of Salt River & about 5 Miles below the Mouth of the said Creek to include his improvment Satisfactory proof being made to the Court they are of Opinion that the s'd Armstrong has a right to a preemption of 1000 Acres of land to include the s'd improvement & that a Cert issue accordingly.

(Cert issd for 1000 fees &c pd D. D.)

Arthur Denton by Thos Denton this day claimed a preemption of 1000 Acres of Land at the State price in the district of Kentucky on Acc't of Marking & improving the same in the year 1775 lying on the Ohio river between the Mouth of Salt river & Mill Creek to include an improvment at a Spring with the two first letters of the said Dentons Name Cut on a tree at the s'd Spring Satisfactory proof being made to the Court they are of Opinion that the s'd Denton has a right to a preemption of 1000 Acres of land to include the s'd improvement & that a Cert issue accordingly.—

Then the Court adjourned untill tomorrow Morning 10 Oclock

William Fleming.

A GENTLEWOMAN OF KENTUCKY

(Editor's Note)

We are deeply grateful to Rev. F. W. Eberhardt, of Georgetown, Ky., for his kindness in sending us for this issue the appreciation of the late Mrs. Lister Witherspoon, which we are publishing herewith. Mrs. Witherspoon had been for many years a faithful officer of the Historical Society, never missing a meeting either of the Society or its Executive Committee, until failing health made it impossible for her to attend. Her interest in the Society extended over a long period of years, and in the trying days of its re-organization, when its financial condition was often a matter of grave concern her loyalty took a very substantial turn.

At the time of her death, she was a Vice-President of the Society and a member of the Executive Committee. The loss of her wise counsel and never failing interest will be keenly felt.

Martinette Viley Witherspoon
1851-1923

King Lemuel, maker of oracles, writing with the pen of inspiration, has given us God's ideal of the perfect woman. The four cardinal virtues she exemplifies—wife, mother, homemaker, comforter—are the priceless treasures of humanity, whether in wigwam or palace. Such a woman, wife, mother, homemaker, comforter, and friend—was Martinette Viley Witherspoon, wife of Lister Witherspoon, who died at her home, Loto Wana, near Versailles, Kentucky, January 31, 1923.

Mrs. Witherspoon was the last person in the world to claim the perfection of the inspired oracle, but those who knew her well—her family and her friends—unite in paying to her memory the highest tribute of love and esteem. She was indeed a noble type of a Kentucky gentlewoman.

This brief paper is neither a biography nor a critical, disinterested character delineation. It is an appreciation from one who, for thirty years, has felt the gracious influence of her life and the sympathetic encouragement of her wise counsel; who was privileged ofttimes to be a guest in the charming home over which she presided; and who found within its friendly walls a golden stairway luring his earth-treading feet up to the shining portals of the Eternal Home.

Born and reared amid the sylvan loveliness of "Stonewall," in the fairest region of the Bluegrass, she was connected by blood ties with many of the most distinguished families in the State and nation. Her own life added luster to her heritage. Her father was Major Warren Viley, her mother Jane Martin Viley. Mrs. Paul Lansing of Lexington is a sister, and Captain Breckenridge Viley, recently deceased, a brother. She grew up amid the happy influences she herself so well described in a paper on the Viley family, published in the Register of Kentucky State Historical Society for May 1909: "Warren Viley's lovely home has always been the seat of cordial hospitality, and there have been entertained the most prominent men of the day. Its famous woodland has been the scene of a number of big barbecues, which have marked great epochs in Kentucky politics. . . . . Warren Viley was a splendid type of Kentuckian at his best; noble hearted, courageous and upright, of knightly courtesy, hospitable and generous, simple and kindly."

Fifty-three years ago she was united in marriage with Lister Witherspoon. Their Golden Wedding celebrated a few years ago, was one of the most distinguished events in the social annals of Central Kentucky. Her husband and children—Warren V. of Lexington, Mrs. M. A. Buffington, of Fall River, Massachusetts, and Mrs. O. L. Alexander of New York City—cherish her memory and call her blessed. Another son, Lister, Jr., a young man full of the noblest promise died some years ago.

Mrs. Witherspoon was a high minded, high spirited, brave and generous woman. She was tender hearted as a little child, but capable of flaming indignation in the presence of injustice. Her sympathy was ever ready, whether to weep with those who weep or to rejoice with those who rejoice—ever ready to share the troubles of others, open handed in the use of her time and means.

Loyalty and sincerity were outstanding traits of her life. Pretense and hypocrisy she despised. Though always courteous, she seldom attempted to disguise her real attitude toward truth.

Her fidelity to husband and children manifested itself in unfaltering devotion; her life was a constant outpouring of love for them. She planned for them, ministered to them in sickness and health by day and by night; encouraging them, restraining them, urging them ever to the noblest goal, and leading the way. It has been said that the modern man wants in his wife a friend and a partner, where his grandfather wanted a housekeeper. In the best sense of these terms Mrs. Witherspoon was all three.

The same loyalty was shown to her friends. She was herself a perfect expression of the sentiment written with her own hand, in a book sent as a gift:

"My friend in the dark days,
My friend in the bright days,
My friend always."

From her honored father she inherited a passionate ardor for the ideals and heroes of the Confederacy, and was ever and always a Kentuckian.

In the sphere of religion her loyalty was most beautiful. The crucified, risen, and glorified Son of God was her Master as well as her Savior. The Bible was His revealed will, the chart and compass for the sea of her life. The simple, spirtual organization of a New Testament Church was to her the sphere of Divine service. No matter if the brotherhood was exalted or lowly, they were His and so was she, and persistently she gave of her best in doing "what she could" for Him. Like the sage of Uz she guarded the faith of her family. When her children made their homes in far distant cities, how solicitious she was that they should first of all find the right church affiliation in the new environment! One simply could not visualize her conforming church membership to social expediency. With her loyalty in religion she combined a noble faith in Divine Providence. Grief was no stranger to her and sorrow, anguish, and loss drove her nearer to God. Well she knew that, "To those that love God all things work together for good."

There was a prophet's chamber in her home, prepared at all times for the minister of her family, and other true men of God.

She was ambitious, coveting earnestly the best gifts for her loved ones, her friends, and herself. Her ambition however, was not that inordinate craving for wealth and preferment which has marred so many lives, but rather for the things of abiding value in time and eternity

Her kindly consideration for the feelings of others made her efforts to help those in need of help wonderfully effective. When the writer, then a young preacher just out of school, became the minister of the Church to which her family belonged she assisted him in numberless ways; always with the most delicate kindness; never at any time allowing it to appear that she was acting as mentor or critic.

As already indicated Mrs. Witherspoon was by birth and rearing a woman of refinement. She was *cultivated* in all the arts and graces of polite society, but more than these she was a woman of the truest *culture.* Endowed by nature with a strong intellect and pleasing personality she improved these by careful observation, wide reading, and close study. She was never an imitator of others. Honoring her own individuality and knowing that improvement of the real self is a duty one owes to God and humanity, she did not place undue value on outward forms. The successful gardener looks first of all to the preparation of the soil, otherwise the cultivation of that which the soil produces will yield but meager fruitage. The perfect honesty of Mrs. Witherspoon's life revealed itself in the sincerity of her culture, so that the longer one knew her the more her accomplishments were appreciated, and the more one realized that the charm of her manner was the real fruitage of her heart, and not the artificial, galvanized affectation of heartless custom.

Because of this sincerity of her intellectual being she maintained a fresh and vigorous interest in life, even when her physical strength had become enfeebled through illness. Like the poet Longfellow she endeavored "each year to grow a little new wood."

She was a delightful conversationalist, always having something worth while to say and saying it in an alert, happy manner. There was always a glint of wit in her talk which at times bubbled over in droll mimicry. A timid member of any group where she was present felt himself drawn out by her tactful interest and patient attention.

I never knew a better letter writer: perfect in form and wonderfully free and interesting in subject matter, the letters, written in a beautiful copper plate hand, were in themselves the finest expression of a gifted mind.

The old home at Glenartney as I knew it was a striking example of good taste in furnishing and decoration; furniture, carpets, hangings, napery, silver, china, and etc. were all of the finest, but everything harmonious. The house itself was old but by its setting of magnificent forest trees, well arranged shrubbery and sloping lawns, it was to me one of the loveliest spots in all Kentucky. Mrs. Witherspoon was a Nature lover. Trees, flowers, birds, squirrels, and even dogs had a large place in her affections, while horses were to her a particular delight.

A love of music entered into the enrichment of her life—not necessarily the commercialized music of the concert hall or opera house, though the best of this was not without its appeal. Unfortunately for our day all the elements of culture and recreation have become so commercialized that we seem to have lost the capacity for spontaneous enjoyment at home or abroad. To her, music was more than an art; it was a source of spiritual uplift and consolation. She loved the standard heart songs of all lands, particularly those of the South. For years she served as organist of the Church with which she and all her family were identified, where the nobler hymns of Christian worship were invariably selected by her for the service of praise.

Her literary appreciation was broad and comprehensive. She read widely and discerningly, the best of the old writers. The standard literary magazines were to be found in her home. These she read and marked and discussed with friends; forming her own opinion without waiting for the decision of the critics. She was the first of my acquaintances to recognize the literary artistry of the Dean of Kentucky letters and the promise of greatness revealed in his first stories. She was the first also to discern his lapse from the high ideals of his earlier visions under the influence first, of pagan hedonism, and afterwards, of scholastic rationalism. There was always in her mind a keen regret that one who was so gifted in *portraying* our distinctive Bluegrass social system, should be so blind to its truest *interpretation*. We are waiting still for the prophet he might have been, the seer who shall reveal to the world the soul of that culture which more than a hundred years ago blossomed and bore fruit in this fair garden of the Lord, shut in by the Cotton Kingdom of the South, the Industrial Empire of the North; isolated by the mountain ramparts of the East, and the uninhabited lands of the West; composite of the pioneer culture of two hundred years of Cavalier, Puritan, Huguenot, and Celtic Americanism.

To Mrs. Witherspoon the writer is also indebted for his first acquaintance with such Kentucky authors as John Fox and Alice Hegan Rice; also to Thomas Nelson Page and Henry Van Dyke, deep pools of quiet restfulness even now, when surfeited with the tumult of the turgid sea of modern realism and brutal naturalism.

Mrs. Witherspoon's interest in history was a natural consequence of her interest in literature. Careful study of her own family records led her through many avenues of county, state, national, and world wide research. Her connection with many historical organizations was an added stimulus. She was identified with practically every hereditary society for Southern women—Colonial Dames, Daughters of the American Revolution, Daughters of the Confederacy, Huguenots, National Society of the Daughters of the Barons of Runnymede, charter member of River Raisin Chapter of the Daughters of 1812, and a national officer in the Order of the Crown. For many years she was one of the vice-presidents of the Kentucky State Historical Society. Her book on the genealogy of her family will undoubtedly prove of real historic value.

After all however, the beauty of Mrs. Witherspoon's life was to be found in the sweet winsomeness of her personality, in the home and among her friends. These all join in crowning her memory, not with the blazing coronet of public acclamation, but with the modest sprays of for-get-me-nots and amaryllis in the chaplet of amaranth:

A Gentlewoman of Kentucky.

F. W. Eberhardt.

MY ANCESTORS

By Martinette Viley Witherspoon.

The leisure moments of the busy, useful life of Martinette Viley Witherspoon were occupied in an earnest effort to collect and put into permanent form all available material pertaining to a distinguished ancestry.

On the last Christmas of her earthly existence she placed in the hands of her children her finished work—"My Ancestors." It is a full sheaf, gleaned from innumerable sources.

In this valuable work we have chronicled many of the most distinguished families of Colonial times with authentic data concerning their European origin and in some instances, indubitable evidence of many generations preceding the American immigration.

The accounts of the pioneer Kentuckians are of much interest also, but the singular charm of the book is the author's personal recollections of her own kindred and their times—representative Blue Grass families, just prior to, and following the Civil War.

The volume is from the press of Chas. H. Potter & Co., Inc., Washington, D. C.

George C. Downing.

THE BOONE FAMILY.

By Hazel Atterbury Spraker.

The Historical Society has been recently enriched by the addition to its library of a new volume of Boone history entitled "The Boone Family." The work was compiled by a descendent of the family, Hazel Atterbury Spraker (Mrs. James Randolph Spraker), of No. 64, Dorchester Road, Buffalo, New York. Quarto, half leather and buckram, 691 pages, splendidly illustrated, including 36 full page portrait plates and many other illustrations pertaining to the family history. Price $15.00. Address compiler at the address given above, or the publishers, The Tuttle Company, 11-13 Centre Street, Ruthland, Vt.

The main portion of the book is devoted to a genealogy of the Boone family and its collateral lines, and will be very highly prized by the descendants of all the lines, and will be a valuable addition to genealogical libraries. The biographical sketch of Daniel Boone is exceedingly interesting, and will be much appreciated by Kentuckians generally, regardless of whether they are of the Boone blood.

The work is compiled along standard genealogical lines, and yet is so carefully arranged and well written as to be interesting to any lover of history, even though he may not ordinarily care for genealogy. The name index, covering some 42 pages is excellent, the illustrations are artistic and printing, binding and paper unusually attractive. To be brief, the work is high class, reflecting great credit on the compiler (only love of the task could have challenged her to the great labor of research necessary to the splendid results), and also upon the publishers for such a contribution to good book-making.

We recommend it to all Kentucky libraries, especially to descendants of the Boone line, direct or collateral, and to lovers of history generally.—(Ed.)

MILITARY CERTIFICATES NO. 1.

Another "Source Book" of great value has been found among the State Archives.

While looking for some records in the file room of the Adjutant General's office the secretary of the Historical Society discovered among some old Roster Books a leather bound volume, apparently of great age, and marked "Military Certificate, No. 1."

Upon examination this book proved to contain a record of the services of the men who served under General George Rogers Clark and Col. Benjamin Logan against the various Indian Tribes who harassed the settlers in Kentucky between 1785 and 1800. These services were mainly against the Shawnee and Wabash Indians, but in a few cases against the Cheegaumaugas and "Southern Indians" and "on the Frontiers."

An alphabetical arrangement of the names is now being made which will be published in the Register as soon as space permits.

OFFICERS

of the

KENTUCKY STATE HISTORICAL SOCIETY

SUBSCRIPTIONS.

Subscription, Yearly, $2.00 — Current Number, 75c Per Copy.
Back Numbers, $1.00 Per Copy.

Subscriptions must be sent by check, or money order. All communications for The Register should be addressed to H. V. McChesney, Editor, Frankfort, Kentucky.

H. V. McCHESNEY, Editor and Business Manager.
MRS. JOUETT TAYLOR CANNON, Associate Editor

TO SUBSCRIBERS.

If your copy of The Register is not received promptly please advise us. It is issued in January, May and September.

Entered as second class matter September 17, 1919, at the Post Office at Frankfort, Kentucky, under the Act of August 24, 1912.

THE STATE JOURNAL COMPANY
FRANKFORT, KY.

REGISTER

Kentucky State Historical Society

Vol. 21 | September, 1923 | No. 63

CERTIFICATE BOOK OF THE VIRGINIA LAND COMMISSION 1779-80—Continued.

At a Court Cont'd & held at Harrodsburg for adjusting Titles to unpattented lands by the Commissioners of Kentucky district the 4 day of Feb'y 1780.—

Present
Wm Fleming Stephen Trigg
Edmund Lyne—Gent'n

(Cert issd for 1400 fees &c pd D. D.)

[1]Uriah Stone by Wm Stafford this day claimed a settlem't & prempt to a tract of land in the district of Kentucky on acc't of raising a Crop of Corn in the Country in the year 1776 lying on Gass fork of Brashiers Creek adjoining Above Thos. Daughertys satisfactory proof being made to the Court they are of Opinion that the s'd Stone has a right to a settlem't of 400 Acres of land to include the above location & the preempt. of 1000 Acres adjoining & that a Cert. issue accordingly.—

(Cert issd for 1400 fees &c pd D. D.)

Wm Stafford Assee of Lew Brown this day claimed a settlement & preemption to a tract of land in the district of Kentucky on acc't of the s'd Browns raising a Crop of Corn in the Country in the year 1776 lying on Marble Creek adjoining Colo Southall on the North & Ross on the East running up from Southalls line on both sides of the Creek & with Ross's line for quantity—Satisfactory proof being made to the Court they are of Opinion that the s'd Stafford &c has a right to a settlement of 400 Acres of Land to include the above Location & the preempt'n of 1000 Acres adjoining & that the Cert issue accordingly.

(Cert issd for 400 fees &c pd D. D. to Jas Hawkins)

Charles Inglish this day claimed a preemption of 400 Acres of land at the State price in the district of Kentucky on Account of Making an Actual settlem't in the Month of March 1779 lying on the Waters of Dicks river Known by the Name of Pettitts where the s'd Inglish Now lives satisfactory proof being made to the Court they are of Opinion that the s'd Inglish has a right to a preempt'n of 400 Acres of land to include

[1] Collins, Vol. 2, p. 417.

the above location & that a Cert issue accordingly.

(Cert issd for 1000 fees &c pd D. D. to Jas Willy)

Henry Holeman this day claimed a preempt'n of 1000 Acres of land at the State price in the district of Kentucky on Acc't of Marking & improving the same in the year 1776 on the head of the North fork of Clear Creek to include his improvements satisfactory proof being made to the Court they are of Opinion that the s'd Holeman has a right to a preemption of 1000 Acres of land to include the s'd improvement & that a Cert'e issue accordingly.

(Cert issd for 400 fees &c pd D. D. to Jas Willy)

James Beaty by Edw'd Holeman this day claimed a preempt of 400 Acres of Land at the State price in the district of Kentucky on Acc't of Making an Actual settlem't in the Month of May 1779 lying on the Second branch above Clear Creek on the Waters of Breashears Creek joining the lands s'd to claimed by Ash Emession on the one side & Peter Sight on the other side satisfactory proof being made to the Court they are of Opinion that the s'd Beaty has a right to a preempt'n of 400 Acres of Land to include the above location & that a Certificate issue accordingly.

(Cert issd for 400 fees &c pd D. D. to Jno. Kennady)

John Clury this day claimed a preempt'n of 400 Acres of land at the State price in the district of Kentucky on Acc't of making an Actual settlement in the Month of April 1778 lying on the dividing ridge between the waters of Dicks river & Seags (Scaggs?) Creek to include a Spring at the head of Seags Creek about 1 Mile East of the old Trace from Weathleys (Whitleys?) to the settlement to Holstons satisfactory proof being made to the Court they are of Opinion that the s'd Clury has a right to a preempt'n of 400 Acres of land to include the above location & that a Cert issue accordingly—

(Cert issd for 400 fees &c pd D. D. to Jno Kenady)

Wm Clury by John Clury this day claimed a preempt of 400 Acres of Land at the State price in the district of Kentucky on Acc't of Making an Actual settlem't in the Month of April 1778 lying on the dividing ridge between the Waters of Dicks river & Seags Creek adjoining the land of John Clury Satisfactory proof being made to the Court they are of Opinion that the said Clury has a right to a preemption of 400 Acres of land to include the above location & that a Cert issue accordingly.

(Cert issd for 400 fees &c pd D. D. to Wm Wheathey)

John Anderson this day claimed a preempt of 400 Acres of Land at the State price in the district of Kentucky on Acc't of Making an Actual settle't in the Month of March 1779 lying on the Waters of Gilberts Creek No. West of Julias Sanders lands satisfactory proof being made to the Court they are of Opinion that the s'd Anderson has a right to a preempt'n of 400 Acres of land to include the above location & that a Certificate issue accordingly.—

(Cert issd for 1000 fees &c pd D. D.)

[2]Thomas Kennady by [3]Jno Kennady this day claimed a preempt'n of 1000 Acres of land at the State price in the district of Kentucky on Acc't of Marking & improving the same in 1775 lying on Dicks River Known by the name of Hawkins improv't satisfactory proof being made to the Court they are of Opinion that the s'd Kennady has a right to a preemption of 1000 Acres of land to include the s'd improvement & that a Cert issue accordingly.—

(Cert issd for 400 fee &c pd D. D. to Jno Kennady)

Elisha Clury this day claimed a preempt'n of 400 Acres of land at the State price in the district of Kentucky on Acct of Making an actual settlem't in the Month of Ap'l 1779 lying about ½ a Mile below the Sugar Loaf lick on the Waters of a Creek known by the name of Logans Creek Satisfactory proof being made to the Court they are of Opinion that s'd Clury has a right to a preempt of 400 Acres of land to include the above location & that a Cert issue accordingly.

(Cert issd for 400 fees &c pd D. to Jno Kenady)

Wm Hicks this day claimed a preempt'n of 400 Acres of land at the state price in the district of Kentucky On Acc't of making an Actual settlement in April 1779 lying about ½ a Mile from the Clay lick near the head of Gilmours Creek the Waters of Dicks river West of Gilmours Lick satisfactory proof being made to the Court they are of Opinion that the s'd Hicks has a right to a preemption of 400 Acres of land to include the above Location & that a Cert. issue accordingly.

(Cert issd for 400 fees &c pd D. D. to Anniah Davis)

Stephenson Huston this day claimed a preempt of 400 Acres of land at the State price the district of Kentucky on Acc't of Making an Actual settlem't in the year 1778 lying on the North side of Green River at the Mouth of Carpenter Creek, Satisfactory proof being made to the Court they are of Opinion that the s'd Huston has a right to a preemption of 400 Acres of land to include the above location & that a Cert. issue accordingly.

(Cert issd for 400 fees &c pd D. D. to Capt'n Harlen)

Geo'e Feater by [4]Silas Harlen this day claimed a preemption of 400 Acres of land at the State price in the district of Kentucky on Acc't of Making an Actual settlem't in the Month of April 1779 lying on a small branch of Dicks River about 3 Miles North E. of Clark Station to include his improvement—Satisfactory proof being made to the Court they are of Opinion that the s'd Feater has a right to a preemption of 400 Acres of Land to include the s'd improvement & that a Cert. iss'e accordingly.

(Cert issd for 400 fees &c pd D. D. to Jno Kennady)

John Wilkinson this day claimed a

[2] Collins, Vol. 2, pp.71, 81, 827.
[3] Collins, Vol. 2, p. 71.
[4] Collins, Vol. 2, p. 19, and index; Reg. Vol. 20, p. 280.

preemption of 400 Acres of land at the State price in the district of Kentucky on Acc't of making an Actual settlem't in the Month of Ma'ch 1779 lying about 3 Miles North West of Harrods Lick on a small Creek that empties into Hingstons fork of licking Creek on both sides of the s'd Creek for Quantity satisfactory proof being made to the Court they are of Opinion that the s'd Wilkerson has a right to a preempt'n of 400 Acres of land to include the above location & that a Cert issue accordingly.—

(Cert issd for 400 fees &c pd D. D. to Jno Kenady)

Lachariah (Zachariah?) Clarey This day claimed a preemption of 400 Acres of Land at the State price in the district of Kentucky on Acc't of Making an Actual settlem't in the Month of March 1779 lying about 1 Mile E. of the Sugar Loaf lick & near Elisha Clareys land satisfactory proof being made to the Court they are of Opinion that the s'd Clarey has a right to a preempt'n of 400 400 Acres of land to include the above location & that a Certificate issue accordingly.—

(Cert issd for 1000 fees &c pd D. D.)

John Miller by [5]Rich'd Burk this day claimed a preempt of 1000 Acres of land at the State price in the district of Kentucky on Acc't of Marking & improving the same in the year 1777—lying on the South side of Millers creek Waters of the Beech fork of Salt River on the Hunters Trace to include his improvement satisfactory proof being made to the Court they are of Opinion that the s'd Miller has a right to a preemption of 1000 Acres of land to include the said improvement & that a Cert issue accordingly.

(Cert issd for 1000 fees &c pd D. D. to Thos. Denton)

Joseph Hington this day claimed a preemption of 1000 of Acres of Land at the State price in the District of Kentucky on Acc't of Marking & improving the same in the year 1776 lying on a fork of Glens Creek that heads towards Leestown joining the Lands of [6]Cyrus McCraken to include his Cabbin Satisfactory proof being made to the Court they are of Opinion that the s'd Hinton has a right to a preemption of 1000 Acres of land to include the s'd improvement & that a Cert. issue accordingly

(Cert issd for 400 fees &c pd D. D. to Cap'n Harlen)

John Young this day claimed a preempt'n of 400 Acres of Land at the State price in the district of Kentucky by making an Actual settlem't in March 1779 lying on the No. fork of the Rowling fork of Salt River just below a Cabbin built by Thos. Harrod satisfactory proof being made to the Court they are of Opinion that the s'd Young has a right to a preemption of 400 Acres of land to include the above location & that a Cert. issue accordingly.

(Cert issd for 400 fees &c pd D. to Capt. Harlan)

Mary Ears this day claimed a preempt'n of 400 Acres of land at the State

[5] Collins, Vol. 2, p. 367.

[6] Col. Vol. 2, p. 20.

price in the district of Kentucky on Acc't of Making an Actual settlement in March 1779 lying on the North fork of the Rowling fork of Salt River adjoining the land of John Young above satisfactory proof being made to the Court they are of Opinion that the s'd Ears has a right to a preemption of 400 Acres of land to include the above location & that a Certificate issue accordingly.

(Cert issd for 400 fees &c pd D. D. to Capt. Harlan)

Charles Forgerson This day claimed a preemption of 400 Acres of Land at the State price in the district of Kentucky on Acc't of Making an Actual settlem't in the Month of March 1779 lying on the docters fork of Salt River at the forks to include an improvement Satisfactory proof being made to the Court they are of Opinion that the s'd Forguson has a right to a preempt'n of 400 Acres of Land to include the above Location & that a Cert issue accordingly.—

(Cert issd for 400 fees &c pd D. D. to George Smith)

Dan'l Trabue this day claimed a preempt'n of 400 Acres of land at the State price in the district of Kentucky on Acc't of making an Actual settlem't in the year 1778 lying on a branch of Salt River on the North side of the s'd River 4 Miles from Floyds fork between Brashears creek & the said fork to include a Cabbin at the head of a Spring satisfactory proof being made to the Court they are of Opinion that the s'd Trabue has a right to a preempt. of 400 Acres of land to include the above location & that a Cert. issue accordingly.—

Then the Court adjourned untill tomorrow Morning 9 Oclock—Wm Fleming.

At a Court Cont'd & held at Harrodsburg for adjusting Titles to unpattented land by the Commissioners of Kentucky district the 5th day of February 1780—

Present

Wm Fleming Stephen Trigg & Edmund Lyne—Gent.

(Cert issd for 1200 fees &c pd D. D.)

[7]Wm Wheatley this day as Assee of Valentine Hammons this day claimed a settlem't & preemption to a tract of land in the district of Kentucky on Acc't of the said Hammonds raising a Crop of Corn in the year 1775 lying on the Waters of Dicks river known by the Name of Weathleys Station to include the same satisfactory proof being made to the Court they are of Opinion that the s'd Weathley has a right to a settlem't of 400 Acres of land to include the above Location & the preemption of 1000 Acres adjoining & that a Cert issue accordingly.

(Cert issd for 400)

Wm Rowan by Wm Weathley this day claimed a preempt'n of 400 Acres of Land at the State price in the District of Kentucky on acc't of making an Actual settlem't in the Month of April 1779 lying between Hawkins's branch & Boonsborough road & about 1 Mile from Dicks river satisfactory proof being made to the Court they are of Opinion that the said Rowan has a right to a preemption of 400 Acres of land to in-

[7] (Whitley) Collins, Vol. 2, p. 180 and index.

clude the above Location & that a Cert issue accordingly.

(Cert issd for 1400 fees &c pd D. D. to Colo Fleming fees &c pd D. D. to Thos Arbuckle.)

*James Douglass came into Court & Moved to have a re-hearing with regard to his claim granted at Bryants Station on Elkhorn Creek which is granted him now comes into & Claimes a right to a settlem't & preemption to a tract of land in the District of Kentucky on Acc't of residing in the Country before the year 1778 lying at the head of Jasemine Creek 5 or 6 miles below Hickmans Creek a branch of Kentucky at a remarkable Camping place to include his improvement satisfactory proof being made to the Court they are of Opinion that the s'd Douglass has a right to a settlem't of 400 Acres of land to include the s'd improvement &c.—

(Cert issd for 1400 fees &c pd D. D. to Colo Fleming)

James Douglas Admr of James Ferry Dec'd this day claimed a settlem't & preempt'n of a tract of Land in the district of Kentucky on Acc't of the s'd dec'd raising a Crop of Corn in the Country in the year 1775 lying below the Mouth of Harrods Creek on the Ohio river about 8 Miles above the Falls of Ohio satisfactory proof being made to the Court they are of Opinion that the s'd Douglass Admins'r &c has a right to a settlement of 400 Acres of land to include the above Location & the preemption of 1000 Acres Adj'g & that a Cert. issue accordingly.

*Col. Vol. 2, pp. 52-53; McAfee Mss.

(Cert issd for 1400 fees &c pd D. D. Wm McBrid)

Sam'l Givens this day claimed a settlem't & preemption to a tract of Land in the district of Kentucky on Acc't of raising a Crop of corn in the Country in the year 1776 lying on Clarks run on the North side thereof to include a Spring Known by the Name of Blevis Spring adjoining the Lands of James Brown satisfactory proof being made to the Court they are of Opinion that the s'd Givens has a right to a settlement of 400 Acres of Land to include the above Location & the preemption of 1000 Acres of land adjoining & that a Certificate issue accordingly—

(Cert issd for 1000 fees &c pd D. D.)

Rob't Bogs this day claimed a preemption of 1000 Acres of Land at the State price in the district of Kentucky On Acct of Mark'g & improving the same in the year 1775 lying on Stoners fork of licking Creek about 4 or 5 Miles E. from Strodes Station at a high bank where the high Land joins the Creek on the North side thereof running South for quantity at a large Bend ½ a Mile below the high bank satisfactory proof being made to the Court they are of Opinion that the s'd Bogs has a right to a preempt'n of 1000 Acres of land to include the above location & that a Cert. issue accordingly.—

(Cert iss for 1400 fees &c pd D. D.)

[8]Sam'l Ingrum by [9]John Gordon this day claimed a settlem't & preemption to a tract of land in the district of Kentucky on Acc't of raising a Crop of Corn

[8] Collins, Vol. 2, p. 519.
[9] Collins, Vol. 2, pp. 624, 657, 663.

in the Country in the year 1775 lying on the Middle fork of Shannons run adj'g Rob't Slaughter Jr. on the N. W. & running half way between his improvement & Davis's Cabbin on which Matthias Yocum has laid a settlem't satisfactory proof being made to the Court they are of Opinion that the said Ingrum has a right to a settlem't of 400 Acres of Land to include the above location & the preemption of 1000 Acres adjoining & that a Cert. issue accordingly.

Ordered that Matthias Yocums Cert. granted him issue.

(Cert issd for 1400 fees &c pd D. D.)

[10]Levi Todd Adm'r of [11]Wm Poag Dec'd for & in behalf of Rob't Poags Heir at law to the s'd Decedent this day claimed a settlement & preemption to a tract of land in the district of Kentucky on Acc't of the s'd Decedents raising a Crop of Corn in the Country in the year 1776 lying on floyds fork of Salt River on both sides thereof about 20 Miles from the falls of Ohio & about 20 Miles from the Mouth of the s'd Creek satisfactory proof being made to the Court they are of Opinion that the s'd Rob't Poag has a right to a settlem't of 400 Acres of land to include the above location & the preemption of 1000 Acres ad joining & that a Cert. issue accordingly.

(Cert issd for 1400 fees &c pd D. D.)

Asel Davis came into Court & Moved the Court to have his Claim reheard which is granted him & now claims a settlem't & preempt'n to a tract of land in the district of Kentucky on Acc't of raising a crop of Corn in the Country in the year 1776 living on the No. East side of Dicks river on Clear Creek to include his improvement Satisfactory proof being made to the Court they are of Opinion that the s'd Davis has a right to a settlement of 400 Acres of land to include the above location & the preemption of 1000 Acres adjoining & that a Cert. issue accordingly.—

(Cert issd for 400 fees &c pd D. D.)

Alex'r Douglass this day claimed a preempt to 400 Acres of Land at the State price in the District of Kentucky on Acc't of Actual settlement in the Month of April 1779 lying on the So. side of Dicks River adjoining the Crab Orchard land below the Mouth of Crab Orchard Creek satisfactory proof being made to the Court they are of Opinion that the s'd Douglass has a right to a preemption of 400 Acres of Land to include the above Location & that a Certificate issue accordingly.—

(Cert issd for 400 fees &c pd D. D. to Wm Wheatley.)

[12]Peter Higgins this day claimed a preemption of 400 Acres of land at the State price in the district of Kentucky On Acc't of Making an Actual settlem't in March 1779 lying on Weathleys Creek a branch of Dick River about 1 Mile above James Davis Station satisfactory proof being made to the Court they are of Opinion that the s'd Higgins has a right to a preempt'n of 400 Acres of land to include the above Location & that a Cert. issue accordingly.

[10] Collins, Vol. 2, p. 22 and index; Con. N. W. English, p. 253.

[11] Collins, Vol. 2, p. 301 and index.

[12] Collins, Vol. 2, pp. 177, 326.

Then the Court Adj'd untill Tomorrow Morning 9 Oclock

Wm Fleming

At a Court Con'd & held at Harrodsburg 8th day of Feb'y 1780 for Adjusting Titles to unpattented Land by the Commissioners of the Kentucky District.

Present

Wm Fleming Stephen Trigg & Edmund Lyne—Gent'n.

(Cert issd for 1400 fees &c pd D. D. to John Jorden)

Wm Grayson heir at Law to Ambrose Grayson dec'd this day claimed a settlement & preempt'n to a tract of land in the District of Kentucky on Acc't of the s'd decedents raising a Crop of Corn in the Country in the year 1776 lying on Chaplins fork of salt river & joining James Harbesons land above satisfactory proof being made to the Court they are of Opinion that the s'd Grayson has a right to a settlem't of 400 Acres of land to include the above location & the preemption of 1000 Adjoining & that a Cert. issue accordingly.

(Cert issd for 1400)

Rob't Slaugher Jun'r by Hankerson Reed this day claimed a settlement & preempt'n to a tract of land at the State price in the district of Kentucky on Acc't of raising a Crop of Corn in the Country in the year 1776 lying on Bensons Creek adjoining the lands of George Slaughter below satisfactory proof being made to the Court they are of Opinion that the s'd Slaughter has a right to a settlem't of 400 Acres of land to include the above location & the preemption of 1000 Acres Adjoining & that a Cert. issue accordingly.—

(Cert issd for 1400)

[13]George Slaugher by Hank'n Reed this day claimed a settlement & preemption to a tract of land in the district of Kentucky on Acc't of raising a Crop of Corn in the Country in the year 1776 lying on the head of the left branch of Bensons Creek lying about 6 or 7 Miles from Capt'n Baileys land satisfactory proof being made to the Court they are of Opinion that the s'd Slaugher has a right to a settlem't of 400 Acres of land to include the above location & the preemption of 1000 acres Adjoining & that a Cert. issue accordingly.—

(Cert issd for 1400)

Rob't Slaughter Sen'r this day claimed a settlem't & preemption of a tract of Land in the district of Kentucky on Acc't of raising a crop of Corn in the Country in the year 1776 lying between the Waters of Cane run & Elkhorn joining the lands claimed by Escile (Ezekiel) Field & running down for Quantity satisfactory proof being made to the Court they are of Opinion that the s'd Slaughter has a right to a settlement of 400 Acres of land to include the above location & the preempt'n of 1000 Acres adjoining & that a Cert issue accordingly.—

(Cert issd for 1400)

Lawrence Slaughter Assee of [14]Thos. Slaughter this day claimed a settlement & preemption to a tract of land in the district of Kentucky on Acc't of the

[13] Collins, Vol. 2, pp. 183, 371; Con. N. W. English, p. 691.
[14] Collins, Vol. 2, p. 337 and index.

s'd Thos Slaughter raising a Crop of Corn in the Country in the year 1776 on the North side of Elkhorn Creek adjoining the Lands said to be claimed by Ezekiel Field Commonly called the Spice Woods satisfactory proof being made to the Court they are of opinion that the s'd Slaughter has a right to a settlement of 400 Acres of land to include the above location & the preemption of 1000 Acres of land adjoining & that a Cert. issue accordingly.

(Cert iss for 1400)
Wm Slaughter Jun'r by Hank'n Reed this day claimed a settlem't & preempt'n to a tract of land in the district of Kentucky on Acc't of raising a Crop of Corn in the Country in the year 1775 lying on the North side of Kentucky river on the upper side of the Junction of Eagle Creek & the s'd Kentucky river satisfactory proof being made to the Court they are of Opinion that the s'd Slaughter has a right to a settlem't of 400 Acres of land to include the above Location & the preemption of 1000 Acres adjoining & that a Cert. isse accordingly.

(Cert issd for 1400)
Rob't Jones Heir at Law to [15]Gabriel Jones Dec'd by Hank'n Reed this day claimed a settlement & preempt'n to a tract of land in the district of Kentucky on Acc't of the s'd decedents raising a Crop of Corn in the Country in the year 1775 lying on the North side of Kentucky adjoining Wm Slaughters land satisfactory proof being made to the Court they are of Opinion that the s'd Rob't Jones has a right to a settlem't of 400 Acres of land to include the above location & the preempt'n of 1000 Acres adjoining & that a Cert issue accordingly.

(Cert issd for 1400)
George Slaughter Jun heir at Law to Francis Slaughter Dec'd this day claimed a settlement & preempt'n to a tract of land in the district of Kentucky on Acc't of the s'd Decedents raising a Crop of Corn in the Country in the year 1775 lying beginning in the fork of 10 Mile Creek Near the Ohio including the heads of the South Branch of the s'd Creek to extend towards Harrods Creek for quantity satisfactory proof being made to the Court they are of Opinion that the s'd Slaughter has a right to a settlement of 400 Acres of land to include the above location & the preemption of 1000 Acres adjoining & that a Cert issue accordingly.—

(Cert issd for 1400)
[16]Wm Bryan this day claimed a settlement to a tract of land in the district of Kentucky on Acc't of raising a Crop of Corn in the Country in the year 1775 lying on the South branch of Hingstons fork of licking Creek Called Bowmans Creek about 3 Miles from Ebenezer Sovrens Land to include an improvement made by James Bowman satisfactory proof being made to the Court they are of Opinion that the s'd Bryan has a right to a settlement of 400 Acres of land to include the above Location & the preemption of 1000 Acres adjoining & that a Cert issue accordingly.

[15] Collins, Vol. 2, pp. 466, 656.

[16] Collins, Vol. 2, pp. 186, 241.

(Cert issd for 400 fees &c pd D. D. to Jacob Myers)

[17]Joseph Cartright this day claimed a preemption of 400 Acres of land at the State price in the district of Kentucky on Acc't of making an Actual settlement in the year 1778 lying on the North fork of Elkhorn Creek adjoining Patrick Henrys survey above the fork on the west side & down the s'd Creek for quantity satisfactory proof being made to the Court they are of Opinion that the s'd Cartright has a right to a preemption of 400 acres of land to include the above location & that a Cert. issue accordingly.

(Cert issd for 1400 fees &c pd D. D.)

Jacob Myers Assee of James Hays Heir at law of [18]John Hays dec'd this day claimed a settlement & preemption to a tract of land in the district of Kentucky on Acc't of the s'd decedents raising a Crop of Corn in the Country in the year 1776 lying on the North side of Green River adjoining the Falls of the said river & running up & down the s'd river for Quantity satisfactory proof being made to the Court they are of Opinion that the s'd Myers has a right to a settlement of 400 Acres of Land to include the above location & the preemption of 1000 Acres Adjoining & that a Cert. issue accordingly.—

(Cert issd for 1000 Fees &c pd D. D.)

Presley Smith by [19]Wm Bailey Smith this day claimed a preemption of 1000 Acres of land at the State price in the district of Kentucky on Acc't of marking & improving the same in the year 1776—lying on panther Creek Waters of Green river below the land of William Bailey Smith on the s'd Creek to include a Spring Marked with EH & LH on the lower side of the Creek satisfactory proof being made to the Court they are of Opinion that the s'd Smith has a right to a preemp'n of 1000 Acres of land to include the above location & that a Cert. issue accordingly.—

(Cert issd for 1400 fees &c pd D. D.)

Peter Smith by Wm Bailey Smith this day claimed a preemption of 1000 Acres of land at the State price in the district of Kentucky on Acc't of Marking & improving the same in the year 1776 lying on Panther Creek adjoining the lands of Presley Smith on the lower side Satisfactory proof being made to the Court they are of Opinion that the s'd Smith has a right to a preemption of 1000 Acres of Land to include the above Location & that a Cert iss'e accordingly.—

(Cert issd for 1400 fees &c pd D. D.)

Martin Hammond by Nath'l Henderson this day claimed a settlement & prempt'n to a tract of land in the district of Kentucky on Acc't of residing in the Country 12 Month before the year 1778 lying on a small Creek that runs into licking Creek about 10 or 12 Miles above the Upper Salt Spring Known by the Name of the Flat Creek beg's about ¾ of a Mile above where a big Buffalo path crosses the Creek including some improvements made by Colo Wm Lynn &c satisfactory proof being made to the Court they are of Opinion that the s'd Hammond has a right to a settlement

[17] Collins, Vol. 2, p. 624.
[18] Collins, Vol. 2, p. 624.
[19] Collins, Vol. 2, pp. 526, 528.

of 400 Acres of Land to include the above Location & the preempt'n of 1000 Acres adjoining & that a Certificate issue accordingly.

(Cert issd for 1400 fees &c pd D. D.)

[20]Wm Henderson by Nath'l Henderson this day claimed a settlement & preemption to a tract of land in the district of Kentucky on Acc't of raising a crop of Corn in the Country in the year 1776 lying Adjoining Martin Hammonds Land above on both sides the s'd Creek satisfactory proof being made to the Court they are of Opinion that the s'd Wm Henderson has a right to a settlem't of 400 Acres of land to include the above location & the preempt'n of 1000 Acres adjoining & that a Cert. issue accordingly.—

(Cert issd for 1400 fees &c pd D. D.)

Thomas Carlane by Nath'l Henderson this day claimed a settlem't & preemption to a tract of land in the district of Kentucky on Acc't of residing in the Country 12 Months before the year 1778 lying on a small Creek on the South side of the Middle fork of Salt River about 10 Miles from Bulletts Lick including John Kenadys Name Cut on a Beach tree on the side of a large Buffaloe road dated July 1775 on s'd Tree satisfactory proof being made to the Court they are of Opinion that the s'd Carlane has a right to a settlem't of 400 Acres of land to include the above location & the preempt. of 1000 Acres adjoining & that a Cert issue accordingly.—

(Cert issd for 1400 fees &c pd D. D. to Capt. Henderson)

Wm Stagg by Nath'l Hart this day claimed a settlem't & preempt. to a tract of Land in the district of Kentucky on Acc't of raising a Crop of Corn in the Country in the year 1775 & 1776 lying on the West side of Panther Creek about 8 or 9 Miles from the Mouth thereof adjoining Dan'l Hogans on the North & West satisfactory proof being made to the Court they are of Opinion that the s'd Stagg has a right to a settlement of 400 Acres of Land to include the above Location & the preempt. of 1000 Acres adjoining & that a Cert. issue accordingly.

(Cert issd for 1000 fees &c pd D. D.)

John Gray Blount this day claimed a preempt. of 1000 Acres of Land at the State price in the district of Kentucky on Acc't of Marking & improving the same in the year 1776 lying Breashears Creek on the Bullskin Fork of same on the East side thereof near Dentons Trace to include his improvement satisfactory proof being made to the court they are of Opinion that the s'd Blount has a right to a preempt of 1000 Acres of Land to include the above Location & that a Cert. issue accordingly.—

(Cert issd for 1000 fees &c pd D. D. to [21]Alex'r Black)

James Cloyd this day claimed a preempt'n of 1000 Acres of Land at the State price in the district of Kentucky on Acc't of Marking & improving the same in the year 1776 lying on both sides the rowling fork of Salt River about 1½ Miles from the Shawnee Lick

[20] Collins, Vol. 2, p. 172.

[21] Collins, Vol. 2, p. 367.

on a small Creek on the South side the s'd fork to include his improvement satisfactory proof being made to the Court they are of Opinion that the s'd Cloyd has a right to a preemption of 1000 Acres of Land to include the above Location & that a Cert. issue accordingly.—

(Cert issd for 1000 fees &c pd D. D. to Alex Black)

Sam'l Lawrence this day claimed a preempt of 1000 Acres of land at the State price in the district of Kentucky on Acc't of Marking & improving the same in the year 1776 lying on both sides of the Rowling Fork of Salt River adjoining the Land of James Cloyd above to include his improvement satisfactory proof being made to the Court they are of Opinion that the s'd Lawrence has a right to a preempt'n of 1000 Acres of Land to include the above Location & that a Cert issue accordingly.

(Cert issd for 1000 fees &c pd D. D. to Alex. Black)

Solmon Lawrence this day claimed a preemption of 1000 Acres of land in the district of Kentucky on Acc't of Marking & improving the same in the year 1776 lying on the South side of the Rolling fork of Salt River between 2 small Creeks & 4 Miles from Jas. Cloyds Land to include his improvement Satisfactory proof being made to the Court they are of Opinion that the s'd Lawrence has a right to a preempt'n of 1000 Acres of Land to include the above location & that a Cert. iss'e accordingly.—

(Cert issd for 1000 fees &c pd D. D. to Alex Black)

John Lawrence this day claimed a preemption of 1000 Acres of land at the State price in the district of Kentucky on Acc't of Marking & improving the same in the year 1776 lying on both Sides of the Rolling Fork of Salt River about 2 Miles above Solmon Lawrences Land to include his improvm't satisfactory proof being made to the Court they are of Opinion that the s'd Lawrence has a right to a preemption of 1000 Acres of Land to include the Abo'e location & that a Cert. iss'e accordingly.—

(Cert issd for 1000 fees &c pd D. D. to Alex Black)

David Lawrence this day claimed a preempt'n 1000 Acres of Land at the State price in the district of Kentucky on Acc't of Marking & improving the same in the year 1776 lying on the Waters of the Rolling Fork of Salt river Adjoining the land of James Cloyd & Sam'l Lawrence to include his improv't satisfactory proof being made to the Court they are of Opinion that the s'd Lawrence has a right to a preempt of 1000 Acres of land to include the above Location & that a Cert. issue accordingly.

(Cert issd for 1000 fees &c pd D. D. to Alex Black)

Henry Brusher (Brasher?) this day claimed a preempt'n of 1000 Acres of land at the State price in the district of Kentucky on Acc't of Marking & improving the same in the year 1776 lying on the Rolling fork of Salt River on both sides thereof adjoining the Lands of Sam'l Lawrence above to include his improvement satisfactory proof being made to the Court they are of Opinion that the s'd Brusher has a right to a preemption of 1000 Acres of land to include the above location & that a Cert. issue accordingly.

(Cert issd for 1400 D. D.)

[22]John Bowman this day claimed a settlem't & preemption to a tract of land in the district of Kentucky on Acc't.of raising a Crop of Corn in the Country in the year 1776 lying on the Waters of Harrods run on the So. side thereof adjoining the South line & East line of Edw'd Bullgers to include a Cabbin built by one McConnell & the s'd Bowman satisfactory proof being made to the Court they are of Opinion that the s'd Bowman has a right to a settlem't of 400 Acres of land to include the above location & the preemption of 1000 Acres adjoining & that a Cert. issue accordingly.—

(Cert issd for 1000 D. D.)

[23]Abraham Bowman this day claimed a settlem't & preempt to a tract of land in the district of Kentucky on Acc't of raising a Crop of Corn in the Country in the year 1775 lying on a small branch of Goose Creek a branch of the Ohio on the North side thereof Adjoining the Lands s'd to be claimed by Isaac Hite satisfactory proof being made to the Court they are of Opinion that the s'd Bowman has a right to a settlement of 400 Acres of Land to include the above Location & the preempt'n of 1000 Acres adjoining & that a Cert issue accordingly.

(Cert issd for 1400 fees &c D. D.)

Isaac Hite Sen'r this day claimed a settlem't & preempt'n to a tract of Land in the district of Kentucky on Acc't of raising a Crop of Corn in the Country in the year 1776 lying adjoining Harrodsburg on the East side thereof to include an improvement made by James Harrod at a Sinking Spring satisfactory proof being made to the Court they are of Opinion that the s'd Hite has a settlement of 400 Acres of Land to include the above Location & the preemption of 1000 Acres Adjoining & that a Cert. issue accordingly.—

(Cert issd for 1400 D. D.)

John Bowman Assee of Edw'd Jackson this day claimed a settlement & preemption to a tract of land in the district of Kentucky on Acc't of the s'd Jackson residing in the Country 12 Months before the year 1778 lying on the Waters of Dicks river it being the Land whereon the s'd Bowman now lives satisfactory proof being made to the Court they are of Opinion that the said Bowman has a right to a settlme't of 400 Acres of land to include the above location & the preemption of 1000 Acres adjoining & that a Cert. issue accordingly.—

(Cert issd for 1400 D. D.)

John Isaacks by Colo Bowman this day claimed a settlement & preemption to a tract of land in the district of Kentucky on Acc't of settling in the Country in the year 1777 & residing 12 Months since the s'd settlement lying on both Sides of Wilson Run adjoining the Lands of [24]Thos. Wilson below & to include his improvement satisfactory

[22] Collins, Vol. 2, p. 183 and index.
[23] Collins, Vol. 2, p. 475.
[24] Collins, Vol. 2, p. 511, 518.

proof being made to the Court they are of Opinion that the s'd Isaacks has a right to a settlem't of 400 Acres of land to include the above location & the preemption of 1000 Acres adjoining & that a Cert. issue accordingly.—

(Cert issd for 1000 D. D.)

The Heir of [25]Nathan Hammond Dec'd by John Bowman this day claimed a preemption to a tract of land at the State Price in the district of Kentucky on Acc't of Marking & improving the same in the year 1775 lying on Hammons run Waters of Kentucky adjoining the lands of Jacob Coffman to include his improvement satisfactory proof being made to the Court they are of Opinion that the s'd Heir of N. Hammond has a right to a preempt'n of 1000 Acres of land to include the s'd improvement & that a Cert. issue accordingly.

Then the Court Adjourned untill tomorrow Morning 9 Oclock—Wm Fleming.

At a Court Continued & held at Harrodsburg this 9th day of Feb'y 1780 for adjusting Titles to unpatented Lands by the Commissioners for Kentucky District

Present

Wm Fleming Stephen Trigg Edmund Lyne—Gents—

(Cert issd for 1400 D. D.)

[26]Isaac Bowman this day claimed a settlement & preemption to a tract of Land in the district of Kentucky on acc't of raising a Crop of Corn in the Country in the year 1776 lying on the Ohio river at the lower end of the Yellow Bank above Green River & extending up the river & back for quantity about 30 Miles above the Mouth of Green River satisfactory proof being made to the Court they are of Opinion that the s'd Bowman has a right to a settlement of 400 Acres of land to include the above location & the preempt'n of 1000 Acres of land adjoining & that a Cert issue accordingly.

(Cert issd for 1400 D. D.)

James Ross by Colo Bowman this day claimed a settlement & preempt'n to a tract of Land in the district of Kentucky on Acc't of residing in the Country 12 Months before the year 1778 lying on the Ohio river joining the Lands of Isaac Bowman on the upper side to extend up the River & back for quantity satisfactory proof being made to the Court they are of Opinion that the s'd Ross has a right to a settlem't of 400 Acres of land to include the above location & the preemption of 1000 Acres adjoining & that a cert. issue accordingly.

(Cert issd for 400 D. D.)

Wm Bryan heir at law to David Bryan Dec'd this day claimed a preemption of 400 acres of land at the State price in the district of Kentucky on Acc't of the s'd decedents making an Actual settlement in the Month of March 1779 lying on the Waters of Cane run Known by the Name of the White Oak Spring satisfactory proof being made to the Court they are of opinion that the s'd Bryan has a right to a preemption of 400 Acres of land to include the above location & that a Cert. issue accordingly.

[25] Collins, Vol. 2, pp. 337, 501, 519.
[26] Collins, Vol. 2, p. 624.

(Cert issd for 1400 D. D.)

The heirs of James Douchester Jun'r dec'd this day claimed a settlement & preemption to a tract of Land (Colo Bowman Ad'ms to the estate of the s'd Decedent) in the District of Kentucky on Acc't of the s'd decedents raising a Crop of Corn in the Country in the year 1776 lying on the North Fork of Hingstons Creek Waters of licking Creek about 6 miles from Riddles Station Satisfactory proof being made to the Court they are of Opinion that the s'd Heirs of the Dec'd has a right to a settlem't of 400 Acres of land to include the above location & the preemption of 1000 Acres of land adjoining & that a Cert. issue accordingly.

(Cert issd for 1400 D. D.)

The Heirs of [27]Wm Myers dec'd by John Bowman Admr of the Estate of the s'd decedents this day claimed a settlement & preemption to a tract of land in the district of Kentucky on Acc't of the s'd dec'd raising a Crop of Corn in the year 1776 lying Wilsons run near the head thereof a branch of Dicks river to include the dec'd improvement & to run & down the run for quantity satisfactory proof being made to the Court they are of Opinion that the s'd Heirs &c has a right to a settlem't of 400 Acres of Land to include the said improvement & the preempt of 1000 Acres adjoining & that a Cert. issue accordingly.

(Cert issd for 1400 fees &c pd D. D.)

Hannah Soverain Now the Wife of [28]Benj Linn this day claimed the settlem't & preemption to a tract of land in the district of Kentucky on Acc't of the s'd Hannah Soverain residing 12 Months before the year 1778 Wh'h was before the enter Marriage with the said Lynn lying on the Ohio river at the Upper end of the Yellow Banks which includes the Mouth of a branch & to extend down the river and back for quantity Satisfactory proof being made to the Court they are of Opinion that the s'd Hannah Soverain has a right to a settlement of 400 acres of land to include the above location & the preemption of 1000 acres Adjoining & that a Cert issue accordingly.—

(Cert issd for 1400 fees &c pd D. D.)

[29]Vangelist Harden by Isaac Hite this day claimed a settlme't & preempt'n to a tract of land in the district of Kentucky on Acc't of raising a Crop of Corn in the Country in the year 1775 lying on the Ohio river adjoining the lands of Hannah Soverign on the lower side to extend down the River & back for quantity satisfactory proof being made to the Court they are of Opinion that the s'd Harden has a right to a settlement of 400 Acre of land to include the above location & the preemption of 1000 Acres of land adjoining & that a Cert issue accordingly.

(Cert issd for 1400 fees &c pd D. D.)

[30]Wm Linn Assee of Michael Wolf this day claimed a preemption of 400 Acres of Land in the district of Kentucky on Acc't of making an Actual settlement in May 1779 lying on the head of the dry run of Beargrass ad-

[27] Collins, Vol. 2, p. 511.
[28] Collins, Vol. 2, pp. 467, 615, 616.
[29] Collins, Vol. 2, p. 519.
[30] Collins, Vol. 2, pp. 358, 371.

joining Wares line on the N. E. to include the place whereon the s'd Linn Now lives satisfactory proof being made to the Court they are of the Opinion that the s'd Linn has a right to a preemption of 400 Acres of land to include the above Location & that a Cert. issue accordingly.

(Cert issd for 400 fees &c pd D. D.)

Wm Linn Assee of Peter Helderbrand this day claimed a preempt. of 400 Acres of land at the State price in the district of Kentucky on Acc't of the s'd Helderbrand Making an Actual settlement in the year 1778 lying on the North side of Harrods Creek adjoining Taylors land & running So. for quantity satisfactory proof being made to the Court they are of Opinion that the said Linn has a right to a preemption of 400 Acres of land to include the above location & that a Cert. issue accordingly.

(Cert issd for 400 fees &c pd D. D.)

Wm Linn Assee of John Helderbrand this day claimed a preemption of 400 Acres of land at the State price in the district of Kentucky on Acc't of the s'd Helderbrand making an Actual settlement in the year 1778 lying on the North side of Harrods Creek adjoining the Lands of the s'd Linn Assee of Peter Helderbrand on the East side & running South for quantity satisfactory proof being made to the Court they are of Opinion that the said Linn has a right to a preemption of 400 Acres of land to include the above location & that a Cert issue accordingly.

(Cert issd for 400 fees &c pd D. D.)

Wm Linn Assee of Henry Bunton this day claimed a preemption of 400 Acres of Land at the State price in the district of Kentucky on Acc't of making an Actual settlement in May 1779 lying on Harrods Creek about 2 Miles above the first forks at the Mouth of a small run on the So. side satisfactory proof being made to the Court they are of the Opinion that the s'd Linn has a right to a preemption of 400 Acres of land to include the above location & that a Certificate issue accordingly.

(Cert issd for 400 fees &c pd D. D.)

Wm Linn Assee of [31]Jno (?) Philips this day claimed a preemption of 400 Acres of Land at the State price in the district of Kentucky on Acc't of the s'd Philips making an Actual settlement in the Month of May 1779 lying on Harrods Creek adjoining Linn Assee of Bunton on the South side Satisfactory proof being made to the Court. They are of Opinion that the s'd Linn has a right to a preemption of 400 Acres of land to include the above location & that a Cert issue accordingly.

(Cert issd for 400 fees &c pd D. D.)

James Linn by Wm Linn this day claimed a preempt of 400 Acres of land in the district of Kentucky at the State price on Acc't of Making an Actual Settlement in the Month of May 1779 lying on the Waters of Harrods Creek adjoining the Lands of Wm Lynn Assee of David Helderbrand satisfactory proof being made to the Court they are of Opinion that the s'd Linn has a right to a preemption of 400 Acres of land to include the above location & that a Cert issue accordingly.

[31] Collins, Vol. 2, p. 435.

(Cert issd for 1000 fees &c pd D. D.)
Charles Howard by Wm Lynn this day claimed a preempt'n of 1000 Acres at the State price in the district of Kentucky on Acc't of marking & improving the same in the year 1777 lying on the Ohio river at the Mouth of a Small Creek about 6 Miles below the Mouth of the Big Maamia River on the So. side of the said Ohio river satisfactory proof being made to the Court they are of Opinion that the s'd Howard has a right to a preempt of 1000 Acres of Land to include the above Location & that a Cert. issue accordingly.

(Cert issd for 1000 fees &c pd D. D.)
Francis Cunningham by Wm Linn this day claimed a preempt'n of 1000 Acres of land at the State price in the district of Kentucky on Acc't of marking & improving the same in the year 1777 lying on the South side of the river adjoining the Lands of Charles Howard above at 2 Miles above the Mouth of Stony Creek satisfactory proof being made to the Court they are of the Opinion that the s'd Cunningham has a right to a preemption of 1000 Acres of land to include the above location & that a Cert. issue accordingly.

(Cert issd for 1000 fees &c pd D. D.)
Wm Philips by Wm Lynn this day claimed a preemption of 1000 Acres of Land at the State price in the district of Kentucky on Acc't of marking & improving the same in the year 1777 lying on the So. side of the Ohio about 2 Miles below the mouth of Stony Creek to include his improvement satisfactory proof being made to the Court they are of Opinion that the s'd Philips has a right to a preempt'n of 1000 Acres of land to include the above location & that a Cert issue accordingly.

(Cert issd for 1000 fees &c pd D. D.)
Thos Brazer by Wm Linn this day claimed a preemption of 1000 Acres of Land at the State price in the district of Kentucky on Acc't of Marking & improving the same in the year 1777 lying on Stoner (Stony) Creek about 2 Miles from the Mouth of waters of the Ohio to include his improvement satisfactory proof being made to the Court they are of Opinion that the s'd Brazer has a right to a preempt of 1000 Acres of land to include the above location & that a Cert. iss'e accordingly.

(Cert isse for 1000 fees &c pd D. D.)
Simon Burney by Wm Linn this day claimed a preempt of 1000 Acres of land at the State price in the district of Kentucky on Acc't of Marking & improving the same in the year 1777 lying on the Waters of Stoney Creek adjoining the Lands of Charles Howard on the N. E. to include his improvement satisfactory proof being made to the Court they are of Opinion that the said Burney has a right to a preempt of 1000 Acres of land to include the above location & that a Cert issue accordingly.

(Cert issd for 1000 fees &c pd D. D.)
Geo Every by Wm Linn this day claimed a preempt of 1000 Acres of land at the State price in the district of Kentucky on Acc't of marking & improving the same in the year 1777 lying on Stoner Creek above the land of Simon Burney to include his improvement satisfactory proof being made to the Court

they are of Opinion that the s'd Every has a right to a prempt. of 400 Acres of land to include the above location & that a Cert issue accordingly.

(Cert issd for 1000 fees &c pd D. D. to McCarty)

[32]Isaac Preechard by Thos. McCarty this day claimed a preempt of 1000 Acres of Land at the State price in the District of Kentucky on Acc't of Marking & improving the same in the year 1776 lying on the dividing ridge of the South fork of Clear Creek & Jasemin Creek to include his Cabbin & spring & a Mill seat on Jasemin Creek satisfactory proof being made to the Court they are of Opinion that the said Preechard has a right to a preemption of 1000 Acres of land to include the above location & that a Cert Iss'e accordingly.

(Cert issd for 1000 fees &c pd D. D. to McCarty)

Rich'd Swan by Thos McCarty this day claimed a preempt of 1000 Acres of land at the State price in the district of Kentucky on Acc't of marking & improving the same in the year 1778 lying on the upper forks of Pleasant run a branch of Salt River adjoining Basil Prather on the lower side to include his improvement satisfactory proof being made to the Court they are of Opinion that the s'd Swan has a right to a preempt of 1000 Acres of land to include the above location & that a Cert iss accordingly.

(Cert iss for 400 fees &c pd D. D. to McCarty)

Sam'l Martin by Thos McCarty this day claimed a preempt of 400 Acres of land at the State price in the district of Kentucky on Acc't of Making an Actual settlement in May 1779 lying on Chinath run No. branch of Floyds Fork of Salt River adjoining Rob't Galloways up the said run & down the forks for quantity satisfactory proof being made to the Court they are of Opinion that the said Martin has a right to a preempt of 400 Acres of land to include the above location & that a Cert issue accordingly.

(Cert issd for 400 fees &c pd D. D. to McCarty)

Thos McCarty Assee of Rob't Galloway this day claimed a preemption of 400 Acres of land at the state price in the district of Kentucky on Acct of Making an Actual settlement in the Month of April 1779 lying on Chineths run a No. branch of Floyds Fork of Salt River adjoining the lands of James Asturgus down the said run &c Sam'l Martin up the said run satisfactory proof being made to the Court they are of Opinion that the s'd McCarty has a right to a preempt of 400 Acres of land to include the above Location & that a Cert issue accordingly.

(Cert issd for 400 fees &c pd D. D. to McCarty)

Thos Owens by Thos McCarty this day claimed a preempt of 400 Acres of land at the State price in the district of Kentucky on Acc't of making an Actual settlement in the Month of April 1779 lying on the North side of Floyds fork on the head of the East fork of Cheneths run satisfactory proof being made to the Court they are of Opinion

[32] (Pritchard) Collins, Vol. 2, p. 511.

that the s'd Owens has a right to a pre-empt'n of 400 Acres of land to include the above location & that a Cert issue accordingly.

(Cert iss for 400 fees &c pd to McCarty)
Thos Hargess by Thos. McCarty this day claimed a preemption of 400 Acres of land at the State price in the district of Kentucky on Acc't of making an Actual settlement in the Month of April 1779 lying about 5 Miles from the Mouth of Salt River & Three or 4 Miles from the Ohio Known by the Name of the Walnut Bottom—Satisfactory proof being made to the Court they are of Opinion that the said Hargess has a right to a preemption of 400 Acres of land to include the above location & that a Cert isse accordingly.—

(Cert issd for 400 fees &c pd To McCarty)
John Venson by Thos McCarty this day claimed a preempt of 400 Acres of land at the State price in the district of Kentucky on Acc't Making an Actual settlement in the Month of April 1779 lying on Floyds fork of Salt river on a small run on the E. side to include his improvement satisfactory proof being made to the Court they are of Opinion that the s'd Venson has a right to a preempt of 400 Acres of land to include the above location & that a Cert issue accordingly.

(Cert issd for 400 fees &c pd D. D. to McCarty)
Jno Nicholas by Thos. McCarty this day claimed a preempt of 400 Acres of land at the State in the district of Kentucky on Acc't of Making an Actual settlement in the Month of April 1779 lying on Chineath run about ½ a Mile below the fork on both sides of the s'd run to include his improvement satisfactory proof being made to the Court they are of Opinion that the s'd Nicholas has a right to a preemption of 400 Acres of land to include the above location & that a Cert issue accordingly.

(Cert issd for 1400 fees &c pd D. D. to Wm Lynn)
The Heir of [33]Silas Train dec'd this day claimed a settlement preemption to a tract of land (by Wm Linn) in the district of Kentucky on Acc't of the s'd dec'd raising a Crop of Corn in the Country in the year 1775 lying on Hingstons Mill Seat Creek about 3 Miles from Riddles Station on a Buffaloe path to include his improvement satisfactory proof being made to the Court they are of Opinion that the s'd Heir &c has a right to a settlem't of 400 acres of land to Include the above location & the preempt of 1000 Acres adjoining & that a Cert issue accordingly.

Then the Court adjourned untill tomorrow 9 Oclock—

Wm Fleming

At a Court Contin'd & held at Harrodsburg this 10 day of Feb'y 1780 For adjusting Titles to unpatentted Lands by the Commissioners of Kentucky district

Present

Wm Fleming Steph'n Trigg Edm'd Lyne—Gent.

[33] Collins, Vol. 2, p. 325.

(Cert issd for 1000 fees &c pd D. D. to Izbarn (?) Sprigg)

James Cruck by Peter Asturgus this day claimed a preemption of 1000 Acres of Land at the State price in the district of Kentucky on Acc't of Mark'g & improving the same in the year 1776 lying on Fox run a branch of Brashiers Creek to include his improvement satisfactory proof being made to the Court they are of Opinion that the s'd Cruck has a right to a preemption of 1000 Acres of land to include the s'd improvement & that a Cert iss accordingly.

(Cert issd for 1000 fees &c pd D. D.)

[34]Elias Tolin by [35]Thos. Clark this day claimed a preempt of 1000 Acres of land at the state price in the district of Kentucky on Acc't of Marking & improving the same in the year 1775 lying on the No. Branch of the Middle fork of Hingstons fork of licking Creek about ¾ of a mile above a Lick on the So. W. side of the s'd branch adjoining the lands of John Soverains to include his improvement satisfactory proof being made to the Court they are of the Opinion that the s'd Tolin has a right to a preempt of 1000 Acres to include the said improvement & that a Cert issue accordingly.

(Cert issd for 400 fees &c pd D. D.)

Wm Scott this day claimed a preemption of 400 Acres of land at the state price in the District of Kentucky on Acc't of Making & Actual settlement in the year 1778 lying on the Water of licking Creek upon a branch that runs into flat Creek about 1 Mile above where a Buffaloe road leaves the s'd Creek on the East side of the s'd Creek & about 10 Miles above the upper Blue licks Satisfactory proof being made to the Court they are of Opinion that the s'd Scott has a right to a preemption of 400 Acres of land to include the Above location & that a Cert issue accordingly.

(Cert issd for 400 fees &c pd D. D.)

[36]Paul Froman by Jacob Myers this day claimed a preempt of 400 Acres of land at the State price in the District of Kentucky on Acc't of Making an Actual settlem't in the Month of May 1779 lying on Fromans Creek a branch of Chaplin fork of Salt River about 20 Miles above Bulletts Salt Lick to include his improvement satisfactory proof being made to the Court they are of Opinion that the s'd Froman has a right to a preemption of 400 Acres of land to include the above location & that a Cert issue accordingly.

(Cert issd for 1000 fees &c pd D. D.)

James Rogers by Jacob Myers this day claimed a preempt of 1000 Acres of land at the State price in the district of Kentucky on Acc't of Marking & improving the same in the year 1775 lying on the No. side of the Rowling Fork of Salt River between & near the head of the Bearches (?) Wh'ch heads Near 2 a large Deer lick the branch running South into the s'd Rolling fork satisfactory proof being made to the Court they are of Opinion that the s'd Rogers has a right to a preempt of 1000 Acres of land to include the—

[34] Collins, Vol. 2, p. 47.
[35] Collins, Vol. 2, pp. 47, 551.

[36] Collins, Vol. 2, p. 183.

(Cert issd for 400 fees &c pd D. D.)

Jonathan Rogers by Jacob Myers this day claimed a preempt of 400 Acres of land at the State price in the district of Kentucky on Account of Making an Actual settlem't in the Month of May 1779 lying on a Creek that runs into Green River & about 3 Miles West of Hardens settlement to include his improvement satisfactory proof being made to the Court they are of Opinion that the s'd Rogers has a right to a preempt of 400 Acres to include the above location & that a Cert. issue accordingly.

(Cert issd for 1000 fees &c pd D. D. to Capt. Owens)

[37]Joseph Waller Assee of [38]Charles Lecompt this day claimed a preempt of 1000 Acres of land at the State price in the district of Kentucky on Acc't of the s'd Lecompts Marking & improving the same in the year 1775 lying on the North fork of Elkhorn Creek on the North side thereof on a Small branch on the Buffaloe road about 6 Miles from where the Buffaloe road Crosses the s'd No. fork of Elkhorn Creek to include his improvement satisfactory proof being made to the Court they are of Opinion that the s'd Wallen has a right to a preemption of 1000 Acres of land to include the s'd improvement & that a Cert iss'e accordingly.

(Cert issd for 400 fees &c pd D. D.)

Philip Taylor by Jno. Cocky Owens this day claimed a preempt of 400 Acres of land at the State price in the district of Kentucky on Acc't of Making an Actual settlement in the Month of May 1779.—lying on the left hand branch of Hammonds Creek a branch of Salt River & about 5 Miles from the Mouth of s'd Creek adjoining the Lands of John Asturgus below satisfactory proof being made to the Court they are of Opinion that the s'd Taylor has a right to a preempt. of 400 Acres to include the above location & that a Cert iss Accordingly.

(Cert issd for 400 fees &c pd D. D.)

Ben'j Taylor by John Cocky Owens this day claimed a preempt'n of 400 Acres of land at the State price in the District of Kentucky on Acc't of Making an Actual settlement in the Month of May 1778 lying on the left hand fork of Hammonds Creek a branch of Salt River adjoining the lands of Philip Taylor below satisfactory proof being made to the Court they are of Opinion that the s'd Taylor has a right to a preemption of 400 Acres of land to include the above location & that a Cert. issue accordingly.

(Cert issd for 400 fees &c pd D. D.)

[39]Benj'n Price by John Cocky Owens this day claimed a preempt of 400 Acres of land at the State price in the District of Kentucky on Acc't of Making an Actual settlement in the year 1778 lying on the Rolling Fork of Salt River about Six Miles below Sam'l Pottengers Cabbin at the Mouth of a Creek to include his improvement satisfactory proof being made to the Court they are of Opinion that the s'd Price has a right to a preempt'n of 400 Acres of land to in-

[37] Collins, Vol. 2, p. 172.
[38] Collins, Vol. 2, pp. 176, 549, 698.
[39] Collins, Vol. 2, p. 367.

clude the above location & that a Cert. issue accordingly.

(Cert issd for 1000 fees &c pd D. D.)

John Sicks by Sam'l Brown this day claimed a preempt of 1000 Acres of land at the State price in the district of Kentucky on Acc't of Marking & improving the same in the year 1776 lying on the Waters of licking Creek near a large Mud lick adjoining the Mountains to include his improvement satisfactory proof being made to the Court they are of Opinion that the s'd Sicks has a right to a preemption of 1000 Acres of land to include the above location & that a Cert. issue accordingly.

(Cert issd for 1000 fees &c pd D. D.)

Lewis Bunnett this day by Sam'l Brown claimed a preempt of 1000 Acres of Land at the State price in the district of Kentucky on Acc't of Marking & improving the same in the year 1776 lying on the waters of licking Creek about 3 Miles West of a large Mud Lick on a Buffaloe road leading to the s'd Lick to include his improvement satisfactory proof being made to the Court they are of Opinion that the s'd Bunnett has a right to a preemption of 1000 Acres of land to include the s'd improvement & that a Cert issue accordingly.

(Cert issd for 1000)

Rich'd Burk for & on behalf of John Miller Moves to remove a location of the s'd Millers which was granted the 4th day of Feb'y it appearing to the Court that there is sufficient cause for a removal it is Granted him & now locates the same on the So. E't side of Fox run a branch of Breashears Creek adjoining the Lands of Evin Hinton & that a Cert. issue accordingly.

(Cert issd for 1400 fees &c pd D. D.)

The right of settlement & preempt'n which [40]Hugh McGary obtained the 19th day of Oct'r 1779 as Assee of Ralph Williams being detained untill the last Day of the setting of this Court appeared to the Court from a Conveyance of the s'd Right from the s'd Williams to Rich'd Henderson to be Vestified in the s'd Henderson therefore it is ordered that the s'd McGary &c Claim be set aside the s'd Rich'd Henderson Assee of Ralph Williams Now claims a right to a settlement & preempt'n to a tract of land in the district of Kentucky on Acc't of the s'd Williams raising a crop of Corn in the Country in the year 1775 lying on Otter Creek Adjoining the land of the s'd Henderson claimed in his own Name So. Eastwardly satisfactory proof being made to the Court they are of Opinion that the said Henderson has a right to a settlement of 400 Acres of land to include the above location & the preempt of 1000 Acres adjoining & that a Cert. issue accordingly.

(Cert issd for 400 fees &c pd D. D. to Jos. Brown)

Sam'l Ozburns this day claimed a preemption of 400 Acres of land at the State price in the district of Kentucky On Acc't of Making an Actual settlem't in the Month of May 1779 lying on a branch on the No. side of Second Creek above the Mouth of Green River to include his improvement satis-

[40] Collins, Vol. 2, p. 368 and index.

factory proof being made to the Court they are of Opinion that the s'd Ozburns has a right to a preempt of 400 Acres of land to include the above Location & that a Cert. issue accordingly.

(Cert issd for 1000 fees &c pd D. D.)

John Baker Assee of And'w Camlick this day claimed a preempt'n of 1000 Acres of land at the State price in the district of Kentucky on Acc't of the s'd Camlick Marking & improving the same in the year 1776 lying on A Creek emptying into Salt River on the So. side thereof about 10 Miles above the Fall of the s'd River & about 5 or 6 Miles above the Mouth of the s'd Creek to include his improvement satisfactory proof being made to the Court they are of Opinion that the s'd Baker &c has a right to a preempt'n of 1000 Acres of Land to include s'd improvement & that a Cert. issue accordingly.

(Cert issd for 1000 fees &c pd D. D.)

John Baker Assee of Francis Kamlick this day claimed a preempt'n of 1000 Acres of Land at the State price in the district of Kentucky On Acc't of the s'd Kamlick Mark'g & improving the same in the year 1776 lying on a Creek emptying into Salt River on the South side thereof about 10 Miles above the falls of s'd river adjoining the Lands of Baker Assee of Andrew Kimlick to include his improv't satisfactory proof being made to the Court they are of Opinion that the s'd Baker has a right to a preempt'n of 1000 Acres of land to include the above location & that a Cert. issue accordingly.

(Cert issd for 400 fees &c pd D. D.)

Adam Pain by Wm Aldridge this day claimed a preempt of 400 Acres of Land at the State price in the district of Kentucky On Acc't of Making an Actual settlement in the Month of May 1779. lying on a Small Branch of Bull Creek a branch of Breasheirs Creek on the West side thereof about 6 Miles from the forks of the s'd Creek & running West for quantity to include his improv't satisfactory proof being made to the Court they are of Opinion that the s'd Pain has a right to a preemption of 400 Acres of Land to include the s'd improv't & that a Cert. issue accordingly.

EDITOR'S NOTE

The next entry in the book is evidently under date of April 18th 1780 as an adjournment order "untill tomorrow Morning 9 Oclock" following about fifteen or sixteen entries is immediately followed by a "Court continued and held" order under date of the 19th of April, 1780. About 90 pages further along in the book appear to be the remainder of the entries made under date of February 10th, 1780, date under which last entry above was made. We are therefore running next in order remainder of entries under date of February 10th and following through to an adjournment of the Court on February 26, 1780. As will be seen when this adjournment order is reached the Court considered that it was adjourning sine die. Entries made in the book under dates in April later on appear to have been made at a subsequent session of the Court and another "final adjournment" was made on April 26, 1780. At the page in the book where the remainder of the entries under February 10th are made the book begins with a heading as set out below.

BOOK NO. 2

(Cert issd for 400 D. D.)

Wm Adridge this day claimed a preempt'n of 400 Acres of land at the State price in the district of Kentucky on Acc't of making an Actual settlement in may 1779 lying on the South fork of Breasheirs Creek about 4 Miles above the forks to include his improvement Satisfactory proof being made to the Court they are of Opinion that the s'd Adridge has a right to a preemption of 400 Acres of Land to include the above location & that A Cert. issue accordingly.

(Cert for 400)

Jno Cocky Owens Assee of Jos'e Brown this day claimed a preemption of 400 Acres of Land at the State price in the District of Kentucky On Acc't of making an Actual settlement in April 1779 Lying on wolf Creek about 3 or 4 Miles from the Mouth, waters of the Ohio about 70 Miles below the falls including a large Spring on the West side of the s'd Creek satisfactory proof being made to the Court they are of Opinion that the s'd Owens has a right to a preemption of 400 Acres of Land to include the above location & that a Cert. issue accordingly.

(Cert issd for 400)

James Stewart this day claimed a preempt'n of 400 Acres of Land at the State price in the district of Kentucky on Acc't of Making & Actual settlem't in April 1779 lying on the waters of Salt River adjoining the Lands of Jas Stewart on the South west to include a large Spring satisfactory proof being made to the Court they are of Opinion that the s'd Stewart has a right to a preempt'n of 400 Acres of Land to include the above location & that a Cert. issue accordingly.

(Cert issd for 1000)

The Heirs of Joshua Hughes by [41]Wm Shepherd Adm'r to the Deceased this day claimed a preempt'n of 1000 Acres of Land at the State price in the district of Kentucky on Acc't of the s'd Decedents marking & improving the same in the year 1776 lying on the head of a small branch that runs into flat Creek where a large Buffaloe road leaves the s'd Creek waters of Licking Creek to include the improvement satisfactory proof being made to the Court they are of Opinion that the s'd Heirs &c has a right to a preemption of 1000 Acres of Land to include the above location & that a Cert issue accordingly.—

(Cert issd for 1000)

Jno Whiteledge by [42]Thomas Whiteledge this day claimed a preempt'n of 1000 Acres of Land at the State price in the District of Kentucky on Acc't of marking & improving the same in the year 1776 lying near the head of a small branch of the south fork of licking Creek on a plan marked and improved for Nich's & Pressly Anderson satisfactory

[41] Collins, Vol. 2, p. 511.
[42] Collins, Vol. 2, pp. 70, 327.

proof being made to the Court they are of Opinion that the s'd Whiteledge has a right to a preempt'n of 1000 Acres of Land to include the above location & that a Certificate issue accordingly.

(Cert issd for 400)
Jeremiah Stark by [43]Wm Calk this day claimed a preempt'n of 400 Acres of Land at the State price in the district of Kentucky on Acc't of making an Actual settlement in April 1779 lying on the East fork of Howards upper Creek to include his improvement satisfactory proof being made to the Court they are of Opinion that the s'd Stark has a right to a preempt'n of 400 Acres of Land to include the above location & that a Cert. issue accordingly.

Jeremiah Spiller by Wm Calk this day claimed a preempt'n of 400 Acres of Land in the district of Kentucky Rejected.—

(Cert issd for 400)
Jno Leright by Wm Calk this day claimed a preempt'n of 400 Acres of Land at the State price in the district of Kentucky on Acc't of making an Actual settlem't in April 1779 lying near the head of a Branch on the So. fork of Licking Creek above the Lands of Jno Whiteledge to include his improvm't Made for Lewis Runoe at a small Spring satisfactory proof being made to the Court they are of Opinion that the s'd Leright has a right to a settlem't of 400 Acres to include the above location & that a Cert. issue accordingly.

(Cert issd for 400)
Spencer Reed by Wm Calk this day claimed a preempt'n of 400 Acres of Land at the State price in the district of Kentucky On Acc't of Making an Actual settlement in April 1779 lying on the Waters of licking Creek to include his improvement Satisfactory proof being made to the Court they are of Opinion that the s'd Reed has a right to a preempt of 400 Acres of Land to include the above & that a Cert issue accordingly.

Then the Court adjourned untill tomorrow Morning 9 Oclock
Wm Fleming

At a Court Cont'd & held by the Commissioners of the Kentucky District for adjusting Titles to unpattented lands at Harrodsburg the 11 day of Feb'y 1780—
Present
Wm Fleming Step'n Trigg & Edmund Lyne—Gen

(Cert issd for 1000)
Anthony Sodusky by [44]Jacob Sodusky this day claimed a preempt'n of 1000 Acres of Land at the State price in the District of Kentucky on Acc't of marking and improving the same in the year 1776 lying on the East fork of Jessemine Creek adjoining the Lands of Jacob Sodusky No. Easterly Satisfactory proof being made to the Court they are of Opinion that the s'd Sodusky has a right to a preemption of 1000 Acres of Land to include the above Location & that a Cert issue accordingly.

(Cert issd for 1400)
[45]Edw'd Bulger this day claimed a

[43] Collins, Vol. 2, pp. 47, 516, 633.

[44] Collins, Vol. 2, p. 467.
[45] Collins, Vol. 2, p. 624 and index.

settlement & preemption to a tract of Land in the District of Kentucky on Acc't of raising Corn in the Country in the years 1775 & 1776 lying on Harrods run below the Lands of Thomas Quirk to include his improvem't Satisfactory proof being made to the Court they are of Opinion that the s'd Bulger has a right to a settlement of 400 Acres of Land to include the above location & the preempt of 1000 Acres adjoining & that a Cert. issue accordingly.

(Cert issd for 1400)

Abraham James this day claimed a settlement & preemption of a tract of land in the District of Kentucky on Acc't of raising a Crop of Corn in the Country in the year 1776 lying on the West branch of the hanging fork of Dicks River about 3 Miles North Easterly from Gordens Lick to include his improvm't satisfactory proof being made to the Court they are of Opinion that the s'd James has a right to a settlem't of 400 Acres of Land to include the above Location & the preempt'n of 1000 Acres adjoining and that a Cert issue accordingly.—

(Cert issd for 1000)

Jos'h James by Edw'd Bulger this day claimed a preempt'n of 1000 Acres of Land at the State price in the Districk of Kentucky on Acc't of marking & improving the same in the year 1776 lying on a branch of the hanging fork of Dicks River about 3½ Miles from the Knobb Lick adjoining the land of the Heirs of Burr Harrison deceased & Isaac Shelby to include his improvem't satisfactory proof being made to the Court they are of Opinion that the s'd James has a right to a preempt of 1000 Acres of Land to include the above Location & that a Cert. issue Accordingly.

(Cert issd for 1000)

Dan'l Bulger by Edw'd Bulger this day claimed a preempt'n of 1000 Acres of Land at the State price in the district of Kentucky on Acc't of marking & improving the same in the year 1776, lying on a branch of the Hanging fork of Dicks River including a Lick known by the name of Bulgers Lick, to include his improvement, satisfactory proof being made to the Court they are of Opinion that the s'd Bulger has a right to a preempt of 1000 Acres of land to include the above Location & that a Cert. issue accordingly.

(Cert issd for 400)

[46]Wm Holdman by Edw'd Bulger this day claimed a preempt'n of 400 Acres of Land at the State price in the District of Kentucky on Acc't of mark'g & improving the same in the year 1776 & making an Actual settlem't in May 1779 Lying about 7 Miles south of the Fall of Ohio above the Trace on the East side that leads to Bullett Lick to include his improvement satisfactory proof being made to the Court they are of Opinion that the s'd Oldham has a right to a preempt. of 400 Acres to include the above Location & that a Cert. issue accordingly.

(Cert issd for 1000)

Abraham Miller by Edw'd Bulger

[46] (Oldham) Collins, Vol. 2, p. 367 and index.

this day claimed a preempt'n of 1000 Acres of Land at the State price in the District of Kentucky on Acc't of marking & improving the same in the year 1775 lying on the West side of the Hanging fork of Dicks River above the Trace Leading from this place to St. Asaphs & above ¾ of Mile of the forks of s'd Creek to include his improvem't satisfactory proof being made to the Court they are of Opinion that the s'd Miller has a right to a preempt'n of 1000 Acres of Land to include the above location & that a Cert. issue accordingly.—

(Cert issd for 1400)

Henry Scaggs this day claimed a settlem't & preempt'n to a tract of Land in the District of Kentucky On Acc't of raising Corn in the Country in the year 1775 lying on the North side of Green River near to a Creek that runs into the s'd river about 7 or 8 Miles above the Elk Lick satisfactory proof being made to the Court they are of Opinion that the s'd Scaggs has a right to a settlem't of 400 Acres of land to include the above Location & the preempt'n of 1000 Acres of Land adjoining & that a Cert issue accordingly.

(Cert issd for 1400)

Hugh McGary Assee of Jos'h Robertson this day claimed a settlem't & preemption to a tract of land in the District of Kentucky on Acc't of raising a crop of Corn in the Country in the year 1775 lying about 27 miles south from the Locust Bent, on a branch of Silver Creek including a honey Locust flat also a small Buffaloe Lick on the s'd branch satisfactory proof being made to the Court they are of Opinion that the s'd McGary has a right to a settlement of 400 acres of Land to include the above Location & the preempt'n of 1000 Acres adjoining & that a Cert. issue accordingly.—

It appearing to the Court that Samuel Givens & Jacob Poplan Located their rights on the same piece of Land ordered that they be summoned to Appear before this Court for a rehearing—

(Cert issd for 1000)

Jno Jones this day claimed a preempt'n of 1000 Acres of Land at the State price in the District of Kentucky on Acc't of mark'g & improving the same in the year 1776, lying on a flat branch on the North fork of the South fork of Licking Creek about 2 Miles West of the trace from the Lower Blue Licks to Boonsborough to include his improvem't satisfactory proof being made to the Court they are are of Opinion that the s'd Jones has a right to a preempt'n of 1000 Acres of Land to include the above location & that a Cert. issue accordingly.

(Cert issd for 1000)

Garret Bolen by Jno Jones this day claimed a preempt'n of 1000 Acres of Land at the State price in the district of Kentucky on Acc't of mark'g & improving the same in the year 1776 lying on the east side of the Upper road leading to Cabbin Creek on the Lick fork of Licking Creek to include his improvement satisfactory proof being made to the Court they are of Opinion that the s'd Bolen has a right to a preempt'n of 1000 Acres of Land to include the above Location & that a Certificate issue accordingly.—

(Cert issd for 1400)

[47]Jno Williams Jun'r Assee of Patrick Wall (Wull?) this day claimed a settlement & preempt'n to a tract of Land in the district of Kentucky on Acc't of the s'd Wall settling in the Country in the year 1777 & residing ever since lying on both sides of Jessemine Creek joining Innis Daugherty land on the lower line to extend eastward & down the Creek for Quantity satisfactory proof being made to the Court they are of Opinion that the s'd Williams has a right to a settlement of 400 Acres of Land to include the above Location & the preempt of 1000 Acres adjoining and that a Cert. issue accordingly.—

(Cert issd for 1000)

James Johnson by Andrew Johnson this day claimed a preempt'n of 1000 Acres of Land at the State price in the district of Kentucky on Acc't of mark'g & improving the same in the year 1776 lying on Cartright Creek the waters of Salt River below the Lands of [48]Dan'l Brown satisfactory proof being made to the Court they are of Opinion that the s'd Johnson has a right to a preempt 1000 Acres of Land to include the above Location & that a Cert. issue accordingly.—

(Cert issd for 1400)

Andrew Dodds this day claimed a preempt'n of 400 Acres of Land at the State price in the district of Kentucky on Acc't of making an Actual settlement in May 1779 lying on the forks of givens Creek a branch of Dicks River to include his improvement Satisfactory proof being made to the Court they are of Opinion that the s'd Dodds has a right to a preemption of 400 Acres of Land to include the above location & that a Cert. iss'e accordingly.

(Cert isd for 1000)

Jno Muldrough this day claimed a preempt of 1000 Acres of Land at the State price in the District of Kentucky on Acc't of marking & improving the same in the year 1776 lying on both sides of the Rowling fork of Salt River about 6 Miles below the Shawnee Lick, running up & down the s'd River for quantity to include his improvem't satisfactory proof being made to the Court they are of Opinion that the s'd Muldrough has a right to a preempt'n of 1000 Acres of Land to include the s'd improvement & that a Cert. issue accordingly.—

(Cert issd for 1000)

Hugh Mildrough Assee of Samuel McMurry this day claimed a preempt'n to a tract of Land at the State price in the district of Kentucky on Acc't of the s'd McMurrys Marking & Improving the s'd Land in the year 1776 lying on both sides of the Rolling fork of Salt River about 1½ Mile from the Shawnee Lick to include the s'd McMurrys improvem't satisfactory proof being made to the Court they are of Opinion that the s'd Mildrough &c has a right to a

[47] Collins, Vol. 2, p. 172.
[48] Collins, Vol. 2, p. 552.

preempt'n of 1000 Acres of Land to include the above location & that a Cert. issue accordingly.

(Cert issd for 1000)

Hugh Malborough this day claimed a preempt'n of 1000 Acres of Land at the State price in the district of Kentucky on Acc't of Marking & improving the same in the year 1776 lying on a branch of the town fork of Salt River about 15 Miles from McCowns Station including a Small Buffaloe Lick & his improvement satisfactory proof being made to the Court they are of Opinion that the s'd Malborough has a right to a preemption of 1000 Acres of Land to include the above Location & that a Cert. issue accordingly.—

(Cert issd for 1000)

John Simpson this day claimed a preemption of 1000 Acres of Land at the State price in the District of Kentucky on Acc't of marking & improving the same in the year 1776 lying on a branch of the Rolling fork of Salt River that runs in on the South side adjoining the Land of Solomon & Jno Lawrence to include his improvement satisfactory proof being made to the Court they are of Opinion that the s'd Simpson has a right to a preempt'n of 1000 Acres of Land to include the above Location & that a Cert. issue accordingly.—

(Cert issd for 1000)

Thomas Simpson by Jno Malborough this day claimed a preempt'n of 1000 Acres of Land at the State price in the District of Kentucky on Acc't of marking & improving the same in the year 1776 lying on a branch of the Town fork of Salt River adjoining the Lands of Hugh Malborough on the South East to include his improvement satisfactory proof being made to the Court they are of Opinion that the s'd Simpson has a right to a preempt'n of 1000 Acres of Land to include the above location & that a Cert. issue accordingly.

(Cert issd for 1000)

John McMurry by Jno Mildrough this day claimed a preemption of 1000 Acres of Land at the State price in the district of Kentucky on Acc't of Marking & improving the same in the year 1776 lying on the South side of the South fork of the Rolling fork of Salt River adjoining the Land of John Lawrence & Jno Simpson to include his improvement satisfactory proof being made to the Court they are of Opinion that the s'd McMurry has a right to a preempt'n of 1000 Acres of Land to include the above Location & that a Cert. issue accordingly—

(Cert issd for 1000)

Alex'r Black this day claimed a preemption of 1000 Acres of Land at the State price in the district of Kentucky on Acc't of Marking & improving the same in the year 1776 lying on both sides of the Rolling fork of Salt River near where the hunters trace crosses satisfactory proof being made to the Court they are of Opinion that the s'd Black has a right to a preemption of 1000 Acres of Land to include the above location & that a Cert. issue accordingly.—

(Cert issd for 1000)

Willi'm Black by Alex'r Black this day claimed a preempt'n of 1000 Acres of Land at the State price in the District of Kentucky on Acc't of Marking & improving the same in the year 1776 lying on a branch of the Town fork of Salt River adjoining the lands of Thomas Simpson on the North side and above the Lands of Hugh Malborough to include his improvement satisfactory proof being made to the Court they are of Opinion that the s'd Black has a right to a preemption of 1000 Acres of Land to include the above location & that a Cert. issue accordingly.—

(Cert issd for 1400)

Adam Hite by Isaac Hite this day claimed a settlem't of 400 Acres & a preempt'n of 1000 Acres of Land at the State price in the district of Kentucky on acc't of marking and improving the same in the year 1776 & raising a crop of Corn in the Country lying on the head of the North fork of Goose Creek a branch of the Ohio to include a Spring known by the name of Cove spring satisfactory proof being made to the Court they are of Opinion that the said Hite has a right to a settlem't of 400 Acres of Land to include the above location & the preempt'n of 1000 Acres of Land adjoining & that a Cert. issue accordingly.—

(Cert issd for 1400)

[49]Abraham Hite Jun'r by Isaac Hite this day claimed a settlem't & preempt'n to a tract of Land in the District of Kentucky on Acc't of raising a crop of Corn in the Country in the year 1774 lying on goose Creek below the Land of Abraham Hite Sen'r to include 2 improvem't one on the said Creek & the other about 1 Mile North of the same satisfactory proof being made to the Court they are of Opinion that the s'd Hite has a right to a settlem't of 400 Acres of Land to include the above Location & the preemption of 1000 of Land adjoining & that a Cert. issue accordingly.

(Cert issd for 1400)

Joseph Hite by Isaac Hite this day claimed a settlem't & preemption to a tract of Land in the District of Kentucky on Acc't of Marking & improving the same & raising a crop of Corn in the Country in the year 1774 Lying on the waters of Howards Creek on the south side thereof about 2½ Miles from the Mouth of Harrods Creek Near &c adjoining the Lands of abraham Bowman satisfactory proof being made to the Court they are of Opinion that the s'd Hite has a right to a Settlem't of 400 Acres of Land to include the above Location & the preemption of 1000 Acres adjoining & that a Cert. issue accordingly.—

(Cert issd for 1400)

Peter Hogg this day claimed a settlem't & preempt'n of a tract of Land in the District of Kentucky on Acc't of raising a crop of Corn in the Country in the year of 1776 lying on the South side of Kentucky River adjoining the lower line of the Land of Drenings Lick survey and to extend back for Quantity satisfactory proof being made

[49] Collins, Vol. 2, p. 367 and index.

to the Court they are of Opinion that the s'd Hogg has a right to a settlement of 400 Acres of land to include the above Location & the preempt of 1000 Acres adjoining & that a Cert. issue accordingly.—

Then the Court adjourned untill to-morrow 9 Oclock

Wm Fleming

At a Court continued and held by the commissioners of the Kentucky for adjusting titles to unpatented Lands at Harrodsburgh this 12th day of Feb'y 1780.

Present

Wm Fleming Stephen Trigg & Edmund Lyne—

Abraham Price this day claimed a settlement & preempt'n to a tract of Land in the District of Kentucky on Acc't of raising a crop of Corn in the Country in the year 1776 on the Bigg Meadow on cumberland River on the South side of s'd River whereon the s'd Price now lives it appearing to the Court from the evidence offered that the s'd Price raised Corn in that part of the Country reserved for the Use of the Army and having made no settlement or improvm't in any other part of the Country they are of Opinion as the Law has made no provision for persons in that situation that they are not authorised to grant a Cert. for the same.—

Benj. Moses, Aron, & Sam'l Price this day claimed a settlement & preemp'n to a tract of Land in the District of Kentucky on Acc't of raising a crop of Corn in the Big Meadow on Cumberland River on the South side thereof in the year 1775 & 1776 it being a Land whereon they now live It appearing to the Court from the Evidence offered that the s'd Benj. Moses, Aron & Sam'l Price raised the corn in that part of the Country reserved for the use of the Army & having made no settlem't or improvment in any other part of the Country they are of Opinion as the Law has made no provision for persons in that situation that they are not Authorized to grant Certificates for the same.

(Cert issd for 1000)

William Davis this day claimed a preempt'n of 1000 Acres of Land at the State price in the District of Kentucky on Acc't of marking & improving the same in the year 1776 lying on the North side of Dicks River adjoining the Lands of David Finley & Azeil Davis to include his improvement satisfactory proof being made to the Court they are of Opinion that the s'd Davis has a right to a preempt'n of 1000 Acres of Land to include the above improvment & that a Cert issue accordingly.

(Cert issd for 1400)

Isaac Hite this day claimed a settlem't & preemption to a tract of Land in the District of Kentucky on Acc't of making an Actual settlement on the premises in the year 1774 & residing in the Country 12 Months before the year 1778 lying on the Town Fork of Salt River on the East side thereof to include a small spring & his improvement known by the name of the fountain Bleaw & also a spring on the West side of the Cainbreak East from the s'd improvt satisfactory proof being made to the Court they are of Opinion that the s'd Hite has a right to a settlement of 400 Acres of Land to include the above Location & the preempt'n of 1000 Acres of Land adjoining & that a Cert. issue accordingly.—

(Cert issd for 400)

Jno Curry this day claimed a preempt'n of 400 Acres of Land at the State price in the district of Kentucky on Acc't of making an Actual settlement in March 1779 lying on both sides of Salt River adjoining the Lands of [50]Sam'l Adams below & [51]Wm McAfee above to include his improvem't satisfactory proof being made to the Court they are of Opinion that the s'd Curry has a right to a preemption of 1000 Acres include the s'd improvement & that a Cert. issue accordingly.

(Cert issd for 1400)

Jno Shanklin by Rich'd Shanklin this day claimed a settlem't & preempt'n to a tract of Land in the district of Kentucky on Acc't of raising a Crop of Corn in the Country in the year 1776 on the waters of Floyds fork of Salt River on the West side thereof about 3 or four Miles from Bulletts Lick & about 1 Mile East from the road leading from Beargrass to the s'd Lick to include his improvement satisfactory proof being made to the Court they are of Opinion that the s'd Shanklin has a right to a Settlem't of 400 Acres of Lands to include the above location & the preempt of 1000 Acres adjoining & that a Cert. issue accordingly.—

(Cert issd for 1400)

Gower Soverns this day claimed a settlem't & preemption to a tract of Land in the district of Kentucky on Acc't of residing 12 Months in the Country before the year 1778 lying on the South side of the Beech fork of Salt River to include the Cedar Spring and back for quantity satisfactory proof being made to the Court they are of Opinion that the s'd Soverns has a right to a settlement of 400 Acres of Land to include the above Location & the preempt'n of 1000 Acres adjoining & that a Cert. issue accordingly.—

(Cert issd for 1400)

The Heirs of [52]Eli Gerrard (Garrard) by Benj'n Linn this day claimed a settlem't & preemption to a tract of Land in the district of Kentucky on Acc't of residing 12 Months in the Country before the year 1778 lying on the South side of the Rolling fork of Salt River about 5 Miles below the Mouth of Pottengers Creek to include a large Cain bottom & to extend up for Quantity satisfactory proof being made to the Court they are of Opinion that the said Heirs &c has a right to a settlement of 400 Acres of Land to include the above Location & the preemption of 1000 Acres adjoining & that a Cert. issue accordingly.—

(Cert issd for 400)

Benham Shaw by Isaac Hite this day claimed a preemption of 400 Acres of

[50] Collins, Vol. 2, p. 53 and index.
[51] Collins, Vol. 2, pp. 475, 519.
[52] Collins, Vol. 2, p. 616.

Land at the State price in the district of Kentucky on Acc't of Making an Actual Settlem't in May 1779 lying on the Rolling fork of Salt River adjoining the upper Line of the Land of the heirs of Eli Gerrard dec'd to extend up for quantity satisfactory proof being made to the Court they are of Opinion that s'd Shaw has a right to a preempt'n of 400 Acres of Land to include the above location & that a Cert. issue accordingly.

(Cert issd for 1000)

Joseph Read this day claimed a preempt'n of 1000 Acres of Land at the State price in the District of Kentucky on Acc't of Marking & improving the same in the year 1776 lying on the South fork of the Rolling fork of Salt River about ¾ of a Mile below [53]Thomas Dentons Station Camp running down on both sides of the said fork for quantity satisfactory proof being made to the Court they are of Opinion that the s'd Reed has a right to a preempt'n of 1000 Acres of Land to include the above Location & that a Cert. issue accordingly.—

(Cert issd for 1400)

[54]Dav'd Glen by [55]William Stewart this day claimed a settlem't & preempt'n of a tract of Land in the District of Kentucky on Acc't of raising a crop of Corn in the Country in the year 1776 lying on Glens Creek known by the name of the Trough Spring to include his improvement satisfactory proof being made to the Court they are of Opinion that the s'd Glen has a right to a settlem't of 400 Acres of Land to include the above location & the preempt'n of 1000 Acres adjoining & that a Cert. issue accordingly.—

(Cert issd for 1400)

Jno Peters by Wm Stewart this day claimed a settlem't & preempt'n to a tract of Land in the district of Kentucky on Acc't of settling & residing 12 Months before the year 1778 Lying at a sinking Spring on the North side of the South fork of Elkhorn Creek 2 Miles North of the forks of the South fork satisfactory proof being made to the Court they are of Opinion that the s'd Peters has a right to a settlem't of 400 Acres of land to include the above location & the preemption of 1000 Acres adjoining & that a Cert. issue accordingly.—

(Cert issd for 1400)

Patrick Dowlan by Wm Stewart this day claimed a settlem't & preempt'n of a tract of Land in the District of Kentucky on Acc't of raising a crop of Corn in the Country in the year 1775 & 1776 lying at a sinking Spring adjoining the Lands of Henry prether on the South side on the Waters of Shawnee run to include his improvement satisfactory proof being made to the Court they are of Opinion that the s'd Doulan has a right to a settlme't of 400 Acres of Land to include the above Location & the preempt'n of 1000 Acres adjoining & that a Cert. issue accordingly.—

(Cert issd for 400)

James Boyd this day claimed a pre-

[53] Collins, Vol. 2, pp. 518, 519.
[54] Collins, Vol. 2, p. 467 and index.
[55] Collins, Vol. 2, p. 275 and index.

empt'n of 400 Acres of Land at the State price in the District of Kentucky on Acc't of making an Actual settlem't of May 1779 lying above 2 Miles East from the Mouth of Givens Run to include his improvement satisfactory proof being made to the Court they are of Opinion that the s'd Boyd has a right to a preempt'n of 400 Acres of Land to include the above Location & that a Cert. issue accordingly.—

(Cert issd for 1400)

Wm Belleau (Bellaw?) by Wm Stewart this day claimed a settlem't & preempt'n to a tract of Land in the district of Kentucky on Acc't of raising a Crop of Corn in the Country in the year 1775 lying on Greers the head thereof Waters of Kentucky river satisfactory proof being made to the Court they are of Opinion that the s'd Belleau has a right to settlem't of 400 Acres of Land to include the above Location & the preempt'n of 1000 Acres of Land adjoining & that a Cert. issue accordingly.—

(Cert issd for 1400)

Martin Stall by William Stewart this day claimed a settlme't & preempt'n to a tract of Land in the district of Kentucky on Acc't of raising a Crop of Corn in the Country in the year 1775 Lying on the Town Fork of Salt River on both sides thereof to include a large Spring of Silas Harlen running up the River for Quantity. Satisfactory proof being made to the Court they are of Opinion that the s'd Stall has a right to a settlem't of 400 Acres of Land to include the above Location & the preempt'n of 1000 Acres.

(Cert issd for 1400)

[56]Joseph Blackford by Wm Stewart this day claimed a settlme't & preempt'n to a tract of Land in the District of Kentucky on Acc't of raising a crop of Corn in the Country in the year 1775 & 1776 and lying on the North fork of the South fork of Clear Creek about 2 Miles from a large Pond & to include an improvement satisfactory proof being made to the Court they are of Opinion that the s'd Blackford has a right to a settlement of 400 Acres of Land to include the above Location & the preemption of 1000 Acres adjoining & that a Cert. issue accordingly.—

(Cert issd for 1400)

[57]James Davis this day claimed a preempt of 400 Acres of Land at the State price in the District of Kentucky on Acc't of making an Actual settlement in the year 1778 lying on the South side of the Beech Fork of Salt River adjoining Adj'g the Land of Go'er Soverns below satisfactory proof being made to the Court they are of Opinion that the s'd Davis has a right to a preempt'n of 400 Acres of Land to include the above Location & that a Cert. issue Accordingly.—

(Cert issd for 1000)

[58]Edward Davis this day claimed a settlem't & preempt'n to a tract of Land in the District of Kentucky on Acc't of Settling in the Country in the year 1777

[56] Collins, Vol. 2, p. 177 and index.
[57] Collins, Vol. 2, p. 127 and index.
[58] Collins Vol. 2, p. 624.

& residing 12 Months after the s'd settlem't & improving Lands in the year 1776 lying on the North side of Dicks River adjoining the Waters of Sugar Creek to include his improvment it appearing to the Court from the evidence offered that the s'd Davis came to this Country as a soldier of the Militia of Mongumery County & that he did not reside here 12 Months after he was discharged therefore the Court are of Opinion that the s'd Davis has a right to a preempt'n only of 1000 Acres to include the above Location & that a Cert. issue accordingly.—

(Cert issd for 1400 to Edw'd Davis)

Jno Boils this day claimed a settlement & preempt to a tract of Land in the District of Kentucky on Acc't of raising a Crop of Corn in the Country in the year 1776 lying on the North of Dicks River adjoining the Lands of Asel Davis to the South West to include his improvement satisfactory proof being made to the Court they are of Opinion that the s'd Boils has a right to a settlem't of 400 Acres to include the above Location & the preemption of 1000 Acres adjoining & that a Cert. issue accordingly.—

(Cert issd for 1400 to Capt. Wathington)

It being proved to the Court that it was proved the 3d of November 1779 that Jas. Fenn was intitled to a settlement & preempt'n for residing in the Country 12 Months before the year 1778 & Now Locates the same on Wilson Creek a branch of Salt River adjoining the Lands of James Sam'l above ordered that a Cert. issue accordingly.—

(Cert issd for 1400 to Capt. Wathington)

Patrick Shone by Edw'd Wathington this day claimed a settlement & preempt'n to a tract of Land in the district of Kentucky on Acc't of raising a Crop of Corn in the year 1776 lying about 1 Mile partly an East course from Givens Station On the waters of the Hanging fork of Dicks River at a rock spring to include a Cabbin built by [59]Arch'd McNeil satisfactory proof being made to the Court they are of Opinion that the s'd Shone has a right to a settlem't of 400 Acres of Land to include the above Location & the preempt'n of 1000 Acres adjoining & that a Cert. issue accordingly.—

Then the Court Adjourned untill tomorrow Morning 9 Oclock

Wm Fleming

At a Court continued & held by the Commissioners of the Kentucky District for adjusting Titles to unpatented Land at Harrodsburgh this 14th day of Feb'y 1780

Present

Wm Fleming Steph'n Trigg &
Edm'd Lyne

(Cert issd for 400 to Jno Clark?)

Joseph Ryan Heir at Law to Patrict Ryan Dec'd this day claimed a preemption of 400 Acres of Land at the State price in the District of Kentucky on Acc't of the s'd dec'ts making an Actual settlem't in the year 1778 lying on both sides of Cartrights Creek a branch of the Beech fork of Salt River about 1½

[59] Collins, Vol. 2, pp. 519, 615.

Miles above the Mouth of the s'd Creek satisfactory proof being made to the Court they are of Opinion that the s'd Ryan has a right to a preemp'n of 400 acres of Land to include the above location & that a Cert'e issue accordingly.—

(Cert isd for 400)

[60]Wm Harrison this day claimed a preempt of 400 Acres of Land at the State price in the District of Kentucky on Acc't of Making an Actual settlement in May 1779 lying on the North side of the Beech fork of Salt River about 1½ Mile from the s'd fork to include his improvment Satisfactory proof being made to the Court they are of Opinion that the s'd Harrison has a right to a preemption of 400 Acres of Land to include the above Location and that a Certif'e issue accordingly.

(Cert issd for 1000 to John Clark)

James Roberson by [61]Jno. Clark this day claimed a preemption of 1000 Acres of Land at the State price in the district of Kentucky on account of marking & improving the year 1775 lying on both sides of Cartrights Creek a branch of the beach fork of Salt River about two Miles below Hardens cabbin to include his improvement satisfactory proof being made to the Court they are of Opinion that the s'd Roberson has a right to a preemption of 1000 Acres of Land to include the above Location & that a Cert. issue accordingly.—

(Cert issd for 400)

[62]Henry Thomas by John Clarke this day claimed a settlement & preempt'n to a tract of Land in the district of Kentucky on Acc't of raising a crop of Corn in the Country in the year 1776 lying on the town Fork of Salt River adjoining Samuel Adams & Isaac Hite on the South side to include an improvement at the mouth of a dry run on the West side of the s'd River made by James Berry satisfactory proof being made to the Court they are of Opinion that the s'd Thomas has a right to a settlem't of 400 Acres of Land to include the above location & the preemption of 1000 Acres adjoining & that a Cert. issue accordingly.—

(Cert issd for 400)

James Anderson this day claimed a preempt'n of 400 Acres of Land at the State price in the District of Kentucky on Acc't of making an Actual settlem't in April 1779 lying on the North side of Green River on a Creek that runs into the s'd River & about 5 Miles from the same and one Mile above a Buffaloe satisfactory proof being made to the Court they are of Opinion that the s'd Anderson has a right to a preemption of 400 Acres of Land to include the above Location & that a Cert. issue accordingly.—

(Cert issd for 1000)

Beazel Preather this day by Henry Preather claimed a preempt'n of 1000 Acres of Land at the State price in the District of Kentucky on Acc't of marking & improving the same in the year 1775 lying on both sides of pleasant run a branch of the Beach Fork of Salt River near where the Hunters Trace

[60] Collins, Vol. 2, p. 552.
[61] Collins, Vol. 2, pp. 172, 517.
[62] Collins, Vol. 2, p. 511.

crosses the same to include his improvement satisfactory proof being made to the Court they are of Opinion that the s'd Preather has a right to a preempt'n of 1000 Acres of Land to include the above Location & that a Cert. issue accordingly.—

(Cert issd for 1400)

It being proved to the Court that David Cowen Heir at Law to James Cowen dec'd the 4th of November 1779 is intituled to a settlem't & preempt'n on Acc't of the said decedents raising a Crop of Corn in the Country in the year 1774 now comes into Court & locates the same lying on the Waters of Chaplins Fork of Salt River near a South West Course of Silas Harlen and about 3 or 4 Miles distance including a large Cove Spring in the run & a Cabbin s'd to be built by Wm Garrott Ordered that a Cert. issue accordingly.—

(Cert issd for 1400 to Edw'd Hammond)

[63]Jno Hinkston by Jno Haggen this day claimed a settlement & preempt'n to a tract of Land in the district of Kentucky on Acc't of raising a crop of Corn in the Country in the year 1775 & 1776 lying on the South side of the South fork of Licking Creek adjoining the Land of Riddles Station to include his improvement satisfactory proof being made to the Court they are of Opinion that the s'd Hinkston has a right to a settlem't of 400 Acres of Land to include the above Location & the preempt of 1000 Acres adjoining & that a Cert. issue accordingly.

[63] Collins, Vol. 2, p. 19, and index.

(Cert issd for 1400 to Edw'd Hammond)

Jno Wood by Jno Haggen this day claimed a settlem't & preemption to a tract of Land in the district of Kentucky on Acc't of raising a Crop of Corn in the Country in the year 1776 lying on a large Buffaloe Road on the Waters of the South fork of Licking Creek adjoining the Lands of Jno Hingston on the South West to include his improvement satisfactory proof being made to the Court they are of Opinion that the s'd Wood has a right to a settlem't of 400 Acres of Land to include the above Location & the preemption of 1000 Acres adjoining & that a Cert. issue accordingly.

(Cert issd for 1400 Edw'd Hammond)

John Sillars by Jno Haggin this day claimed a settlement & preempt'n to a tract of Land in the District of Kentucky on Acc't of raising a Crop of Corn in the Country in the year 1776 lying on the North side of the South fork of Licking Creek about 4 Miles below Riddles Station to include his improvement satisfactory proof being made to the Court they are of Opinion that the s'd Sillas has a right to a settlem't of 400 Acres of Land to include the above Location & the preempt of 1000 Acres adjoining & that a Cert. issue accordingly.—

(Cert issd for 1400 to Edward Hammond)

William McCune by John Haggin this day claimed a settlem't & preempt'n to a tract of Land in the district of Kentucky on Acc't of raising a crop of Corn in the Country in the year 1776 lying near the head of Hingstons Creek waters of the South fork of Licking Creek on the road leading from Riddles Station to Elkhorn satisfactory proof being made to the Court they are of Opinion that the s'd McCaun has a right to a settlem't of 400 Acres of Land to include the above Location & the preempt'n of 1000 Acres adjoining & that a Cert. issue accordingly.—

(Cert issd for 1400 to Edw'd Hammond)

Wm Huskins by Jno Haggins this day claimed a settlem't & preempt'n to a tract of Land in the District of Kentucky on Acc't of raising a Crop of Corn in the Country in the year 1775 & 1776 lying on Huskins run on a Buffaloe road that leads to McClellens fort & adjoining the Lands of Jno Woods to include his improvements satisfactory proof being made to the Court they are of Opinion that the s'd Huskins has a right to a settlem't of 400 Acres of Land to include the above Location & the preempt of 1000 Adjoining & that a Cert. issue accordingly.—

[64]James McAfee Sen'r by [65]Rob't McAfee this day claimed a preemption of 1000 Acres of Land at the State price in the district of Kentucky. Rejected—

(Cert issd for 1000)

James Bartlett by [66]Wm Bartlett this day claimed a preemption to a tract of Land in the district of Kentucky on Acc't of Marking and improving the same in the year 1776 lying at a sinking Spring about 1 Mile south of the Trough Spring on Glens Creek waters of Kentucky to include his improvement satisfactory proof being made to the Court they are of Opinion that the s'd Bartlett has a right to a preempt of 1000 Acres of Land to include the above Location & that a Cert. issue accordingly.

(Cert issd for 1000)

Jno. Banks by Wm Bartlett this day claimed a preempt'n of 1000 Acres of Land at the State price in the District of Kentucky on Acc't of Marking & improving the same in the year 1776 lying on the North fork of Greers Creek adjoining the Land of Jas Bartlett to include his improvement satisfactory proof being made to the Court they are of Opinion that the s'd Banks has a right to a preempt of 1000 Acres of Land to include the above Location & that a Cert. issue accordingly.—

(Cert issd for 400)

[67]James Wood this day claimed a preempt'n of 1000 Acres of Land at the State price in the District of Kentucky on Acc't of making an Actual settlem't in March 1779 lying on the Town fork of Salt River adjoining the Land of Wm Adams above & [68]Jas McCoun Jun below satisfactory proof being made to the Court they are of Opinion that the s'd Wood has a right to a preempt'n of 400 Acres of Land to include the above Location & that a Cert. issue accordingly.—

[64] Collins, Vol. 2, p. 53 and index.
[65] Collins, Vol. 2, p. 53 and index.
[66] Collins, Vol. 2, p. 550.
[67] Collins, Vol. 2, p. 183.
[68] Collins, Vol. 2, p. 519.

(Cert issd for 1000 to Mr Allison)

[69]Jeremiah Tilford this day claimed a preempt of 1000 Acres of Land at the State price in the District of Kentucky on Acc't of mark'g & improving the same in the year 1775 lying on the Waters of the Town fork of Salt River adjoining the Land of Jas McAfee on the East side to include his improvement satisfactory proof being made to the Court they are of Opinion that the s'd Tilford Has a right to a preempt'n of 1000 Acres of Land to include the above Location & that a Cert. issue accordingly.—

(Cert issd for 400)

Jesse Davis by Isaac Davis this day claimed a preempt'n of 400 Acres of Land at the State price in the District of Kentucky on Acc't of making an Actual settlem't in May 1779 lying on the North side of Chaplins fork of Salt River adjoining the Lands of Wm Harrison to include a small sinking Spring & his improvem't satisfactory proof being made to the Court they are of Opinion that the s'd Davis has a right to a preempt'n of 400 Acres of Land to include the above location & that a Cert. issue accordingly.—

(Cert issd for 400)

Jacob Harlen by Silas Harlen this day claimed a preempt'n of 400 Acres of Land at the State price in the District of Kentucky on Acc't of making an Actual settlement in April 1779 lying on the fork of the Rolling fork of Salt River where the North & South forks meet together and to extend upwards for Quantity Satisfactory proof being made to the Court they are of Opinion that the s'd Harlen has a right to a preemption of 400 Acres of Land to include the above Location & that a Cert. issue accordingly.—

(Cert issd for 1400)

[70]Barney Stagner Heir at Law to Barney Stagner Dec'd by James Barney this day claimed a settlem't & preempt'n of a tract of Land in the district of Kentucky on Acc't of raising a Crop of Corn in the year 1776 lying on both sides of Cartrights Creek waters of the Beech fork of Salt river adjoining the Lands of Robertson below satisfactory proof being made to the Court they are of Opinion that the s'd Stagner has a right to a settlement of 400 Acres of Lands to include the above location & that the preempt'n of 1000 Acres of Land adjoining & that a Cert issue accordingly.—

(Cert issd for 400)

[71]Jno Wilson this day claimed a preempt'n of 400 Acres of Land at the State price in the District of Kentucky on Acc't of Making an Actual settlem't in March 1779 lying on both sides of Fromans Creek a branch of Chaplins fork of Salt river to include his improvem't satisfactory proof being made to the Court they are of Opinion that the s'd Wilson has a right to a preempt'n of 400 Acres of Lands to include the above Location & that a Cert. isse accordingly.—

(Cert issd for 1400)

Jno McAllester Assee of [72]Rich'd

[69] Collins, Vol. 2, p. 183.

[70] Collins, Vol. 2, pp. 520, 616.
[71] Collins, Vol. 2, pp. 517, 519, 663.
[72] Collins, Vol. 2, pp. 518, 519.

Benson this day claimed a settlment & preempt'n to a tract of Land in the District of Kentucky on Acc't of the s'd Bensons raising a Crop of Corn in the Country in the year 1775 lying on Bensons run near the Mouth waters of the Kentucky River to include his improvement satisfactory proof being made to the Court they are of Opinion that the s'd McAllester has a right to a settlem't of 400 Acres of Land to include the above Location & the preempt of 1000 Acres adjoining & that a Cert. issue accordingly.

Then the Court adjourned untill tomorrow Morning 9 Oclock

Wm Fleming

At a Court continued & held by the Commissioners of Kentucky District for adjusting titles to unpatented lands at Harrodsburgh this 15th day of Feb'y 1780

Present

Wm Fleming Steph'n Trigg & Edm'd Lyne—Gent

Order'd that the Surveyor of this County attend this Court with his book to day as there is some claimes already granted upon hands Wh'ch appears has been entered by Virtue of Military Warrants.

(Cert issd for 400)

James Phinax this day claimed a preempt of 400 Acres of Land at the State price in the district of Kentucky on Acc't of making an Actual settlem't in the year 1778 lying on the South fork of Hardens Creek waters of the Beech fork of Salt River about 1 Mile above the Mouth and to run up the s'd Creek for quantity satisfactory proof being made to the Court they are of Opinion that the s'd Phinax has a right to a preempt'n of 400 Acres of land to include the above Location & that a Cert. issue accordingly.—

(Certificate issd for 400)

[73]Jas McCollack this day claimed a preemption of 400 Acres of Land at the State price in the District of Kentucky on Acc't of making an Actual settlem't in the year 1778 lying on the Waters of Licking Creek a branch of Green River on the North side thereof about 7 Miles from the s'd River to include a Spring marked on a Tree TD Satisfactory proof being made to the Court they are of Opinion that the s'd McCullack has a right to a preemption of 400 Acres to include the above Location & that a Cert. issue accordingly.—

(Cert issd for 1000)

[74]James Brown heir at Law to Jno Brown Dec'd this day claimed a preempt'n of 1000 Acres of land at the State price in the district of Kentucky on Acc't of s'd decedents marking & improving the same in the year 1774 lying on Clarks run adjoining the Lands of Givens below & Logan Above to include his improvement satisfactory proof being made to the Court they are of Opinion that the s'd Brown has a right to a preempt of 1000 Acres of Land to

[73] (McCollach) Collins, Vol. 2, pp. 517, 624.
[74] Collins, Vol. 2, pp. 476, 517, 519.

include the above Location & that a Cert. issue accordingly.

(Cert issd for 400)

Francis McBrid this day claimed a preempt of 400 Acres of Land at the State price in the district of Kentucky on Acc't of making an Actual settlement in April 1779 lying on the South fork of Licking Creek about 5 or 6 Miles below riddles Station including a small branch of Licking below the Salt Spring satisfactory proof being made to the Court they are of Opinion that s'd McBrid has a right to a preempt'n of 400 Acres of Land to include the above Location & that a Cert issue accordingly.—

(Cert issd for 1000)

Jno Deremiah by Wm Stewart this day claimed a preempt of 1000 Acres of land at the State price in the district of Kentucky on Acc't of Marking & improving the same in the year 1775 lying on the waters of Buffaloe Creek a branch of Beech fork of Salt River lying on both sides of the Forks of the s'd Creek to include his improvement satisfactory proof being made to the Court they are of Opinion that the s'd Deremiah has a right to a preemption of 1000 Acres of Land to include the above Location & that a Cert. issue accordingly.—

(Cert issd for 1400)

It being proved to the Court that [75]Wm White heir at Law [76]Charles White Dec'd intituled to a settlem't & preemption to a tract of Land by the s'd dec'dts raising a Crop of Corn in the Country in the year 1776 the 1st of Nov'r 1779 Now comes into Court & locates the same lying on Hardens Creek at the mouth of the south fork and to run down for quantity joining Bunton Camp or Prenixland on the West & that a Cert. issue accordingly.—

(Cert issd for 1400)

Thos. Wilson by Jno Cowan this day claimed a settlem't & preempt'n to a tract of Land in the district of Kentucky on Acc't of raising a Crop of Corn in the Country in the year 1776 lying on Wilsons run adj'g the Lands of Wm Morgen on the s'd run below to include a spring & improvement & to extend down the Creek for quantity satisfactory proof being made to the Court they are of Opinion that the s'd Wilson has a right to a settlement of 400 Acres of Land to include the above Location & the preempt of 1000 Acres adjoining & that a Cert. issue accordingly—

(Cert issd for 1000)

Owen Devere this day claimed a preemption of 1000 Acres of Land at the State price in the district of Kentucky on Acc't of mark'g & improving the same in the year 1776 lying on the water of the Hanging fork of Dicks River on the Lower side of the road leading from this to Logans Fork to include an improvement made by James Brown in the year 1772 (?) satisfactory proof being made to the Court they are of Opinion that the s'd Devere has a right to a preempt of 1000 Acres of Land to include the above Location & that a Cert. issue accordingly.

[75] Collins, Vol. 2, p. 550.
[76] Collins, Vol. 2, p. 178.

(Cert issd for 1000)

[77]Henry Miller by Edw'd Bulger this day claimed a preempt'n of 1000 Acres of Land at the State price in the district of Kentucky lying on the left hand branch of Clear Creek about 4 Miles from the head to include his Cabbin & improvement on acc't of Marking & improving the same in the year 1776 satisfactory proof being made to the Court they are of Opinion that the s'd Miller has a right to a preempt of 1000 Acres of land to include the s'd improvem't & that a Cert. issue.

Wm Fleming Assee of Jas Ross withdraws the location made by s'd Ross on the Ohio River on the yellow Banks as it appears to the Court that the s'd Lands are in dispute—

[78]Geo'e May Surveyor for this County in consequence of an Order of this Court requiring him to attend them with his books accordingly Attended—Jno Bowman & Jno Hite being personally in Court imform'd them that having Obt'd Certificates from this Court in the name of Isaac Bowman, Hannah Soverins & Vangelist Harden for settlem't & preempt'n each, which they had Located on the Yellow Banks on the Ohio River above the Mouth of Green River being informed by the surveyor that entrys Now made by Virtue of Military Warrants on the s'd Land they apply to the Court to have their rights of claim Determined upon examining the surveyors books which finds the lands above Mentioned to be entered by Geo. May for and in behalf of [79]Jno May, Thos Mann Randolph & Jos'h Woods Exec'rs of Lenard Price dec'd & Theodrick Bland Jun'r who acknowledged himself there acting Attorney for the purpose of making the s'd entries but now objects to the Courts authority in determining the rights of claim to the s'd Lands it being the opinion of the Court that they are fully empowered & authorised to adjust & settle all titles of claims to unpatented Lands under the present and former Government thought proper to examine sundry witnesses in consideration of which the Court are of Opinion that the s'd entries made by Virtue of Military Warrants & preempt'n rights are good & that the Location of the s'd persons be withdrawn.—

(Cert issd for 1000)

Patrick Wall Assee of Conrad Baker this day claimed a preempt of 1000 Acres of Land at the State price in the district of Kentucky on Acc't of the s'd Bakers marking & improving the same in the year 1775 lying on the lower end of sinking Creek a branch of the South fork of Elkhorn joining the lands of Colo Andrew Lewis & James on satisfactory proof being made to the Court they are of Opinion that the s'd Wall has a right to a preempt'n of 1000 Acres of Lands to include the above Location & that a Cert. issue accordingly.—

(Cert issd for 1400)

Peter Phillips by Jno Bowman this day claimed a settlement & preempt'n to a tract of land in the district of Kentucky on Acc't of raising a Crop of Corn in the Country in the year 1775.

[77] Collins, Vol. 2, pp. 309, 310.
[78] Collins, Vol. 2, pp. 101, 183. 368.
[79] Collins, Vol. 2, p. 547 and index.

lying on the south side of the Town fork of Salt River about 5 or 6 Miles from Bulletts Lick on the 1st Creek below the Lick and near the fork of the s'd Creek to include a Tree marked IH 1776 satisfactory proof being made to the Court they are of Opinion that the s'd Philips has a right to a settlement of 400 Acres to include the above Location & the preempt of 1000 Acres adjoining & that a Cert. issue accordingly.—

(Cert issd for 400)

Jno Bunton Sen'r by Jno Bunton Jun'r this day claimed a preemption of 400 Acres of Land at the State price in the district of Kentucky on Acc't of making an Actual settlement in December 1778 lying about 1½ Miles this side Harrods Landing on the road leading from this to the s'd landing including and improvement made by James Sodusky satisfactory proof being made to the Court they are of Opinion that the s'd Bunton Sen'r has a right to a preempt of 400 Acres of land to include the above location & that a Cert. issue accordingly.—

(Cert issd for 400)

Jas Bentley this day claimed a preempt of 400 Acres of Land at the State price in the district of Kentucky on Acc't of making an Actual settlem't in May 1779 lying on the South side of the Rolling fork of Salt river about 15 Miles from Bulletts Lick to include his improvement satisfactory proof being Made to the Court they are of Opinion that the s'd Bentley has a right to a preemption of 400 Acres of Land to include the above Location & that a Cert. issue accordingly.

(Cert issd for 400 &c)

Wilson Mattox this day claimed a preempt'n of 400 Acre of Land at the State price in the district of Kentucky on Acc't of making an Actual settlem't in 1778 lying on a Creek about 12 Miles from Green River to include his improvement satisfactory proof being made to the Court they are of Opinion that the s'd Mattox has a preempt of 400 Acres of Land to include the s'd improvement & that a Cert issue accordingly.—

(Cert issd for 400 &c)

Thos Arbuckle this day claimed a preempt'n of 400 Acre of Land at the State price in the district of Kentucky on Acc't of Making an Actual settlement in April 1779 lying on the Rolling fork of Salt River on both sides thereof between the Lands of Henry Bristo & Solomon Laurance satisfactory proof being made to the Court they are of Opinion that the s'd Arbuckle has a right to a preemption of 400 Acres of Land to include the above Location & that a Cert issue accordingly.

(Cert issd for 400 &c)

It appearing to the Court that there is sufficient reason for removing Henry Darthetys Claim which was located the 5 of Nov'r 1779 now comes into Court and locates the same lying on the North side of Green River near where William Glover now lives Ord'd that a Cert. issue accordingly.—

(Cert issd for 1000 &c)

Jos'h Daugherty by Jno Daugherty

this day claimed a preempt of 1000 Acres of Land at the State price in the district of Kentucky on Acc't of marking & improving the same in the year 1776 lying on a branch about 1¼ mile North Eastwardly from Poff Mill Seat between Beargrass & Howards Creek to include a large Spring & a beech tree with the two 1st Letter of Jos'h Dotherty & a Cabbin satisfactory proof being made to the Court they are of Opinion that the s'd Daugherty has a right to a preemption of 1000 Acres of land to include the above location & that a Cert issue accordingly.

(Cert issd for 1000 fees &c pd D. D. to Jno Kennedy)

James Crockett this day claimed a preemption of 1000 Acres of Land at the State price in the District of Kentucky on Acc't of marking & improving the same in the year 1775 lying on the North side of Silver Creek about 2 Miles from the s'd Creek on a small branch called Stone lick Creek satisfactory proof being made to the Court they are of Opinion that the s'd Crockett has a right to a preemption of 1000 Acres of Land to include the above location & that a Cert issue accordingly.—

Then the Court adjourned untill tomorrow Morning 9 Oclock

Wm Fleming

At a Court continued and held by the commissioners of Kentucky District For Adjusting Titles to unpatented lands at Harrodsburgh this 16th day of Feb'y 1780

present

Wm Fleming Stephen Trigg & Edmund Lyne—Gentlemen

(Cert issd for 400 &c to W. Wilson)

James Scott this day claimed a preemption of 400 Acres of Land at the State price in the district of Kentucky on Acc't of making an Actual settlem't in April 1779 lying between sinking Creek and shannons run the waters of Elkhorn joining the Lands of Patrick Wall to include the Buffaloe spring satisfactory proof being made to the Court they are of Opinion that the s'd Scott has a right to a preemption of 400 Acres of Land to include the above location & that a Cert. issue accordingly.—

(Cert issd for 400)

Jno Allason this day claimed a preempt of 400 Acres of Land at the State price in the district of Kentucky on Acc't of making an Actual settlement in April 1779 lying on both sides of Salt River below the fork to include an improvement made by Thos Denton above Silas Harlens Lands and adjoining the Lands of George Culwell Assee of Jas Hoys Land on the Lower side satisfactory proof being made to the Court they are of Opinion that the s'd Allison has a right to a preempt of 400 Acres of Lands to include the above Location & that a Cert issue accordingly.—

(Cert issd for 1000 &c)

Rich'd Woods by [80]Charles Campbell this day claimed a preempt of 1000 Acres of land at the State price in the district of Kentucky on Acc't of Marking & improving the same in the year 1776 lying on the waters of the town Fork of Salt River between the s'd

[80] Collins, Vol. 2, p. 476.

Fork & Breashiers Creek on Coxes settlement to include his improvement satisfactory proof being made to the Court they are of Opinion that the s'd Woods has a right to a preempt of 1000 Acre of Lands at the State price in the District of Kentucky to include the s'd improvement & that a Cert. issue accordingly.—

(Cert issd for 1000 &c)

Stephen Groves by Charles Campbell this day claimed a preemption of 1000 Acres of Land at the State price in the district of Kentucky on Acc't of mark'g & improving the same in the year 1776 lying on the waters of the town fork of Salt River between the s'd fork & Breashiers Creek to include his improvement on Coxes Settlement satisfactory proof being made to the Court they are of Opinion that the s'd Groves has a right to a preemption of 1000 Acres of land to include the s'd Improvement & that a Cert issue accordingly.—

(Cert issd for 1000 &c)

Jno Woodrow by Charles Campbell this day claimed a preemption of 1000 Acres of Land at the State price in the district of Kentucky on Acc't of marking and improving the same in the year 1776 lying on the waters of the Town fork of Salt River between the s'd Fork & breashiers Creek in Cox's Settlement to include his improvement satisfactory proof being made to the Court they are of Opinion that the s'd Woodrow has a right to a preemption of 1000 Acres of Land to include the above Location & that a Cert issue accordingly.—

(Cert issd for 1000 &c)

Jno Ross by Charles Campbell this day claimed a preempt'n of 1000 Acres of Land at the State price in the district of Kentucky on Acc't of marking and improving the same in the year 1776 lying on the waters of the Town fork of Salt River between the s'd fork & Breasheirs Creek in Coxes settlement to include his improvement satisfactory proof being made to the Court they are of Opinion that the s'd Ross has a right to a preempt of 1000 Acres of Land to include the s'd Improvement & that a Cert issue accordingly.—

(Cert issd for 1400 &c to John Dorterthy)

Jno Wilson this day claimed a settlement & preempt'n to a tract of land in the District of Kentucky on acc't of raising a Crop of Corn in the County in the year 1776 lying on a dividing ridge between the waters of Kentucky & Dicks River to include part of both waters & his improvement satisfactory proof being made to the Court they are of Opinion that the s'd Wilson has a right to a settlement of 400 Acres of Land to include the above location & the preempt of 1000 Acres adjoining & that a Certificate issue accordingly.

(Cert issd for 1400 to John Deatherty)

Rob't Wilson this day claimed a settlement & preempt'n of a tract of Land in the District of Kentucky on Acc't of raising Corn in the Country in the year 1776 lying on the North side of Green River on the Waters of Crooked Creek adjoining henry Daughertys Land Satisfactory proof being made to the Court they are of Opinion that the s'd

Wilson has a right to a settlement of 400 Acres of Land to include the above Location & the preemption of 1000 Acres adjoining & that a Cert issue accordingly.—

(Cert issd for 1000 &c to John Deatherty)

Andrew Cowan this day claimed a preemption of 1000 Acres of land at the state price in the district of Kentucky on Acc't of marking & improving the same in the year 1776 lying on a dividing Ridge between the waters of Dicks River & Kentucky adjoining the Lands of Jno Wilson on the North side to include his improvement satisfactory proof being made to the Court they are of Opinion that the s'd Cowan has a right to a preemption of 1000 Acres of land to include the s'd improvement and that a Cert. issue accordingly.

(Cert issd for 1000 &c)

Jno Bentley by Jno Bently Jun'r this day claimed a preemption of 1000 Acres of land at the State price in the district of Kentucky on Acc't of marking & improving the same in the year 1776 lying on the North side of Dicks river opposite the Lands said to be claimed by Rich'd Jackson to include his improvement satisfactory proof being made to the Court they are of Opinion that the s'd Bentley has a right to a preempt of 1000 Acres of land to include the above Location & that a Cert. issue accordingly.—

(Cert issd for 1400 &c to John Bentley)

Marquis Helms Assee of Jno Falloway this day claimed a settlement & preempt'n to a tract of Land in the district of Kentucky on Acc't of raising a crop of Corn in the district of Kentucky in the year 1775 lying on a branch of Green River Called Elk Garden about 15 Miles from Gordens Lick to include an improvement made by Edm'd Bulger Satisfactory proof being made to the Court they are of Opinion that the s'd Helms has a right to a settlement of 400 Acres of Land to include the above Location & the preempt'n of 1000 acres Adjoining and that a Cert. issue accordingly.

(Cert issd for 1400)

Isaac Hite comes into Court and moves to Order the location of Land claimed by him in favor of Vangelist Harden which is granted him lying on the head of a branch of the Ohio known by the name of Finn Creek about 12 Miles from the falls of Ohio to include an improvement & spring known by the name of the Joseph Solerains Spring.

(Cert issd for 1400 pd)

Wm Fleming moves to locate the lands claimed by Jas Ross which he withdrew yesterday beginning on the head Waters of a small branch that empties into the Ohio near the upper end of the 3 Islands thence with Griffins East line to the branches of Howards Creek a Cert issue accordingly.—

(Cert issd for 400 pd &c)

[81]Edw'd Bulger in behalf of Wm Oldham[82] moves for leave to Alter the Location of the lands claimed by the said Holman 11th Inst. sufficient cause appearing for the same it is granted him

[81] Collins, Vol. 2, pp. 624, 663.
[82] Collins, Vol. 2, pp. 667, 668.

now locates the said lands lying on the waters of Salt River about 4 Miles from Bulletts Lick including an improvement made by Isaac McBrid on the North side of the s'd river & that a Cert. issue accordingly.

(Cert issd for 1000 pd to Capt. Sanders)

[83]Jno Fitzgarrel this day claimed a preempt of 1000 Acres of Land at the State price in the district of Kentucky on Acc't of Marking & improving the Same in the year 1776 lying on the South Side of the North fork of Licking Creek at the mouth of the Creek called Mill Creek on the Lower side to include his improvement satisfactory proof being made to the Court they are of Opinion that the s'd Fitzgarrard has a right to a preemption of 1000 Acres of Land to include the above Location & that a Cert issue accordingly.

(Cert issd for 1400 pd &c to Colo Logan)

Rich'd Jackman by Colo Logan this day claimed a settlem't & preempt'n to a tract of Land in the district of Kentucky on Acc't of Making an Crop of Corn in the Country in the year 1775 lying on the South side of Dicks River about 1½ Mile of the Land of Wm Craig to include his improvm't satisfactory proof being made to the Court they are of Opinion that the s'd Jackman has a right to a settlm't of 400 Acres of Land to include the above Location & the preempt. of 1000 Acres adjoining & that a Cert. issue accordingly.—

(Cert issd for 1400 pd &c to Colo Logan)

John Jackman by Colo Logan this day claimed a settlement and Preemption to a tract of Land in the District of Kentucky on account of Raising a Crop of Corn in the Country in the year 1776 lying on Elkhorn Creek a branch of Dicks River (?) on the north Side thereof adjoining Bertholomew Fanton on the East to Include his improvement satisfactory proof being made to the Court they are of oppinion that the s'd Jackman has a right to a settlement of 400 acres to include the s'd improvement & the preemption of 1000 acres adjoining & that a Certificate issue accordingly.—

(Obt'd a Cert before)

Sam'l Kirkman this day claimed a preempt of 400 Acres of Land at the State price in the District of Kentucky on Acc't of making an Actual settlement in March 1779 lying on both side of the Hanging fork of Dicks River within a mile of Jas Lagins including a Spring marked WM and a cabbin marked thus IG Satisfactory proof being made to the Court they are of oppinion that the said Hickman has a right to a preemption of 400 acres to include the above Location and that a certe Issue accordingly.—

(Cert iss for 1400 pd &c to Simon Canton)

[84]Thomas Williams by Simon Canton[85] this day claimed a settlement and preemption to a tract of Land in the District of Kentucky on Acc't of residing in the Country 12 Months before the year 1778 lying on the second right hand fork of Lawrences Creek that heads with the waters of licking to include his

[83] Collins, Vol. 2, p. 551.

[84] Collins, Vol. 2, p. 84, &c.
[85] Collins, Vol. 2, p. 84, &c.

improvem't Made by Charles Lacompt. satisfactory proof being made to the Court they are of Opinion that the s'd Williams has a right to a settlement of 400 Acres of land to include the above Location & the preempt'n of 1000 Acres adjoining & that a Cert. issue accordingly.—

Then the Court adjourned untill to-morrow Morning 9 Oclock

Wm Fleming

At a court Continued and held by the Commissioners of Kentucky District for adjusting Titles to unpatented Lands at Harrodsburgh this 17th day of Feb'y 1780

Present

Wm Fleming, Stephen Trigg & Edmund Lyne

(Cert issd for 1400 pd &c)

[86]Isaac Hite moves to remove a location made by Hannah Soverins now the wife of [87]Benj'n Lynn sufficient reason appearing to the Court for the same it is granted now locates it lying on the South fork of Beargrass to include a spring just below a Buffaloe path & to extend up the branch to include 2 Springs marked in the year 1774. Order'd that a Cert. issue.

(Cert issd for 1400 pd &c to Isaac Hite)

Martin Fowler has proof to the Court that he was intitled to a settlem't & preempt'n by residing in the Country 12 Months before the year 1778 at the falls of Ohio the 23 day of Nov'r 1779 which was not Located Isaac Hite come into Court & locates the same lying on the main fork of Elkhorn Creek about 6 Miles from the forks to include an Improvement made by Nathaniel Randolph & two springs one Large the other small waters of the South fork of Elkhorn Order'd that a Cert. issue accordingly.—

(Cert issd for 1400 pd &c)

It Appearing to the Court that the Lands Claimed by Roger Topp Assee of Thos Gibson is within an Officers Survey Benj'n Logan in behalf of the said Topp moves to alter the Location of the s'd Lands which is granted him lying on the waters of Breasheirs Creek on the last branch that the old trace Crosses that leads to falls of Ohio at a Camp called Bulskin ordered that a Cert. issue accordingly.—

(Cert issd for 400 pd &c to Colo Logan)

Jos'h Martin Moves to the Court to have the location that he obtained the 29th of Jan'y 1780 removed it appearing to the Court that there was sufficient cause for the same it is granted he now locates the same lying on the side of the Hanging fork of Dicks River on a branch that runs at Rob't Barnetts improvem't adjoining the Lands of the s'd Barnetts improvem't above Ordered that a Cert. issue accordingly.—

It appearing to the Court that John Higgins was a Servant to [88]Robert McAfee during his residence in this Country and untill he died ordered that a Claim of Dan'l Higgins heir at Law to the s'd Jno Higgins be set aside.—

[86] Collins, Vol. 2, p. 176, &c.; Conquest of the N. W., Vol. I, p. 65, &c. (Reg., May, 1922, p. 170).

[87] Collins, Vol. 2, p. 457; Conquest of the Northwest, Vol. I, p. 79.

[88] Collins, Vol. 2, p. 605, &c.; McAfee Papers, &c.

(Cert issd for 1400 pd &c to Geo May)

It being proved to the Court that Thos Rowlin Assee of Mordecai Reed who was Assee of Jno Love the 6th day of Nov'r 1779 was intitled to a settlem't & preemption tho did not locate the same now comes into Court & locates the same lying on Hickmans Creek adjoining abraham Hite on the East side to include a spring about $\frac{3}{4}$ of a Mile from the s'd Hites Line ordered that a Cert issue accordingly.—

It appearing to the Court that Sam'l Givins & Jacob Coplin has located the same piece of land the parties being both present witnesses being sworn & Exam'd the Court are of Opinion that the s'd Givens has a right to this Land & that Coplins Location of the s'd Lands be withdrawn.—

(Cert issd for 1400 pd &c)

The Heirs of Jas Bunton dec'd this day claimed a settlem't & preempt'n to a tract of land in the district of Kentucky on Acc't of the Decd't making an Actual settlement in the year 1777 Lying on the dividing ridge between Jessemine Creek and the head of the South fork of Clear Creek to include a Sinking Spring marked in the year 1776 by Jno Phelp & to extend down the waters of Clear Creek for quantity satisfactory proof being made they are of Opinion that the s'd Heirs &c has a right to a settlem't of 400 Acres of land to include the above Location & the preempt'n of 1000 Acres adjoining & that a Cert issue accordingly.—

(Cert issd for 1000 pd &c)

Joseph Farrow by [89]Rich'd Masterson this day claimed a preempt'n of 1000 Acres of Land at the State price in the District of Kentucky on Acc't of marking & improving the same in the year 1776 lying on the South side of the North fork of Licking Creek about 9 or 10 Miles above where the road crosses the said fork to include his improvment satisfactory proof being made to the Court they are of Opinion that the s'd Farrow has a right to a preemption of 1000 Acres of land to include the above Location & that a Cert. issue accordingly.—

(Cert issd for 1000 pd &c)

Thos Masterson by Rich'd Masterson this day claimed a preempt'n of 1000 Acres of Land at the State price in the district of Kentucky on Acc't of the s'd Masterson marking & improving the same in the year 1776, lying on the North fork of Licking Creek above a South East course from the Mouth of limestone on the North side of the s'd Creek about 4 Miles above the War road to include his improvement satisfactory proof being made to the Court they are of opinion that the s'd Masterson has a right to a preempt'n of 1000 Acres of Land to include the above improvement & that a Certificate issue accordingly.

(Cert issd for 1000 pd &c)

Rich'd Masterson this day claimed a preempt'n of 1000 Acres of Land at the State price in the district of Kentucky on Acc't of marking & improving the same in the year 1775. lying on the North fork of Licking Creek at the

[89] Collins, Vol. 2, p. 287, &c.

Mouth of a small Creek on the South side beginning at the War road running up said Creek for quantity to include his improvement Satisfactory proof being made to the Court they are of Opinion that the s'd Masterson has a right to a preempt'n of 1000 Acres of Land to include the above Location & that a Cert. issue accordingly.—

(Cert issd for 1000 fees &c pd)

John Masterson by Rich'd Masterson this day claimed a preemption of 1000 Acres of Land at the State price in the district of Kentucky on Acc't of marking & improving the same in the year 1776 lying on the North fork of Licking Creek on the south side about 4 Miles above where the war road Crosses from the Mouth of Limestone to the blue lick to include his improvement satisfactory proof being made to the Court they are of opinion that the s'd Masterson has a right to a preempt'n of 1000 Acres of Land to include the above Location & that a Cert. issue accordingly.—

(Cert issd for 1000 pd &c)

[90]James Batterton by Rich'd Masterson this day claimed a preemption of 1000 Acres of land at the State price in the District of Kentucky on Acc't of marking & improving the same in the year 1776 lying on Mill Creek waters of the North fork of Licking Creek about 2 or 3 Miles from the Mouth of the s'd Creek to include his improvement satisfactory proof being made to the Court they are of Opinion that the s'd Batterton has a right to a preemption of 1000 Acres of Land to include the said improvement.

(Cert issd for 1000 pd &c)

Tho. Champ by Rich'd Masterson this day claimed a preempt'n of 1000 Acres of land at the State price in the District of Kentucky on Acc't of marking & improving the same in the year 1776 lying between the head of Limestone & the North fork of licking Creek near the head of a branch that empties into the said north fork of Licking to include his improvement satisfactory proof being made to the Court they are of Opinion that the s'd Champ has a Right to a preempt of 1000 Acres of Land to include the above Location & that a Cert. issue accordingly.—

(Cert issd for 1000 pd &c)

Jno Churchwell by Rich'd Masterson this day claimed a preemption of 1000 Acres of Land at the State price in the district of Kentucky on Acc't of marking & improving the same in the year 1776 lying on the North side of licking Creek about 8 Miles above where the war road crosses the s'd Creek to include his improvement satisfactory proof being made to the Court they are of Opinion that the s'd Churchwell has a right to a preempt of 1000 Acres of Land to include the above improvem't & that a Cert. issue accordingly.

(Cert issd for 1000 Pd &c)

Rob't Wall by [91]Jas McBride this day claimed a preempt of 1000 Acres of land at the State price in the district of Kentucky on Acc't of Marking & improving

[90] Collins, Vol. 2, p. 551.

[91] Collins, Vol. 2, p. 172, &c.

the same in the year 1776 lying on the West side of Bullskin waters of Breashiers Creek opposite the Mouth of Fox run to include his improvement satisfactory proof being made to the Court they are of Opinion that the s'd Wall has a right to a preemption of 1000 Acres of land to include the said improvement & that a Cert. issue accordingly.—

(Cert issd for 1000 pd &c)
Jas Wall by Jas McBrid this day claimed a preemption of 1000 Acres of Land at the State price in the District of Kentucky on Acc't of marking & improving the same in the year 1776 lying on the East side of Bullskin Creek to include the Mouth of Fox Run to include his improvement satisfactory proof being made to the Court they are of Opinion that the s'd Wall has a right to a preemption of 1000 Acres of Land to include the s'd improvement & that a Cert. issue accordingly.

(Cert issd for 400 to Jas drake pd &c)
Jno Drake heir at Law to [92]Jos'h Drake dec'd by Jno Floyd, this day claimed a preemption of 400 Acres of Land at the State price in the District of Kentucky on Acc't of the s'd Decedents making an actual settlement in the year 1778 lying on the Mouth of Battle Creek about 2 or 3 Miles below the Mouth of the little Kentucky & to extend up the Creek & down the Ohio for quantity—Satisfactory proof being made to the Court they are of Opinion that the s'd Drake has a right to a preemption of 400 Acres of Land to include the above Location & that a Cert. issue accordingly—

(Cert issd for 1000 pd &c)
Wm Williams by [93]Wm Lynn this day claimed a preempt'n of 1000 Acres of Land at the State price in the district of Kentucky on Acc't of marking & improving the same in the year 1777 lying on the Ohio river at the Lower end of a large Pond about 4 Miles above a large Rock & about 10 Miles below the mouth of the big Maamia to run down the River for quantity Satisfactory proof being made to the Court they are of Opinion that s'd Williams has a right to a preempt of 1000 Acres of Land to include the above Location & that a Cert. issue accordingly.

(Cert issd for 1000)
Wm Holloday by Wm Lynn this day claim a preempt'n of 1000 Acres of Land at the State price in the district of Kentucky on Acc't of Marking and improving the same in the year 1777 lying on the Ohio River adjoining Wm Williams Land to include his improvement satisfactory proof being made to the Court they are of Opinion that the s'd Hollody has a right to a preemption of 1000 Acres to include the above Location that a Cert. issue accordingly.

(Cert issd for 1000)
Jno Lewis by Wm Lynn this day claimed a preemption of 1000 Acres of Land at the State price in the district of Kentucky on Acc't of marking & improving the same in the year 1777 lying about ¾ of Mile from the Ohio River at the head of a small Drean adjoining the

[92] Collins, Vol. 2, p. 417; Finley's Hist. of Logan Co., pp. 9-13.

[93] Collins, Vol. 2. pp. 358, 371; Con. of the N. W., Vol. I, p. 97.

Lands of Wm Holloday to include his improvem't satisfactory proof being made to the Court they are of Opinion that the s'd Lewis has a right to a preempt of 1000 Acres of Land to include the above Location & that a Cert. issue accordingly.—

(Cert issd for 1000)

Jno Wyett by Wm Lynn this day claimed a preemption of 1000 Acres of land at the State price in the District of Kentucky on Acc't of marking & improving the same in the year 1777 lying on a small Creek that runs into the Ohio River about 6 or 7 Miles below the Mouth of the Maame on the South side thereof to include his improvement satisfactory proof being made to the Court they are of Opinion that the s'd Wyett has a right to a preemption of 1000 Acres to include the above Location & that a Cert. issue accordingly.—

(Cert issd for 1000)

The heirs of Thos Bryan Dec'd this day claimed a preempt'n of 1000 Acres of Land at the State price in the district of Kentucky on Acc't of the s'd Decedents marking & improving the same in the year 1777 lying on the fork of a Creek that runs into the Ohio about 6 Miles below the Meami adjoining the Lands of Jno Wyatt on the North side to include his improvem't satisfactory proof being made to the Court they are of Opinion that the s'd Heirs &c has a right to a preemption of 1000 Acres of land to include to s'd improvement & that a Cert issue.

(Cert issd for 1000)

[94]Francis McDermid by Rich'd Masterson this day claimed a settlement & preemption to a tract of Land in the district of Kentucky on Acc't of Mak'g a Crop of Corn in the Country in the year 1776 lying on the War road leading from the Mouth of Cabbin Creek to the Upper Blue Licks about 6 Miles from the mouth of the s'd Creek to include a large Lick, satisfactory proof being made to the Court they are of Opinion that the s'd McDermid has a right to a settlement of 400 Acres of Land to include the above Location & the preempt'n of 1000 Acres adjoining & that a Cert. issue accordingly.—

(Cert issd for 1000)

Geo'e Helms Moves to the Court to have a Location removed which he Obt'd as Assee of constance Cade sufficient cause appearing to the Court for the same it is granted him now locates the same lying on a branch of Green River Known by the Name of Elkgarden adjoining the Lands of Marquis Helm below to include an improvement made by Edw'd Bulger Order'd that a Cert issue accordingly.

Then the Court adjourned untill Tomorrow Morning 9 Oclock

Wm Fleming

At a Court continued & held by the Commissioners of Kentucky District for adjusting Titles to unpatented Lands at Harrodsburg this 18th day of Feb'y 1780

Present

Wm Fleming Steph'n Trigg &
Edm'd Lyne

[94] Collins, Vol. 2, p. 172.

(Cert issd for 1000 pd &c)

[95]Van Swearingan by Wm Lynn this day claimed a preempt to a tract of Land in the district of Kentucky on Acc't of Mark'g & improving the same in the year 1776 lying on the dividing ridge between Jessimin & Clear Creek to include an improvment made by Thos Wilson satisfactory proof being made to the Court they are of Opinion that the s'd Swearingin has a right to a preemption of 1000 Acres of Land to include the s'd improvement & that a Cert issue accordingly.—

(Cert issd for 1000 pd &c)

[96]Jacob Drinan by Simon Butler this day claimed a preempt'n of 1000 Acres of Land at the State price in the district of Kentucky on Acc't of Marking & improving the same in the year 1776 lying on the head of Mill Creek eight miles from the lower Blue licks 2½ Miles East of the upper limestone road to include his improvement satisfactory proof being made to the Court they are of Opinion that the s'd Drinan has a right to a preempt'n of 1000 Acres of Land to include the above location & that a Cert. issue accordingly.—

(Cert issd for 1400 pd &c)

Thomas Denton Assee of Eliz'a White who was since enter'd married with [97]Andrew Johnston this day claimed a settlement & preemption to a tract of Land in the District of Kentucky on Acc't of the s'd Elia'h White Settling in the Country 12 Months before the year 1778 which was before her entermarrying with the said Johnson lying on the North side of Green River waters of Sinking Creek to include 2 Cabbins built by the s'd Denton & Wm Stewart & a spring known by the name of a Flat Spring and marked on a Tree IM Satisfactory proof being made to the Court they are of Opinion that the s'd Denton has a right to a settlement of 400 Acres of Land to include the above Location & the preempt'n of 1000 Acres adjoining & that a Cert. issue accordingly.

(Cert issd for 400 pd &c)

Jos'h Reed this day claimed a preempt'n of 400 Acres of Land at the State price in the District of Kentucky on Acc't of making an Actual settlem't in 1s June 1779 lying on Cartrights Creek on the South side thereof about 2 Miles from the s'd Creek on a draft of the same and about 4 Miles from the Indian Lick to include his improvem't satisfactory proof being made to the Court they are of Opinion that the s'd Reed has a right to a preemption of 400 Acres of Land to include the above Location & that a Cert issue accordingly.—

(Cert issd for 400 pd &c)

Jno Boyd this day claimed a preemption of 400 Acres of Land at the State price in the district of Kentucky on Acc't of making an Actual settlement in the year 1778 lying on the North side of Kentucky nearly a South East Course from the shanee run & about 3½ Miles from the same to include 2 Spring near an Old Camping Place Satisfactory proof being made to the Court they are of Opinion that the s'd Boyd has a right to a preemption of 400 Acres of land to

[95] Collins, Vol. 2, p. 131; Life of Maj. G. M. Bedinger, p. 140

[96] Drinan (Drennon) Jacob, Collins, Vol. 2, p. 53, &c.

[97] Collins, Vol. 2, p. 624.

include the above location & that a Cert issue accordingly.

(Cert issd for 400 pd &c)

[98]Wm Breasheir this day claimed a preempt'n of 400 Acres of Land at the State price in the district of Kentucky on Acc't of making an Actual settlem't in May 1779 lying on simpsons Creek at the fork to include his improvement Satisfactory proof being made to the Court they are of Opinion that the s'd Brashier has a right to a preempt'n of 400 Acres of land to include the above Location & that a Cert. issue accordingly.

(Cert issd for 1400 pd &c)

Henry Tilbon by Wm Breasheirs this day claimed a settlem't & preempt'n to a tract of Land in the District of Kentucky on Acc't of raising a Crop of Corn in the Country in the year 1775 lying on the South side of Salt River extending from the first great Crossings above Bulletts Licks to his Cabbin along the Buffaloe path—satisfactory proof being made to the Court they are of Opinion that the s'd Tilbon has a right to a settlement of 400 Acres of Land to include the above Location & the preemption of 1000 Acres adjoining & that a Cert issue accordingly.

(Cert issd for 1000 pd &c)

[99]Jno Harbeson this day claimed a preempt of 1000 Acres of land at the State price in the District of Kentucky on Acc't of Marking & improving the same in the year 1776 lying on the east side of Chaplins fork on a small Branch to include his improvem't satisfactory proof being made to the Court they are of Opinion that the s'd Harbeson has a right to a preempt. of 1000 Acres of land to include the above Location & that a Cert. issue accordingly.

(Cert issd for 1400 pd &c)

The Heirs of [100]Sam'l Cartright Dec'd by Joseph Cartright this day claimed a settlme't & preemption to a tract of Land in the district of Kentucky on Acc't of the s'd Decedents raising a Crop of corn in the year 1776 lying on both sides of Cartrights Creek adjoining the Lands of Isaac McCrakins on the Upper line to include his improvem't Wm McBrid appeared & alledged that he had a right to the Land by Virtue of a purchase from Isaac Shelby who purchased of the s'd Decedents Witnesses being sworn & examined in consideration of which the Court are of Opinion that the s'd Heirs &c has a right to a settlement of 400 Acres of Land to include the s'd improvement & the preempt of 1000 Acres adjoining & that a Cert. issue accordingly.—

(Cert issd for 400 pd &c)

Patrick McGee this day claimed a preempt of 1000 Acres of Land at the State price in the district of Kentucky on Acc't of Making an Actual settlement in April 1779 lying on the East side of Simpson Creek about 4 Miles above the Mouth to include his improvement satisfactory proof being made to the Court they are of Opinion that the

[98] Breashers Station, Collins, Vol. 2, pp. 17, 100.

[99] Collins, Vol. 2, p. 23.

[100] Collins, Vol. 2, pp. 84, 518, 519.

s'd McGee has a right to a preemption of 1000 Acres of Land to include the above Location & that a Cert. issue accordingly.—

(Cert issd for 1400 pd &c)

Jno Lapesly by Chas Campbell this day claimed a settlme't & preemption to a tract of Land in the District of Kentucky on Acc't of raising a Crop of Corn in the Country in the year 1776 lying at the head of the North fork of Gilberts Creek a branch of Dicks River Satisfactory proof being made to the Court they are of Opinion that the s'd Lapesley has a right to a settlement of 400 Acres of Land to include the above Location & the preemption of 1000 Acres of Land adjoining & that a Cert. issue accordingly.—

(Cert issd for 1400 pd &c)

[101]Rich'd Burk Assee of Edw'd Hoggin this day claimed a settlement & preempt. to a tract of Land in the District of Kentucky on Acc't of the s'd Hoggin raising a Crop of Corn in the Country in the year 1775 lying on both sides of Fox run about 1 Miles from the head thereof to include his improvem't—satisfactory proof being made to the Court they are of Opinion that the s'd Burk has a right to a settlement of 400 Acres adjoining & that a Cert. issue accordingly.

(Cert issd for 1000 pd &c)

Thos Preather by Henry Preather this day claimed a preempt'n to a tract of Land at the State price in the district of Kentucky on Acc't of Marking & improving the same in the year 1776 lying on the waters of Harrods Creek a Branch of Dicks River adjoining the lands of James Harrods on the West to include his improvem't satisfactory proof being made to the Court they are of Opinion that the s'd Preather has a right to a preempt of 1000 Acres of Land to include the above Location & that a Cert issue accordingly.—

(Cert issd for 1400 pd &c)

Angus Cameron this day claimed a settlement & preempt to a tract of Land in the District of Kentucky on Acc't of residing in the Country 12 Months before the year 1778 lying on the head of the right hand fork of Wells branch extending South East to the head of a small run that empties into the North fork of Licking including the Spring on the head of both branches about 1½ Miles above the War path that Cross the North fork Satisfactory proof being made to the Court they are of Opinion that the s'd Cameron has a right to a settlement of 400 Acres of Land to include the above Location & the preemption of 1000 Acres adjoining & that a Cert. issue accordingly.—

(Cert issd for 1000 pd &c)

John Cameron by Angus Cameron this day claimed a preemption of 1000 Acres of Land at the State price in the District of Kentucky on Acc't of Marking & improving the same in the year 1776 lying about 8 Miles from the Mouth of Floyds fork extending across the dividing ridge salt river waters & Floyds fork & a large Buffaloe path that run through the Level in the upper part to

[101] Collins, Vol. 2, p. 367.

include his improvem't satisfactory proof being made to the Court they are of Opinion that the s'd Cameron has a right to a preempt'n of 1000 Acres of Land to include the above Location & that a Cert. issue accordingly.—

(Cert issd for 1400 pd &c)

Rueben Guthrey Moves to remove a location granted at Boonsborough as Assee of Thomas Hartgrove Sufficient cause Appearing for the same it is granted him lying about ¼ of a Mile below Buntons Lick lays on the waters of Salt River & running down the Creek on both sides the Creek for quantity Order'd that a Cert. issue accordingly.—

(Cert issd for 1400 pd &c)

Jno Bowman for & in behalf of [102]Isaac Bowman moves to have a Location removed w'h was granted the 1 Inst. sufficient cause Appearing to the Court it is granted lying above the Mouth of Delewere Creek that empties on the upper side of Green River 7 or 8 Miles above the Mouth of Panther Creek Ordered that a Cert issue accordingly.—

(Cert issd for 400 pd &c to Jno Philips)

Jno Stapleton this day claimed a preempt. of 400 Acres of Land at the State price in the district of Kentucky on Acc't of Making an Actual settlem't in the year 1778 lying on a branch that runs into Chaplins fork on the East side about a Mile from the Mouth thereof & about 2 Miles from Hunters road, satisfactory proof being made to the Court they are of Opinion that the s'd Stapleton has a right to a preempt of 400 Acres of Land to include the above Location & that a Cert. issue accordingly.—

Then the Court Adjourned untill To-morrow Morning 9 Oclock

Wm Fleming

At a Court Continued & held by the Commissioners of Kentucky District for adjusting Titles to unpatented Lands at Harrodsburg this 21st day of Feb'y 1780—

present

Wm Fleming, Steph'n Trigg & Edm'd Lyne—

(Cert issd for 1000 pd &c)

Gerred Menefee Sen'r by Gerred Menefee Jun'r this day claimed a preempt'n of 1000 Acres of Land at the State price in the district of Kentucky on Acc't of Marking & improving the same in the year 1777 lying on the head of Cedar Creek adjoining the land of Wm Whetley to include his improvem't satisfactory proof being made to the Court they are of Opinion that the s'd Menefee Sen'r has a right to a preemption of 1000 Acres of Land to include the above Location & that a Cert issue accordingly.—

(Cert issd for 1000 Pd &c)

James Trabue by Dan'l Trabue this day claimed a preemp'n of 400 Acres of Land at the State price in the District of Kentucky on Acc't of Making an Actual settlement in the year 1778 lying on the head of the West branch of Gilberts Creek to include his improvement

[102] Collins, Vol. 2, p. 624.

satisfactory proof being made to the Court they are of Opinion that the s'd Trabue has a right to a preempt of 400 Acres to include the above Location & that a Cert. issue accordingly.—

(Cert issd for 1000 pd &c)

Thos Clarke Sen'r by Thos Clarke Jun'r this day claimed a preempt of 1000 Acres of Land at the State price in the District of Kentucky on Acc't of Marking & improving the same in the year 1776 lying on the waters of Licking Creek about 6 Miles from a large Lick near the Mouth of a small branch that heads in the Mountains adjacent to the Lick & on the East side of a large fork that empties into the main branch of licking & about 30 Miles above the Upper Blue Licks and on the same side of the Creek that the Lick is to include his improvement satisfactory proof being made to the Court they are of Opinion that the s'd Clarke has a right to a preempt of 1000 Acres of land to include the above Location & that a Cert. issue accordingly.—

(Cert issd for 1400)

[103]Wm Kennedy by [104]Jas Douglass this day claimed a settlme't & preempt to a tract of Land in the District of Kentucky on Acc't of settling & residing in the Country 12 Months before the year 1778 lying on the Ohio on the first large Bottom below the Mouth of Kentucky adjoining the Lands of Jno Drake heir at Law to [105]Joseph deceased satisfactory proof being made to the Court they are of Opinion that the s'd Kennedy has a right to a settleme't of 400 Acres to include the above Location & the preemption of 1000 Acres adjoining & that a cert issue accordingly.—

(Cert issd for 1000 pd &c)

Hugh Ladwell by Jno Handley this day claimed a preempt'n of 1000 Acres of land at the State price in the district of Kentucky on Acc't of mark'g & improving the same in the year 1776 lying on the Waters of Licking Creek on the East side of a large fork including a Spring Known by the name of the Elkhorn Spring to include his improvement satisfactory proof being made to the Court they are of Opinion that the said Ledwell has a right to a preempt'n of 1000 Acres to include the above Location & that a Cert. issue accordingly.—

(Cert issd for 1000 pd &c)

Thomas French by Jno Handley this day claimed a preempt of 1000 Acres of Land at the State price in the district of Kentucky on Acc't of Mark'g & improving the same in the year 1776 lying on the waters of Licking Creek near the Mouth of a small branch of a large Fork empting into the main creek about 30 Miles above the upper Blue Licks to include his improvem't Satisfactory proof being made to the Court they are of Opinion that the s'd French has a right to a preemption of 1000 Acres to include the above Location & that a Cert issue accordingly.—

(Cet issd for 1400 pd &c)

[106]Sam'l Pottenger this day claimed a settlem't & preemption to a tract of

[103] Collins, Vol. 2, pp. 326, 466.
[104] Collins, Vol. 2, pp. 52, 53, &c.; McAfee Mss.
[105] Collins, Vol. 2, pp. 417-18, 499.
[106] Collins, Vol. 2, p. 511.

Land in the District of Kentucky on Acc't of raising a Crop of Corn in the Kentucky District in the year 1776 lying on Pottengers Creek beginning about ¼ of a mile below his covered Cabbin and extending up the Creek for quantity they are of Opinion that the s'd pottenger has a right to a settlem't of 400 Acres to include the above Location & the preempt of 1000 Acres adjoining & that a Cert. issue accordingly.

(Cert issd for 1400 fees &c pd to Wm Welm)

Joseph Vance Assee of James McPheran this day claimed a settlme't & preempt to a tract of Land in the district of Kentucky on Acc't of the s'd McPheran raising a Crop of Corn in the Country in the year 1776 lying on the Waters of Green River adjoining the lands of Sam'l Briggs on the South to include McPhersan, improvement satisfactory proof being made to the Court they are of Opinion that the s'd Vance has a right to a settlem't of 400 acres of land to include the above location and the preempt'n of 1000 Acres adjoining & that a Cert. issue accordingly.—

On the Motion of Jno Vance ordered that a summons issue for Jno McKenny to appear before this court in behalf of [107]Arch'd McKenney as appears to this Court that he had laid the s'd Arch'd McKenneys lands on the Lands claimed by said Vance—

(Cert issd for 1000 fees &c pd D. D.)

Alexander Templeton Heir at Law to [108]James Templeton Dec'd by James McBrid this day claimed a preempt'n of 1000 Acres of Land at the State price in the District of Kentucky on Acc't of the s'd Templeton dec'd marking & improving the same in the year 1776 lying between Shannons Run & Glens Creek about one & half Mile from Shannons run to include his improvement satisfactory proof being made to the Court they are of Opinion that the said Templeman &c has a right to a preemption of 1000 Acres of Land to include the s'd improvem't & that a Cert. issue accordingly.—

(Cert issd for 1000 pd &c)

Wm McNutt heir at Law to [109]Joseph McNutt Dec'd by [110]Jas McBride this day claimed a preempt of 1000 Acres of Land at the State price in the District of Kentucky on Acc't of the s'd decedent marking & improving the same in the year 1776 lying between the Middle fork of Elkhorn and the West fork of Cain run adjoining the Lands of [111]Rob't Thompson to include his improvem't satisfactory proof being made to the Court they are of Opinion that the s'd McNutt has a right to a preempt'n of 1000 Acres of Land to include the above Location & that a Cert. issue accordingly.—

(Cert issd for 1000 &c)

[112]Dav'd Mitchell by Jas McBride this day claimed a preemption of 1000 Acres of Land at the State price in the district of Kentucky on Acc't of Mark-

[107] Collins, Vol. 2, p. 21, &c.
[108] Collins, Vol. 2, p. 178.
[109] Collins, Vol. 2, p. 178.
[110] Collins, Vol. 2, p. 172; Ranck's Hist. of Lex., p. 73.
[111] Collins, Vol. 2, p. 172; Ranck's Hist. of Lex., p. 73.
[112] Collins, Vol. 2, p. 172; Ranck's Hist. of Lex., p. 73.

ing & improving the same in the year 1776 lying on both sides of the South fork of Elkhorn Creek adjoining [113]Alex'r McConnell 400 Acre Tract above to include his improvem't satisfactory proof being made to the Court they are of Opinion that the s'd Michell has a right to a Preempt of 1000 Acres of Land to include the above Location & that a Cert. issue accordingly.—

(Cert issd for 1000)

[114]James Carr by Thos. Clark Jun'r this day claimed a preempt of 1000 Acres of land at the State price in the District of Kentucky on Acc't of Mark'g improving the same in the year 1774 lying adjoining the Lands of Elijah Harlen on the North side to include his improvement satisfactory proof being made to the Court they are of Opinion that the s'd Carr has a right to a preemption of 1000 Acres to include the above Location & that a Cert. issue accordingly.—

(Cert issd)

[115]Jno Clarke in behalf of Henry Thomas moves to remove a location wh'ch he obt'd a Cert. in behalf of the s'd Thomas sufficient Cause appearing to the Court it was granted and now locates it lying on Stewarts Creek which empties into the Beech fork of Salt River on the North side of the s'd fork to include his improvement about $\frac{3}{4}$ of a Mile from the Mouth of the s'd Creek & On the lower side Ordered that a Cert. issue accordingly.—

(Cert issd for 50. Acres &c)

Anthony Rogers this day claimed a preempt'n of 250 Acres of land at the State price in the District of Kentucky on Acc't of making an Actual settlement in April 1779 lying on the South East side of the Crab Orchard branch adjoining the Lands of [116]Wm Moore satisfactory proof being made to the Court they are of Opinion that the s'd Rogers has a right to a preempt'n of 250 Acres to include the above Location & that a Cert. issue accordingly.

(Cert issd for 400 pd &c)

Wm Wilson this day claimed a preemption of 400 Acres of Land at the State price in the District of Kentucky on Acc't of making an Actual settlement in March 1779 lying on Clarks run Waters of Dicks river adjoining to Clarke lying on both sides of a branch including an improvement & to extend up from Clarks land for quantity Satisfactory proof being made to the Court they are of Opinion that the s'd Wilson has a right to a preempt of 400 Acres of Land to include the above Location & that a Cert. issue accordingly—

(Cert issd for 1000)

Jos'h Hunter Jun'r by Jno Donne this day claimed a preempt of 1000 Acres of land at the State price in the District of Kentucky on Acc't of Marking & improving the same in the year 1775 lying on the Ohio River on a large Bottom about 5 or 6 Miles below the Mouth of Kentucky to include his improvement satisfactory proof being made to the Court they are of Opinion

[113] Collins, Vol. 2, 172.
[114] (Probably one of Harrod's Company).
[115] Register, Vol. 20, p. 280.

[116] Collins, Vol. 2, p. 501.

that the s'd Hunter has a right to preempt'n of 1000 Acres of Land to include the above Location & that a Cert. issue accordingly.—

(Cert issd for 1000)

Jos'h Hunter Jun. by Jno Donne this day claimed a preemption of 1000 Acres of Land at the State price in the district of Kentucky on Acc't of marking & improving the same in the year 1775 lying on the West side of Kentucky about 3 Miles above the Clay Lick & about 1 Mile South of the big Buffaloe Crossing to include his improvement satisfactory proof being made they are of Opinion that the said Hunter has a right to a preempt'n of 1000 Acres of land to include the above location & that a Cert. issue accordingly.—

Then the Court adjourned untill Tomorrow Morning 9 Oclock

Wm Fleming

At a Court continued and held by the Commissioners of Kentucky District for adjusting titles to unpatented Lands at Harrodsburgh this 22d day of Feb'y 1780

Present

Wm Fleming Stephen Trigg Edmund Lyne—

(Cert issd for 400 pd &c)

Jas Logan this day claimed a preempt of 400 Acres of Land at the State price in the District of Kentucky on Acc't of making an Actual settlement in March 1779 lying on the head of a branch of the Hanging fork of Dicks River between the Lands of Craig & McNeil to include an improvem't made by Wm Todd in the year 1774 Satisfactory proof being made to the Court they are of Opinion that the s'd Logan has a right to a preempt of 400 Acres to include the above Location & that a Cert issue accordingly.—

Wm Swan this day claimed a settlement & preempt'n to a tract of Land at the State price in the District of Kentucky on Acc't of Wm. Woodard residing in the Country 12 Months before the year 1778 at his expence It appearing to the Court that the s'd Woodard has obt'd a Cert. for the same service it is the Opinion of this Court the claime be rejected.

Then the Court adjourned untill tomorrow Morning 9 Oclock

Wm Fleming

At a Court continued & held by the Commissioners for the Kentucky District for adjusting Titles to unpatented lands at Harrodsburg this 23d day of Feb'y 1780

present

Wm Fleming Stephen Trigg Edmund Lyne—

(Cert issd)

[117]Stephen Trigg Moves to the Court to remove a Location he Obt'd a Cert. for the 2d Feb'y sufficient reason Appearing to the Court it is granted & he is Allowed to locate the same lying on the South side of the North fork of Harrods Creek above Dan'l Haggin Land to include a Spring & some im-

[117] Collins, Vol. 2, p. 22.

provm't made by Sam'l Moore &c Ord'd that a Cert. issue accordingly.—

(Cert issd)

[118]Dan'l Hoggan Applies to have his location on Salt River removed sufficient reason appearing to the Court it is granted and he is allowed to locate the same on a fork of the North Fork of Harrods Creek a branch of the Ohio to include some improvm't made by Moore &c Ordered that a Cert. issue accordingly.—

(Cert issd)

Jacob Lodawick begs leave to remove his location wh'ch he obt'd a Cert 5 Jan'y 1778(?) Sufficient cause appearing for the same it is granted him & now locate the same lying on the dividing ridge between [119]Shannons run & Sinking Creek to extend to both Creeks for Quantity Ordered that a Cert. issue accordingly.—

(Cert issd for 400 pd &c)

[120]James Harrods this day claimed a preempt of 400 Acres of Land at the State price in the District of Kentucky on Acc't of Making an Actual settlem't in 1779 lying in the forks of Bullskin Creek a branch of Breashiers Creek to include an improvement made by one Rice satisfactory proof being made to the Court they are of Opinion that the s'd Harrods has a right to a preempt'n of 400 Acres of Land to include the above Location & that a Cert. issue Accordingly.—

(Cert issd for 400 pd &c)

Francis Wilson Heir At Law to [121]Hugh Wilson by James Harrod this day claimed a settlment of 1000 Acres of Land on Acc't of the s'd Decedent residing in the Country 12 Months before the year 1778 lying on the Rolling fork of Salt River including part of a large lick called the Ceder Lick and on both sides of the said fork satisfactory proof being made to the Court they are of Opinion that the s'd Wilson has a right to a settlement of 400 Acres of land to include the above location & that a Cert. issue accordingly.—he refusing to claim the preemption.

(Cert issd for 1400 pd &c)

[122]Wm Field by [123]James Harrod this day claimed a settlem't & preempt to a tract of Land in the district of Kentucky on Acc't of raising a crop of Corn in the Country in the year 1776 lying on the head of Wilsons Run and adj'g the lands of Rev'd Charles Cummans on the west & thos Harrod on the East to include his improvement satisfactory proof being made to the Court they are of Opinion that the s'd Field has a right to a settlem't of 400 Acres of Land to include the above Location & the preemption of 1000 Acres adjoining & that a Cert issue accordingly.—

(Cert issd for 1400 pd &c)

Ann McDonnald now the wife of James Harrod this day claimed a settlem't & preempt'n to a tract of Land in the district of Kentucky on Acc't of the s'd Ann Harrod residing in the

---

[118] (Haggin) Collins, Vol. 2, p. 22.
[119] Dividing line between Fayette and Woodford.
[120] Collins, Vol. 2, p. 19, &c.

[121]Collins, Vol. 2, p. 615.
[122] Collins, Vol. 2, pp. 511, 624, 663.
[123] Collins, Vol. 2, p. 517.

Country 12 Months before the year 1778 which was before her entermarring with the s'd Harrod lying on the Ohio River at the Mouth of the first large Creek below the . . . about 50 Miles below the falls of the Ohio Satisfactory proof being made to the Court they are of Opinion that the s'd Ann Mcdonald now the wife of James Harrod has a right to a settlme't of 400 Acres of Land to include the above Location and the preempt'n of 1000 Acres adjoining & that a Cert issue accordingly.—

(Cert issd for 1400)

[124]Jno Moore by Jas Harrod this day claimed a preempt'n to a tract of Land in the District of Kentucky on account of raising a Crop of Corn in the Country in the year 1775 lying on both sides of the rowling fork of Salt river about four miles below the lands claimed . . . . ? Wilson satisfactory proof being made to the Court they are of opinion that the s'd moore has a right to a settlement of 400 acres of Land to include the above Location and the preemption of 1000 Acres adjoining and that a certificate issue accordingly.—

(Cert issd for 400 pd &c)

[125]Rob't Gilbert by Jas Harrod this day claimed a preemption of 1000 Acres of Land at the State price in the district of Kentucky on Acc't of Marking & improving the same in the year 1774 lying on the Ohio adjoining the lower side of the Lands of Ann McDonald now the wife of James Harrod satisfactory proof being made to the Court they are of Opinion that the said Gilbert has a right to a preemption of 1000 Acres of land to include the above location & that a Cert issue accordingly.—

(Cert issd for 400 pd &c)

Sam'l Garden by Jno Wilkerson this day claimed a preempt'n of 400 Acres of Land at the State price in the district of Kentucky on Acc't of Making an Actual settlement in March 1779 lying on the North side of Dicks River on a small branch of the s'd River and about 1 Mile from the same between the Lands of Wm Menefee & Henry Boffman Satisfactory proof being made to the Court they are of Opinion that the s'd Gorden has a right to a preemption of 400 Acres of Land to include the above Location & that a Cert. issue accordingly.

(Cert issd for 1400 pd &c)

Hezekiah Applegate by Ben'n Lynn this day claimed a settlement & preemption to a tract of Land in the district of Kentucky on Acc't of residing 12 Months before the year 1778 lying on Plumb Creek a branch of Salt River about 4 Miles from the mouth of the s'd Creek to improve his improvement Satisfactory proof being made to the Court they are of Opinion that the s'd Applegate has a right to a settlem't of 400 Acres of Land to include the above Location & the preempt of 1000 Acres adjoining & that a Cert. issue accordingly.—

(Cert issd for 1000)

Thos Powell by [126]Jno Floyd this day

[124] Collins, Vol. 2, p. 511.
[125] Collins, Vol. 2, p. 517.
[126] Collins, Vol. 2, p. 18 and index.

claimed a preempt of 1000 Acres of Land at the State price in the District of Kentucky on Acc't of Mark'g & improving the same in the year 1775 lying on the Ohio River including the Mouth of a small Creek about 10 Miles below the falls satisfactory proof being made to the Court they are of Opinion that the s'd Powell has a right to a preempt'n of 1000 Acres of Land to include the above Location & that a Cert. issue accordingly.—

(Cert issd for 1000 pd &c)

Rob't McCoy this day claimed a preempt of 1000 Acres of Land at the State price in the district of Kentucky on Acc't of Marking & improving the same in the year 1776 lying on Ro—e run on the south side near the head thereof to include his improvement & running Eastwardly for quantity satisfactory proof being made to the Court they are of Opinion that the s'd McCoy has a right to a preempt of 1000 Acres of Land to include the above location & that a Cert. issue accordingly.—

(Cert issd for 1000 pd &c)

Thos Beard by Wm Stewart this day claimed a preempt of 1000 Acres of Land at the State price in the district of Kentucky on Acc't of Marking & improving the same in the year 1776 lying on Stewarts Creek a branch of Chaplins fork of Salt River to include his improvement satisfactory proof being made to the Court they are of Opinion that the s'd Beard has a right to a preempt of 1000 Acre of land to include the above Location & that a Cert issue accordingly.—

(Cert issd for 1000 pd &c)

Charles Stewart Jun'r by Wm Stewart this day claimed a preemption of 1000 Acres of Land at the State price in the District of Kentucky on Acc't of Mark'g & improving the same in the year 1775 lying on both sides of Mill Creek to include his spring & Cabbin on the North side Water of Chaplins fork of Salt River satisfactory proof being made to the Court they are of Opinion that the s'd Stewart has a right to a preemption of 1000 Acres of Land to include the above Location & that a Cert. issue accordingly.—

Then the Court adjourned untill tomorrow Morning 9 Oclock

Wm Fleming

At a Court continued & held by the Commissioners of the Kentucky District for adjusting Titles to unpatented Lands at Harrodsburgh this 24th day of Feb'y 1780

Present

Wm Fleming Stephen Trigg &
Ed'd Lyne—

(Cert issd for 1400)

Peter Casey by Isaac Hite this day claimed a settlement & preemption to a tract of Land in the district of Kentucky on Acc't of raising a Crop of Corn in the Country in the year 1776 lying on the waters of Shawnee run adjoining Hugh McGarys Settlement on the West side to include his improvem't satisfactory proof being made to the Court they are of Opinion that the s'd Casey has a right to a settlem't of 400 Acres of Land to include the above location & the preempt'n of 1000 Acres of Land adj'g & that a Cert. issue accordingly.—

(Cert issd for 1400)

[127]Dav'd Williams by Isaac Hite this day claimed a settlement & preemption to a tract of Land in the District of Kentucky on Acc't of raising a Crop of Corn in the Country in the year 1775 lying on the Main Fork of Harrods Creek about 3 Miles above the fork to include an improvem't made by Peter Casey in the year 1775 Satisfactory proof being made to the Court they are of Opinion that the s'd Williams has a right to a settlement of 400 Acres of Land to include the above Location & the preempt of 1000 Acres adjoining & that a Cert issue accordingly.—

(Cert issd for D. D.)

Jacob Poplan comes into Court & Offers to locate a peice of land which he obtained a Cert. for — day of Feb'y —— which is granted lying on the South side of the Rolling of Salt River below the Mouth of Pottengers Creek adjoining the lands of Jno Walton & to extend up the River for Quantity Ordered that a Cert. issue accordingly.—

(Cert issd for 1400)

[128]Edw'ds Williams by Isaac Hite this day claimed a settlement & preempt'n to a tract of Land in the district of Kentucky on Acc't of raising a Crop of Corn in the Country in the year 1775 lying on the waters of Floyds fork of Salt River about 5 or 6 Miles from Bulletts Lick on the right hand of the path from the s'd Lick to Beargrass to include and improvem't made by [129]Wm & Peter Casey Satisfactory proof being made to the Court they are of Opinion that the s'd Williams has a right to a settlement of 400 Acres of Land to include the above location & the preemption of 1000 Acres adjoining & that a Cert. issue accordingly.—

(Cert issd for 1400)

Peter Higgins by Isaac Hite this day claimed a settlement & preempt'n to a tract of land in the district of Kentucky on Acc't of raising a crop of Corn in the Country in the year 1776 lying on the path from Harrodsburgh to Harrods landing of Kentucky about 2 Miles from Harrodsburgh to include his improvem't satisfactory proof being made to the Court they are of Opinion that the s'd Higgins has a right to a settlement of 400 Acres of land to include the above Location & the preemption of 1000 Acres of land adjoining & that a Cert. issue accordingly.—

(Cert issd for 400)

Jno Rennocks by Isaac Hite this day claimed a settlem't & preempt to a tract of land in the District of Kentucky on Acc't of raising a Crop of Corn in the Country in the year 1776 lying on the South side of Dick River about ½ a Mile from the mouth of Gilberts to include an improvem't made by J. Sanders Satisfactory proof being made to the Court they are of Opinion that the said Rennocks has a right to a settlement of 400 Acres of Land to include the above Location & the preempt of 1000 Acres

[127] Collins, Vol. 2, p. 177 and index.
[128] Collins, Vol. 2, pp. 519, 634.
[129] Collins, Vol. 2, pp. 124, 775.

adjoining & that a Cert. issue accordingly.—

(Cert issd for 1400)

[130]Henry Higgins by Isaac Hite this day claimed a settlem't & preempt'n to a tract of Land in the district of Kentucky on Acc't of residing in the Country 12 Months before the year 1778 lying on the right hand side of the path leading from this place to Harrodsburg on Kentucky about 3 Miles from Harrodsburgh to include an improvement made by Wm Mattimore satisfactory proof being made to the Court they are of Opinion that the s'd Higgins has a right to a settlemnt of 400 Acres of Land to include the above Location & the preemption of 1000 Acres adj'g & that a Cert. issue accordingly.—

Rob't Traves (Travers) by Isaac Hite this day claimed a settlement & preempt to a tract of Land in the District of Kentucky on Acc't of residing 12 Months in the Country before the year 1778 satisfactory proof being made to the Court they are of Opinion that the s'd Travers has a right to a settlement of 400 Acres to include the above location & the preemption of 1000 adj'g & that a Cert issue accordingly.—

(Cert issd for 1000)

James McCanly by [131]Francis McConnel this day claimed a preempt of 1000 Acres of land at the State price in the District of Kentucky on Acc't of marking & improving the same in the year 1776 lying on the head branch of the east fork of licking Creek on the East side of the s'd Branch to include his improvem't satisfactory proof being made to the Court they are of Opinion that the s'd McCanly has a right to a preempt of 1000 Acres of land to include the above Location & that a Cert issue accordingly.—

(Cert issd for 1000)

Thos Johnson by [132]Sam'l Moore this day claimed a preempt of 1000 Acres of Land at the State price in the district of Kentucky on Acc't of Mark'g & improving the same in the year 1776 lying on the forks of Clear creek on the North side of Kentucky beginning at the point formed by the North & South fork of the s'd Creek & extending up each fork so as to include his Cabbin satisfactory proof being made to the Court they are of Opinion that the s'd Johnson has a right to a preempt of 1000 Acres of Land to include the above Location & that a Cert issue accordingly—

(Cert issd for 400)

[133]Wm Pope Assee of [134]Joshua Archer this day claimed a preempt'n of 400 Acres of Land at the State price in the district of Kentucky on Acc't of Making an Actual settlem't in the Month of May 1779 lying on the South side of Salt River about 3 Miles from Bulletts Lick at the Buffaloe Crossing to include his improvement about 3 or 400 yards from the River satisfactory proof being made to the Court they are of Opinion that the s'd Pope has a right to a preempt of 400 Acres of Land to include

[130] Collins, Vol. 2, pp. 467, 519.
[131] Collins, Vol. 2, p. 172 and index.
[132] Collins, Vol. 2, p. 445 and index.
[133] Collins, Vol. 2, p. 360 and index.
[134] Collins, Vol. 2, pp. 231, 655.

the above location & that a Cert issue accordingly.—

(Cert issd for 400 pd &c to Sam'l Moore)

Henry Hall this day claimed a preempt of 1000 Acres of Land at the State price in the District of Kentucky on Acc't of making an Actual settlement in April 1779 lying on Otter Creek waters of Salt River about 2 Miles above the Buffaloe Lick 4 Miles from the mouth of the s'd Creek & on the East side to include his improvement satisfactory proof being made to the Court they are of Opinion that the s'd Hall has a right to a preempt of 400 Acres of Land to include the above Location & that a Cert. issue accordingly.—

(Cert issd for 1000 pd &c)

Martin Hawkins by [135]Jno Todd this day claimed a preempt of 400 Acres of Land at the State price in the District of Kentucky on Account of making an Actual settlement in May 1779 lying on the East fork of Hickmans Creek adj'g Bolls Land on the South west including a Cabbin built by one Roberson satisfactory proof being made to the Court they are of Opinion that the said Hawkings has a right to a preempt of 400 Acres of Land to include the above Location & that a Cert issue accordingly.

(Cert issd for 1000 pd &c)

Jesteman Swan by Wm Swan this day claimed a preemption of 1000 Acres of Land at the State price in the district of Kentucky on Acc't of marking & improving the same in the year 1776 lying on the North side of the North fork of Elkhorn Creek on the waters of Lecompts run to include his improvement satisfactory proof being made to the Court they are of Opinion that the s'd Swan has a right to a preempt of 1000 Acres of Land to include the above Location & that a Cert issue accordingly.—

James Lapesly by [136]Wm McBrid this day claimed a settlem't & preempt'n to a tract of land in the district of Kentucky on Acc't of raising a Crop of Corn in the Country in the year 1775 lying on the East fork of Paint lick creek to include a spring marked W. M. B. by a small Lick satisfactory proof being made to the Court they are of Opinion that the s'd Lapsley has a right to a settlem't of 400 Acres of land to include the above Location & the preempt'n of 1000 Acres adjoining & that a Cert issue accordingly & reconsidering the above claim they are of oppinion from the evidence that the above Order be set aside.

(Cert issd for 1400 pd &c)

[137]Wm Steel by Wm Stewart this day claimed a settlement & preemption to a tract of Land in the District of Kentucky on Acc't of residing in the Country 12 Months before the year 1778 lying on the North side of the North fork of Elkhorn Creek on the waters of a Creek that runs into Elkhorn Opposite to McClellens fort in the fork to include two Cabbins one built by Wm Stewart the other Jno Gabriel Jones Satisfactory proof being made to the Court they are of Opinion that the s'd

135 Collins, Vol. 2, p. 110 and index.

136 Collins, Vol. 2, p. 475 and index.

137 Collins, Vol. 2, p. 173 and index.

Steel has a right to a settlement of 400 Acres of Land to include the above Location & the preemption of 1000 Acres adjoining & that a Cert issue accordingly.—

(Cert issd for 1400 pd &c)

George McClure by Wm Stewart this day claimed a settlem't & preempt to a tract of Land in the district of Kentucky on Acc't of residing in the Country 12 Months before the year 1778 lying on both sides of Bullskin a branch of Breasheirs Creek about 2 Miles above the forks to include his improvement satisfactory proof being made to the Court they are of Opinion that the s'd McClure has a right to a settlement of 400 Acres of Land to include the above Location & the preempt of 1000 Acres adjoining & that a Cert issue accordingly.

(Cert issd for 1000 pd &c)

[138]Wm McConnell Sen'r by Frat McConnell this day claimed a preempt'n of 1000 Acres of land at the State price in the district of Kentucky on Acc't of marking & improving the same in the year 1775 lying on the middle branch of Lawrence Creek adjoining a settlem't & preempt'n granted Joseph Frazer to include his improvement satisfactory proof being made to the Court they are of Opinion that the s'd McConnell Sen'r has a right to a preempt of 1000 Acres to include the above Location & that a Cert issue accordingly.—

(Cert issd for 1000 pd &c)

[139]Andrew Steele by Levi Todd this day claimed a preempt of 1000 Acres of Land at the State price in the District of Kentucky on Acc't of Mark'g & improving the same in the year 1775 lying on the North fork of Elkhorn ½ Mile above its Junction with the South fork to include his improvement satisfactory proof being made to the Court they are of Opinion that the s'd Steele has a right to a preempt of 1000 Acres to include the above location & that a Cert issue accordingly.—

(Cert issd for 1000 pd &c)

[140]Samuel Boggs by [141]David Vance this day claimed a preemption to a tract of Land at the State price in the District of Kentucky on Acc't of marking & improving the same in the year 1776 lying on the waters of the East Fork of Licking Creek upon a branch called Mill Creek adjoining [142]John Vance to include his improvement satisfactory proof being made to the Court they are of Opinion that the s'd Bogs has a right to a preempt'n of 1000 Acres of Land to include the above Location & that a Cert issue accordingly.

(Cert issd for 1000 pd &c)

Adam Young by James McCollock this day claimed a preempt of 1000 Acres of Land at the State price in the district of Kentucky on Acc't of Mark'g & improving the same in the year 1775 lying on the north fork of Hammons Creek a branch of Salt River including the head of the North fork of the Said Creek and his improvement Satisfactory proof being made to the Court they

[138] Collins, Vol. 2, p. 172 and index.
[139] Collins, Vol. 2, p. 173 and index.
[140] Collins, Vol. 2, p. 550.
[141] Collins, Vol. 2, p. 172.
[142] Collins, Vol. 2, p. 177 and index.

are of Opinion that the s'd Young has a right to a preempt of 1000 Acres of Land to include the above Location & that a Cert issue accordingly.—

(Cert issd for 1000 pd &c)

Philip Young McCallock this day claimed a preempt of 1000 Acres of Land at the State price in the district of Kentucky on Account of Mark'g & improving the same in the year 1776 lying on the head waters of Bensons Creek waters of Kentucky River near the Fork of the said Creek to include his improvement satisfactory proof being made to the Court they are of Opinion that the s'd Young has a right to a preempt of 1000 Acres of land to include the above Location & that a Cert issue accordingly.—

(Cert issd for 1000 pd &c)

Shadorick McLamore by Jas McCallock this day claimed a preempt of 1000 Acres of Land at the State price in the District of Kentucky on Acc't of marking & improving the same in the year 1774 lying on the west side of Simpsons Creek a branch of Salt River five Miles above the Mouth of the s'd Creek satisfactory proof being made to the Court they are of Opinion that the s'd McLamore has a right to a preempt of 1000 Acres of Land to include the above location & that a Cert issue accordingly.—

(Cert issd for 1400 pd &c)

Wm Steele by [143]Jno Martin this day claimed a settlement & preempt'n to a tract of Land in the District of Kentucky on Acc't of raising a Crop of Corn in the Country in the year 1776 lying on the North side of Middle fork of Licking Creek between a large Buffaloe road & the creek to include his improvement satisfactory proof being made to the Court they are of Opinion that the s'd Steele has a right to a settlem't of 400 Acres of land to include the above location & the preempt of 1000 Acres adjoining & that a Cert issue accordingly.—

(Cert issd for 1400 pd &c)

[144]Wm Miller by Jno Martin this day claimed a settlement & preempt'n to a tract of Land in the District of Kentucky on Acc't of raising a crop of Corn in the Country in the year 1776 lying on the Waters of the Middle fork of Licking Creek on a large Buffaloe road to include his improvement satisfactory proof being made to the court they are of Opinion that the s'd Miller has a right to a settlement of 400 Acres of Land to include the above Location & the preempt of 1000 Acres adj'g & that a Cert issue accordingly.

(Cert issd for 1400 pd &c)

[145]Jno Miller by Jno Martin this day claimed a settlement & preempt'n to a tract of land in the district of Kentucky on Acc't of raising a Crop of Corn in the Country in the year 1776 lying on the North side of the Middle fork of Licking Creek to include his improvement adjoining the Lands of [146]Alexander Polock Satisfactory proof being made to the Court they are of Opinion

[143] Collins, Vol. 2, p. 20 and index.

[144] Collins, Vol. 2, p. 326.
[145] Collins, Vol. 2, p. 21 and index.
[146] Collins, Vol. 2, p. 326.

that the s'd Miller has a right to a settlement of 400 Acres of Land to include the above Location & the preempt of 1000 Acres of Land adjoining & that a Cert issue accordingly.—

(Cert issd for 1400 pd &c)

Alexander Pollock by Jno Martin this day claimed a settlement & preempt to a tract of land in the district of Kentucky on Acc't of raising a Crop of Corn in the year of 1776 lying on the North side of the Middle fork of Licking Creek adjoining the lands of Jno Miller to include his improvement satisfactory proof being made to the Court they are of Opinion that the s'd Pollock has a right to a settlement of 400 Acres of land to include the above Location & the preempt of 1000 Acres adjoining & that a Cert issue accordingly.—

(Cert issd for 1400 pd &c)

[147]Wm Nisbit by Jno Martin this day claimed a settlement & preempt'n to a tract of land in the district of Kentucky on Acc't of raising a crop of Corn in the Country in the year 1776 lying on the North side of the Middle Fork of Licking Creek between a buffaloe Road & the s'd Creek adjoining of the Lower side of Wm Steeles land to include his improvement Satisfactory proof being made to the Court they are of Opinion that the s'd Nisbit has a right to a settlement of 400 Acres of land to include the above Location & the preemption of 1000 Acres of land adjoining & that a Cert. issue accordingly.—

(Cert issd for 1400 pd &c)

[148]Sam'l Nisbit by Jno Martin this day claimed a settlement & preempt to a tract of land in the district of Kentucky on Acc't of raising a crop of Corn in the Country in the year 1776 lying between the Middle & South fork of Licking creek on a buffaloe path on a branch of the Middle fork to include his improvement Satisfactory proof being made to the Court they are of Opinion that the s'd Nisbit has a right to a settlement of 400 Acres of Land & the preempt of 1000 Acres adjoining & that a Cert. issue accordingly.—

(Cert iss for 1400 pd &c)

[149]Sam'l Wilson by Jno Martin this day claimed a settlem't & preempt'n to a tract of land in the district of Kentucky on Acc't of raising a Crop of Corn in the Country in the year 1775 lying on the North side of the Middle Fork of Licking Creek about 3 Miles from Riddles Station to include his improvement satisfactory proof being made to the Court they are of Opinion that the s'd Wilson has a right to a settlement of 400 Acres of land to include the above Location & the preemption of 1000 Acres adjoining & that a Cert issue accordingly.—

(Cert issd for 1000 pd &c)

[150]Jno Lacey by Jno Martin this day claimed a preempt'n of 1000 Acres of Land at the State price in the district of Kentucky on Acc't of marking & improving the same in the year of 1775 lying on the South side of the South fork Licking Creek including a Spring on a High Bank and his improvem't

147 (Nesbitt) Collins, Vol. 2. p. 326.
148 (Nesbitt) Collins, Vol. 2, p. 326.
149 Collins, Vol. 2, p. 325.
150 Collins, Vol. 2, p. 326.

Satisfactory proof being made to the Court they are of Opinion that the s'd Lacey has a right to a preemption of 1000 Acres to include the s'd improvement & that a Cert issue accordingly.—

(Cert issd for 1400 pd &c)

Archabald Martin by Jno Martin this day claimed a preempt of 1000 Acres of Land at the State price in the district of Kentucky on Acc't of marking & improving the same in the year 1775 lying on the South side of the South fork of Licking Creek about 2½ Miles from Jno Martins Land to include a Spring & improvem't satisfactory proof being made to the Court they are of Opinion that the s'd Martin has a right to a preempt of 1000 Acres of Land to include the above Location & that a Cert issue accordingly.

(Cert issd for 1400 pd &c)

Jno Dunley by Jno Martin this day claimed a settlement & preempt to a tract of Land in the District of Kentucky on Acc't of residing in the Country 12 Months before the year 1778 lying West of the Sycamore Forest on a Branch of Licking Creek includ'g Locust ridge Satisfactory proof being made to the Court they are of Opinion that the s'd Dunley has a right to a settlem't of 400 Acres of land to include the above Location & the Preemption of 1000 Acres adjoining & that a Cert issue accordingly.—

(Cert issd for 1000 pd &c)

Peter Jorden by [151]Patrick Jorden this day claimed a preempt'n of 1000 Acres of Land at the State price in the District of Kentucky on Acc't of Marking & improving the same in the year 1776 lying on a branch that runs into Hustons fork of licking Creek to include his improvment to run West & North West for quantity Satisfactory proof being made to the Court they are of Opinion that the s'd Jorden has a right to a preempt of 1000 Acres of Land to include the above Location & that a Cert issue accordingly.

(Cert issd for 1000)

Peter Jorden Jun'r by Patrick Jourden this day claimed a preempt'n of 1000 Acres of Land at the state price in the District of Kentucky on Acc't of Mark'g & improving the same in the year 1776 lying on the North side of Elkhorn Creek about 1 Mile from the forks partly Opposite on a small branch that runs into the s'd Creek to include made by Patrick Jourden satisfactory proof being made to the Court they are of Opinion that the s'd Jorden Jun'r has a right to a preempt'n of 1000 Acres to include the above Location & that a Cert. issue accordingly.—

Then the Court adjourned untill tomorrow Morning 9 Oclock

Wm Fleming

At a Court continued & held by the Commissioners of Kentucky District for adjusting Titles to unpatented Lands at Harrodsburgh the 25th day of Feb'y 1780

Present

Wm Fleming Stephen Trigg & Edmund Lyne—Gent—

[151] Collins, Vol. 2, p. 177 and index.

(Cert issd for 400)

George May Assee of Joshua Willis this day claimed a preempt'n of 400 Acres of Land at the State price in the district of Kentucky on Acc't of making & Actual settlement in April 1779 lying on the North side of Green River about 2 or 3 Miles above the Mouth of Panther Creek to include the Cypress Springs running up and down the river for Quantity satisfactory proof being made to the Court they are of Opinion that the s'd May Assee of Joshua Willis has a right to a preempt'n of 400 Acres to include the above Location & that a Cert issue accordingly.

(Cert issd for 400)

Ezecle Morris this day claimed a preemption of 400 Acre of Land at the State price in the district of Kentucky on Acc't of mak'g and Actual settlement in the year 1778 lying at the mouth of Hardens Creek a branch of the Beech fork of Salt River to include an improvement satisfactory proof being made to the Court they are of Opinion that the s'd Morris has a right to a preemption of 400 Acres of Land to include the above Location & that a Cert issue accordingly.—

(Cert issd for 1400)

Hugh McGary by Rich'd Porter this day claimed a settlement & preemption to a tract of land in the District of Kentucky on Acc't of the s'd Porters residing in the Country 12 Months before the year 1778 lying on the Kentucky River to include Harrods Landing Satisfactory proof being made to the Court they are of Opinion that the s'd McGarry has a right to a settlement of 400 Acre of Land to include the above Location & the preemption of 1000 Acres adjoining & that a Cert issue accordingly.

(Cert issd for 400 pd &c to And'w Jorden)

Jno Jackson this day claimed a preemption of 400 Acres of Land at the State price in the district of Kentucky on Acc't of Mak'g an Acc't settlement in April 1779 lying near the head of Hardens Creek a branch of the Beech fork of Salt River to include an improvement made by Thos Denton & a small spring above the improvement marked on a tree D Satisfactory proof being made to the Court they are of Opinion that the s'd Jackson has a right to a preemption of 400 Acres of land to include the above Location & that a Cert issue accordingly.

(Cert issd for 1000)

Wm McMurry by Jno Muldrough this day claimed a preempt'n of 1000 Acres of land at the State price in the district of Kentucky on Acc't of mark'g & improving the same in the year 1776 lying on the Rolling fork of Salt river about 3 Miles below Jno Muldoroughs Land satisfactory proof being made to the Court they are of Opinion that the s'd McMurry has a right to a preempt of 1000 Acres to include the above Location & that a Cert issue accordingly.

(Cert issd for 400)

Andrew Hines by Wm Freeman this day claimed a preempt of 1000 Acres of land at the State price in the District of Kentucky on Acc't of making an

Actual settlement in April 1779 in Soverins Valley waters of Green River adjoining Hines Land on his East line to include his improvement satisfactory proof being made to the Court they are of Opinion that the s'd Hines has a right to a preempt of 1000 Acres to include the above Location & that a Cert issue accordingly.

(Cert issd for 400)

Micheal Goodnight this day claimed a preempt of 400 Acres of land at the State price in the District of Kentucky on Acc't of making an Actual settlement in Feb'y 1779 lying at the Mouth of the Docters fork of Chaplins fork of Salt River on both sides of the s'd Creek Satisfactory proof being made to the Court they are of Opinion that the said Goodnight has a right to a preempt of 400 Acres of Land to include the above Location & that a Cert issue accordingly.—

(Cert issd for 400)

Jean Benton this day claimed a preempt of 400 Acres of Land at the State price in the district of Kentucky on Acc't of the s'd Benton mak'g an Actual settlement in the year 1778 lying on the west side of Hardens Creek waters of the Beech fork of Salt River about 5 or 6 Miles partly a North West Course from James Pheonix's Land Satisfactory proof being made to the Court they are of Opinion that the s'd Benton has a right to a preempt of 400 Acres of Land to include the above Location & that a Cert issue accordingly.

(Cert issd for 1000)

Jno Hall by Wm McBride this day claimed a preempt of 1000 Acres of land at the State price in the District of Kentucky on Acc't of mark'g & improv'g the same in the year 1775 lying on the waters of the Dicks River about 4 Miles from the flat Lick Near the Knobbs to include his improvement Satisfactory proof being made to the Court they are of Opinion that the s'd Hall has a right to a preempt of 1000 Acres of Land to include the s'd improvement & that a Cert. issue accordingly.—

(Cert issd for 400)

Francis McMeans by And'w McBride this day claimed a preemp'n of 400 Acres of land at the State price in the district of Kentucky on Acc't of Making an Actual settlement in May 1779 lying on the Beech fork of Salt River on the West side thereof about 4½ Miles below the Mouth of Chaplins fork Satisfactory proof being made to the Court they are of Opinion that the s'd McMeans has a right to a preempt of 1000 Acres of Land to include the above Location & that a Cert issue accordingly.—

(Cert issd D. D.)

Arch'd McKenney came into Court & moves to alter his location & his former one was taken from him by a prior improvement which is granted him lying on Stoners fork of Licking Creek above Stoners Land at a Buffaloe path running North for quantity Ordered that a Cert issue accordingly.

(Cert issd for 400)

Rob't McMean this day claimed a preempt'n of 400 Acres of Land at the

State price in the District of Kentucky on Acc't of making an Actual settlement in May 1779 lying on the North side of the Beech fork of Salt River about 3 or 4 Miles from the s'd fork to include his improvement satisfactory proof being made to the Court they are of Opinion that the s'd McMean has a right to a preemp'n of 400 Acres of Land to include the above location & that a Cert issue accordingly.

(Cert issd for 400)

Andrew McMean this day day claimed a preemption of 400 Acres of Land at the State price in the district of Kentucky on Acc't of making an Actual settlement in May 1779 lying on the Beech fork of Salt river on the west side thereof & about 4 Miles below the mouth of Chaplins fork to include his improvement satisfactory proof being made to the Court they are of Opinion that the s'd McMean has a right to a preempt of 400 Acres of Land to include the above Location & that a Cert issue accordingly.—

(Cert issd for 400)

Jas Young this day claimed a preempt of 400 Acres of Land at the State price in the District of Kentucky on Account of making an Actual settlement in May 1779 lying on the Beech fork of Salt river on the West side thereof about 2 Miles from the s'd fork and about 5 Miles below the Mouth of Chaplin Fork to include his improvement Satisfactory proof being made to the Court they are of Opinion that the s'd Young has a right to a preempt of 400 Acres of Land to include the above Location & that a Cert issue accordingly.

(Cert issd for 1000)

Isaac Sparks by George Smith this day claimed a preempt of 1000 Acres of land at the State price in the District of Kentucky on Acc't of marking and improving the same in the year 1777 lying on Breasheirs Creek on the West waters of the same adjoining Harrodsburgh Trace to include an improvement made by George Smith satisfactory proof being made to the Court they are of Opinion that the s'd Sparks has a right to a preempt of 1000 Acres of Land to include the Above Location & that a Cert. issue accordingly.—

(Cert issd for 1400)

Joseph Cartright this day claimed a settlement & preemption to a tract of Land in the District of Kentucky on Acc't of settling in the Country in the year 1777 & residing in the Country 12 Months since the s'd settlement lying on both sides of pleasant run waters of Beech fork of Salt River to include an improvem't made by [152]Sam'l Cartright & running down the Creek for quantity Satisfactory proof being made for the Court they are of Opinion that the s'd Cartright has a right to a settlement of 400 Acres to include the above location & the preemption of 1000 Acres adjoining & that a Cert issue accordingly.—

Ordered that the former claime of s'd Cartright be set aside.

(Location Altered)

[153]Sam'l Porter this day claimed a

[152] Collins, Vol. 2, pp. 84, 518, 519.
[153] Collins, Vol. 2, p. 367.

preemption of 400 Acres of Land at the State price in the district of Kentucky on Acc't of mak'g an Actual settlement in the year 1778 lying on the South side of Jessemine Creek adjoining the Lands of Edw'd Brandly to include his improvement satisfactory proof being made to the Court they are of Opinion that the s'd Porter has a right to a preempt of 400 Acres of Land to include the above location & that a Cert issue accordingly.—

(Cert issd for 400)

Wm Casey by Joseph Vance this day claimed a preemption of 400 Acres of land at the State price in the district of Kentucky on Acc't of making an Actual settlement in the Month of Jan'y 1779 lying on the waters of the Hanging fork of Dicks river adjoining the lands of Sam'l Briggs on the North side to include an improvement made by James McPheran satisfactory proof being made to the Court they are of Opinion that the s'd Casey has a right to a preemption of 400 Acres of land to include the above location & that a Cert issue accordingly.—

(Cert issd for 1000)

Andrew Bunton by Thos Denton this day claimed a preempt'n of 1000 Acres of Land at the State price in the District of Kentucky on Acc't of marking & improving the same in the year 1775 lying on the North side of Green River on sinking Creek that runs into the s'd River in the forks of the s'd Creek marked on a tree A. B. at a Spring Satisfactory proof being made to the Court they are of Opinion that the s'd Bunton has a right to a preemption of 1000 Acres of land to include the above Location & that a Cert issue accordingly.

(Cert issd for 400 Pd &c)

Henry Bryan by Jno Martin this day claimed a preempt'n of 400 Acres of Land at the State price in the district of Kentucky on Acc't of making an Actual settlement in March 1779 lying on Dicks River on the South side thereof on a branch at a place known by the name of Boons Mill seat on both sides of the s'd Branch satisfactory proof being made to the Court they are of Opinion that the s'd Bryan has a right to a preempt'n of 400 Acres of Land to include the above Location & that a Cert issue accordingly.—

Ord'd that the Several Certificates which was Obtained by order of this Court be issued.

(Cert issd for 400)

[154]Jno Todd Jun'r by Wm Stafford this day claimed a preempt'n of 400 Acres of Land at the State price in the district of Kentucky on Acc't of making an Actual settlement in the year 1778 lying on the head waters of the South fork of Harrods Creek including his spring & improvement made by Moore & Hughs Satisfactory proof being made to the Court they are of Opinion that the s'd Todd has a right to a preemtion of 400 Acres of land to include the above Location & that a Cert issue accordingly.

[154] Collins, Vol. 2, pp. 371, 427.

(Cert issd for 400)

Jno Todd Jun'r Assee of [155]Dan'l Griffin this day claimed a preempt of 400 Acres of land at the State price in the district of Kentucky on Acc't of Marking and improving the same in the year 1779 lying on the waters of the Mulberry fork of Beargrass Creek adjoining the Lands of Jno Floyd on the North to include an improvement made by One Hughes satisfactory proof being made to the Court they are of Opinion that the s'd Todd &c has a right to a preempt of 400 Acres of Land to include the above location & that a Cert issue accordingly.—

(Cert issd for 400)

Jno Todd Jun'r Assee of [156]Patrick Owens this day claimed a preempt of 400 Acres of Land at the State price in the district of Kentucky on Acc't of the s'd Owens making an Actual settlement in May 1779 lying on the head waters of the main fork of Cain Run on the South end of a tract of Land marked for him in the year 1775 adjoining McConnells Land on the North including an improvem't by [157]Rob't Patterson Satisfactory proof being made to the Court they are of Opinion that the s'd Todd has a right to a preempt of 400 Acres of Land to include the above Location & that a Cert issue accordingly.—

(Cert issd for 1400)

Jno Todds Jun'r Assee of Jno May this day claimed a settlme't & preemption to a tract of Land in the district of Kentucky on Acc't of the S'd Jno May raising a Crop of Corn in the Country at his expence in the year 1775 lying on the head waters of the South Fork of Elkhorn at McConnells Fork including a Cabbin made by [158]Jno McCracken about 1 Mile North West of Mansfield satisfactory proof being made to the Court they are of Opinion that the s'd Todd has a right to a settlement of 400 Acres of land to include the above Location & the preemption of 1000 Acres adjoining & that a Cert issue accordingly.—

Jno Todd Jun'r made application to the Court for a preempt of 1000 Acres of land on . . . . Assee of [159]Wm Shields & it appearing to the Court that a Certain Jas Higgins has already Obt'd a Cert. for settlem't & preemption for the same service it is the Opinion of the Court that they cannot now (enter) into and examination of both parties cannot be present & that the s'd Todd can only set the Cert aside in General Court.

(Cert iss for 1400)

Domnenick Flanagen by Jno Todd Jun'r this day claimed a settlement & preemption to a tract of land in the district of Kentucky on Acc't of raising a Crop of Corn in the Country in the year 1775 lying on Cane run North of the preempt granted Jno Todd Jun Assee of Patrick Owens to include and improvement at a Sink'g Spring Satisfactory proof being made to the Court they are of Opinion that the s'd Flangen has a right to a settlement of 400 Acres of land to include the above Loca-

[155] Collins, Vol. 2, p. 435.
[156] Collins, Vol. 2, p. 173.
[157] Collins, Vol. 2, p. 170 and index.
[158] Collins, Vol. 2, p. 178.
[159] Collins, Vol. 2, p. 325.

tion & the preemption of 1000 Acres adjoining.

(Cert issd)

Geo May in behalf of [160]Pemberton Rollings moves to alter a location which he had obtained a Cert sufficient reason appearing to the Court for the same it is granted now Locates lying on the head of the West fork of Clear creek including the head branches thereof to extend towards Kentucky and the head of Glens Creek for quantity Ordered that a Cert issue accordingly.—

Isaac Hite in behalf of [161]Robt Travis proves to the Court that the s'd Travis was intitled to a settlem't & preempt'n the 24 Inst in the District of Kentucky his land being taken by one Craig now refers (prefers) to locate the same as he thinks that the s'd Travis's only redress is to be had in the General Court.

(Cert issd for 1400)

Geo'e Hart by Jno Todd Jun'r this day claimed a settlem't & preempt'n to a tract of Land in the District of Kentucky on Acc't of settling in the Country in the year 1777 and residing ever since lying on the North side of chaplins fork of Salt River adjoining the Land of Wm Beard to include his improvem't made by Wm Stewart satisfactory proof being made to the Court they are of Opinion that the s'd Hart has a right to a settlement of 400 Acres of Land to include the above Location & the preempt'n of 1000 Acres of Land adjoining & that a Cert. issue accordingly.—

[160] Collins, Vol. 2, pp. 514, 664.
[161] Con. N. W., En., Vol. I, pp. 145-50-51.

Then the Court adjourned untill tomorrow Morning 9 Oclock

Wm Fleming

At a Court continued & held by the Commissioners of Kentucky District for adjusting Titles to unpatented Lands at Harrodsburg this 26th day of Feb'y 1780

Present

Wm Fleming Steph'n Trigg & Edm'd Lyne.

(Cert issd for 400)

Jno Miller this day claimed a preempt of 400 Acres of Land at the State price in the District of Kentucky on Acc't of settling in May 1779 lying on the 2d South fork of clear Creek to include a Cabbin by Wm Feild Satisfactory proof being made to the Court they are of Opinion that the s'd Miller has a right to a preempt of 400 Acres of Land to include the above location & that a Cert. issue accordingly.—

(Cert issd for 400)

[162]Wm Mitchell by Gilbert Marshall this day claimed a preempt'n of 400 Acres of land at the State price in the district of Kentucky on Acc't of making an Actual settlem't in April 1779 lying on the fork between Dicks River & Kentucky at a place Know by the name of the Elk Lick about 2 Miles from Kentucky River satisfactory proof being made to the Court they are of Opinion that the s'd Mitchell has a right to a preempt'n of 400 Acres of Land to include the above Location & that a Cert issue accordingly.—

[162] Collins, Vol. 2, pp. 172, 771.

(Cert issd for 1400)

Thos. OBryan by [163]Edw'd Wathington this day claimed a settlem't & preempt'n to a tract of Land in the district of Kentucky on Acc't of raising a crop of Corn in the Country in the year 1775 lying on both sides of Fox run a branch of Breashers Creek waters of Salt River adjoining Jno Millers Land on the Lower side to include his improvem't—It running down the s'd Run for quantity Satisfactory proof being made to the Court they are of Opinion that the s'd OBryan has a right to a settlem't of 400 Acres of Land to include the above Location & the preempt of 1000 Acres adjoining & that a Cert issue accordingly.—

Thos. Carland came into court and on Oath declares he never impowered Nathan'l Henderson or any other person for him to lay in his claim for a settlem't of 400 Acres of Land & the preempt. of 1000 Acres & that he cannot accept of the Location made for him by the s'd [164]Nathan'l Henderson the 8th Inst as it deprives him the s'd Carland of the Location he has a just right to from an Actual settlem't made on the s'd Land lying at a sinking Spring Known by the name Carlands spring & about a Mile from the Jessemine Spring & for which Lands a cert has been granted to Dav'd Gass & that Cert. for the s'd Gass the Court is informed is sent down to the Registers Office the s'd Carland protest against Nath'l Henderson proceedings in his behalf before the Court as he hopes by entering the protests to obtain the Location of his claim to a settlem't & preempt'n before the General Court wherein his present circumstances he can only be redressed—It is the opinion of this Court that s'd Thomas Carland protest be entered & that the Clark give the s'd Carland a Copy of this order—

(Cert issd for 400)

Jno Handley this day claimed a preempt'n of 1000 Acres of Land at the State price in the District of Kentucky on Acc't of Marking & improving the same in the year 1776 lying on a branch of floyds fork of Salt River about 4 Miles East from Linns Garrison to include his improvement satisfactory proof being made to the Court they are of Opinion that the s'd Handley has a right to a preemption of 400 Acres of land to include the above Location & that a Cert issue accordingly.—

(Cert iss for 400 fees &c to Capt'n)

Jno Handley Assee of Levi Theel this day claimed a preempt'n of 400 Acres of land at the State price in the District of Kentucky on Acc't of Making an Actual settlem't in the year 1778 lying on the Middle fork of Licking the preempt of 400 Acres above of one Joseph Essex Satisfactory proof being made to the Court they are of Opinion that the s'd Handly &c has a right to a preempt. of 400 Acres to include the above Location & that a Cert issue accordingly.—

(Cert issd for 400)

[165]And'w Hends Assee of [166]James Piggett this day claimed a preempt'n of

[163] (Probably Worthington) See Con. N. W. En., p. 81, &c.
[164] Collins, Vol. 2, p. 291.
[165] (Hinde) Reg., Vol. 21, p. 53.
[166] Collins, Vol. 2, p. 40; Con. N. W. En., p. 1067.

400 Acres of Land at the State price in the district of Kentucky on Acc't of the s'd Piggetts making an Actual settlem't in May 1779 lying on the Waters of Salt River about 1½ Miles from Salt River Station to include the s'd Piggets improvem't satisfactory proof being made to the Court they are of Opinion that the s'd Hends &c has a right to a preempt of 400 Acres of Land to include the above Location & that a Cert issue accordingly.—

(Cert iss for 400)

Joseph Warford by Andrew Hends this day claimed a preemption of 400 Acres of Land at the State price in the district of Kentucky on Acc't of making an Actual settlem't in may 1779 lying on Mill Creek at a Sulphur Lick where the Buffaloe Road crosses the s'd Creek & about 15 Miles South of Bulletts Lick to improve his improvem't satisfactory proof being made to the Court they are of Opinion that the s'd Warford has a right to a preempt'n of 400 Acres of Land to include the above Location & that a Cert. issue accordingly.—

(Cert issd for 400)

Joseph Combs by And'w Hinde this day claimed a preempt'n of 400 Acres of Land at the State price in the District of Kentucky on Acc't of making an Actual settlem't in May 1779 lying on the Beech fork of Salt River about 6 Miles from the mouth on the second Creek above the Mouth to include his improvement satisfactory proof being made to the Court they are of Opinion that the said Combs has a right to a preempt, of 400 Acres of Land to include the above Location & that a Cert. issue accordingly.—

(Cert issd for 400)

Zebelen Collins by And'w Hindes this day claimed a preempt. of 400 Acres of Land at the State price in the district of Kentucky on Acc't of making an Actual settlem't in May 1779 lying on the North fork of Beargrass adjoining the Lands of [167]Wm Linn & on the South side of [168]Colo Fleming Satisfactory proof being made to the Court they are of Opinion that the s'd Collins has a right to a preempt of 400 Acres of Land to include the above Location & that a Cert. issue accordingly.—

(Cert issd for 400)

Conrod Oyler by And'w Hinde this day claimed a preempt'n of 400 Acres of Land at the State price in the District of Kentucky on Acc't of Mak'g and Actual settlem't in May 1779 lying on Rolling fork of Salt River on the South side thereof above the Mouth of the Beech fork about 4 or 5 Miles to include his improvem't Satisfactory proof being made to the Court they are of Opinion that the s'd Oyler has a right to a preempt of 400 Acres of Land to include the above Location & that a Cert. issue accordingly.—

(Cert issd for 400)

Mark Oyler by And'w Hinde this day claimed a preempt'n. of 400 Acres of Land at the State in the District of Kentucky on Acc't of making an Actual settlement in May 1779 lying about 4

[167] Con. N. W. En., p. 143; Rev. on Up. Ohio., p. 144. &c.
[168] Reg., Vol. 21, p. 168.

Miles above the long lick Creek waters of Salt River to include his improvement satisfactory proof being made to the Court they are of Opinion that the s'd Oyler has a right to a preempt of 400 Acres of Land to include the above Location & that a Cert. issue accordingly.

(Cert issd for 400)

Mark Oyler Jun'r by And'w Hinde this day claimed a preempt'n of 400 Acres of Land at the State price in the district of Kentucky on Acc't of making an Actual settlem't in May 1779 lying on the long lick Creek and about 2 Miles above Mark Oylers Land to include his improvement satisfactory proof being made to the Court they are of Opinion that the s'd Oyler has a right to a preemption of 400 Acres to include the above Location & that a Cert. issue accordingly.—

(Cert issd for 400 pd &c D. D.)

Sam'l Porter came into court & moves to alter a Location he made the 25th Inst sufficient cause appearing for the same it is granted him Now locates lying on the North side of Kentucky on the first Bottom below Millers Creek to include an improvement made by Jno Martin Order'd that a Cert. issue accordingly—

(Cert issd for 400)

And'w Hinde Assee of Dan'l Miller this day claimed a preempt'n of 400 Acres of Land at the State price in the district of Kentucky on Acc't of making an Actual settlement in May 1779.— lying on the Rolling fork of Salt River on the South side thereof on a run called Millers run to include his improvement satisfactory proof being made to the Court they are of Opinion that the s'd Hinde has a right to a preemption of 400 Acres of Land to include the above Location & that a Cert. issue accordingly.—

(Cert issd for 1400)

Jno Halloday this day claimed a settlem't & preempt'n to a tract of land in the district of Kentucky on Acc't of settling in the Country in the year 1777 & residing ever since lying on the West fork of licking Creek & below the Rolling fork of Salt River & Green River on the North side of the Creek to include Pottengers Camp & running down the Creek for quantity satisfactory proof being made to the Court they are of Opinion that the s'd Holloway has a right to a settlem't of 400 Acres of Land to include the above Location & the preempt of 1000 Acres adjoining & that a Cert. issue accordingly.—ordered that the former entry of the s'd Hollaways claim be set aside.

(Cert issd for 1000)

Moses Ashbrook Ass'ee of Wm Bartley this day claimed a preempt of 1000 Acres at the State price in the District of Kentucky on Acc't of marking & improving the same in the year 1776 lying on Simpsons Creek about 2 Miles above the forks extending up the Creek for quantity waters of Salt River Satisfactory proof being made to the Court they are of Opinion that the s'd Ashbrook has a right to a preemption of 1000

Acres of Land to include the above location & that a Cert issue accordingly.—

(Cert issd for 400)

Nathan Allen by Edw'd Wathington this day claimed a preempt'n of 400 Acres of Land at the State price in the district of Kentucky on Acc't of making an Actual settlem't in May 1779 lying on the Waters of Otter Creek on the West side thereof adjoining to the [169]Barrens of Salt River to include a Spring issuing out of the Barrens Hill & also his cabbin & other improvement satisfactory proof being made to the Court they are of Opinion that the s'd Allen has a right to a preempt of 400 Acres of Land to include the above Location & that a Cert. issue accordingly.—

(Cert issd for 1400)

[170]Lewis Hombs by Hugh McGarry this day claimed a settlem't & preempt. to a tract of Land in the District of Kentucky on Acc't of raising a crop of Corn in the Country in the year 1776 lying on the Waters of Shanee run adjoining the Lands of [171]Peter Casey on the South West Satisfactory proof being made to the Court they are of Opinion that the s'd Hombs has a right to a settlement of 400 Acres to include the Above Location & the preempt of 1000 Acres adjoining & that a Certificate issue accordingly—

(Cert issd for 1000)

Abraham Keller by [172]Jno. Bowman this day claimed a preempt'n of 400 Acres of Land at the State price in the district of Kentucky on Acc't of Mark'g & improving the same in the year 1776 lying on a branch of Higstons fork of Licking Creek Known by the name of Bowmans Creek to include an improvement made by [173]Burr Harrison.

Satisfoctory proof being made to the Court they are of Opinion that the s'd Keller has a right to a preemption of 400 Acres of land to include the above Location & that a Cert. issue accordingly.—

(Cert issd for 400)

Eliz'eth Allen by Jno Bowman this day claimed a preempt'n of 400 Acres of Land at the State price in the District of Kentucky on Acc't of making an Actual settlement in March 1779 lying on the North side of Dicks River on a run that empties into the s'd River opposite to where Colo Bowman now lives Satisfactory proof being made to the Court they are of Opinion that the s'd Allen has a right to a preemption of 400 Acres of Land to include the above Location & that a Cert. issue accordingly.—

(Cert issd for 400 pd &c D. D. to Jno Shelp)

Joseph Acres by Colo Bowman this day claimed a preempt'n of 400 Acres of Land at the State price in the district of Kentucky on Acc't of making an Actual settlem't in March 1779 lying on the South side of the Middle fork of Licking Creek on a branch adjoining the Lands of [174]Jno Shelp & about 3

[169] Reg., Vol. 21, p. 158.
[170] (Holmes) Collins, Vol. 2, pp. 518, 519.
[171] Collins, Vol. 2, p. 367; Con. N. W., p. 961.
[172] Con. N. W. En., p. 65, &c.
[173] Con. N. W. En., p. 580.
[174] Collins, Vol. 2, pp. 517-19; Reg., Vol. 20, p. 280.

Miles from Harrods Lick to include an improvement made by Jno Shelp Satisfactory proof being made to the Court they are of Opinion that the s'd Acres has a right to a preempt'n of 400 Acres of Land to include the above Location & that a Cert. issue accordingly.—

(Cert issd for 400)

Jno. Pearcy moves to alter a location wh'ch he Obt'd a Cert. for the 29th Jan'y 1780 sufficient cause appearing for the same it was granted him Now locates lying on the Middle fork of licking Creek beginning on the line of Wm Hays & running its length on the s'd line Ord'd that a Cert. issue accordingly.—

(Cert issd for 400)

Jno. Scott by Joseph Carsweller this day claimed a preempt'n of 400 Acres of Land at the State price in the district of Kentucky on Acc't of making an actual settlem't in March 1779 lying on the South side of Harrods run about ½ a Mile from the Mouth satisfactory proof being made to the Court they are of Opinion that the s'd Scott has a right to a preempt'n of 400 Acres of Land to include the above Location & that a Cert. issue accordingly.

(Cert issd for 1000)

Geo'e Bellow by Wm Stewart this day claimed a preempt'n of 1000 Acres of Land at the State price in the district of Kentucky on Acc't of marking & improving the same in the year 1776 lying on a branch of a large fork of licking Creek about 2 Miles from Sam'l Brown Land including a large spring Mill seat & his improvem't satisfactory proof being made to the Court they are of Opinion that the s'd Bellow has a right to a preempt'n of 1000 Acres of Land to include the above Location & that a Cert. issue accordingly—

(Cert issd for 1400)

[175]Lott Wood by Edw'd Hammond this day claimed a settlem't & preempt to a Tract of Land in the district of Kentucky on Acc't of raising a Crop of Corn in the Country in the year 1777 lying on the East fork of Paint Lick to include a Spring by a small Lick Marked with W. M. B. & I. K. on a tree satisfactory proof being made to the Court they are of Opinion that the s'd Wood has a right to a settlement of 400 Acres of Land to include the above Location & the preempt'n of 1000 Acres adjoining & that a Cert. issue accordingly.

(Cert issd for 400)

[176]Jacob Mayers this day claimed a preempt of 400 Acres of Land at the State price in the district of Kentucky on Acc't of Making an Actual settlement in March 1779 lying on the hanging forks of Dicks River adj'g Robert Bennett on the lower side & running down the Creek for quantity satisfactory proof being made to the Court they are of Opinion that the s'd Mayers has a right to a preempt'n of 400 Acres of Land to include the above Location & that a Cert. issue accordingly.—

(Cert issd for 400)

Jno Hawkins Assee of Wm Johnson

[175] Collins, Vol. 2, p. 624.
[176] (Myers?) Collins, Vol. 2, p. 113.

this day claimed a preempt'n of 400 Acres of Land at the State price in the district of Kentucky on Acc't of Making an Actual settlem't in April 1779 lying on the north side of Green River on Buffaloe Creek about 2 Miles from the River & about 1 Mile below the Buffaloe Lick to include his improvement satisfactory proof being made to the Court they are of Opinion that the s'd Hawkins has a right to a preemption of 400 Acres to include the above Location & that a Cert. issue accordingly.—

(Cert issd for 1400)

James Wallis by Jas McCullock this day claimed a settlem't & preempt'n to a tract of Land in the District of Kentucky on Acc't of raising a Crop of Corn in the Country in the year 1776 lying on the waters of Hardens Creek adjoining the Lands of Phenex on the West waters of the Beech fork of Salt River Satisfactory proof being made to the Court they are of Opinion that the s'd Wallis has a right to a settlement of 400 Acres of Land to include the above Location & the preempt of 1000 Acres adjoining & that a Cert. issue accordingly.—

(Cert issd for 400)

Jacob Pyall by Jno Handley this day claimed a preempt'n of 400 Acres of Land at the State price in the District of Kentucky on Acc't of making an Actual settlement in May 1779 lying on a branch of Floyds fork of salt River within about 3 Miles of Jno Handleys preempt'n an East course & to include his improvement made by Jno Handley Satisfactory proof being made to the Court they are of Opinion that the s'd Pyall has a right to a preempt'n of 400 Acres of land to include the above Location & that a Cert. issue accordingly.

(Cert issd for 400)

Jno Todd Jun'r in behalf of Jno Todd Sen'r Moves to the Court to have the s'd Todds claim reheard wh'h is granted him Witnesses being sworn & examined the Court are of Opinion that the s'd Jno Todd has a right to a settlement of 400 Acres of Land adjoining his improvement on Hickmans Creek for which a Cert for a preempt of 1000 Acres has been before granted Ordered that a Cert issue accordingly.

(Cert issd for 400)

Thos Christy by Jno Todd Jun'r this day claimed a preemption of 400 Acres of Land at the State price in the district of Kentucky on Acc't of making an Actual settlement in the Month of March 1779 lying on Hingstons Mill Seat Creek about 8 Miles from Riddles Station to include an improvem't made by Jno. Townsend satisfactory proof being made to the Court they are of Opinion that the s'd Christy has a right to a preempt'n of 400 Acres of Land to include the above Location & that a Cert issue accordingly.

(Cert issd for 400)

[177]Margarett Pendergrass Assee of Edward Wilson by Jno Todd Jun'r this day claimed a preempt'n of 400 Acres of Land at the State price in the district of Kentucky on Acc't of the s'd Wilson making an Actual settlem't

[177] Reg., Vol. 21, pp. 45, 47, 52.

in the year 1778 lying on a small branch of Wilson Creek on the North side of a branch of the Rolling fork of Salt River about 10 or 12 Miles South East of Bulletts Lick to include the s'd Wilsons improvement Satisfactory proof being made to the Court they are of Opinion that the s'd Pendergrass has a right to a preemption of 400 Acres to include the above Location & that a Cert. issue accordingly.

(Cert issd for 1400)

[178]James Waters by Jno Todd Jun'r this day claimed a settlem't & preempt'n to a tract of Land in the district of Kentucky on Acc't of raising a Crop of Corn in the Country in the year 1776 lying on the waters of the East fork of licking Creek adjoining the Settlem't & preempt'n of Jno. William Jun'r on the West including an improvement satisfactory proof being made to the Court they are of Opinion that the s'd Waters has a right to a settlement of 400 Acres of Land to include the above Location & the preempt'n of 1000 Acres of Land Adj'g & that a Cert. issue accordingly.—

(Cert iss for 400 pd D. D.)

James Polly this day claimed a preempt. of 400 Acres of Land at the State price in the District of Kentucky on Acc't of making an Actual settlement in March 1779 lying on the South side of Kentucky about 8 Miles from Colo. Bowman & about 5 Miles above the Mouth of Dicks River in a large Bent of Kentucky to include a Spring Satisfactory proof being made to the Court they are of Opinion that the s'd Polly has a right to a preempt of 400 Acres of Land to include the above Location & that a Cert. issue accordingly.

(Cert issd for 1000)

Abell Randall by Isaac Hite this day claimed a preempt'n of 1000 Acres of Land at the State price in the district of Kentucky on Acc't of Mark'g & improving the same in the year 1775 lying on the Waters of the town fork of Salt River on the south side thereof about 30 Miles from this place to include his improvem't & a tree mark'd M. Satisfactory proof being made to the Court they are of Opinion that the s'd Randall has a right to a preempt'n of 1000 Acres of land to include the above Location & that a Cert. issue accordingly.

The Heirs of [179]Dan'l Bryan this day claimed a settlem't & preempt. to a Tract of Land. (by Isaac Hite) in the district of Kentucky on Acc't of the s'd decedents residing in the Country 12 Months before the year 1778 lying on Jesemine Creek adjoining the lands of John Williams & Adams Stephen to include an improvement made by Isaac Hite & Company Satisfactory proof being made to the Court they are of Opinion that the s'd Heirs of Bryan has a right to a settlement of 400 Acres of land to include the above Location & the preempt'n of 1000 Acres adjoining & that a Cert. issue cccordingly.—

(Cert issd for 1400)

It being proved to the Court that dan'l whelen was intitled to a settle-

[178] Collins, Vol. 2, p. 551.

[179] Con. N. W. En., p. 581.

ment & preemption to a tract of Land in the district of Kentucky on acc't of raising a Crop of Corn in the Country in the year 1776 the 3d of Nov'r 1779 Tho did not locate it Now comes into Court and locates the same lying on the head of Mill Creek a branch of licking Creek adjoining the lands of Jacob Dunin on the East to include a cabbin built by [180]Simon Butler ordered that a Cert. issue accordingly.—

(Cert issued)

Wm Stewart in behalf of John Peters (moved) the Court to remove a location for which the s'd Peters had obt'd a Cert. for sufficient causes Appearing for the same it is granted him & now locates lying on a Buffalo road that leads from the upper Blue Licks 7 Miles North West from said lick including a Cabbin built by Simon Butler & running up and down for quantity Ordered that a Cert. issue accordingly.—

(Cert issd for 1400)

[181]Peter Flin by Thos Carland this day claimed a settlem't & preempt'n to a tract of land in the district of Kentucky on Acc't of residing in the Country 12 Month before the year 1778 at the Mouth of Breasheirs Creek in the Forks between the s'd Creek & Salt River & crossing the s'd Creek to include a pond Satisfactory proof being made to the Court they are of Opinion that the s'd Flin has a right to a settlement of 400 Acres of Land to include the above Location & the preempt'n of 1000 Acres adjoining & that a Cert. issue accordingly.—

Jessee Evans by Moses Archbrook this day claimed a settlem't & preempt to a tract of Land in the District of Kentucky as Assee of Low (Lew) Brown by Virtue of a bill of sale from the s'd Brown to the s'd Evans but the Bill of Sale having Appeared to this Court from the s'd Brown to Wm Stafford previous to the present claim upon which a Cert. was granted to the s'd Stafford the Court are of Opinion that they cannot grant another for the same.—

(Cert issd for 1400)

Jno Bowman Admrs of Jno Preston Dec'd this day claimed a settlement & preemption to a tract of Land in the district of Kentucky on Acc't of the s'd decedents residing in the Country 12 Months before the year 1778 lying on Jessemine Creek adjoining the Lands of Jno Williams & Adams Stephens to include an improvement made by Isaac Hite &c satisfactory proof being made to the Court they are of Opinion that the s'd Bowman has a right to a settlement of 400 Acres of Land to include the above Location & the preempt'n of 1000 Acres of Land to include the above Location & that a Cert. issue accordingly.—

Ordered that the Clerk issue all the Certificates that are not yet given Out.—

The Commissioners for Kentucky District having compleated the business of the s'd District and their power expired this present 26th day of Feb'y.

[180] Collins, Vol. 2, p. 551.
[181] Collins, Vol. 2, p. 615.

—Agreeable to an Act of General Assembly, Intituled an Act. for Adjusting & settling the Titles of Claimers to unpatented Lands under the present & former Government previous to the Establishment of the Commonwealths Land Office—After publick proclamation at the Court house door The Court accordingly broke up—

William Fleming
Stephen Trigg
Edm'd Lyne

EDITOR'S NOTE.

The last entry above shows a sine die adjournment on February 26, 1780. The original Act creating the Commission provided for its adjournment on February 26. A subsequent act gave an extension of time to the Commission and the entries that follow were made when the commission reassembled. The first entry made at the April session does not carry a date but the first adjournment in the April session "untill tomorrow Morning" is followed immediately by a Court order under date of April 19, 1780, so it is clear that the Court reassembled on April 18, 1780.

Present

William Fleming Stephen Trigg & Edmund Lyne—Gent.

Wm Hoy by Dan'l Gass this day claimed a settlem't & preemption in the district of Kentucky to a tract of Land the Testimony being heard the Court are of Opinion that the claim be rejected.—

William Pendleton Assee of [182]William McClary by Craven Peyton this day claimed a preemption of 1000 Acres of Land in the district of Kentucky on Acc't of Marking & improving the same in the year 1776 lying on the East fork of Licking about 3 or 4 Miles below the upper fork of s'd branch joining to an improvement of John . . . on which there is a large encampment supposed to have been made by the Indians. Satisfactory proof being made by the Court they are of Opinion that the s'd Pendleton has a right to a preemption of 1000 Acres to include the above location & that a Certificate issue accordingly.—

Joseph Holmes Assee of Patrick Pendleton who was Assee of John Fleming by Craven Peyton this day claimed a preemption of 1000 Acres of Land in the district of Kentucky. It not being made appear to this Court that the s'd Fleming had not taken the oaths of Fedillity & Allegence to this State the claim was —— further inquired into—

Francis Peyton by Craven Peyton this day claimed a preemption of 1000 Acres of Land in the district of Kentucky in Support of which the deposition of John Fleming was read in consideration thereof the Court are of Opinion that this claim be rejected.—

John Smith by [183]Azeriah Davis this day claimed a settlem't & preemption to a tract of land in the district of Kentucky It not being made appear to the Court that the s'd Smith had taken the Oaths of Fidellity & Allegence to this

[182] Collins, Vol. 2, pp. 466, 551.

[183] Collins, Vol. 2, p. 501; Reg., Vol. 20, p. 280.

State the s'd Claim was not further inquired into—

Solomon Corn this day claimed a preempt'n of 1000 Acres of Land in the district of Kentucky on Acc't of Marking & improving in the year 1775 lying on the North side of the North fork of Elkhorn and on the waters of Lecomps run adjoining the Lands where John Deal has an improvem't and like wise the lands of John Williams Jun'r—Satisfactory proof being made to the Court they are of Opinion that the s'd Corn has right to a preempt'n of 1000 Acres of Land to include his improvement and that a Certificate issue accordingly.—

George Corn by Simeon Corn this day claimed a preempt'n of 1000 Acres of Land in the district of Kentucky on Acc't of Marking & improving the same in the year 1775 lying about one Mile from the white oak spring about a North West course from the same on the head of a dry run to include his improvem't satisfactory proof being made to the Court they are of Opinion that the s'd Geo'e Corn has a right to a preempt'n of 1000 Acres to include his improvement & that a Certificate issue accordingly.—

——— [184]Rees this day claimed a preemption of 1000 Acres of Land in the district of Kentucky on Acc't of Marking and improving the same in the year 1774 & 1775 lying near the Knob Lick Isaac Shelby having Obtained a Cert. for the ———.

Hogan—

John Keller this day claimed a preemption of 1000 Acres of Land in the district of Kentucky on Acc't of marking & improving the same in the year 17— lying on the last fork of Coopers run on one of the head Springs thereof on the East side of a branch near a large Cane break to include his improvement satisfactory proof ———

[185]Cuthbert Bullett Devisee of his brother [186]Thos. Bullett this day claimed a settlement & preemption to a tract of land in the District of Kentucky on Acc't of the s'd decedents having had a Crop of Corn raised in the Country in the year 1776 lying on the Ohio beginning at the Lower Corner of Cuthbert Bulletts settlement & preemption running down the s'd river & back for quantity satisfactory proof being made to the Court they are of Opinion that the s'd Bullett has a right to a settlement of 400 Acres to include the above Location & the preemption of 1000 Acres adjoining & that a Cert. issue accordingly.—

Andrew Kincannon by Geo'e Adams this day claimed a preempt'n of 1000 Acres of Land in the district of Kentucky on Acc't of marking and improving the same in the year 1775 & 1776 lying on Silver Creek where the old tract (trace) at Boonesborough crosses s'd Creek & on both sides of the s'd road running down the Creek as low as the

[184] (Azor?) Collins, Vol. 2, p. 517; Reg., Vol. 20, p. 280, Note.

[185] Collins, Vol. 2, p. 376.

[186] Collins, Vol. 2, p. 18; Filson Club Pub., No. 8, p. 23.

Blue lick branch to include his improvements Satisfactory proof being made to the Court they are of Opinion that the s'd Kincannon has a right to a preempt'n of 1000 Acres of Land to include his improvement & that a Cert. issue accordingly.—

John Campbell Assee of Wm Deal Heir at Law to Wm Deal Dec'd this day claimed a preemption of 1000 Acres of Land in the district of Kentucky on Acc't of the s'd Decedents marking and improving the same in the year 1775 lying on a branch of Lecompts run adjoining the Lands of Lecompts below and the Lands of Solomon Corn on the North side of the North fork of Elkhorn to include his improvm't.

Joel Walker came into Court and offered to locate a tract of Land to include the Cave Spring about one Mile South of Cane Run adjoining James Carrs improvement on Acc't of an improvment made thereon by him in 1775. It appearing to the Court from the records that John Bunton has obtained a Cert. for settlement & preemption on the s'd Land ordered that a summons issue for John Bunton to appear before this Court on Saturday the 22d Inst.

Charles Cliffton Heir at law to John Cliffton Dec'd this day claimed a settlement & preempt'n to a tract of Land in the district of Kentucky It appearing to the Court that a Cert. has been granted by Virtue of s'd Cliffton raising a Crop of Corn in the year 177—.

Micheal Smith by Peter Watts this day claimed a settlment & preemption to a tract of land in the District of Kentucky Witnesses being examined in consideration of which the Court are of Opinion that this claim be rejected.

Adam Smith by Peter Watts this day claimed a settlem't & preemption to a tract of land in the District of Kentucky it not being made appear to the Court that the s'd Smith had taken the Oaths of Fidillity & Allegence to this State the claim was not further enquired into.—

Avender Gordon this day claimed a preemption of 400 Acres of Land in the district of Kentucky.—

[187]William Hickman by [188]George Stovel Smith this day claimed a preempt'n of 1000 Acres of land in the district of Kentucky on Acc't of Marking & improving the Land in the year 1776 lying in the head of the Middle fork of the next Creek that runs into Salt River below Breashiers Creek on the North side of the s'd ———— Satisfactory proof being made to the Court they are of Opinion that the s'd Hickman has a right to a preempt'n of 1000 Acres of land to include the above Location & that a Cert. issue accordingly.

[189]George Scott by Thos Carland this day claimed a preempt'n to a tract of land in the district of Kentucky on Acc't of Marking & improving the same in the year 1775 lying on the head of a Creek that empties in below Jessemine

---

[187] Hist. Ky. Bap., Vol. 1, pp. 13, 155, 159.

[188] George Stovel (or Stokes) Hist. Ky. Bap., Vol. 1. p. 159; Collins, Vol. 2, p. 515.

[189] Collins, Vol. 1, p. 12.

Creek into Kentucky River where a Buffaloe Road crosses s'd River to include two Springs. Satisfactory proof being made tó the Court they are of Opinion that the s'd Scott has a right to a preemption of 1000 Acres of land to include the above location & that a Cert. issue accordingly.—

Wm Rowan Assee of Joseph Moore this day claimed a settlem't & preemption to a tract of Land in the district of Kentucky ——— rejected.

Sam'l Davis Assee of Wm Crawford this day claimed a preempt'n of 400 Acres of land in the district of Kentucky. ——— rejected.—

Ordered that the Court adjourn untill tomorrow Morning 9 Oclock.—

Wm Fleming

At a Court continued and held by the Commissioners of the Kentucky District for adjusting Titles to unpatented lands at St. Asaphs the 19th day of April 1780.

Present

Wm. Fleming Stephen Trigg & Edmund Lyne—Gent.

John Fagert Assee of Micheal Fagert who was surviving joint Tenement (Tenant) of Sam'l Hunter Dec'd this day claimed a settlement & preemption to a tract of land in the district of Kentucky on Acc't of the s'd Decedents residing in the Country 12 Months before the year 1778 & improving lands lying on the West Fork of Buck lick Creek near the head thereof a branch of the South fork of Licking Creek about 12 Miles from the upper Blue licks party a South West Course to include the s'd Decedents improvement satisfactory proof being made to the Court they are of Opinion that the s'd Fagert has a right to a settlement of 400 Acres of land to include the above Location & the preemption of 1000 Acres adjoining & that a Cert. issue accordingly.—

Martin Nall Jun'r this day claimed a settlement & preempt'n to a tract of land in the district of Kentucky on Acc't of raising a Crop in the Country in the year 1775 & 1776 lying on the Ohio above the Mouth of the Big Kentucky 9 Miles & adjoining the land of Adam ——— on his lower line satisfactory proof being made to the Court they are of Opinion that the s'd Nall has a right to a settlement of 400 Acres of land to include the above location & the preemption of 1000 Acres adjoining & that a Certificate issue accordingly.—

Martin Nall Sen'r by Martin Nall Jun'r this day claimed settlement & preemption to a tract of Land in the District of Kentucky on Acc't of having a Crop of Corn raised for him in the year 1776 lying on the first Creek that empties into Salt River below the lower [190]McAfee Station on the South side of the s'd River and about 1½ Mile up the s'd Creek, satisfactory proof being made to the Court they are of Opinion that the s'd Nall has a right to a settlement of 400 Acres of Land to include the above Location & the preemp-

[190]Collins, Vol. 2, p. 20.

tion of 1000 Acres adjoining & that a Certificate issue accordingly.—

John Briscoe this day claimed a settlement & preemption to a tract of Land in the District of Kentucky on Acc't of having had a crop of Corn raised in the Country in the year 1775 & 1776 lying on the Ohio about 10 or 12 Miles above the Big Bone licks beginning at the Mouth of a Small Creek which has very steep Banks & extend up the River for quantity Satisfactory proof being made to the Court they are of Opinion that the s'd Briscoe has a right to a settlement of 400 Acres of land to include the above Location & the preemption of 1000 Acres of Land and that a Certificate issue accordingly.—

Thomas Carland came into Court & waved his Objection made to the Claim laid in by him for Nathaniel Henderson, On David Gass's coming into Court & agreeing to take that location in exchange for one made by him near the head of Jasemine Creek which he gives up to the s'd Carland.—

[191]John Harden this day claimed a preempt'n of 1000 Acres of Land at the State price in the district of Kentucky on Acc't of marking & improving the same in the year 1775 lying on pleasant run a branch of the Beech Fork of Salt River about 3 Miles from the Mouth of the s'd Run to include a small Deer lick on a branch & his improvem't satisfactory proof being made to the Court they are of Opinion that the s'd Harden has a right to a preempt'n of 1000 Acres of Land to include the above Location & that a Cert. issue accordingly.—

[192]Mark Harden by John Harden this day claimed a preemption of 1000 Acres at the State price in the district of Kentucky on Acc't of Marking and improving the same in the year 1775 lying on Hardens Creek a branch of the Rolling fork of Salt River about 6 or 7 Miles from the Indian lick to include his improvement satisfactory proof being made to the Court they are of Opinion that the s'd Mark Harden has a right to a preemption of 1000 Acres of land to include the above Location & that a Certificate issue accordingly.—

John Askins Heir at Law to George Askins Dec'd this day claimed a preemption of 1000 Acres of Land at the State price in the district of Kentucky on Acc't of the s'd Decedents marking & improving the same in the year 1776 lying on the West side of Hardens Creek a branch of the West fork of Salt River above the Lands claimed by Mark Harden about 1½ or 2 Miles to include his improvement satisfactory proof being made to the Court they are of Opinion that the s'd Askins has a right to a preemption of 1000 Acres of land to include the above location & that a Certificate issue accordingly.—

John Askins this day claimed a preempt of 1000 Acres of Land at the State price in the district of Kentucky on Acc't of marking & improving the same in the year 1776 lying on the East branch called the last fork of Cart-

[191] Collins, Vol. 2, p. 315.

[192] Collins, Vol. 2, p. 749.

rights Creek to include his improvement satisfactory proof being made to the Court they are of Opinion that the s'd Askins has a right to a preempt'n of 1000 Acres of Land to include the above location & that a Cert issue accordingly.—

[193]Jacob Froman by John Keller this day claimed a settlement & preempt'n to a tract of Land in the district of Kentucky It not being made appear to the Court that the s'd Froman had taken the Oaths of Fidellity & Allegence to the State the claim was not further enquired into.—

Joseph Keller by John Keller this day claimed a preemption of 1000 Acres of Land at the State price in the district of Kentucky. ———— Rejected.—

Jacob Newland this day claimed a preempt'n of 1000 Acres of Land at the State price in the district of Kentucky on Acc't of marking & improving the same in the year 1775 lying on Pleasant run adjoining the Land of Cartright—Basil Preather to include his improvement satisfactory proof being made to the Court they are of Opinion that the s'd Newland has a right to a preemption of 1000 Acres of land to include the above Location & that a Certificate issue accordingly.—

Edward Smith by Jos. Newland this day claimed a preemption of 1000 Acres of land at the State price in the district of Kentucky it not being made appear to the Court that the s'd Smith had taken the Oaths Fidelity and Allegence to this State the s'd Claim was not further enquired into.—

Peter Keller by John kendrer Assee of John Williams was not enquired into there was not proof of their having taken the Oaths of Fidelity & Allegence to State.—

Peter Buttler by Martin Nall Jun'r this day claimed a settlement & preempt'n to a tract of Land in the district of Kentucky on Acc't of raising a Crop of Corn in the Country in the year 1775 lying on a Creek that runs into Salt River on the South side below the lower McAfee Station joining the lands of Martin Nall Sen'r above Satisfactory proof being made to the Court they are of Opinion that the s'd Buttler has a right to a settlement of 400 Acres of Land to include the above Location & the preempt of 1000 Acres adjoining & that a Cert. issue accordingly.—

Adam Rough Heir at Law to Nich's Rough by Patrick Davis this day claimed a settlement & preemption to a tract of Land in the District of Kentucky on Acc't of the s'd decedents raising a crop of Corn in the year 1776 lying on the head of Roughs run a branch of Kentucky River on the North side of the s'd River about 5 Miles above the Mouth of Collins Creek to include an improvement made by Patrick Dawbin, satisfactory proof being made to the Court they are of Opinion that the s'd Adam Rough has a right to a settlement of 400 Acres of Land to include the above Location & the preemption of 1000 Acres

[193] Collins, Vol. 2, p. 245.

adjoining & that a Cert. issue accordingly.—

John Briscoe Sen'r by John Briscoe Jun'r this day claimed a settlement & preemption to a tract of Land in the district of Kentucky on Account of having had a Crop of Corn in the Country in the year 1776 lying on the North side of the Kentucky river adjoining the lands of David Glen to include the falling Springs his improvement which was made in April 1775 satisfactory proof being made to the Court they are of Opinion that the s'd Briscoe has a right to a settlement of 400 Acres of Land to include the above Location & the preemption of 1000 Acres adjoining & that a Certificate issue accordingly.—

[194]Parnemus Briscoe by John Briscoe Jun'r this day claimed a settlement and preempt'n to a tract of land in the district of Kentucky on Acc't of having had a crop of Corn raised in this district in the year 1776 Lying on a branch of Salt River adjoining the Lands of Martin Shell and Silas Harlen agreeable to the lines agreed upon between the parties in the year 1775 to include the boiling springs and his improvement which was made in the year 1774 satisfactory proof being made to the Court they are of opinion that the s'd Briscoe has a right to a settlement of 400 Acres of land to include the above Location & the preemption of 1000 Acres of land and that a Certificate issue accordingly.—

Joseph Tomleson this day claimed a settlement & preempt'n to a tract of Land in the district of Kentucky It appearing to the Court that the s'd Tomleson had obtained a Certificate for a settlement & preempt'n in the district of Monongalia therefore the Court are of Opinion that he has no right to claim in this district:—

Alexander Moore claimes was not inquired into as it does not Appear to the Court that he has taken the Oaths of Fidelity & Allegence to the State.—

(Cert issue for 1000)

Joseph Dixon by William Stewart this day claimed a preemption of 1000 Acres of Land at the State price in the district of Kentucky on Acc't of Marking & improving the same in the year 1775 lying on the branch of the Rolling fork of Salt River adjoining the Lands of James Phenix to extend over the waters of Harden Creek to include his improvement & satisfactory proof being made to the Court they are of Opinion that the s'd Dixon has a right to a preemption of 1000 Acres of Land to include the above Location & that a Cert. issue accordingly.—

Samuel Lyon Heir at Law to Dan'l Lyon dec'd this day claimed a settlement & preempt'n to a tract of Land in the district of Kentucky on Acc't of improving Lands in the year 1776 & residing 12 Months in the Country before the year 1778 postponed untill tomorrow or next day.—

(Cert. issd for 1000)

Joel Rees came into Court and desired

[194] Collins, Vol. 2, p. 765.

that the Sums (summons) ordered for John Bunten on his Motion be dismissed and offered to Locate his land lying on the Rolling fork of Salt River on the Old Hunters trace between the Sulpher & Indian Licks including an old improvem't marked T D Ordered that a Certificate issue accordingly.—

Alexander Rallery by James Douglass claimes a preemption of 1000 Acres of Land in the District of Kentucky.—Rejected.—

John Moore by Sam'l Moore this day claimed a preemption of 1000 Acres of land in the District of Kentucky.—Rejected.

Ordered that the Court be adjourned untill Tomorrow Morning 9 Oclock.
William Fleming.

At a Court continued & held by the Commissioners of Kentucky District for adjusting titles to unpatented lands at St Asaphs the 20th day of April 1780
Present
William Fleming, Steph'n Trigg
& Edmund Lyne.

(Cert issd for 1400 Acres d. d. to Stephen Trigg)
Solomon Kendrick Assee of Gallant Lemare this day claimed a settlement & preemption to a tract of Land in the district of Kentucky on Acc't of settling in the Country in the year 1777 & residing upwards of 12 Months after s'd Settlement lying on Shawnee run where Gordens fork & the Middle fork meet to include a large spring on the East side the run & to extend up and down the Creek for quantity satisfactory proof being made to the Court they are of Opinion that the s'd Kendrick has a right to a settlement of 400 Acres of Land to include the above Location & the preempt'n of 1000 Acres adjoining & that a Certificate issue accordingly.

Wm Curry this day claimed a preemption of 1000 Acres of Land in the district of Kentucky. Rejected.

(Cert issd for 1000)
Robert Hartness by Joseph Tomlinson this day claimed a preemption of 1000 Acres of Land at the State price in the District of Kentucky on Acc't of Marking & improving the same in the year 1776 Lying on the North side of the North fork of Elkhorn on a Branch that run into the s'd North fork About 8 miles above McClellands Fort to include his improvement satisfactory proof being made to the Court they are of Opinion that the s'd Hartness has a right to a preempt'n of 1000 Acres of Land to include the above Location & that a Cert. issue accordingly.—

(Cert issd for 1000)
Mary Hartness Heir at Law to [195]Jacob Greathouse by Joseph Tomleson this day claimed a preemption of 1000 Acres of Land at the State price in the district of Kentucky on Account of the s'd Decedents marking & improving the same in the year 1776 lying on the North side of the North fork of Elkhorn on a branch that runs into the

[195] Collins, Vol. 2, p. 84.

s'd North Fork about 4 Miles above McClellans Fort and about 1½ Miles above the s'd Branch to include the said decedents improvement Satisfactory proof being made to the Court they are of Opinion that the s'd Hartness has a right to a preempt'n of 1000 Acres of Land to include the above Location & that a Certificate issue accordingly.—

John Carpenter by Jos'h Tomleson this day claimed a preemption of 1000 Acres of Land in the district of Kentucky it not being made appear to this Court that the Claiment has taken the Oath of Fidelity and Allegence to the State therefore the Court did not enquire into the Claim.—

(Cert issd for 1000)
Dan'l Gallasby by Joseph Tomleson this day claimed a preemption of 1000 Acres of Land in the district of Kentucky on Acc't of Marking & improving the same in the year 1776 lying on a branch of Licking that runs in on the South of Higstons fork of Licking near hingstons improvement about 14 or 15 Miles up the s'd Branch to include his improvem't Satisfactory proof being made to the Court. They are of Opinion that the s'd Gallesby has a right to a preemption of 1000 Acres of Land to include the above Location & that a Certificate issue accordingly.—

Abiger McClane by Jos'h Tomleson this day claimed a preemption of 1000 Acres of land at the State price in the district of Kentucky on Acc't of marking & improving the same in the year 1776 lying on the branch that runs into the North fork of Elkhorn Creek on the North side thereof about 3 Miles above the Lands of Mary Hartness Heir to Jacob Greathouse to include his improvm't satisfactory proof being made to the Court they are of Opinion that the s'd McClane has a right to a preemption of 1000 Acres of Land to include the above Location & that a Certificate issue accordingly.

[196]Sam'l Campbell Assee of [197]James Mitcheal Heir at Law to John Mitchell Dec'd this day claimed a settlem't & preempt'n to a tract of Land in the district of Kentucky on Acc't of the said decedents raising a Crop of Corn in the Country in the year 1776 lying about one Mile and a half from a Lick on a Buffaloe road near to Salt River including an improvement made by Sam'l Moore in 1774 & 1775 Satisfactory proof being made to the Court they are of Opinion that the s'd Campbell has a right to a settlement of 400 Acres of Land to include the above Location & the preempt'n of 1000 Acres adjoining & that a Cert. issue accordingly.—

James Deoger this day claimed a preemption of 400 Acres of Land in the District of Kentucky rejected.—

Zacheriah Doeger this day claimed a preempt of 400 Acres of land in the district of Kentucky—rejected.—

(Cert iss for 1400)
Solomon Kendrick Assee of Wm Dortens this day claimed a settlement and

[196] Collins, Vol. 2, p. 524.
[197] Collins, Vol. 2, 173.

preemption to a tract of Land in the District of Kentucky on Acc't of the said Dortens raising a Crop of Corn in the Country in the year 1775 Lying on the North side of Silver Creek about 2 Miles from the Little fort & there is DW. and M. S. below on a trace to include a Spring that runs out among a parcel of rocks Satisfactory proof being made to the Court they are of Opinion that the s'd Kendrick has a right to a settlement of 400 Acres to include the above Location & the preemption of 1000 Acres adjoining & that a Cert issue accordingly.—

(Cert issd for 1000)
[198]Waller Overton this day claimed a settlement & preemption to a tract of Land in the district of Kentucky on Acc't of Marking and improving the same in the year 1776 and raising lying on the East fork of Hickmans to include the said Overtons lower improvem't on the said Creek adjoining the Lands of John Hickman Assee of [199]Dan'l Turner Witnesses being sworn & examined in consideration of which the Court are of Opinion that the s'd Overton is only Intituled to a preempt'n of 1000 Acres of Land to include the above Location & that a Certificate issue accordingly.—

(Cert issd for 1000)
Joseph McClane by [200]John Maxwell this day claimed a preemption of 1000 Acres of Land at the State price in the district of Kentucky on Acc't of Marking & improving the same in the year 1776 lying about 2 Miles above the Mouth of grears Creek on the s'd Creek waters of Kentucky Satisfactory proof being made to the Court they are of Opinion that the s'd McClane had a right to a preempt'n of 1000 Acres of Land to include the above Location & that a Cert. issue accordingly.—

[201]James Masterson this day claimed a preemption of 400 Acres of Land in the district of Kentucky Rejected.—

(Cert issd for 1000)
Thomas Maxwell by John Maxwell this day claimed a preemption of 1000 Acres of Land at the State price in the District of Kentucky on Acc't of marking & improving in the year 1776 lying on the waters of the North fork of licking on the lower Buffaloe road that crosses the said North fork and about 2 Miles from the same to include a Cabbing built by [202]Alexander McClellen Satisfactory proof being made to the Court they are of Opinion that the s'd Maxwell has a right to a preemption of 1000 Acres of Land to include the above Location & that a Cert. issue accordingly.—

(Cert issd for 1000)
Adam Rough this day claimed a settlem't and preemption to a tract of Land in the district of Kentucky on Acc't of raising a Crop of Corn in the Country in the year 1775 lying on the North side of the Kentucky river on Roughs run a branch of the said River to include his improvement satisfactory proof being made to the Court they are of the

[198] Collins, Vol. 2, p. 183.
[199] Collins, Vol. 2, p. 624.
[200] Collins, Vol. 2, p. 178 and index.
[201] Collins, Vol. 2, p. 172.
[202] Collins, Vol. 2, p. 176.

Opinion that the said Rough has a right to a settlem't of 400 Acres of Land to include the above Location & the preemption of 1000 Acres of Land adjoining & that a Certificate issue accordingly.—

(Cert issued for 1000)

[203]Edward Mitchell by John Maxwell this day claimed a settlement & preemption to a tract of Land in the district of Kentucky on Acc't of marking & improving & raising a Crop of Corn in the year 1776 lying on clear Creek a branch of Kentucky about 1½ Miles from [204]Isaac Greers improvement to include an improvem't purchased by James Greer Witnesses being sworn & examined in consideration of which the Court are of Opinion that the s'd Mitchell has a right to a settlement of 400 Acres of Land to include the above Location & the preempt of 1000 Acres adjoining & that a Cert. issue accordingly.—

John Hutton this day claimed a preemption of 1000 Acres of Land at the State price in the district of Kentucky rejected.—

(Cert issd for 1400)

Aron Higgins this day claimed a settlement & preemption to a tract of Land in the District of Kentucky on Acc't of raising a Crop of Corn in the year 1776 lying on Buck lick Creek a branch of the South fork of Licking including a small Deer lick and his improvement satisfactory proof being made to the Court they are of Opinion that the s'd Higgins has a right to a settlem't of 400 Acres of Land to including the above Location & the preemption of 1000 Acres adjoining & that a Cert. issue accordingly.—

(Cert issd for 1400)

Sam'l Lyon Heir at Law to Dan'l Lyon Dec'd this day claimed a settlement & preemption to a tract of Land in the District of Kentucky on Acc't of improving lands in the year 1776 and residing in the Country twelve Months before the year 1778 Thos. Cartmot came into Court and Alleged that he purchased the s'd Deceased Right in his lifetime of him whereupon witnesses were sworn and examined in consideration of which the Court are of Opinion that the s'd Sam'l Lyon has a right to a settlement of 400 Acres of Land & preempt'n of 1000 As heir at Law to the said decedents lying on the Waters of Hingstons fork of Licking Creek on a branch that empties in about 8 miles above the s'd Hingstons fork on the same side known by the name of Mortons Creek joining the Lands of Patrick ———den and Mathew Sullever including John Lyons improvement and three big springs Ordored that a Cort. issuo accordingly.—

Ordered that the Court adjourn untill tomorrow Morning 9 Oclock

Wm Fleming.

At a Court Continued and held by the Commissioners of Kentucky District for Adjusting titles to unpatented

[203] Collins, Vol. 2, p. 178.
[204] Collins, Vol. 2, p. 178.

Lands at St Asaphs the 21 day of April 1780.

Present

Wm Fleming Stephen Trigg & Edmund Lyne—Gent.

(Cert for 1000)

[205]John Fleming this day claimed a preemption of 1000 Acres of land at the State price in the district of Kentucky on Acc't of marking & improving the same in the year 1776 lying on the Waters of a Creek that empties into Licking Creek between the upper and lower Blue licks about 3 or 4 Miles nearly North East from the said upper Blue lick to include his improvement satisfactory proof being made to the Court they are of Opinion that the s'd Fleming has a right to a preemption of 1000 Acres of Land to include the Above Location & that a Cert. issue accordingly.—

John Vantress Assee of John Maddeson who was Assee of Thos. Ogle this day claimed a preemption of 1000 Acres of Land at the State price in the district of Kentucky on Acc't of Marking & improving the same in the year 1776 lying on the Rolling fork of Salt River rejected for want of sufficient proof.—

John Vantress Assee of John Corbley this day claimed a preempt'n of 1000 Acres of Land in the district of Kentucky, Rejected for want of Sufficient proof.—

(Cert issd for 1000)

John Hutton this day came into Court and moved to have his (cert.) which was granted him now claimes a preempt'n of 400 Acres of Land at the State price in the District of Kentucky on Acc't of making and Actual settlement in May 1779 lying on the North side of the North fork of Licking a branch about 8 or 9 Miles from Riddle Station to include his improvement Satisfactory proof being made to the Court they are right to a preempt of 400 Acres of Land and that a Certificate issue accordingly.—

(Cert issd for 1400 Location removed & Assigned to Wm Stewart)

Ephraim Peyton Assee of Wm Jennings this day claimed a settlem't & preempt'n to a tract of Land in the District of Kentucky on Acc't of the s'd Jennings raising a crop of Corn in the Country in the year 1775 Lying on Cedar Creek a branch of Chaplins fork of Salt River including a Cabbin built by Wm Stewart & Wm Beard adjoining Bairds preemption to include a small Spring Satisfactory proof being made to the Court they are of Opinion that the s'd Peyton has a right to a settlement of 400 Acres of Land to include the above Location & the preemption of 1000 Acres adjoining & that a Certificate issue accordingly.—

Willi'm Flyner by Robt Johnson this day claimed a preemption of 1000 Acres of Land in the District of Kentucky on Acc't of marking and improving the same in the year 1775 on the waters of Licking Creek rejected for want of proof.—

Thos. Gest by Robt Johnson this day

[205] Collins, Vol. 2, p. 233 and index.

claimed a preemption of 1000 Acres of Land at the State price in the district of Kentucky rejected.—

Benj'm Johnson by Robt Johnson this day claimed a settlement & preempt'n to a tract of Land in the District of Kentucky on Acc't of Lewis Holmes raising a crop of Corn in the Country in the year 1775 rejected as a Cert. was granted to the said Holmes for the same service.—

Edward Rolling Assee of Wm McCleary this day claimed a preempt'n of 1000 Acres of Land at the State price in the District of Kentucky rejected as it appears that there (was) a preemption already granted to Phillip Assee of the s'd Cleary for the same service.—

(Cert issd for 1400)
James Higgins by Aron Higgins this day claimed a preemption to a tract of Land in the District of Kentucky on account of having had a crop of Corn raised in the Country in the year 1776 lying on Buck Lick Creek a branch of the South Fork of Licking Creek adjoining above the s'd Creek the Lands of Aron Higgins Satisfactory proof being made to the Court they are of Opinion that the s'd Higgins has a right to a settlement of 400 Acres of Land to include the above Location & the preemption of 1000 Acres of land adjoining & that a Cert. issue accordingly.—

John Swan by Rich'd Swan this day claimed a preemption of 1000 Acres of Land in the district of Kentucky rejected as it Appeared to the Court that he had obtained a Certificate for a settlem't & preemption in the District of Manongilia &c.

(Cert issd for 1000)
John Swan Jun'r this day claimed a preempt of 1000 Acres of Land at the State price in the district of Kentucky on Acc't of Marking & improving the same in the year 1776 lying on the South fork of the Rolling fork of Salt River about 2 or 3 Miles from the Mouth of the s'd Fork about 2 Miles from where a large Buffaloe road crosses the Rolling fork to include his Improvem't Satisfactory proof being made to the Court they are of Opinion that the s'd Swan has a right to a preempt'n of 1000 Acres of Land to include the above Location & that a Cert. issue accordingly.

(Cert issd for 1000)
Charles Swan by Rich'd Swan this day claimed a preemption of 1000 Acres of Land at the State price in the District of Kentucky on Acc't of marking & improving the same in the year 1776 lying on a branch of the South fork of Clear Creek near the head & adjoining Lands of Van Swearingen to include his improvement satisfactory proof being made to the Court they are of Opinion that the said Swan has a right to a preemption of 1000 Acres of Land to include the above Location & that a Cert. issue accordingly.—

Wm Swan by Rich'd Swan this day claimed a preemption of 1000 Acres of Land at the State price in the district of Kentucky rejected.—

(Cert issd for 1000)

Thomas Hughes by Swan this day claimed a preemption of 1000 Acres of land at the State price in the district of Kentucky on Acc't of Marking & improving the same in the year 1776 lying on a Branch of the Rolling fork of Salt River on the North side thereof about one Mile from the head of Plesant run to include his improvement Satisfactory proof being made to the Court they are of Opinion that the said Hughes has a right to a preemption of 1000 Acres of Land to include the above Location & that a Certificate issue accordingly.

(Cert issd for 1000)

Joseph Hughes this day claimed a preempt of 1000 Acres of Land at the State price in the District of Kentucky on Acc't of marking & improving the same in the year 1776 lying on a branch of Salt River that runs in on the South side thereof near the head of the said Branch about 1½ or 2 Miles south from Silas Harlens Land to include his improvement satisfactory proof being made to the Court they are of Opinion that the said Hughes has a right to a preempt of 1000 Acres of Land to include the above Location & that a Cert issue accordingly.—

(Cert issd for 1000)

Sam'l Swan heir at Law to Thos Swan deceased this day claimed a preemption of 1000 Acres of Land at the State price in the District of Kentucky on Account of the said decedents having had the said Land Marked and improved in the year 1776 lying on the North fork of the Rolling fork of Salt River about 4 Miles below the Clay Lick on the said fork to include the s'd Decedents improvement Satisfactory proof being made to the Court they are of Opinion that the said Swan has a right to a preempt of 1000 Acres of Land to include the above Location & that a Cert. issue accordingly.—

(Cert issd for 1000)

Nich's McCarty by Rich'd Cheneth this day claimed a preempt'n of 1000 Acres of Land at the State price in the District of Kentucky on Acc't of Marking & improving the same in the year 1776 Lying on the waters of Floyds of Salt River 6 or 7 Miles from Linns Station near a South East Course satisfactory proof being made to the Court they are of Opinion that the s'd McCarty has a right to a preemption of 1000 Acres of Land to include the above Location & that a Cert. issue accordingly.—

(Cert issd for 1000)

Rob't Jones by Rich'd Cheneth this day claimed a preempt of 1000 Acres of Land at the State price in the District of Kentucky on Acc't of Marking & improving the same in the year 1776 lying on Pottengers Creek waters of the Rolling fork of Salt River including an improvement made by Rich'd Cheneth near the head of the s'd Creek Satisfactory proof being made to the Court they are of Opinion that the said Jones has a right to a preempt'n of 1000 Acres of Land to include the above Location & that a Certificate issue accordingly.—

(Cert issd for 1000)

James Stewart by Rich'd Cheneth

this day claimed a preempt'n of 1000 Acres of Land at the State price in the District of Kentucky on Acc't of Marking and improving the same in the year 1776 lying on the North side of the North fork of Elkhorn on the Buffaloe road that crosses the s'd North fork about 3 Miles below the Mouth of McConnells branch to include an improvement made by Jos'h Dandrey Satisfactory proof being made to the Court they are of Opinion that the s'd Stewart has a right to a preemption of 1000 Acres of Land to include the above Location & that a Cert. issue accordingly.—

(Cert issd for 1000)

George Neil by Rich'd Cheneth this day claimed a preempt'n of 1000 Acres of Land at the State price in the District of Kentucky on Acc't of Marking & improving Lands in the year 1776 lying on the Waters of the Beech Fork of Salt River on the South side thereof about 18 Miles from the Mouth and about 3 Miles from the Knobbs Satisfactory proof being made to the Court they are of Opinion that the s'd Neil has a right to a preemption of 1000 Acres of Land to include the above Location & that a Cert issue accordingly.—

(Cert issd for 1000)

Edward Mooredock by Rich'd Cheneth this day claimed a preemption of 1000 Acres of Land at the State price in the district of Kentucky on Acc't of Marking and improving the same in the year 1776 lying on the Waters of Clear Creek a branch of Breashiers Creek about 2 Miles and a half from the punching camp nearly a North West Course to include his improvement Satisfactory proof being made to the Court they are of Opinion that the s'd Mooredock has a right to a preemption of 1000 Acres of Land to include the above Location & that a Cert. issue accordingly.—

Bezin (Rezin) Vergen (Virgin) by Sam'l Lyon this day claimed a preemption of 1000 Acres of Land at the State price in the District of Kentucky upon the Testimony offered in evidence it appears to the Court that he obtained a Certificate from the Commissioners of the District of the Monongalia &c for Lands nor does it Appear that he had taken the Oaths of Fidelity & Allegence to the State therefore his claim is rejected.—

(Cert issd for 1000)

[206]John Lyon by Sam'l Lyon this day claimed a preemption of 1000 Acres of Land at the State price in the district of Kentucky on Acc't of Marking & improving the same in the year 1776 lying on the South Branch of Licking Creek known by a Creek called Martins Creek to include his improvement Satisfactory proof being made to the Court they are of Opinion that the s'd Lyon has a right to a preemption of 1000 Acres to include the above Location & that a Certificate issue accordingly.—

(Cert issd for 1000)

John Jones by John Fleming this day claimed a preemption of 1000 Acres of Land at the State price in the District of Kentucky on Acc't of Marking & improving the same in the year 1776 lying

[206] Collins, Vol. 2, pp. 327, 551.

on a branch of Licking Creek about 8 Miles from the Upper Blue licks nearly a North East course to include his improvement Satisfactory proof being made to the Court they are of Opinion that the s'd Jones has a right to a preemption of 1000 Acres of Land to include the above Location & that a Cert. issue accordingly.—

(Cert issd for 1000)

Patrick Allison by John Fleming this day claimed a preemption of 1000 Acres of Land at the State price in the district of Kentucky on Acc't of marking & improving the same in the year 1776 Lying on a branch of licking creek about 12 Miles from the upper Blue Licks nearly a North Course to include his improvement Satisfactory proof being made to the Court they are of Opinion that the said Allison has a right to a preemption of 1000 Acres of land to include the above Location & that a Cert. issue accordingly.

(Cert issd for 1000)

[207]Wm Garrott this day claimed a preempt of 1000 Acres of Land at the State price in the district of Kentucky on Acc't of marking & improving the same in the year 1776 lying on one of the East branches of Clear Creek about three miles from the forks of the s'd Creek to include his improvement satisfactory proof being made to the Court they are of opinion that the s'd Garrott has a right to a preemption of 1000 Acres of land to include the above Location & that a Certificate issue accordingly.—

John Hume this day claimed a preemption of 1000 Acres of Land at the State price in the district of Kentucky rejected as it appears he made his improvement on warranted Land.—

(Cert issd for 1000)

John Hume Assee of John Chambers claimes a preemption of 1000 Acres of Land at the State price in the district of Kentucky on Acc't of the said Chambers marking & improving the same in the year 1776 lying on the waters of Salt River near the head of the first big Creek that empties into the said river above Floyds fork to include said Chambers improvement satisfactory proof being made to the Court they are of Opinion that the said Humes (Assee) of Chambers has a right to a preempt'n of 1000 Acres of Land to include the above Location & that a Cert. issue accordingly.—

(Cert issd for 1000)

John Andrew Miller this day claimed a preemption of 1000 Acres of Land at the State price in the district of Kentucky on account of Marking & improving the same in the year 1776 lying on the North side of the North fork of Elkhorn on the fourth run above McClellens Spring about 1½ Miles up the said run to include his improvement satisfactory proof being made to the Court they are of Opinion that the said Miller has a right to a preemption of 1000 Acres of Land to include the above Location & that a Cert. issue accordingly.—

[207] (Garrett) Collins, Vol. 2, p. 177.

Ordered that the Court adjourn untill tomorrow Morning 9 Oclock

Wm Fleming.

At a Court continued & held by the Commissioners of Kentucky District for adjusting titles to unpatented land at St. Asaphs the 22 day of April 1780

Present

Wm Fleming Steph'n Trigg & Edmund Lyne—Gentle.—

(Cert issd for 400)

Rich'd May this day claimed settlem't & a preempt'n to a tract of Land in the district of Kentucky on Acc't of settling in the Country in the year 1777 lying on the West fork of Cane run near the Mouth adjoining the Lands Survey'd [208]Wm Henry including his improvem't made by the Lexenton Trustees witnesses being made to the Court they are of Opinion that the s'd May to a preemption only of 1000 Acres to include the above Location & that a Cert. issue accordingly.—

James Brown this day claimed a settlement & preemption to a tract of Land in the district of Kentucky rejected.—

James Bard this day claimed a preemption of 1000 Acres of Land at the State price in the district of Kentucky rejected.—

(Cert issd for 1400)

Joseph Blackford Heir at Law to Sam'l Blackford dec'd David Grear this day claimed a settlement & preemption to a tract of Land in the District of Kentucky on Acc't of the said decedents raising a Crop of Corn in the year 1775 lying on the North fork of Glens Creek including an improvement of Joseph Blackford & David Glens corn field Satisfactory proof being made to the Court they are of Opinion that the s'd Blackford' has a right to a settlement of 400 Acres of Land to include the above Location & the preempt'n of 1000 Acres adjoining & that a Cert. issue accordingly.—

(Cert issd for 1000)

The Heirs of Thos. Glen dec'd by David Glen this day claimed a preemption of 1000 Acres of Land at the State price in the district of Kentucky on acc't of mark'g and improving the Lands in the year 1774 lying on the first fork of Glens Creek about 2 Miles above the forks including a small Sinking Spring & improvement made by David Glen Satisfactory proof being made to the Court they are of Opinion that the said Heirs &c has a right to a preemption of 1000 Acres of Land to include the above Location & that a Cert issue accordingly.—

Anthony Rollings this day claimed a preemption of 1000 Acres of Land at the State price in this district of Kentucky on Acc't of Marking & improving the same in the year 1775 lying on the head of the North fork of Clear Creek Waters of Kentucky including a Large Spring & his improvement Satisfactory proof being made to the Court they are of Opinion that the said Rollins has a right to a preemption of 1000 Acres of Land to include the Above location &

[208] Collins, Vol. 2, p. 476 and index.

that the Certificate issue accordingly.—
(Cert issd for 1000)

Wm McMeckhant by [209]James Galloway this day clamed a preemption of 1000 Acres of Land at the State price in the district of Kentucky on Acc't of marking & improving the same in the year 1776 lying on one of the West branches of the Main fork of Licking Creek about 12 Miles from the upper Blue Licks to include his improvement Satisfactory proof being made to the Court they are of Opinion that the s'd Meckhant has a right to a preemption of 1000 Acres to include the above Location & that Cert issue accordingly.

(Cert issd for 400)

Geo'e Hart Jun'r this day claimed a preemption of 400 Acres of Land at the State price in the district of Kentucky on Acc't of Marking & improving the same in the year 1779 & making an Actual settlement in the Spring lying on Breashiers Waters of Salt River of the s'd Creek adjoining the Lands of [210]Evan Hinton on the Creek and a place of Wekerham up the s'd Creek satisfactory proof being made to the Court they are of the Opinion that the said Hart has a right to a preemption of 400 Acres of land to include the above Location & that a Cert. issue accordingly.—

(Cert issd for 1000)

[211]Wm Gallaway by James Gallaway this day claimed a preemption of 1000 Acres of Land at the State price in the district of Kentucky on Acc't of marking & improving the same in the year 1776.—Lying on Stoners fork of Licking Creek adjoining the Mouth of —— Creek that comes in below Michael Stoners Land about 3 or 4 Miles and running east for quantity to include his improvement Satisfactory proof being made to the Court they are of Opinion that the s'd Gallaway has a right to a preemption of 1000 Acres of Land to include the above Location & that a Cert. issue accordingly.—

(Certificate issd for 1000)

James Hendrick by Joseph Tomleson this day claimed a preemption of 1000 Acres of Land at the State price in the district of Kentucky on Acc't of marking & improving the same in the year 1776 lying on the waters of Hingston fork of Licking Creek supposed to be about 20 Miles above Hingstons settlement on a branch of that comes from the East and near 3 Miles from the Mouth of the s'd Creek joining lands of Sam'l Tomleson Ebenezer Coan & Lizmon Basey to include his improvement satisfactory proof being made to the Court they are of Opinion that the s'd Hendrick has a right to a preempt. of 1000 Acres of land to include the above Location & that a Cert. issue accordingly.—

(Certificate issd for 1000)

Joseph Tomleson Heir at Law to Sam'l Tomleson Dec'd this day claimed a preemption of 1000 Acres of Land at the State price in the district of Kentucky on Acc't of the s'd decedents marking & improving the lands in the year 1776 Lying on the North side of

[209] Collins, Vol. 2, p. 327.
[210] Collins, Vol. 2, pp. 517, 710.
[211] Collins, Vol. 2, p. 173.

Elkhorn Creek on a branch that empties into the said North Fork about 4 Miles above McClellens fort & about 1 Mile & a half up the said branch to include Joseph Tomleson improvement where there is a Cabbin built and land cleared Satisfactory proof being made to the Court they are of Opinion that the said Tomleson has a right to a preempt of 1000 Acres of Land to include the above Location & that a Cert. issue accordingly.—

(Cert issd for 1000)

John Wilson by Joseph Tomleson this day claimed a preemption of 1000 Acres of Land at the State price in the district of Kentucky on Acc't of Marking & improving the lands in the year 1775 lying on a branch of hingston fork some little distance above the s'd Hingstons and about 14 Miles up the said branch near the lands of Dan'l Gelasby to include an improvement made by John Hartness satisfactory proof being made to the Court they are of Opinion that the s'd Wilson has a right to a preemption of 1000 Acres of Land to include the above Location & that a Cert. issue accordingly.

The Heirs of Henry Carlter by Joseph Tomleson this day claimed a preemption of 1000 Acres of Land at the State price in the district of Kentucky Rejected as it Appears that the said Heir has not taken the Oaths of Fidelity & Allegence.—

(Cert issd for 1000)

James Davis by Joseph Tomleson this day claimed a preemption of 1000 Acres of Land at the State price in the District of Kentucky on Acc't of Marking & improving the same in the year 1776 lying on the Forks of Hingstons fork of Licking Creek near the Land of James Hendricks to include his improvement Satisfactory proof being made to the Court they are of Opinion that the said Davis has a right to a preemption of 1000 Acres of Land to include the above Location & that a Cert. issue accordingly.—

(Cert issued for 1000)

Isaac Greyers this day claimed a preemption of 1000 Acres of Land at the State price in the district of Kentucky on Acc't of Marking & improving the same in the year 1776 lying on the head of the 2d branch of Clear Creek waters of Kentucky to include a large Spring & his improvement satisfactory proof being made to the Court they are of Opinion that the s'd Greyers has a right to a preemption of 1000 Acres of Land to include the above location & that a Cert. issue accordingly.—

(Cert issd for 1000)

Alexander Mitchell by Wm Mitchell this day claimed a preemption of 1000 Acres of Land at the State price in the district of Kentucky on Acc't of marking and improving the same year 1776 lying on a small branch that runs into clear Creek on the North side about 3 Miles below a place called Greyers Camp to include his improvement Satisfactory proof being made to the Court they are of Opinion that the s'd Michell has a right to a preempt'n of 1000 Acres of land to include the above

Location & that a Cert. issue accordingly.—

(Cert issd for 1000)

Adam Coones by James Gallaway this day claimed a preemption of 1000 Acres of Land at the State price in the district of Kentucky on Acc't of marking & improving the same in the year 1776 lying on a run that empties into the West branch of Licking and running south for quantity and adjoining the land of Wm Gallaway to include his improvement Satisfactory proof being made to the Court they are of Opinion that the s'd Coones has a right to a preemption of 1000 Acres of Land to include the above Location & that a Cert issue accordingly.—

(Cert issd for 1000)

Geo'e Sitlemore by Rich'd Bard this day claimed a preemption of 1000 Acres of land at the State price in the district of Kentucky on Acc't of marking & improving the same in the year 1776 lying on the waters of Kentucky River between 10 & 15 Miles south from Drenning Lick on a large Buffaloe road to include his improvement satisfactory proof being made to the Court they are of Opinion that the s'd Sittlemore has a right to a preemption of 1000 Acres of Land to include the above Location & that a Cert. issue accordingly.—

(Cert issd for 1000)

Charles Stewart by Rich'd Bard this day claimed a preemption of 1000 Acres of Land at the State price in the district of Kentucky on Acc't of marking & improving the same in the year 1776 lying on the waters of Kentucky about 8 or 10 Miles from Leestown partly a south course to include his improvement Satisfactory proof being made to the Court they are of Opinion that the s'd Stewart has a right to a preemption of 1000 Acres of Land to include the above Location & that a Cert. issue accordingly.

Sam'l Potter by Rich'd Bard this day claimed a preempt'n of 1000 Acres of Land at the State price in the district of Kentucky on Acc't of marking & improving the same in the year 1776 lying on the Waters of Kentucky adjoining the Lands of Geo'e Sittlemore to include his improvement Satisfactory proof being made to the Court they are of Opinion that the s'd Potter has a right to a preemption of 1000 Acres of Land to include the above Location & that a Cert. issue accordingly.—

(Cert issd for 1000)

Rich'd Bard this day claimed a preempt'n of 1000 Acres of Land at the State price in the district of Kentucky on Acc't of Marking & improving the same in the year 1776 lying between Benson upper & lower Creek waters of Kentucky to include his improvement Satisfactory proof being made to the Court they are of Opinion that the s'd Bard has a right to a preempt of 1000 Acres of Land to include the above Location & that a Cert. issue accordingly.—

It appearing to the Court that Pemberton Rollings has sold his right of Settlement & preemption in the District of Kentucky to John Craig ordered that the s'd Craig be entered as Assee of the s'd Rollings & that on the old Certificate was granted to the s'd Rolling being produced to this Court Ordered that a Cert. issue accordingly.—

(Cert issd for 1400)

[212]John Lawrey this day claimed a settlement & preemption to a tract of Land in the district of Kentucky on Acc't of raising a Crop of Corn in the Country in the year 1776 lying on McCowns fork waters of the North fork of Elkhorn about 1½ or 2 Miles above the Stamping Ground on a small branch of the said Run adjoining the land said to be claimed by [213]Steph'n Lawrey and Wm McConnell to include his improvement Satisfactory proof being made to the Court they are of Opinion that the said Lawrey has a right to a settlement of 400 Acres of Land to include the above Location & that a Cert. issue accordingly.—

(Cert issd for 1000)

Robt. Foaker by Moses Cherry this day claimed a preemption of 1000 Acres of Land at the State price in the district of Kentucky on Acc't of marking and improving the same in the year 1776 lying on little Kentucky River about 15 Miles from the Mouth on the 2d fork above the Mouth to include his improvement Satisfactory proof being made to the Court they are of Opinion that the s'd Foaker has a right to a preemption of 1000 Acres of Land to include the above Location & that a Cert. issue accordingly.

(Cert issd for 1000)

Moses Cherry this day claimed a preempt of 1000 Acres of land at the State price in the district of Kentucky on Acc't of Marking & improving the same in the year 1776 lying on the North side of Elkhorn Creek on the 2d branch above McClellens fort to include his improvement Satisfactory proof being made to the Court they are of Opinion that the s'd Cherry has a right to a preempt of 1000 Acres of Land to include the above location & that a Cert. issue accordingly.—

(Cert issd for 1000)

Stephen Archer this day claimed a preempt'n of 1000 Acres of land at the State price in the district of Kentucky on Acc't of Marking & improving the same in the year 1776 lying on the North side of the North branch of Elkhorn about 5 Miles above McClellens fort to include a spring & his improvement Satisfactory proof being made to the Court they are of Opinion that the said Archer has a right to a preempt'n of 1000 Acres of land to include the above Location & that a Cert. issue accordingly.—

(Cert issd for 1400)

Rob't Foeman this day claimed a settlem't & preempt'n to a tract of land in the district of Kentucky on Acc't of Marking & improving the same in the year 1776 and raising a Crop of Corn in the Country lying on Fox run a branch of Breashiers Creek above & adjoining the lands of Evan Hinton to include a large Rocky Spring & his improvement Satisfactory proof being made to the Court they are of Opinion that the s'd Foarman has a right to a settlement of 400 Acres of land to in-

[212] (Lowrey) Collins, Vol. 2, p. 178.
[213] (Lowrey) Collins, Vol. 2, p. 178.

clude the above Location & the preempt'n of 1000 Acres of land adjoining & that a Cert. issue accordingly.—

(Cert issd for 1000)
Ash Emmerson by Stephen Archer this day claimed a preempt'n of 1000 Acres of land at the State price in the district of Kentucky on Acc't of marking & improving the same in the year 1776 lying on the head waters of the Dry run that empties into the North fork of Elkhorn 1 Miles above McClellens fort in the first fork of the run from the head to include a large Spring and his improvement Satisfactory proof being made to the Court they are of Opinion that the s'd Emeson has a right to a preempt'n of 1000 Acres of Land to include the above Location & that a Cert. issue accordingly.—

(Cert issd for 1000)
Hugh Emmerson by Steph'n Archer this day claimed a preempt'n of 1000 Acres of Land at the State price in the district of Kentucky on Acc't of marking & improving the same in the year 1776 lying on the North side of the North fork of Elkhorn about 1 Mile above Stephen Archers land & adjoining the same to include a large Spring & his improvement Satisfactory proof being made to the Court that the said Emerson has a right to a preempt'n of 1000 Acres to include the above Location & that a Cert. issue accordingly.

(Cert issd for 1000)
James Gallaway this day claimed a preempt'n of 1000 Acres of land at the State price in the district of Kentucky on Acc't of marking & improving the same in the year 1776 lying on Stoners fork of Licking Creek adjoining the lands of [214]Michel Stoner on the No. to include a spring & his improvem't satisfactory proof being made to the Court they are of Opinion that the s'd Gallaway has a right to a preempt'n of 1000 Acres of Land to include the above location & that a Cert. issue accordingly.—

(Cert issd for 1000)
[215]Ebenezer Corn this day claimed a preempt'n of 1000 Acres of Land at the State price in the district of Kentucky on Acc't of marking & improving the same in the year 1776 lying on a small West branch of the Main fork of licking & running east for quantity adjoining the lands of James Hendricks to include his improvem't satisfactory proof being made to the Court they are of Opinion that the s'd Corn has a right to a preempt'n of 1000 Acres of land to include the above Location & that a Cert. issue accordingly.—

(Cert issd for 1000)
John Reed by James Gallaway this day claimed a preempt'n of 1000 Acres of land at the State price in the district of Kentucky on Acc't of Marking & improving the same in the year 1776 lying on Stoners fork of licking Creek about 4 or 5 Miles below Stoners settlem't opposite the Mouth of the first large Creek that runs in below the s'd settlement to include a large Spring on the side of the s'd fork & his improvem't on the No. side Satisfactory proof being made to the Court they are of Opinion

[214] Collins, Vol. 2, p. 70 and index.
[215] Collins, Vol. 2, p. 615.

that the s'd Reed has a right to a pre-empt. of 1000 Acres of land to include the above Location & that a Cert. issue accordingly—

(Cert issd for 1000)

Bazel Stoker by James Gallaway this day claimed a preempt'n of 1000 Acres of Land at the State price in the District of Kentucky on Acc't of marking & improving the same in the year 1776 lying on a West branch of the East side of licking Creek including a large sinking Deer lick about ¼ of a mile from his cabbin about 6 Miles from an old indian Town Satisfactory proof being made to the Court they are of Opinion that the s'd Stoker has a right to a preempt'n of 1000 Acres of land to include the above Location & that a Cert issue accordingly.

Anthony Junkin by Jas. Gallaway this day claimed a preempt'n of 1000 Acres of land at the State price in the district of Kentucky rejected.

(Cert issd for 1400)

Andrew Miller this day claimed a settlem't & preempt'n to a tract of land at the State price in the District of Kentucky on Acc't of raising Corn in the Country in the year 1775 lying on the waters of Dolans run emptying into glens Creek including an improvem't Known by the name of the Linn spring & running So. for quantity Satisfactory proof being made to the Court they are of Opinion that the said Miller has a right to a settlem't of 400 Acres to include the above Location & the preemp'n of 1000 Acres adjoining and that a Cert issue accordingly.—

(Cert issd for 1400)

Benj'm Roberts Jun'r this day claimed a settlem't & preempt'n to a tract of land in the district of Kentucky on Acc't of raising a Crop of Corn in the country in the year 1775 lying about 6 or 7 Miles near a South West Course to include a large Meadow from the falls of Ohio to include his improvem't satisfactory proof being made to the Court they are of Opinion that the s'd Roberts has a right to a settlem't of 400 Acres of land to include the above Location & the preempt'n of 1000 Acres adjoining and that a Cert issue accordingly.—

(Cert issd for 1000)

Rich'd Shankler this day claimed a preempt'n of 1000 Acres of land at the State price in the district of Kentucky on Acc't of Marking & improving the same in the year 1775 lying on the fork of the Beech fork & Chaplins fork of Salt River about 1 Miles above the forks on the Beech fork Satisfactory proof being made to the Court they are of Opinion that the s'd Shankler has a right to a preempt'n of 1000 Acres of land to include the above Location & that a Cert. issue accordingly.—

Ordered that this Court adjourn to-morrow Morning 7 Oclock

William Fleming.

(To be continued.)

EDITOR'S NOTE.

In order to complete the "Certificate Book" for binding in volume 21 a supplement to this issue will be published about October 1, 1923.

OFFICERS

of the

KENTUCKY STATE HISTORICAL SOCIETY

SUBSCRIPTIONS.

Subscription, Yearly, $2.00 Current Number, 75c Per Copy.

Back Numbers, $1.00 Per Copy.

Subscriptions must be sent by check, or money order. All communications for The Register should be addressed to H. V. McChesney, Editor, Frankfort, Kentucky.

H. V. McCHESNEY, Editor and Business Manager.
MRS. JOUETT TAYLOR CANNON, Associate Editor

TO SUBSCRIBERS.

If your copy of The Register is not received promptly please advise us. It is issued in January, May and September.

Entered as second class matter September 17, 1919, at the Post Office at Frankfort, Kentucky, under the Act of August 24, 1912.

The State Journal Company
Frankfort, Ky.

REGISTER

Kentucky State Historical Society

Vol. 21 September, 1923 No. 63—Supplement

CERTIFICATE BOOK OF THE VIRGINIA LAND COMMISSION 1779-80—Concluded.

At a Court Continued & held by the Commissioners of Kentucky District for Adjusting Titles to unpatented lands at St. Asaphs this 22nd day of April 1780—

Present

Wm Fleming Stephen Trigg & Edm'd Lyne—

Capt'n John Craig came into court & declared that it is not in his power to comply with an order of this Court entered the 22nd Inst the Cert. granted to Pemberton Rollings being sent to Williamsburg and the Court being fully Satisfied that the land Granted by the s'd Cert was purchased from the s'd Rollings by the s'd Craig and the s'd Rollings being since killed by the Indians and there being no Heir in this Country to Assign over the s'd Cert. therefore that Justice may be done the said Craig it is the Opinion of this Court that the Survey & preemp'n Warrant for the s'd Land ought to issue in the name of John Craig Assee &c & that the same be Certified Accordingly.

(Cert issd for 1400)

Rich'd Graham by John Crittenden this day claimed a settlem't & preemption to a tract of Land in the District of Kentucky on Acc't of having had a Crop of Corn raised in the Country in the year 1776 lying on the Ohio River and adjoining the Lands of Thos. Powell to run down the River 400 poles & back for quantity Satisfactory proof being made to the Court they are of Opinion that the S'd Graham has a right to a settlement of 400 Acres of Land to include the above Location & the preemption of 1000 Acres of Land adjoining & that a Cert issue accordingly—

(Cert issd for 1400)

John Conner by Jno. Crittenden this day claimed a settlem't & preemption to a tract of Land in the District of Kentucky on Acc't of having had a crop of Corn raised in the Country in the year 1776 & improving Land lying on the North fork of the South fork of Licking Creek below & adjoining the Lands of Anthony Buckner on his lower line to include an improvement Satisfactory proof being made to the Court they are of Opinion that the s'd Conner has a right to a settlem't of 400 Acres of Land to include the above Location & the preempt'n of 1000 Acres adjoining & that a Cert issue accordingly.—

(Cert issd for 1400)

Luke Conner by John Crittenden this day claimed a settlement & preempt'n to a tract of land in the district of Kentucky on Acc't of improving land & raising a crop of Corn in the Country in the year 1776 lying on the North fork of the South fork of licking adjoining John Conners lower line to include an improvem't satisfactory proof being made to the Court they are of Opinion that the s'd Conner has a right to a settlem't of 400 Acres to include the above Location & the preempt'n of 1000 Acres of Land adjoining & that a Cert. issue accordingly.—

(Cert issd for 1400)

[1]Wm Bennett by Crittenden this day claimed a settlem't & preempt'n to a tract of land in the District of Kentucky on Acc't of improving lands & raising a Crop of Corn in the Country in the year 1776 lying on a small branch of the South fork of Elkhorn Known by the name of Crittenden Camp to include an improvement satisfactory proof being made to the Court they are of Opinion that the s'd Bennett has a right to a settlement of 400 Acres of land to include the above Location & the preemption of 1000 Acres adjoining & that a Cert. issue accordingly—

[1] Collins, Vol. 2, p. 553.

(Cert issd for 1000)

[2]Thornton Farrow by Jno Crittendon this day claimed a preempt'n of 1000 Acres of land at the State price in the District of Kentucky on Acc't of Marking & improving the same in the year 1776 lying on Buck lick Creek a branch of the North fork of the South fork of licking to include his improvem't satisfactory proof being made to the Court they are of Opinion that the s'd Farrow has a right to a preempt'n of 1000 Acres of land to include the above Location & that a Certificate issue accordingly.

(Cert issd for 1000)

[3]Timothy Payton by Jno Crittendon this day claimed a preempt'n of 1000 Acres of Land at the State price in the district of Kentucky on Acc't of Marking & improving the same in the year 1776 lying on the head waters of licking Creek about 4 Miles nearly South West from the Lands of John Cannon to include a Rock spring & his improvement Satisfactory proof being made to the Court they are of Opinion that the s'd Payton has a right to a preempt'n of 1000 Acres of land to include the above Location and that a Cert issue accordingly—

[4]Mathew Walker this day claimed a preempt'n of 400 Acres at the State price in the District of Kentucky rejected.

(Cert issd for 1000)

John McClellen by Alex'r McClellen this day claimed a preemption of 1000

[2] Collins, Vol. 2, p. 172.
[3] Collins, Vol. 2, p. 172.
[4] Collins, Vol. 2, p. 172.

Acres of land at the State price in the District of Kentucky on Acc't of marking & Improving the same in the year 1775 lying about 1½ or 2 Miles North East from Lees town on a small path that leads to Bartletts Fitgarrard & [5]andrew McConnells to include his improvem't Satisfactory proof being made to the Court they are of Opinion that the s'd McClellen has a right to a preempt of 1000 Acres of Land to include the above Location & that a Cert. issue accordingly—

(Cert issd for 1000)

John McClellen by Alex'r McClellen this day claimed a preempt'n of 1000 Acres of land at the State price in the District of Kentucky on Acc't of marking & improving the same in the year 1775 lying on the North branch of the North fork of licking Creek near to Lees Creek to include his improvement satisfactory proof being made to the Court they are of Opinion that the said McClellen has a right to a preempt'n of 1000 Acres of land to include the above Location & that a Cert. issue accordingly—

(Cert issd for 1000)

The Heirs of Benj'n Casey Dec'd by David Williams this day claimed a preempt'n of 1000 Acres of land at the State price in the District of Kentucky on Acc't of the s'd Decedents marking & improving the same in the year 1776 Lying on the 2d Buffaloe Crossing on the Middle Creek of Stoners fork of licking Creek to include his improvement Satisfactory proof being made to the Court they are of Opinion that the s'd Heirs &c has a right to a preempt'n of 1000 Acres of land to include the above Location and that a Cert. issue accordingly—

(Cert issd for 1000)

The Heirs of Rich'd Ryand dec'd late of Whelen by David Williams this day claimed a preempt'n of 1000 Acres of Land at the State price in the district on Acc't of marking & improving the same in the year 1776 lying on a small Creek that runs into the Ohio below the Mouth of licking about 3 Miles from the s'd River to include his improvem't Satisfactory proof being made to the Court they are of Opinion that the s'd Heirs &c has a right to a preempt'n of 1000 Acres of Land to the above Location & that a Cert issue accordingly—

Vincent Williams by David Williams this day claimed a preempt'n of 1000 Acres of land at the State price in the District of Kentucky on Acc't of marking & improving the same in the year 1774, 1775 & 1776 and Offered to locate the same on Salt River adjoining the lands of Isaac Hite it appearing to the Court that the s'd Williams improved the s'd land as above mentioned they are of Opinion that he is entitled to a preempt'n of 1000 Acres of land but the Court having granted a Cert. for the said land to Jno McGee they are of Opinion they cannot issue another Cert. for the s'd location nor can they determine the priority of the claim as McGee is not present & cannot be summoned to Appear before the Court till the Au-

[5] Collins, Vol. 2, p. 172 and index.

thority of the Court expires it appearing to them that Williams must proceed for redress by way of Caveat.

(Cert issd for 1000)
Ennis Harden by David Williams this day claimed a preempt'n of 1000 Acres of land at the State price in the district of Kentucky on Acc't of marking & improving the same in the year 1775 lying on the head of the main fork of Stoners fork of licking Creek about 5 Miles above douglasses Survey on the s'd Creek to include his improvement Satisfactory proof being made to the Court they are of Opinion that the s'd Harden has a right to a preempt' of 1000 Acres of Land to include the above Location & that a Cert. issue accordingly—

John Peaxcall by Dav'd Williams this day claimed a preempt'n of 1000 Acres of land at the State price in the district of Kentucky It not appearing to the Court that the claimant had taken the Oaths of Fidelity and Allegence to the State therefore they did not examine further into the Claim.

(Cert issd for 1000)
Peter Coleman by Wm Spangle this day claimed a preempt'n of 1000 Acres of Land at the State price in the district of Kentucky on Acc't of Marking & improv'g Lands in the year 1776 lying on a run that empties into Floyds fork of Salt River the Run heads near Bullskin to include his improvement Satisfactory proof being made to the Court they are of Opinion that the s'd Coleman has a right to a preempt'n of 1000 Acres of land to include the above Location & that a Cert. issue accordingly.—

(Cert issd for 1000)
James Beard this day claimed a preempt'n of 1000 Acres of land at the State price in the District of Kentucky on Acc't of marking & improving the same in the year 1776 lying on the East fork of Licking on a branch called McGrew's Mille Seat to include his improvem't Satisfactory proof being made to the Court they are of Opinion that the s'd Beard has a right to a preempt'n of 1000 Acres of land to include the above Location & that a Cert. issue accordingly—

Cadwallader Slaughter this day claimed a settlem't & preempt'n of a tract of land in the district of Kentucky rejected for want of proof—

(Cert issd for 1000 Acres)
Berkley Fitzgerald this day claimed a settlem't & preempt'n to a tract of land in the District of Kentucky on Acc't of Marking & improving the same in the year 1775 lying on the main fork of Elkhorn about 2½ Miles below the forks to include his improvem't Satisfactory proof being made to the Court they are of Opinion that the s'd Fitzgerald has a right to a preempt'n of 1000 Acres of land to include the above Location & that a Cert issue Accordingly—

Lenifield Sharp By [6]Benj'n Rob'ts Jun'r this day claimed a settlem't &

[6] Collins, Vol. 2, p. 357.

preemption to a tract of Land in the District of Kentucky it not appearing to the Court that he had taken the Oaths of Fidelity & Allegance the State therefore the claim was not further enquired into.

(Cert issd for 1000 Acres)

Zecheriah Archer by Stephen Archer this day claimed a preempt'n of 1000 Acres of land at the State price in the District of Kentucky on Acc't of Marking & improving the same in the year 1776 lying on the North side of the little Kentucky River on the first large Bend about 5 Miles Above the Mouth of the s'd River Satisfactory proof being made to the Court they are of Opinion that the s'd Archer has a right to a preempt'n of 1000 Acres of Land to include the above Location & that a Cert. issue accordingly.—

(Cert. issd for 1000 Acres)

Lewis Thomas by John Askins this day claimed a preempt'n of 1000 Acres of land at the State price in the district of Kentucky on Acc't of Marking & improving the same in the year 1776 lying on Harden Creek a branch of the Rolling fork of Salt River on a point where another small Creek runs to include both sides of the Creek about 2 Miles below Mark Hardens land to include his improvem't Satisfactory proof being made to the Court they are of Opinion that the s'd Thomas has a right to a preempt of 1000 Acres of Land to include the above location and that a Cert. issue accordingly.

(Cert issd for 1000 Acres)

[7]James McConnell Jun'r by Wm McConnell Sen'r this day claimed a preempt'n & settlem't to a tract of Land in the district of Kentucky on Acc't of raising a crop of Corn in the Country in the year 1776 lying on the East side of the North fork of Elkhorn on a run that empties into the said North fork about 1 Mile above Deale Lick to include his improvem't satisfactory proof being made to the Court they are of Opinion that the s'd McConnell has a right to a settlem't of 400 Acres of land to include the above Location & the preempt'n of 1000 Acres adjoining and & that a Cert. issue accordingly.

(Cert issd for 1000 Acres)

Adam McConnell this day claimed a preempt'n of 1000 Acres of land at the State price in the District of Kentucky on Acc't of Marking and improving the same in the year 1775 lying about 1½ Miles up the Timber Ridge on the East fork of the East side including a small Spring and his improvem't about a ¼ of a mile from the s'd Run Satisfactory proof being made to the Court they are of Opinion that the s'd McConnell has a right to a preempt'n of 1000 Acres of land to include the above Location & that a Cert issue accordingly—

(Cert for 400 Acres)

Wm McConnell Sen'r having obtained a Cert. for a preempt of 1000 Acres in the district of Kentucky the day of Feb'y 1780 and now comes into Court & makes it appear that he is intitled also to a settlem't by Virtue of raising a Crop of corn in the Country in the year

[7] Collins, Vol. 2, p. 172 and index.

1776 lying on McConnells run a branch of the North fork of Elkhorn abo't ½ a Mile below the Buffaloe road including a large spring & his improvem't ordered that a Cert issue accordingly.—

(Cert issd for 1000 Acres)

[8]Geo'e Dirkins this day claimed a preempt'n of 1000 Acres of Land at the State price in the District of Kentucky on Acc't of Marking & improv'g the same in the year 1776 lying on a branch of the North fork of licking Creek which heads up with the middle fork of Lawrends Creek beginning a ¼ of a Mile below Harrod Smith Corn field extending West to include his improvem't Satisfactory proof being made to the Court they are of Opinion that the s'd Dirkins has a right to a preempt'n of 1000 Acres of land to include the above Location & that a Cert. issue accordingly—

(Cert issd for 1400 Acres)

James Nevil by Rich'd Jackson this day claimed a settlem't & preempt'n to a tract of land in the district of Kentucky on acc't or raising a crop of corn in the year 1775 lying adjoining the lands of Rich'd Jackman in the forks of Dicks River runing towards Hawkins Creek to the Top of a High Ridge leading towards the Hanging fork Satisfactory proof being made to the Court they are of Opinion that the s'd Nevill has a right to a settlem't of 400 Acres of land to include the above Location & the preempt'n of 1000 Acres adjoining & that a Cert. issue accordingly—

[8] Collins, Vol. 2, p. 551.

Dav'd Buckhannon this day claimed a preempt of 1000 Acres of land at the State price in the District of Kentucky rejected—

Rob't Woods Assee of Simon Buttler this day claimed a preempt'n of 1000 Acres of land at the State price in the District of Kentucky rejected.

(Cert issd for 1000 Acres)

Rob't Woods by Jno Crittendon this day claimed a preempt'n of 1000 Acres of land at the State price in the District of Kentucky on Acc't of Marking and improving the same in the year 1774 lying on the Ohio River about 25 Miles above the mouth of Sioto to include his improvem't satisfactory proof being made to the Court they are of Opinion that the s'd Woods has a right to a preempt'n of 1000 Acres of land to include the above Location & that a Cert. issue accordingly.—

(Cert issd for 1000 Acres)

[9]John Woods by Jno Crittendon this day claimed a preempt'n of 1000 Acres of land at the State price in the district of Kentucky on Acc't of marking & improving the same in the year 1773 lying on the Ohio River adjoining the Lands of Rob't Wood to include his improvement Satisfactory proof being made to the Court they are of Opinion that the s'd Woods has a right to a preempt of 1000 Acres of land to include the above Location & that a Cert. issue accordingly.—

(Cert issd for 1000 Acres)

David Mitchell Assee of Jno Greyer this day claimed a preempt'n of 1000

[9] Collins, Vol. 2, p. 325.

Acres of land at the State price in the district of Kentucky on Acc't of the s'd Greyer marking & improving the same in the year 1776 lying on the North fork of Clear Creek about 1 Mile above the forks including the s'd Greyers improvem't Satisfactory proof being made to the Court they are of Opinion that the s'd Mitchell has a right to a preempt'n of 1000 Acres of land to include the above Location & that a Certificate issue accordingly.—

Wm Mitchell by Dav'd Mitchell this day claimed a preempt'n of 1000 Acres of land at the State price in the district of Kentucky rejected—

(Cert issd for 1000 Acres)
On Motion of Dav'd Mitchell for leave to remove a location for which he has obt'd a Certificate sufficient appearing for the same it is granted him & Now locates the same lying on the head water of the South fork of Cane run adjoining the Lands of McDowell to include his improvem't ordered the Cert. not to issue untill the one that has already been granted be returned.—

Rueben Powell by Jno Porter this day claimed a preempt'n of 1000 Acres of land at the State price in the District of Kentucky.—rejected—

Michael Findley Sen'r by Wm Bard this day claimed a preempt'n of 1000 Acres of land at the State price in the District of Kentucky It not being made appear to the Court that the Claiment had taken the Oaths of Fidelity & Allegance to the State therefore the Court did not enquire further into the Claim.—

Micheal Findley Sen'r by Wm Bard this day claimed a preempt'n of 1000 Acres of land at the State price in the district of Kentucky.—rejected—

(Cert issd for 400)
It being made appear to this Court that Edward Camp was intituled to a preemption of 1000 Acres land at the State price in the district of Kentucky the day of Feb'y tho not located now comes into Court & locates the same lying about 2 Miles from the flat lick between the falls & Bulletts lick and nearly a North West Course to include his improvem't ordered that Cert issue accordingly.—

(Cert issd for 1000 Acres)
Hugh Alexander by Wm Alexander this day claimed a preempt'n of 1000 Acres of land at the State price in the District of Kentucky on Acc't of Mark'g & improving the same in the year 1776 lying in the forks of Elkhorn about 4 or 5 Miles above a large pond spring to include his improvem't Satisfactory proof being made to the Court they are of Opinion that the s'd Alexander has a right to a preempt'n of 1000 Acres of land to include the above Location & that a Cert. issue accordingly.—

(Cert issd for 1000 Acres)
Wm Alexander this day claimed a preempt'n of 1000 Acres of Land at the State price in the district of Kentucky on Acc't of Marking & improving the same in the year 1776 lying in the forks of Elkhorn adjoining above the lands of Hugh Alexander to include his improvem't Satisfactory proof being made

to the Court they are of Opinion that the s'd Alexander has a right to a preempt of 1000 Acres of Land to include the above Location & that a Cert issue accordingly.—

Charles Harrah Assee of Isaac Greyer by Jno Maxwell this day claimed a preemption of 1000 Acres of land at the State price in the District of Kentucky, rejected as the s'd Greyer has obtained a preempt'n in his own name.—

(Cert issd for 1000 Acres)
Rob't Davison by John Maxwell this day claimed a preempt'n of 1000 Acres of land at the State price in the district of Kentucky on Acc't of marking & improving the same in the year 1776 lying on a small branch that runs into the North fork of Clear Creek waters of Kentucky about 1 Mile below the head of the s'd North fork to include a Spring & his improvem't Satisfactory proof being made to the Court they are of the Opinion that the s'd Davison has a right to a preempt'n of 1000 Acres of Land to include the above Location & that a Cert. issue accordingly—

(Cert issd for 1000 Acres)
James Power Assee of Wm Cooks by Jno. Maxwell & Rob't Patterson his Attorneys this day claimed a preempt of 1000 Acres of land at the State price in the district of Kentucky on Acc't of the s'd Cooks improving the same in the year 1776 lying on a small branch that runs into Kentucky Called Buck Run about Mile from the Mouth of the s'd branch to include his Improvement & a spring Satisfactory proof being made to the Court they are of Opinion that the s'd Power has a right to a preemption of 1000 Acres of Land to include the above Location & that a Cert issue accordingly.—

(Cert issd for 1000)
Wm Gray Heir at Law to Geo'e Gray Dec'd by Jno Maxwell this day claimed a preempt of 1000 Acres of land at the State price in the District of Kentucky on Acc't of Marking & improving the same in the year 1775 lying on the North fork of Hingston fork of Licking Creek about 5 or 6 Miles from Riddle Station to include an improvem't Satisfactory proof being made to the Court they are of Opinion that the s'd Heir &c had a right to a preempt'n of 1000 Acres of land to include the above Location & that a Cert issue accordingly.—

(Cert issd for 1000 Acres)
Andrew Steele having obt'd a Cert. for a preempt'n of 1000 Acres of land in the District of Kentucky the day of Feb'y 1780 now comes into Court and makes it appear that he intitled also to a settlem't by Virtue of raising a crop of Corn in the year 1776 lying about 2 Miles up from the mouth of Steel run waters of the South fork of Elkhorn to include a large Rocky Spring & his improvem't ordered that a Cert. issue accordingly.—

(Cert issd for 1000 Acres)
Wm McConnell Jun'r this day claimed a preempt'n of 1000 Acres of land at the State price in the district of Kentucky on Acc't of Marking & improving the same in the year 1775 lying on the South side of the South fork of Elkhorn

Creek on a trace that Crittenden & Company made from Crittenden Camp to licking Creek and about 6 Miles from Lexington to include a Spring & his improvem't Satisfactory proof being made to the Court they are of Opinion that the s'd McConnell has a right to a preemption to of 1000 Acres of land to include the above location & that a Cert issue accordingly—

(Cert issd for 1000 Acres)

Martha Black by Wm Garrett this day claimed a preempt'n of 1000 Acres of land at the State price in the District of Kentucky on Acc't of marking & improving the same in the year 1774 lying on Lees Creek about ½ a Mile above the forks waters of Ohio about 10 Miles from the Mouth to include his improvem't Satisfactory proof being made to the Court they are of Opinion that the s'd Black has a right to a preempt of 1000 Acres of land to include the above Location & that a Cert. issue accordingly.—

(Cert issd for 1000 Acres)

Gasper Marrivele by Jos'h Wilson this day claimed a preempt'n of 1000 Acres of land at the State price in the District of Kentucky on Acc't of Marking & improving the same in the year 1776 on the heads of the dry run empty ing into the main fork of Elkhorn on the South side where a large Buffaloe road crosses to include his improvem't Satisfactory proof being made to the Court they are of Opinion that the s'd Marrivele has a right to a preempt'n of 1000 Acres of land to include the above Location & that a Cert issue accordingly.—

(Cert issd for 1000 Acres)

John Summall by Jos'e Wilson this day claimed a preempt'n of 1000 Acres of Land at the State price in the District of Kentucky on Acc't of Marking & improving the same in the year 1776 lying on a branch that runs into the East fork of Licking Called Mill Creek about 2 or 3 Miles above the mouth to include his improvem't Satisfactory proof being made to the court they are of Opinion that the s'd Summall has a right to a preempt'n of 1000 Acre of land to include the above location & that a Cert. issue accordingly.—

(Cert issd for 1000)

James Caruthers this day claimed a preempt of 1000 Acres of land at the State price in the district of Kentucky on Acc't of marking & improving the same in the year 1776 lying on a branch of the third run that crosses the Buffaloe Road to include his spring and improvem't Satisfactory proof beng made to the Court they are of Opinion that the s'd Caruthers has a right to a preemption of 1000 Acres of land to include the above Location & that a Cert. issue accordingly.—

(Cert issd for 1000)

Henry Penkerton by Jas Caruther this day claimed a preempt'n of 1000 Acres of land at the State price in the district of Kentucky on Acc't of marking & improving the same in the year 1776 lying South of the stamping ground on the South side of the South fork of Elkhorn about 1½ a mile to include a sinking spring & his improvem't Satisfactory proof being made to the Court they are of Opinion that the s'd

Penkerton has a right to a preempt'n of 1000 Acres of Land to include the above Location & that a Cert issue accordingly.—

(Cert issd for 1000)

[10]Jno Fitzpatrick this day claimed a preemption of 1000 Acres of land on Acc't of Marking & improving the same in the year 1775 lying on the waters of the North fork of Licking Creek to the West and adjoining the Lands of Hugh Shannon to include his improvement Satisfactory proof being made to the Court they are of Opinion that the s'd Fitzpatrick has a right to a preemption of 1000 Acres adjoining & that a Cert. issue accordingly.—

(Cert issd for 1000)

Charles Whiteker by [11]Aquilla Whiteker this day claimed a preemption of 1000 Acres of land at the State price in the district of Kentucky on acc't of marking & improving the same in the year 1776 lying on a dry run that runs into the North of Elkhorn on the North side about 3 Miles above McClellens Fork & about 3 or 4 Miles up the s'd run near the forks of the same to include his improvem't Satisfactory proof being made to the Court they are of Opinion that the s'd Whiteker is intitled to a preempt of 1000 Acres of land to include the above location & that a Cert issue accordingly.

(Cert issd for 1000)

Abraham Whiteker by Aquilla Whitaker this day claimed a preempt'n of 1000 Acres of land at the State price in the district of Kentucky on Acc't of marking & improving the same in the year 1776 lying on a dry run that runs into the North fork of Elkhorn below and adjoining the lands of Charles Whitaker to include his improvem't Satisfactory proof being made to the Court they are of Opinion that the s'd Witcker has a right to a preempt'n of 1000 Acres of land to include the above Location & that a Cert. issue accordingly.—

(Cert issd for 1000)

Aquilla Whiteker this day claimed a preempt'n of 1000 Acres of land at the State price in the district of Kentucky on Acc't of marking & improving the same in the year 1776 lying on Breasheirs Creek on the West side thereof below & adjoining lands of Pendergrass to include his improvem't Satisfactory proof being made to the Court they are of Opinion that the s'd Whiteker has a right to a preempt'n of 1000 Acres of Land to include the above Location & that a Cert issue accordingly.—

Sarah McClellen this day claimed a preempt'n of 1000 Acres of land at the State price in the district of Kentucky. rejected—

(Cert issd for 1400)

[12]Rob't Johnson Assee of Stephen Laway this day claimed a settlem't of 400 Acres & a preempt'n of 1000 Acres of land at the State price in the District of Kentucky on Acc't of raising a crop of corn in the Country in the year 1776 lying on the South West fork of Cane

[10] Collins, Vol. 2, p. 53 and index.
[11] Collins, Vol. 2, pp. 22, 710.
[12] Collins, Vol. 2, p. 193 and index.

run a branch of the North fork of Elkhorn Creek about 6 Miles from Lexington to include 3 Springs & improvem't satisfactory proof being made to the Court they are of Opinion that the s'd Johnson has a right to a settlement of 400 Acres of Land to include the above Location & the preempt'n of 1000 Acres adjoining & that a Cert issue accordingly.—

(Cert issd for 1400)

[13]Benj'n McClellen by Rob't Johnson this day claimed a settlement & preemption to a tract of Land in the district of Kentucky on Acc't of raising a Crop of Corn in the Country in the year 1776 lying on Buckhen run a branch of the North fork of Elkhorn Creek to include his improvem't Satisfactory proof being made to the Court they are of Opinion that the s'd McClellen has a right to a settlem't of 400 Acres of land to include the above Location & the preempt'n of 1000 Acres adjoining & that a Cert. issue accordingly.—

(Cert issd for 1000)

Will'm Stewart by Jas. Power this day claimed a preempt'n of 1000 Acres of land at the State price in the district of Kentucky on Acc't of marking & improving the same in the year 1775 lying on Buckhorn run a branch of the North fork of Elkhorn Creek on the side of a Buffaloe road to include his improvement Satisfactory proof being made to the Court they are of Opinion that the s'd Stewart has a right to a preempt'n of 1000 Acres of land to include the above Location & that a Cert. issue accordingly.—

[13] Collins, Vol. 2, p. 178.

(Cert for 1400)

James Greer by Rob't Patterson this day claimed a settlement & preemption to a tract of land in the District of Kentucky on Acc't of settling & residing in the Country 12 months before the year 1778 lying on the Middle branch of Clear Creek waters of Kentucky about 1½ Miles below Greyers Spring to include his improvement Satisfactory proof being made to the Court they are of Opinion that the s'd Greer has a right to a settlement of 400 Acres of land to include the above Location & the preemption of 1000 Acres of land adjoining & that a Cert. issue accordingly.—

Order'd that the Court be adjourned untill tomorrow Morning 7 Oclock

Wm Fleming

At a Court continued & held by the Commissioners of the Kentucky District for adjusting Titles to unpatented Land at St. Asaphs the 25 day of April 1780

Present

Wm Fleming Stephen Trigg & Edmund Lyne—Gentlemen

(Cert issd for 1000 D. D. to Joseph Wilson)

[14]Henry Thompson by Jno Miller this day claimed a preempt'n of 1000 Acres of land at the State price in the District of Kentucky on Acc't of Marking & improving the same in the year 1775 lying on the Middle fork of licking Creek About 2 Miles from where [15]James Cooper settled & about 10 Miles from the lower Salt Spring nearly a South

[14] Collins, Vol. 2, p. 326.
[15] Collins, Vol. 2, p. 325.

west course below the Buffaloe road about 1 Mile to include his improvem't Satisfactory proof being made to the Court they are of Opinion that the s'd Thompson has a right to a preempt'n of 1000 Acres of land to include the above Location & that a Cert issue accordingly.—

(Cert issd for 1000)

Henry Roads Assee of Wm Plumber by Wm McConnell this day claimed a preempt'n of 1000 Acres of Land at the State price in the District of Kentucky on Acc't of Marking & improving the same in the year 1775 Lying on the North fork of McConnells run about 2½ Miles from stamping ground about ¾ of a Mile above the forks of the s'd run and a Buffaloe Road to include his improvem't Satisfactory proof being made to the Court they are of Opinion that the s'd Roads has a right to a preempt'n of 1000 Acres of land to include the above Location & that a Cert issue accordingly.—

(Cert issd for 1400)

[16]William McClellan by Jno Miller this day claimed a settlem't & preempt'n to a tract of Land at the State price in the District of Kentucky on Acc't of raising a Crop of Corn in the Country in the year 1776 lying on the North fork of the South fork adjoining the land of Wm Miller and on a Buffaloe Road to include a spring on the s'd Road & his improvem't Satisfactory proof being made to the Court they are of Opinion that the s'd McClellen has a right to a settlement of 400 Acre of land to include the above Location & the preempt of 1000 Acres adjoining & that a Cert. issue accordingly.—

Wm Harrod this day claimed a settlement & preempt'n to a tract of land in the district of Kentucky on Acc't of raising a crop of Corn in the Country in the year 1776 upon the Witnesses being examined the Court are of Opinion that the said Harrod has a right to a settlem't of 400 Acres of land and the preempt'n of 1000 Acres adjoining & offered to locate the same on the lower Shawnee Spring adjoining the lands granted to Hugh McGarry it being an improvem't purchase of Benj'n Davis in the year 1776 which has been granted to Dianah Denton heir to Jno Denton dec'd and a Cert. issue for the same the parties not being present and the time being short that they cannot be summoned in time to appear before the Court they are of Opinion that this Court cannot grant the s'd Harrod a Cert for the s'd Land and it appearing to the Court that they s'd Harrod must proceed for redress by way of Caveat.

(Cert issd for 1000)

Jesse Peyman this day claimed a preemption of 1000 Acres of land at the State price in the district of Kentucky on Acc't of marking & improving Lands in years 1774 & 1775 lying on the North side of Clear Creek waters of Kentucky & adjoining the land of Paeteh(?) which he obt'd a Cert. for a preemption Satisfactory proof being made to the Court they are of Opinion that the s'd Poagman has a right to a preempt'n of 1000 Acres of land to include the above Location & that a Cert issue accordingly.—

[16] Collins, Vol. 2, p. 327.

(Cert issd for 1000)

[17]Thos White by [18]Bartlett Fitzgerald this day claimed a preempt of 1000 Acres of land at the State price in the district of Kentucky on Acc't of marking & improving the same in the year 1776 lying on Mill Creek a branch of the East fork of Licking at the mouth of Williams run to include his improvem't Satisfactory proof being made to the Court they are of Opinion that the s'd White has a right to a preempt'n of 1000 Acres of land to include the above Location & that a Cert issue accordingly.—

(Cert issd for 1000)

James Foaker by Moses Cherry this day claimed a preempt'n of 1000 Acres of Land at the State pricce in the district of Kentucky on Acc't of marking and improving the same in the year 1776 lying about four miles from Drening lick between the lick & the little Kentucky to include his improvem't Satisfactory proof being made to the Court they are of Opinion that the s'd Foaker has a right to a preempt'n of 1000 Acres of Land to include the above location & that a Cert issue accordingly.—

(Cert issd for 1000)

Adam McConnell Sen'r by Wm McConnell this day claimed a preempt'n of 1000 Acres of land at the State price in the district of Kentucky on Acc't of Marking & improving the same in the year 1776 lying on the Waters of McConnells run a branch of the North Fork of Elkhorn adjoining the lands of Solomon Coan & Wm McConnell to include his improvem't Satisfactory proof being made to the Court they are of Opinion that s'd McConnell has a right to a preemption of 1000 Acres of land to include the above Location & that a Cert issue accordingly.—

[17] Collins, Vol. 2, p. 550.
[18] Collins, Vol. 2, p. 550.

(Cert issd for 1000 Acres)

Jno Cunningham by Wm McConnell this day claimed a preempt of 1000 Acres of Land at the State price in the district of Kentucky on Acc't of marking & improving the same in the year 1776 lying on Lees Creek waters of the Ohio River adjoining Blacks land to include his improvement.—Satisfactory proof being made to the Court they are of Opinion that the s'd Cunningham has a right to a preempt of 1000 Acres to include the above location & that a Cert. issue accordingly.—

Edward Holdman this day claimed a preempt'n of 1000 Acres of land at the State price in the District of Kentucky. rejected.

(Cert issd for 1000 Acres)

Eli Coulter by Andrew Steele this day claimed a preempt'n of 1000 Acres of land at the State price in the district of Kentucky on Acc't of marking & improving the same in the year 1776 lying on the head of Steeles run waters of the South fork of Elkhorn Creek at the pond spring to include his improvem't Satisfactory proof being made to the Court they are of Opinion that the s'd Coulter has a right to a preemption of 1000 Acres of land to include the above Location & that a Cert issue accordingly.

Arthur Poak by Wm McConnell this day claimed a preemption of 1000 Acres of land at the State price in the district of Kentucky on Acc't of marking & improving the same in the year 1776,—rejected.

Jacob Light this day claimed a preemption of 1000 Acres of Land at the State price in the district of Kentucky.—rejected.

Peter Light by Stephen Archer this day claimed a preempt of 1000 Acres of land at the State price in the District of Kentucky.—rejected.—

(Cert issd for 1400)

Joseph Huston by Jas Power this day claimed a settlem't & preempt'n to a tract of land in the district of Kentucky on Acc't of raising a crop of corn in the Country in the year 1776 lying on the North side of the North fork of the Middle fork of licking Creek on a small run & About ½ a Mile from the mouth & 1½ Miles from where Cooper raised Corn to include his improvem't Satisfactory proof being made to the Court they are of Opinion that the s'd Huston has a right to a settlement of 400 Acres of land to include the above location to the preempt'n of 1000 Acres of land adjoining & that a Cert issue accordingly—

(Cert issd for 1000)

Charles Polke by Thos. Polke this day claimed a preempt of 1000 Acres of land at the State price in the District of Kentucky on Acc't of marking & improving the same in the year 1776 lying on Simpsons Creek a branch of the town fork of Salt River near the head thereof to include his improvem't Satisfactory proof being made to the Court they are of Opinion that the s'd Polke has a right to a preempt of 1000 Acres of land to include the above Location & that a Cert. issue accordingly.—

(Cert issd for 1000)

Rich'd Conner by Thos. Polke this day claimed a preempt'n of 1000 Acres of land at the State price in the District of Kentucky on Acc't of marking & improving the same in the year 1776 lying on simpson Creek waters of the Town fork of Salt River below and adjoining the lands of Charles Polke to include his improvem't Satisfactory proof being made to the Court they are of Opinion that the s'd Conner has a right to a preempt of 1000 Acres of land to include the above Location & that a Certificate issue accordingly.

(Cert issd for 1000)

[19]Wm Triplett by Jno Todd this day claimed a preempt'n of 1000 Acres of land at the State price in the district of Kentucky on Acc't of marking and improving the same in the year 1775 lying on the South side of the East fork of licking Creek No. W. of waters land on the Buffaloe road to include his improvem't Satisfactory proof being made to the Court they are of Opinion that the s'd Triplett has a right to a preempt'n of 1000 Acres of land to include the above Location & that a Cert issue accordingly.—

[19] Collins, Vol. 2, pp. 465, 550.

(Cert issd for 1400)

[20]Charles Mayn Thruston by Jno Todd this day claimed a settlement & preemption to a tract of Land in the district of Kentucky on Acc't of marking & improving the same in the year 1776 lying on the waters of Drenning Lick Creek on the left hand fork about 7 Miles above the lick adjoining the Buffaloe road on the South East side including the improvement made by Geo'e Rogers Clarke Satisfactory proof being made to the Court they are of Opinion that the s'd Thruston has a right to a settlement of 400 Acres of land to include the above Location & the preemption of 1000 Acres adjoining & that a Cert issue accordingly.—

(Cert issd for 1000)

It Appearing to the Court that a Settlem't & preempt'n to a Tract in the District of Kentucky was granted the — day of ——— 1779 to Rich'd Thomas which s'd Land so granted is within the bounds of a tract of land under survey by Virtue of a Military Warrant therefore the Court are of Opinion that the s'd Cert should not carried into execution & that the s'd Thomas have leave to Locate the s'd Settlem't & preempt'n on Mulberry Creek waters of Brashiers Creek adjoining the lands of Mr. Pendergrass on the No. E. on both side of s'd Creek ordered that a Certificate issue accordingly.

(Cert issd for 1000)

James Wilson this day claimed a preempt of 1000 Acres of Land at the State price in the district of Kentucky on Acc't of marking and improving the same in the year 1776 lying on Pleasant run waters of Salt River on the first run that runs into the s'd run below Morton Harden and adjoining the same to include his improvem't Satisfactory proof being made to the Court they are of Opinion that the s'd Wilson has a right to a preemption of 1000 Acres of land to include the above Location & that a Cert. issue accordingly.—

(Cert issd for 1000)

Thos. Wilson by Jas. Wilson this day claimed a preempt'n of 1000 Acres of land at the State price in the district of Kentucky on Acc't of marking & improving the same in the year 1776 lying on Clear Creek waters of Kentucky about 1½ Miles from the mouth of the s'd Creek to include his improvem't Satisfactory proof being made to the Court they are of Opinion that the s'd Wilson has a right to a preemption of 1000 Acres of land to include the above Location & that a Cert issue accordingly.—

(Cert issd for 1000)

Aron Vancleave by Squire Boone this day claimed a settlem't & preempt'n to a tract of land at the State price in the district of Kentucky on Acc't of Marking & improving the same in the year 1776 & planting Corn lying on Bullskin a branch of Breashiers Creek about 3 Miles from the head to include a Camp & Corn field Witnesses being sworn and Examined the Court are of Opinion that the s'd Vancleave is intitled to a preempt only of 1000 Acres of land to include the above Location & that a Cert. issue accordingly.—

---

[20] Collins, Vol. 2, pp. 357, 514.

(Cert issd for 1000)

Mathew Rogers this day claimed a preempt of 1000 Acres of land at the State price in the District of Kentucky on Acc't of marking & improving the same in the year 1775 lying on the Rolling fork of Salt River above & adjoining the land of Rich'd Swan to include his improvem't Satisfactory proof being made to the Court they are of Opinion that the s'd Rogers has a right to a preemption of 1000 Acres of Land to include the above Location & that a Cert issue accordingly.—

(Cert issd for 1000)

[21]Wm Wood Jun'r by Dav'd Glen this day claimed a preempt'n of 1000 Acres of Land at the State price in the District of Kentucky on Acc't of Marking & improving the same in the year 1775 lying Glens Creek adjoining the Lands of Dav'd Glen to the North to include his improvement Satisfactory proof being made to the Court they are of Opinion that the s'd Wood has a right to a preempt'n of 1000 Acres of Land to include the above Location and that a Cert issue accordingly.—

(Cert issd for 1400)

[22]Adam Smith this day claimed a settlement & preempt'n to a tract of Land in the district of Kentucky on Acc't of raising a Crop of Corn in the Country in the year 1776 lying on Cane run to include a Mill Seat adjoining the lands of Harlen & William Bryan Heir to David Bryan to include his improvem't Satisfactory proof being made to the Court they are of Opinion that the s'd Smith has a right to a settlement of 400 Acres of Land to include the above Location & the preempt'n of 1000 Acres of Land adjoining & that a Cert issue accordingly.—

[23]James McKennely Assee of Thos. White this day claimed a preempt'n of 1000 Acres of land at the State price in the district of Kentucky Rejected.

(Cert issd for 1000)

[24]Thos. White Jun'r by David Bohanon this day claimed a preemption of 1000 Acres of Land at the State price in the district of Kentucky on Acc't of Marking & improving the same in the year 1776 lying on Mill Creek waters of the East fork of Licking 2 or 3 Miles below the mouth of Williamsons Run to include his improvem't Satisfactory proof being made to the Court they are of Opinion that the S'd White has a right to a preempt'n of 1000 Acres of Land to include the above Location & that a Cert issue accordingly.

(Cert issd for 1400)

[25]Micheal Thomas by Henry Thomas this day claimed a settlement & preempt'n to a tract of Land in the district of Kentucky on Acc't of raising a Crop of Corn in the year 1776 lying on the South side of Dicks River adjoining Teator to include his improvem't Satisfactory proof being made to the Court they are of Opinion that the s'd Thomas has a right to settlement of 400 Acres of land to include the above location & the preemption of 1000 Acres of land adjoining & that a Cert. issue accordingly.—

[21] Collins, Vol. 2, p. 511.
[22] Collins, Vol. 2, p. 511.
[23] (McKinley) Collins, Vol. 2, pp. 24, 555.
[24] Collins, Vol. 2, p. 550.
[25] Collins, Vol. 2, p. 511.

[26]William Crow this day claimed a settlement & preempt'n to a tract of land in the district of Kentucky on Acc't of raising a crop of Corn in the Country in the year 1776 & improving the Lands in the year 1774 & 1775 & offered to locate the same on Clarks run whereon [27]Geo'e Clarke now lives for which he the s'd Clarke has obt'd a Certificate who appeared & the Parties agreed to submit the matter to the Court Postponed untill tomorrow to be further considered—

(Cert issd for 1000)

Jno. Underwood Heir at Law to Benj. underwood dec'd by William Crow this day claimed a preempt'n of 1000 Acres of land at the State price in the district of Kentucky on Acc't of Marking & improving the same in the year 1776 lying on the Waters of Sunfish Creek waters of Breasheirs Creek near the Lands of [28]Abraham Vanmeters to include an improvement satisfactory proof being made to the Court they are of Opinion that the s'd Underwood has a right to a preemption of 1000 Acres of Land to include the above Location & that a Cert issue accordingly.—

[29]John Crawford this day claimed a preemption of 1000 Acres of land at the State price in the District of Kentucky on Acc't of Marking and improving the same in the year 1774 the witnesses being sworn & examined in consideration of Which the Court are of Opinion that the s'd Crawford has a right to a preempt'n of 1000 Acres and offered to locate the same on the Hanging fork of Dicks River which Lands Sam'l Craig has obt'd a Cert. for 1000 Acres preempt'n therefore the Court are of Opinion that they s'd cannot grant a Cert to the s'd Crawford and that he must proceed for redress by way of Caveat.

(Cert issd for 1000)

[30]James Kelly this day claimed a preempt. of 1000 Acres of land at the State price in the district of Kentucky on Acc't of marking & improving the same in the year 1776 lying on Hingston fork of Licking Creek about 7 Miles above the said Hingstons adjoining the Lands of Wm Steele to include a large Blue Spring and his improvement Satisfactory proof being made to the Court they are of Opinion that the s'd Kelly has a right to a preempt of 1000 Acres of land to include the above Location & that a Cert issue accordingly.—

(Cert issd for 1000)

[31]Peter Paul this day claimed a preempt'n of 1000 Acres of Land at the State price in the district of Kentucky on Acc't of marking & improving the same in the year 1776 lying on Bullskin branch of Breasheirs Creek about 1 Mile below the mouth of Fox run to include his improvement satisfactory proof being made to the Court they are of Opinion that the s'd Paul has a right to a preemption of 1000 Acres of Land to include the above Location & that a Cert issue accordingly.

[26] Collins, Vol. 2, p. 511, 519.
[27] Collins, Vol. 2, pp. 23, 446, 760.
[28] Collins, Vol. 2, pp. 511, 710.
[29] Collins, Vol. 2, pp. 517, 632.
[30] Collins, Vol. 2, pp. 84, 327, 551.
[31] Collins, Vol. 2, pp. 511, 710.

(Cert issd for 1000)

[32]Jno. Paul by Peter Paul this day claimed a preempt of 1000 Acres of Land at the State price in the district of Kentucky on Acc't of marking & improving the same in the year 1776 lying on Bullskin a branch of Breasheir Creek about 1 Mile above the mouth of Fox run to include his improvement Satisfactory proof being made to the Court they are of Opinion that the s'd Paul has a right to a preempt'n of 1000 Acres of land to include the above Location & that a Cert issue accordingly.—

(Cert issd for 1000)

Meridith Holm by Wm Holm this day claimed a preempt'n of 1000 Acres of Land at the State price in the district of Kentucky on Acc't of marking & improving the same in the year 1776 lying on the South side of Tick Creek a branch of Breasheirs Creek about 2 Miles up the s'd Tick Creek from the Mouth to include his improvement satisfactory proof being made to the Court they are of Opinion that the s'd Holm has a right to a preempt of 1000 Acre of land to include the above Location & that a Cert issue accordingly.—

(Cert issd for 1000)

[33]Meredith Helm Heir at Law to [34]Jno Helm Deceased by Wm Helm this day claimed a preempt'n of 1000 Acres of land at the State price in the district of Kentucky on Acc't of marking & improving the same in the year 1776 lying on the South side of Ticks Creek about 2 Miles East of Meridith Helms improvem't to include the s'd dec'd improvem't Satisfactory proof being made to the Court they are of Opinion that the s'd Helm &c has a right to a preemption of 1000 Acres of land to include the above Location & that a Cert issue accordingly.—

(Cert for 1000)

Arthur McConnell by Jas. Cair this day claimed a preempt'n of 1000 Acres of Land at the State price in the district of Kentucky on Acc't of marking & improving the same in the year 1776 lying on the North side of Green River between 15 & 20 Miles above Bryants lick to include his improvement Satisfactory proof being made to the Court they are of Opinion that the s'd McConnell has a right to a preempt of 1000 Acres to include the above Location & that a Cert issue accordingly.—

(Cert for 1000)

[35]Henry Dickerson by Geo'e Cullom this day claimed a preempt'n of 1000 Acres of land at the State price in the District of Kentucky on Acc't of marking & improving the same in the year 1776 lying on Hingstons fork of Licking Creek about 1½ Miles above the Lands of James Kelly to include his improvem't Satisfactory proof being made to the Court they are of Opinion that the s'd Dickerson has a right to a preempt'n of 1000 Acres of land to include the above Location & that a Cert issue accordingly.—

(Cert issue for 1000)

[36]Thomas Dickerson by Geo'e Cullom this day claimed a preempt'n of 1000

[32] Collins, Vol. 2, p. 308.
[33] Collins, Vol. 2, p. 511.
[34] Collins, Vol. 2, p. 511.
[35] Collins, Vol. 2, pp. 327, 551.
[36] Collins, Vol. 2, pp. 327, 551.

Acres of land at the State price in the District of Kentucky on Acc't of marking & improving the same in the year 1776 lying on Hingstons fork of Licking Creek about 1½ Miles from the lands of Henry Dickerson to include his improvem't Satisfactory proof being made to the Court they are of Opinion that the s'd Dickerson has a right to a preempt'n of 1000 Acres of Land to include the above Location & that a Certificate issue accordingly.

Jacob Severton by Jonah Seamas this day claimed a preempt'n of 1000 Acres of land at the State price in the district of Kentucky on Acc't of Marking & improving the same in the year 1776 Rejected the Court having reason to believe he has obtained a Cert for land of the Commissioners of Monogalia &c District.

(Cert issd for 1000)
James Hannah by Jonah Seaman this day claimed a preempt'n of 1000 Acres of Land at the State price in the district of Kentucky on Acc't of Marking & improving the same in the year 1776 on the waters of Drennings lick Creek about 4½ Miles from the lick in the fork of the said Creek including a Cabbin made in the year 1775 by Jacob Newland Satisfactory proof being made to the Court they are of Opinion that the s'd Hannah has a right to a preempt of 1000 Acres of Land to include the above Location & that a Cert issue accordingly.—

Jonah Seaman this day claimed a preempt'n of 1000 Acres of Land at the State price in the district of Kentucky. rejected.

(Cert issd for 1000)
Dav'd Hawkins this day claimed a preempt'n of 1000 Acres of Land at the State price in the district of Kentucky on Acc't of Marking & improving the same in the year 1779 & making & Actual settlem't in the Month of May lying opposite to the Mouth of McCartys Creek Silas Cocks on the South side of Salt River Satisfactory proof being made to the Court they are of Opinion that the s'd Hawkins has a right to a preempt'n of 1000 Acres of land to include the above Location & that a Cert issue accordingly.—

Ordered that the Court adjourn untill tomorrow Morning 6 Oclock
William Fleming

At a Court continued and held by the Commissioners for adjusting Titles to unpatented lands in the district of Kentucky at St. Asaphs the 26 day of April 1780
Present
William Fleming Stephen Trigg
Edmund Lyne—

(Cert issd for 1400)
Jno Kenny by [37]Jas. Kenny this day claimed a settlem't & preempt'n to a Tract of land in the district of Kentucky on Acc't of raising a Crop of Corn in the year 1776 lying on Coopers run waters of licking Creek below & adjoining Wm. McGee's Land & on both sides of the s'd run Satisfactory proof

[37] Collins, Vol. 2, p. 327.

being made to the Court they are of Opinion that the s'd Kenny has a right to a preemp'n of 1000 Acres of Land to include the above Location & that a Cert issue accordingly.—

(Cert issd for 1000)

Dav'd Cox by Isaac Cox this day claimed a preemp'n of 1000 Acres of Land at the State price in the District of Kentucky on Acc't of marking & improving the same in the year 1776 lying on Cox's Creek about 2 Miles below Isaac Coxes land to include his improvem't Satisfactory proof being made to the Court they are of Opinion that the s'd Cox has a right to a preempt of 1000 Acres of land & that a Cert issue accordingly.—

(Cert issd for 1000)

Isaac Cox this day claimed a preemption of 1000 Acres of Land at the State price in the district of Kentucky on Acc't of marking & improving the same in the year 1776 lying on Coxes Creek that empties into the Town fork of Salt River to include his improvement Satisfactory proof being made to the Court they are of Opinion that the s'd Cox has a right to a preemption of 1000 Acres of Land to include the above Location & that a Cert issue accordingly.—

(Cert issd for 1000)

Jacob Decker by Isaac Cox this day claimed a preempt of 1000 Acres of land at the State price in the district of Kentucky on Acc't of marking & improving the same in the year 1776 lying on Cox Creek near the head thereof above & adjoining the Lands of Isaac Cox to include his improvem't Satisfactory proof being made to the Court they are of Opinion that the s'd Decker has a preempt'n of 1000 Acres of land to include the above Location & that a Cert issue accordingly.—

(Cert issd for 1000)

Joseph Cox by Isaac Cox this day claimed a preempt'n of 1000 Acres of land at the State price in the district of Kentucky on Acc't of marking & improving the same in the year 1776 lying on a Branch of the town fork of Salt River about 8 Miles East from Isaac Coxes Land to include his improvement Satisfactory proof being made to the Court they are of Opinion that the said Cox has a right to a preempt'n of 1000 Acres of Land to include the above Location & that a Cert issue accordingly.—

(Cert issd for 1000)

James McDonald by Isaac Cox this day claimed a preemption of 1000 Acres of Land at the State price in the District of Kentucky on Acc't of marking & improving the same in the year 1776 lying on a branch of Coxes run which empties in 4 Miles below Isaac Cox's land to include his improvement Satisfactory proof being made to the Court they are of Opinion that the s'd McDonald has a right to a preemption of 1000 Acres of land to include the above location and that a Cert issue accordingly.—

(Cert issd for 1000)

Benj Cox by Isaac Cox this day claimed a preempt of 1000 Acres of Land at the State price in the District of Kentucky on Acc't of marking & improving the same in the year 1776 lying on Cox's Creek about 3 Miles below Isaac Cox's land to include his improvem't Satisfactory proof being made to the Court they are of Opinion that the s'd Cox has a right to a preempt'n of 1000 Acres of land to include the above Location & that a Cert issue accordingly.—

(Cert issd for 1000)

Jno Ash Sen'r this day claimed a preempt of 1000 Acres of land at the District of Kentucky on Acc't of Marking & improving the same in the year 1776 lying on the Waters of the town fork of Salt River about 2 Miles nearly East from Jos'h Cox's land to include his improvem't satisfactory proof being made to the Court they are of Opinion that the s'd Ash has a right to a preempt'n of 1000 Acres of land to include the above Location & that a Cert issue accordingly.—

(Cert issd for 1000)

Thos. Polke this day claimed a preempt of 1000 Acres of Land at the State price in the District of Kentucky on Acc't of Marking & improving the same in the year 1776 lying on the dividing ridge between the Town fork & the Rolling Fork of Salt River on the head of a Branch of Cox's Creek about 4 Miles S. W. from Isaac Cox land to include his improvem't Satisfactory proof being made to the Court they are of Opinion that the s'd Polke has a right to a preemption of 1000 Acres of land to include the above Location & that a Cert issue accordingly.—

(Cert issd for 1000)

[38]Sam'l Strode this day claimed a preempt'n of 1000 Acres of Land at the State price in the district of Kentucky on Acc't of mark'g & improving the same in the year 1776 lying on a Creek that runs into the West side of Licking between the Upper & lower lick about 8 Miles from the s'd Upper Blue Licks to include his improvem't Satisfactory proof being made to the Court they are of Opinion that the s'd Strode has a right to a preempt'n of 1000 Acres of Land to include the above Location & that a Cert issue accordingly.—

(Cert issd for 1000)

Mercer Beason Heir at Law to [39]Mercer Beason Ded'd this day claimed a preempt of 1000 Acres of land at the State price in the district of Kentucky on Acc't of the s'd Deced'r marking & improving the same in the year 1776 lying on a branch of Licking Creek and 1 Mile East from Sam'l Strodes land to include s'd Decedents improvem't Satisfactory proof being made to the Court they are of Opinion that the s'd Beason has a right to a preempt'n of 1000 Acres of Land to include the above Location & that a Cert issue accordingly.—

(Cert issd for 1000)

Jonah Heaton this day claimed a preempt'n of 1000 Acres of Land at the State price in the district of Kentucky on Acc't of marking & improving the same in the year 1776 lying on Cox's Creek a branch of the Town fork of Salt River about 5 or 6 Miles below Isaac Coxs land to include his improve-

[38] Collins, Vol. 2, pp. 466, 551.
[39] Collins, Vol. 2, p. 553.

ment Satisfactory proof being made to the Court they are of Opinion that the s'd Heaton has a right to a preempt'n of 1000 Acres of Land to include the above Location & that a Cert issue accordingly.—

(Cert issd for 1000)

[40]Benj'n Harrison this day claimed a preempt'n of 1000 cres of land at the State price in the district of Kentucky on Acc't of Marking & improving the same in the year 1776 lying at the head of the West fork of Licking Creek about 3 Miles from Jno Morgans Cabbin on a branch which empties into the Creek & about 1 quarter of a mile above the s'd Cabbins to include his improvement & 2 springs one on each side of the s'd Branch Satisfactory proof being made to the Court they are of Opinion that the s'd Harrison has a right to a preempt of 1000 Acres of land to inclde the above Location & that a Cert issue accordingly.

[41]John Baker this day claimed a preemption of 1000 Acres of land at the State price in this district of Kentucky. Postponed.

(Cert issd for 1000)

John Hughes Assee of [42]Arthur Ingram by [43]Jesse Pigman this day claimed a preemption of 1000 Acres of Land at the State price in the district of Kentucky on Acc't of the s'd Ingram marking &c improving the same in the year 1776 lying on Fox run about 2 Miles from the mouth thereof to include the s'd Ingrums improvem't Satisfactory proof being made to the Court they are of Opinion that the s'd Hughes has a right to a preempt'n of 1000 Acres of Land to include the above Location & that a Cert issue accordingly.—

(Cert issd for 1000)

Nath'l Hogman Triplett by Jno Peters this day claimed a preempt'n of 1000 Acres of land at the State price in the district of Kentucky on Acc't of marking & improving the same in the year 1776 lying upon the East branch of licking about 8 Miles from a Creek called Limestone Creek and adjoining the Lands of [44]William Triplett and Sam'l Webbs to include his improvem't Satisfactory proof being made to the Court they are of Opinion that the s'd Triplett has a right to a preempt of 1000 Acres of Land to include the above Location & that a Cert issue accordingly.—

(Cert issd for 1000)

[45]Willis Edwards by Jno Peters this day claimed a preempt'n of 1000 Acres of land at the state price in the District of Kentucky on Acc't of marking & improving the same in the year 1776 lying on the Ohio River about 10 Miles below the Mouth of the Sioto adjoining some Sand (Land) improved by [46]Jas Triplett to include his improvement satisfactory proof being made to the Court they are of Opinion that the s'd Edwards has a right to a preempt'n of

[40] Collins, Vol. 2, p. 71 and index.
[41] Collins, Vol. 2, p. 417.
[42] Collins, Vol. 2, p. 511.
[43] Collins, Vol. 2, p. 511.
[44] Collins, Vol. 2, pp. 465, 550.
[45] Collins, Vol. 2, p. 465.
[46] Collins, Vol. 2, p. 465.

1000 Acres of Land to include the above Location & that a Cert issue accordingly.—

(Cert issd for 1000)
William Morgan by Jno Peters this day claimed a preempt'n of 1000 Acres of Land at the State price in the District of Kentucky on Acc't of Marking & improving the same in the year 1776 lying on Benson Creek on the North side of Kentucky about 4 or 5 Miles up the Creek from the Mouth where it empties into the Kentucky River to include a spring and his improvem't where there is W. M. cut on a Tree Satisfactory proof being made to the Court they are of Opinion that the s'd Morgan has a right to a preempt'n of 1000 Acres of land to include the above Location & that a Cert issue accordinly.—

(Cert issd for 1400)
[47]John Crow this day claimed a settlement & preemption of 1400 Acres of Land in the district of Kentucky on Acc't of improving the same in the year 1774 & 1777 & Raising a crop of Corn in the year 1776 the s'd Crowe is to Survey a half way between 2 Cabbins with a Square line that the s'd Crowe built in the year 1774 one Cabbin covered South West from Fishers Garrison Known by Rees' Lottery Cabbin the other N. E. from s'd Station and the s'd Fisher is not to go more than half way to another Cabbin that the s'd Crow built in the year Aforesaid which Cabbin lies North from s'd Station Satisfactory proof being made to the Court they are of Opinion that the s'd Crow has a right to a settlement of 400 Acres of Land to include the above Location & the preempt'n of 1000 Acres of Land adjoining & that a Cert issue accordingly.—

[47] Collins, Vol. 2, pp. 18, 517.

(Cert iss for 1000)
John Baker this day claimed a preemption of 1000 Acres of Land at the State price in the district of Kentucky on Acc't of Making an Actual settlem't in May 1779 lying on the Waters of Cedar Creek a branch of Chaplins fork to include his improvem't with the letters JB marked on a tree Satisfactory proof being made to the Court they are of Opinion that the s'd Baker has a right to a preempt'n of 1000 Acres of land to include the above Location & that a Cert issue accordingly.—

(Cert issd for 1000)
Joseph Connerly this day claimed a preemption of 1000 Acres of land at the State price in the district of Kentucky on Acc't of Marking and improving the same in the year 1776 lying on a small branch of Greyers Creek adjoining the lands of Isaac Greyer & Isaac Power to include his improvem't Satisfactory proof being made to the Court they are of Opinion that the s'd Connerly has a right to a preempt'n of 1000 Acres to include the above Location & that a Cert issue accordingly.—

(Cert issd for 1000)
William Eagin this day claimed a preempt of 1000 Acres of Land at the State price in the district of Kentucky on Acc't of marking & improving the same in the year 1775 lying on a branch

that runs into Greyers Creek about ¾ or 1 Miles west of Joseph Connerways to include his improvem't Satisfactory proof being made to the Court they are of Opinion that the s'd Eagin has a right to a preempt of 1000 Acres of Land to include the above Location & that a Cert issue accordingly.—

Joell Rees Motion to have leave to remove a Location which he Obt'd a Certificate the — day of April sufficient cause appearing to the Court for the same it is granted Now locates the same lying on the North side Kentucky river Drennings Lick at a place Known by the name of the Cove to include two Buildings in the year 1775 ordered that a Cert issue accordingly.—

(Cert issd for 1000)

Elisha Lickley by Cornelias Gatter this day claimed a preempt'n of 1000 Acres of Land at the State price in the district of Kentucky on Acc't of Marking & improving the same in the year 1776 lying on a Creek a branch of the Rolling fork of Salt River about 1½ Miles below the fork of Creek to include the improvem't Satisfactory proof being made to the Court they are of Opinion that the s'd Lickley has a right to a preempt of 1000 Acres of Land to include the above Location & that a Cert issue accordingly.—

(Cert issd for 1000)

Cornelias Howard by Cornelias Gatter this day claimed a preempt'n of 1000 Acres of land at the State price in the district of Kentucky on Acc't of Marking & improving the same in the year 1776 lying on the South side of a Creek a Branch of the Rolling fork of Salt River above the lands claimed by Elisha Lickley to include his improvem't Satisfactory proof being made to the Court they are of Opinion that the Said Howard has a right to a preempt'n of 1000 Acres of land & that a Cert. issue accordingly.

(Cert issd for 1000)

Cornelias Gatter this day claimed a preemption of 1000 Acres of land at the State price in the District of Kentucky on Acc't of marking & improving the same in the year 1776 lying on a small branch that empties into Breasheirs Creek & about 6 or 7 Miles from the said Creek to include the improvem't Satisfactory proof being made to the court they are of Opinion that the s'd Getter has a right to a preempt'n of 1000 Acres of Land to include the above Location & that a Cert issue accordingly.

(Cert issd for 1400 to be d. d. to Mr. May)

Jno Warford Assee of Jno Hunt this day claimed a preempt'n of 1000 Acres of Land at the State price in the district of Kentucky on Acc't of mark'g & improving the same in the year 1776 lying on the first branch of Breaseirs Creek below where the three forks meet on the South side of the s'd Creek and about 2½ or 3 Miles from the Mouth of the s'd Branch to include his improvem't they are of Opinion that the s'd Warford has a right to a settlement of 400 & a preempt of 1000 Acres of Land to the above Location and that Cert issue accordingly.

(Cert issd for 1000)

Alex'r Lithgrow by Jno Crittendon this day claimed a preemption of 1000 Acres of Land at the State price in the district of Kentucky on Acc't of Marking & improving the same in the year 1776 Lying on the West fork of licking Creek below an improvem't of Jno Morgans binding upon the lower Line of Benjamin Harrison Land to include his improvement satisfactory proof being made to the Court they are of Opinion that the s'd Lithgrow has a right to a preemption of 1000 Acres of Land to include the above Location & that a Cert issue accordingly.

(Cert issd for 1000)

[48]Jno Hedges Jun'r by Jno Crittenden this day claimed a preempt'n of 1000 Acre of Land at the State price in the district of Kentucky on Acc't of Marking & improving the same in the year 1776 lying on the Ohio River beginning 200 Poles above the Mouth of Turkel Creek & running down the river 400 poles & back for quantity to include his improvem't which is about 50 Miles above the Mouth of licking satisfactory proof being made to the Court they are of Opinion that the s'd Hedges has a right to a preempt of 1000 Acres of Land to include the above Location & that a Certificate issue accordingly.—

(Cert issd for 1000)

Wm Farrow by Jno Crittendon this day claimed a preempt'n of 1000 Acres of Land at the State price in the district of Kentucky on Acc't of marking & improving the same in the year 1776 lying on Buck Lick Creek head of the South fork thereof waters of the south fork of Licking including the upper improvement the said South fork of Buck Lick Creek Satisfactory proof being made to the Court they are of Opinion that the s'd Farrow has a right to a preemption of 1000 Acres of Land to include the above Location that a Cert issue accordingly.—

Jno. Kendrick of Loudon County by John Crittenden this day claimed a preemption of 1000 Acres of land in the district of Kentucky rejected for want of proof of having taken the Oath of Fidelity and Allegence &c.

(Cert issd for 400)

Arthur Blackburn this day claimed a preempt of 400 Acres of land at the State price in the district of Kentucky on Acc't of making an Actual settlement in March 1779 lying on a branch of the hanging fork of Dicks river 2 Miles above the Lands of Sam'l Briggs to include his improvement satisfactory proof being made to the Court they are of Opinion that the s'd Blackburn has a right to a preempt of 400 Acres of land to include the above Location & that a Cert issue accordingly.—

[49]Wm Rice claim for 1000 a preemption is rejected for want of proof of his having taken the Oath of Fidelity &c.

(Cert issd for 1000)

James Logan this day claimed a preemption of 1000 Acres of Land at the State price in the district of Kentucky on Acc't of marking and improving the

[48] Collins, Vol. 2, pp. 94, 549.

[49] Collins, Vol. 2, p. 511.

same in the year 1776 on the North side of the rolling fork about 6 Miles below the Shawnee Lick to include his improvement satisfactory proof being made to the Court they are of Opinion that the s'd Logan has a right to a preemption of 1000 Acres of Land to include the above Location & that a Cert issue accordingly.—

(Cert issd for 1000)
James Adams this day claimed a preempt of 1000 Acres of Land at the State price in the district of Kentucky on Acc't of marking & improving the same in the year 1776 on the East fork of Mill Creek & about 10 Miles from where the s'd Creek empties into the Kentucky river about 7 Miles above the Mouth to include his improvement satisfactory proof being made to the Court they are of Opinion that the s'd Adams has a right to a preempt of 1000 Acres of Land to include the above Location & that a Cert. issue Accordingly.—

(Cert issd for 1000)
Eli Adams by James Adams this day claimed a preempt of 1000 Acres of Land at the State price in the district of Kentucky on Acc't of marking & improving the same in the year 1776 lying on the East fork of Mill Creek adjoining the Lands of Sineca McCrakin and Near to James Adams Land to include his improvement satisfactory proof being made to the Court they are of Opinion that the s'd Adams had a right to a preempt of 1000 Acres.

Wm Adams Claim by Jas. Adams for a preemption of 1000 Acres of Land Rejected.

(Cert issd for 1000)
Edmund Turmond this day claimed a preempt of 1000 Acres of Land at the State price in the district of Kentucky on Acc't of Marking & improving the same in the year 1777 lying on the North side of Colo Callaways land and on the south side of Jno Litrells land on Callaway Creek Satisfactory proof being made to the Court they are of Opinion that the s'd Turmond has a right to a preempt of 1000 Acres of land to include the above Location & that a Cert. issue accordingly.—

(Cert issd for 1400)
Wm Bohanon this day claimed a preemption and settlement in the District of Kentucky on Acc't of settling in the Country in the year 1777 & residing twelve Months at one time lying on the head waters of Paint Lick Creek including a Sulphur Lick Spring joining the White lick—Satisfactory proof being made to the Court they are of Opinion that the s'd Bohanon has a right to a settlement of 400 Acres & a preemption of 1000 Acres of Land to include the above Location & that a Certificate issue accordingly.—

(Cert isd for 1400)
Wm Crow & Geo'e Clarke this day Appeared agreeable to an Order of this court the 25th Inst witnesses being sworn & examined in consideration of which the s'd Crowe has a right to a settlem't of 400 Acres of Land to include the s'd Crows improvem't which is on the land now in dispute & the preempt of 1000 Acres adjoining & that a Cert. issue accordingly.—

Agreed to exchange this Certificate and assign them Accordingly to the Porters (Parties?) Wm Crow came into Court & locates his land lying on the North fork of Licking Creek joining the Middle fork of Laurenes Creek & adjoining George Dickens preemption including three Cabbins of Simon Butlers. Ordered that a Cert. issue accordingly.—

Isaac Romine this day claimed a preempt of 400 Acres of Land at the State price in the District of Kentucky rejected.—

(Cert issd for 1000)
Phillip Lutts this day claimed a preempt of 1000 Acres of Land at the State price in the District of Kentucky on Acc't of marking & improving the same in the year 1776 lying on Bull Creek and adjoining the Lands of Aron Vancleave Satisfactory proof being made to the Court they are of Opinion that the s'd Lutts has a right to a preemption of 1000 Acres of Land to include the above Location & that a Certificate issue accordingly.—

(Cert issd for 1000)
Henry Failwether by Phillip Lutts this day claimed a preempt of 1000 Acres of Land at the State price in the district of Kentucky on Acc't of Marking & improving the same in the year 1776 lying on the dividing Ridge between Clear Creek & Bullskin Creek & about 3 Miles South of the Mouth of Fox Run to include his improvement satisfactory proof being made to the Court they are of Opinion that the s'd Failwether has a right to a preempt of 1000 Acres of Land to include the above Location & that a Cert. issue accordingly.—

(Cert issd for 1400)
Hugh Forbes this day claimed a settlem't & preempt to a tract of Land in the district of Kentucky on Acc't of raising a crop of corn in the Country in the year 1776 lying on both sides of the West fork of Licking Creek and adjoining the Lower lines of the lands of Alexander Lithgrow to include his improvement satisfactory proof being made to the Court they are of Opinion that the s'd Forbes has a right to a settlement of 400 Acres of land to include the above Location & the preempt of 1000 Acres adjoining & that a Cert issue accordingly—

(Cert issd for 1400)
Wm Brent by Hugh Forbes this day claimed a settlem't & preemption in the district of Kentucky on Acc't of raising a crop of Corn in the Country in the year 1776 on the West fork of Licking Creek on a small branch that runs in on the East side above the lands claimed by Benj'n Harrison to include his improvement Satisfactory proof being made to the Court they are of Opinion that the s'd Brent has a right to a settlem't of 400 Acres of Land to include the above Location & the preempt of 1000 Acres of land adjoining & that a Certificate issue accordingly.—
(Cert issd for 1400)

Edward Sprigg by Hugh Forbes this day claimed a settlement & preemption to a tract of Land in the district of Kentucky on Acc't of raising a Crop of Corn in the Country in the year 1776 lying on the waters of the West fork of Licking Creek on both sides above & adjoining the Lands of Wm Brent to include his improvement Satisfactory proof being made to the Court they are of Opinion that the s'd Sprigg has a right to a settlem't of 400 Acres of Land to include the above Location & that a Cert. issue accordingly.—

(Cert issd for 1000)

Dan'l Forbes by Hugh Forbes this day claimed a preempt of 1000 Acres of Land at the State price in the district of Kentucky on Acc't of Marking & improving the same in the year 1776 lying on the West fork of Licking Creek below & adjoining the land of Hugh Forbes to include his improvement satisfactory proof being made to the Court they are of Opinion that the s'd Forbes has a right to a preemption of 1000 Acres of Land to include the above Location & that a Cert issue accordingly.—

(Cert issd for 1400)

Charles Will'm Cross by Hugh Forbes this day claimed a settlement & preeption to a tract of Land in the district of Kentucky on Acc't of raising corn in the Country in the year 1776 lying near the head of Buck Lick Creek where there is a remarkable round Hill to include his improvement satisfactory proof being made to the Court they are of Opinion that the s'd Cross has a right to a settlement of 400 Acres of Land to include the above Location & the preemption of 1000 Acres of Land adjoining & that the Cert issue accordingly.—

(Cert issd for 1000)

The [50]Rev'd Adam Smith by Rich'd Thomas this day claimed a preemption of 1000 Acres of land at the State price in the district of Kentucky on Acc't of marking & improving the same in the year 1776 lying on a branch of Hickmans Creek below & adjoining the Rev'd Jno Todds Land to include his improvement satisfactory proof being made to the Court they are of Opinion that the s'd Smith has a right to a preempt of 400 Acres of Land to include the above Location & that a Certificate issue accordingly.—

(Cert issd for 1400)

Joshua Wright by Squire Boone this day claimed a tract of land in the district of Kentucky on Acc't of raising a Crop of Corn in the Country in the year 1776 lying on the waters of Floyds fork of Salt River about 4 or 5 Miles above their old trace to include a Mark made by Squire Boone satisfactory proof being made to the Court they are of Opinion that the s'd Wright has a settlement of 400 Acres of land to include the above location & the preempt of 1000 Acres of Land adjoining & that a Cert. issue accordingly.—

(Cert issd for 1000)

[51]James Wright by Squire Boone this day claimed a preemption of 1000 Acres of Land at the State price in the district of Kentucky on Acc't of Mark'g & improving the same in the year 1776 lying on the Waters of Breasheirs Creek above & adjoining the lands of Squire Boon & Allens Satisfactory proof being made to

[50] Collins, Vol. 2, p. 511.
[51] Collins, Vol. 2, p. 710.

the Court they are of Opinion that the s'd wright has a right to a preemption of 1000 Acres of Land to include the above location & that a Cert issue accordingly.—

(Cert issd for 1400)

On the Motion of Sam'l Campbell for leave to remove a Location which he Obt'd a Cert for the day of April In't Assee of Jas. Mitchell &c sufficient cause appearing for the same it is granted, now locates lying on both sides of Spring Creek which runs into the North side of the Rolling fork of Salt River including a Spring near a Buffaloe Path ordered that a Cert issue accordingly.—

(Cert issd for 1400)

On the Motion of Wm Stewart for leave to remove a location which was granted to Ephraim Peyton Assee of Wm Ennings the 21 Inst Sufficient cause appearing it is granted him on the right hand fork of Lawrences Creek to join Thos Williams on the West end to extend West for Quantity ordered that a Cert issue accordingly.—& the s'd Stewart to be entered as Assee of Peyton &c as it appears to the Old Cert was Assigned to the s'd Stewart.

(Cert issd for 1000 Acres)

Charles Gatliff heir at Law to Squire Gatliff this day claimed a preemption of 1000 Acres of Land at the State price in the district of Kentucky on Acc't of mark'g & improving the year 1773 lying on the Ohio River on the 3d Large Bottom above the Mouth of Sioto to include his improvement Satisfactory proof being made to the Court they are of Opinion that the s'd Gatliff has a right to a preemption of 1000 Acres of Land to the above Location & that a Cert issue accordingly.—

(Cert issd for 1400)

Adam Whickerham Jun'r this day claimed a settlement & preempt'n to a tract of Land in the district of Kentucky on Acc't of raising a Crop of Corn in the Country in the year 1776 lying near the head of the first branch that empties into Breasheirs Creek below the three forks to include his improvement satisfactory proof being made to the Court they are of Opinion that the s'd Wickerham has a right to a settlement of 400 Acres of land to include the above location & the preemption of 1000 acres adjoining & that a Cert issue accordingly.—

[52]Jacob Wickerham by [53]Adam Wickerham this day claimed a settlement & preemption to a tract of land in the district of Kentucky rejected as it does not appear that the claimant had taken the Oath of Fidelity &c.

Adam Witckerham by Adam Witckerham this day claimed a preempt of 1000 Acres of land at the State price in the district of Kentucky on Acc't of marking & improving the same in the year 1776 Rejected as it Appeared to the Court that he had obt'd a Cert. for lands in Monnongalia District.

(Cert issd for 1000)

Sam'l Applegate by Wm Crow this day claimed a preempt'n of 1000 Acres of Land at the State price in the district of Kentucky on Acc't of marking & im-

[52] Collins, Vol. 2, pp. 319, 710.
[53] Collins, Vol. 2, pp. 319, 710.

proving the same in the year 1776 lying on the Rowling fork of Salt River about 2 Miles above the Mouth of Indian lick run to include his improvement satisfactory proof being made to the Court they are of Opinion that the s'd Applegate has a right to a preempt of 1000 Acres of land to include the above Location & that a Cert issue accordingly.—

(Cert issue for 1000)

James Gilmore this day claimed a preempt of 1000 Acres of land at the State price in the district of Kentucky on Acc't of marking & improving the same in the year 1776 on the head waters of the town fork of Salt River about 1½ Miles west of Knob Lick to include his improvement satisfactory proof being made to the Court they are of Opinion that the s'd Gilmore has a right to a preempt of 1000 Acres to include the above Location & that a Cert issue accordingly.—

(Cert issd for 1000)

Geo'e Smith by Jno Smith this day claimed a preemption of 1000 Acres of land at the State price in the District of Kentucky on Acc't of marking & improving the same in the year 1775 lying on Silver Creek at St. Asaphs Fork on the West side thereof extending up the Creek to include gerushes Grove satisfactory proof being made to the Court they are of Opinion that the s'd Smith has a right to a preemption of 1000 Acres of Land to include the above Location & that a Cert issue accordingly.—

(Cert issd for 1000)

Owen Deven this day claimed a settlement in the district of Kentucky on Acc't of raising a crop of Corn in the Country in the year 1776 lying adjoining a preemption which he obt'd a Cert. for the — day of 1780 Satisfactory proof being made to the Court they are of Opinion that the s'd Devon has a right to a settlement of 400 Acres of land to include the above Location & that a Cert issue accordingly he having at the time he Obt'd his preempt no proof of his being entitled.

Alexander Mchan by [54]Jos'h Wilson this day claimed a preemption of 1000 Acres in the district of Kentucky. rejected.—

(Cert issd for 1000)

Jno Allison by Jno Fleming this day claimed a preempt of 1000 Acres of Land at the State price in the district of Kentucky on Acc't of marking & improving the same in the year 1776 lying on a branch of Licking Creek about 7 Miles from the Upper Blue licks to include a large Dear Lick and his improvement satisfactory proof being made to the Court they are of Opinion that the s'd Allison has a right to a preemption of 1000 Acres of land to include the above Location & that a Cert issue accordingly.

(Cert issd for 1400)

On the Motion of [55]Dav'd Glen this day in behalf of Jos. Blackford to have a location removed which he obtained a Cert. for the 12 of Feb'y 1780 on Acc't of raising a Crop of corn &c in the year 1776 sufficient Cause appearing for the same it his granted him & now

[54] Collins, Vol. 2, p. 550.
[55] Collins, Vol. 2, pp. 467, 517, 624.

locates lying on the North side of Kentucky about 2 or 3 Miles from Benson Crossing to include a sinking Spring & his improvement Ord'd that a Cert. issue accordingly.—

(Cert iss for 1400)

[56]James Sterrat by Jos'h Wilson this day claimed a settlem't & preemption to a tract of land in the district of Kentucky on Acc't of raising Corn in the Country in the year 1776 lying on the waters of Dry Run on the North West side of the North fork of Elkhorn about ¾ of a Mile from the Mouth about 1½ Miles from McClellens fork to include an improvement made by Jno. Lawrey Satisfactory proof being made to the Court they are of Opinion that the s'd Sterrat has a right to a settlement of 400 Acres of land to include the above Location & the preemption of 1000 Acres adjoining & that a Cert issue accordingly.—

[56] Collins, Vol. 2, p. 178.

The Commissioners having finished all the business in this District that has come before them that power expired this day after Public notice being 3 times given by the Sheriff for Claimers to appear this Court of Commissioners for the County of Kentucky is dissolved.

Test

Wm. Fleming
Steph'n Trigg
Edm'd Lyne
Jno Williams Jun'r C. C. C.

A CORRECTION

In the January number (No. 61), page 5, Colonel Stephen Trigg is referred to as the "only son of Abraham Trigg." It should have read "youngest son of Abraham Trigg."

In the same number, pages 26 and 80, mention is made of "Harrods Creek." This should have been "Howards Creek."

LOCATIONS AND WATER COURSES

In preparing the following list of locations and water courses no effort has been made to include all the streams now on the map of Kentucky, but those which are mentioned in the "Certificate Book" of the Virginia Land Commission have, we believe, been located with fair accuracy. In the location of the early Stations and Forts Collins' History and Filson's map of Kentucky have been of great assistance, and for the water courses, Elihu Barker's map of 1795 and J. Russell's map of 1794, with maps of Kentucky showing the present county outlines have been used.

Confusion is likely to occur to some extent on account of the frequent repetition of names, as for instance; Otter Creek, Mill Creek, Wolf Creek, Muddy Creek, Clear Creek, Cedar Creek, Buffaloe Creek, Cane Creek, &c., all of which appear in widely separated parts of the State. It is sometimes possible to determine just which of these creeks is meant by the place of hearing and by examination of the locations of the other claimants whose applications are filed on the same day. For instance if a claim is located "on Muddy Creek" *without other description,* the location of that particular meeting of the Land Commission might help us to decide whether the creek of that name in Madison County or Ohio County was intended. If the sitting of the Commission on that day was at Boonesboro, we should certainly believe it was the former; if at the Falls of the Ohio, it might very well be the latter. If the location was on Otter Creek while the Commission was sitting at Boonesboro, we should not expect to look for the record of the land in McLean, or one of the other counties where there was a creek by that name, but in Madison. If the hearing was at St. Asaphs or Logan's Fort, and the land in question was on Canoe Creek, we should expect to find that it was located in Rockcastle rather than in Henderson County. However, we must not conclude that the claim was *always* filed at the nearest meeting place of the Commission, for on page 12, we find that during a sitting of the Commission at St. Asaph's, October 19 (?), 1779, James Cobun, "Heir-at-law to Samuel Coburn deceased," produced a claim for a tract which is so particularly described that we know it must have been located in the present county of Shelby.

In more than one instance it is apparent that the surveyor has erred in describing a creek as tributary to the wrong stream, but when we consider the dangers and hardships accompanying the making of these early surveys, the difficulties of transportation and navigation, and the interlocking of the headwaters of many of the rivers, the descriptions are wonderfully correct.

Locations

Barrens—Meade and Hardin Cos.

Barrens—Barren, Warren and Edmonson.

Big Forks of Elkhorn—Franklin Co.

"Bigg Meadow"—South of Cumberland River.

Blue Licks (Upper and Lower)—Nicholas Co.

Boiling Springs—Mercer Co.

Boonesborough—Madison Co.

Boones Station—Same as Boonesborough.

Boones Trace—"Wilderness Road" through Cumberland Gap to Boonesborough.

Bowman's Station—Mercer Co.

Brashear's Station—Bullitt Co.

Bryan's Station—Fayette Co. 5 miles from Lexington.

Buffaloe Trace—From Blue Licks to Big Bone Lick through Nicholas, Harrison. Scott, Franklin, Henry, Owen and Boone Cos.

Bullitt's Salt Lick—Bullitt Co.

Carpenter's Station—Lincoln Co.

Clark's Station—Boyle Co.

Clark's Station—Mason Co.

Cooper's Station—Bourbon Co.

Coxes Settlement—Nelson Co.

Crab Orchard—Lincoln Co.

Craig's Station—Garrard Co.

Crittenden's Cabbins—Probably in Bourbon Co.

Crittenden's Camp—Woodford Co.

Crow's Station—Boyle Co.

Drenning's Salt Lick (Drennon)—Henry Co.

English Station—Lincoln Co.

Falls of the Ohio—Louisville, Jefferson Co.

Floyd's Station—Jefferson Co., Mouth of Bear Grass.

Floyd's Station—Jefferson Co. 6 miles from Falls.

Floyd's Fork Station—Oldham Co., 18 miles from Louisville.

Fountain Blue (Fontainebleau)—Mercer Co.

Fort Liberty—Mercer Co.

Glover's Station—Green Co. (Greensburg).

Goar's Station—Franklin Co.

Gordon's Station—Mercer Co.

Grant Station—Fayette Co.

Great Crossings—Scott Co.

Haggin's Station—Mercer Co. Same as Trigg's.

Handcock Taylor's Grave—Madison Co.

Hardin's Station — Hardinsburg, Breckinridge Co.

Harlan's Station—Mercer Co.

Harrodsburg—Mercer Co.

Harrod's Landing—Kentucky River, Mercer Co.

Harrod's Station—Mercer Co., 6 miles from Harrodsburg.

Hart's (White Oak Springs)—Madison Co.

Haycraft Station—Hardin Co.

Hazel Patch—Laurel Co.

Helm's Station—Hardin Co.

Hickory Bottom—Carrol Co.

Higgin's Blockhouse—Harrison Co.

Hinde's (Hynde's)—Hardin Co.

Hinkstones' Station (Hingstone)—Same as Riddles or Ruddles.

Holder's Station—Madison Co.

Hoy's Station—Madison Co.

Huston's Station—Paris, Bourbon Co.

Hynes Station—Same as Hends or Hindes.

Indian Town (Indian Old Fields)—Clark Co.

Irvine's Station—Madison Co.

Jacob Grott's Settlement—Bourbon Co.

Kellar's Station—Jefferson Co.

Kenton's Station—Mason Co.

Kenton's, John, Station—Mason Co.

Kennedy's Station—Garrard Co.

Kinchloe's Station—Spencer Co.

Knob Lick Station—Lincoln Co.

Knocks Buckle.

Kuykendall Station—Jefferson Co.

Leach's Station—Bracken Co.

Leitch's Station—Campbell Co.

Lee's Station—Mason Co.

Leestown—Franklin Co.

Lewis' Station—Mason Co.

Lexington—Fayette Co.

Liberty, Fort—Mercer Co.

Licking Station—Harrison Co.

Lidia Mount.

Limestone—Mason Co.

Linn's Garrison—Jefferson Co.

Littell's Station—Grant Co.

Littell's Station—Pendleton Co.

Little Fort, The—Twetty's Fort, Madison Co.

Locust Thicket Fort—Madison Co.

Logan's Fort (or Station)—St. Asaphs, 1 mile from Stanford, Lincoln Co.

Louden's Station—Probably on Kentucky River in Henry Co.

Lynch's Station, same as Squire Boone's—Shelby Co.

McAfee's Station—Near Harrodsburg, Mercer Co.

McAfee's Station, James—6 or 7 miles from Harrodsburg.

McAfee's Station, William—Mercer Co., on Shawnee Run.

McClellan's Fort or Station—Georgetown, Scott Co.

McConnell's Station—Near Lexington.

McCowan's Station—Mercer Co.

McGary's Station—Mercer Co.

McGee's Station—Fayette Co.

McGuire's Station—Same as McGee's.

McKinney's Station—Lincoln Co.

McMillin's Fort—Bourbon or Harrison.

Marble Creek Station—Madison Co.

Martin's Station—Bourbon Co.

Masterton's Station—Fayette Co.

Maulding Station—Logan Co.

Montgomery Station—Lincoln Co.

Mud Garrison—Shepherdsville, Bullitt Co.

Muddy River Licks—Logan Co.

Nelson, Fort—Louisville, cor. 9th and Ohio River.

New Market—Henry Co.

Old Town—Harrodsburg.

Old Town (Indian)—Greenup Co.

Owen's, Brackett, Station—Near Shelbyville.

Painted Stone—Squire Boone's Station in Shelby Co.

Paint Lick Station—Garrard Co.

Pettitt Station—Lincoln Co.

Phillip's Fort—Larue Co.

Pittman's Station—Green Co.

Poplar Level—Jefferson Co.

Red Banks—Daviess Co.

Reed Station—Near Danville, same as Given's.

Riddle's Station—Same as Ruddles.

Rogers' Station—Clark Co.

Rogers' Station—Nelson Co.

"Rock Dunda."

Ruddles' Station—Harrison Co.

Salt River Garrison.

Sandusky Station—Washington Co.

Scott's Station—Harrison Co.

Shannon's Trace—Scott Co.

Shallow Ford Station—Madison Co.

Skagg's or Skegg's Station—Green Co.

Slate Blockhouse—Bath Co.

Spring Station—Jefferson Co.

Squire Boone's Station—Shelby Co.

St. Asaphs'—Lincoln Co. (Stanford).

Stamping Ground—Scott Co.

Stations on Beargrass—Jefferson Co.

Stevenson's Station—Garrard Co.

Stockfields—Madison Co.

Stoner's Settlement—Bourbon Co.

Strode's Station—Clark Co.

Sturgus (Asturgus) Station—Jefferson Co.

Sullivan's Station—Jefferson Co.

Taylor's Creek Station—Campbell Co.

Tick Creek—Shelby Co.

Todd's Station, Capt.—Jessamine Co.

Trigg's Station (Viney Grove)—Mercer Co.

Twetty's Fort—Madison Co.

Tyler's Station—Shelby Co.

Vance's Station—On Green River, 15 miles from M.

Vanmeter's Fort—Hardin Co.

Vienna—McLean Co.

Viney Grove—Trigg's Station.

War Road—Same as Whitley, Lincoln Co.

Wells Station—Shelby Co.

Wells Station—Mason Co.

Whaley's Station—Mason Co.

Wheatley—Same as Whitley, Lincoln Co.

Whittaker's Station—Bullitt Co.

White Oak Springs (Hart Station)—Madison Co.

Whitley's Station—Lincoln Co., 2 miles from Crab Orchard.

Wilderness—Road from Virginia.

Williamson's Run—Fleming Co.

Wilson Station—Mercer Co.

Woods Station—Madison Co.

Woodstock—"8 miles N. W. from Boonesboro."

Worthington Station—Lincoln Co.

Yellow Banks—Daviess Co.

Water Courses

Barren River—Southern tributary of Green River, between Allen, Monroe, Barren and Warren Counties.

Barton's Creek—Mercer Co.

Barshear's Creek—Same as Brasheares, in Shelby Co. (Bearshears).

Battle Creek—Trimble Co.

Beach Fork (of Salt River) in Nelson and Washington counties.

Beargrass Creek—Jefferson Co.

Benson Creek (Upper and Lower)—Franklin Co.

Big Boiling Spring—Near Harrodsburg in Mercer Co.

Big Blue Lick—Nicholas Co.

Big Forks of Elkhorn Creek—Franklin Co.

Big Bone Lick—Between Boone and Gallatin Counties.

Boggers Fork—Clark Co.

Boffman's Fork of Boon's Creek—Clark Co.

Boiling Spring—Mercer Co.

Boon's Creek—Clark Co.

Boon's Mill Creek—Madison Co.

Bowman's Creek—Bourbon and Montgomery Counties.

Bracken's Creek—Bracken Co.

Bramlet's Lick—Bourbon Co.

Breashier's Creek—Same as Barshears or Brashears, in Shelby Co.

Brush Creek—Casey Co. and Owen Co.

Bryant's Lick—Casey Co.

Brushy Pond Creek—Jefferson Co.

Buck Lick Creek.

Buck Run—Woodford Co.

Buffaloe Creek—Nelson (Washington, Mercer and Boyle).

Bullitt's Salt Lick—3 miles from Shepherdsville in Bullitt Co.

Bull Lick—Madison Co.

Bullskin Creek—Fork of Brearshears in Shelby Co.

Bunton's Creek.

Cabbin Creek—Mason and Lewis Cos.

Calloway Creek—Madison Co.

Cane Run—Scott and Fayette Cos.

Cane Run—Lincoln and Casey Cos.

Cane Run—Mercer Co.

Caney Fork.

Canoe Creek—Henderson and Rockcastle Cos.

Carpenter's Creek—Lincoln and Casey Cos.

Cartwright's Creek—Washington and Marion Cos.

Cedar Creek—Owen Co.

Cedar Creek—Lincoln Co.

Cedar Run—Mercer Co.

Cees (?) Creek—Mason or Bracken Co.

Chinath Run (Chenowith)—Jefferson or Shelby Co.

Chaplin's Fork of Salt River—Between Washington, Nelson and Marion Counties.

Clark Creek—Garrard Co.

Clark's Run—Branch of Dick's River.

Clay Lick.

Clear Creek—Shelby Co.

Clear Creek—Woodford Co.

Combs' Creek—Same as Howard's Creek, Clark Co.

Cooper's Run—Bourbon Co.

Coxes Creek—Nelson Co.

Crooked Creek—Mason, Trigg, Crittenden and Pendleton Cos.

David Jones Fork of Elkhorn—Fayette Co.

Deal's Run—Scott Co.

Delaware Creek—McLean Co.

Dick's River—Branch of Kentucky in Mercer, Boyle, Garrard and Lincoln Cos.

Doctor's Fork of Salt River—Washington Co.

Dowlan's Creek—Branch of Salt River.

Drake Camp Creek—Lincoln and Garrard Cos.

Dreaming Creek—Madison Co.

Drennon's or Drennings Creek—Henry Co.

Drowning Creek or Downing—Madison and Estill Counties.

Dry Fork of Salt River.

Dyx (Dix) River—Dicks River.

Eagle Creek—Carroll and Owen Cos.

Elk Garden Creek—Madison Co.

Elkhorn Creek (Main)—Franklin Co.

Elkhorn Creek (North)—Franklin and Scott Cos.

Elkhorn Creek (South)—Franklin, Woodford and Fayette Cos.

"Elkhorn Creek, a branch of Dick's River," evidently a mistake or intended for the branch of Licking in Knott, Floyd and Letcher Cos.

Elk Lick.

Falling Creek—Branch of Dick's River in Lincoln and Garrard Cos.

Falls of the Ohio—Louisville, Jefferson Co.

Fern Creek—Jefferson Co.

Finn Creek—Probably Fern Creek.

Fish Pools—At the head of Pond River in Jefferson Co.

Flat Creek—Bath Co.

Floyd's Fork of Salt River—Jefferson and Bullitt Cos.

Four Mile Creek—Clark Co.

Fox Run—Shelby Co.

Froman's Creek—Branch of Chaplin's Fork of Salt River in Washington Co.

Fun Creek—Probably Fern Creek in Jefferson Co.

Gasses Creek—Probably Gist's or Guesses Creek.—Harrison Co.

Gilbert's Creek—Anderson Co.

Gilbert's Creek—Garrard Co.

Gilmour's Creek—Lincoln Co.

Glen's Creek—Woodford Co.

Glen's Creek—Washington Co.

Grear's or Greer's Creek or Greyer's Creek—Woodford Co.

Green Creek—Bourbon Co.

Green River—Southern Kentucky through Lincoln, Casey, Green, Adair, Hart, Edmonson, Warren, Butler, Ohio, Muhlenberg, Hopkins, Daviess and Henderson Cos. to Ohio River.

Given's Creek—Branch of Green River in ———.

Gordon's Lick—Lincoln Co.

Goose Creek—Clay Co.

Goose Creek—Jefferson Co.

Goose Creek—Oldham Co.

Hammond's Creek—Anderson Co.

Hanging Fork of Dick's River—Lincoln Co.

Harden's Creek—Breckinridge Co.

Harmon's Creek or Lick—Wayne Co.

Harrod's Creek—Jefferson Co.

Harrod's Lick—Branch of the Licking in Bourbon Co.

Harrod's Run—Mercer Co.

Haskin's Run—Bourbon Co.

Hawkin's Branch of Dick's River.

Hickman's Creek—Jessamine Co.

Hinkson's or Hinkstone's Creek—Bourbon Co.

Howard's Creek—Clark Co.

Howard's Upper Creek—Clark Co.

Huston's Fork of the Licking—Bourbon Co.

Indian Creek—Jackson Co.

Indian Camp Creek—Madison Co.

Indian Camp Creek—Butler Co.

Irvin's Lick—Branch of Tates Creek in Madison Co.

Jessemen Creek—Jessamine and Fayette Cos.

Johnson's Fork of Licking—Robertson Co.

Jouett's Creek—See Duret's Creek.

Kennady's Fork of.

Kentucky River—N. W. through Letcher, Perry, Breathitt, Wolfe, Lee, Estill, Madison, Clarke, Fayette, Jessamine, Garrard, Mercer, Woodford, Anderson, Franklin, Owen, Henry and Carroll Counties.

Knob Creek—Hardin Co.

Knob Lick Creek—Lincoln Co.

Knob Lick—Webster Co.

Lawrence Creek—Mason Co.

Lee's Creek—Mason Co.

Licking River—Northeastern Kentucky.

Lilbergrud—Lulbergrud in Clark.

Limestone Creek or Run—Mason Co.

Linn Camp Creek—Butler Co.

Little Flat Lick—Lincoln Co.

Little Kentucky River—Henry, Carroll and Trimble Cos.

Logan's Creek—Lincoln Co.

Long Run—Jefferson Co.

Lower Blue Licks—Nicholas Co.

Lulbegrud Creek—Clark, Montgomery and Powell Cos.

McClallun's Fork or Fort—Scott Co.

McConnell's Run—Scott and Fayette Co.

Marble Creek—Jessamine Co.

Martin's Creek—"A branch of the S. F. of Licking."

Mill Creek ("Waters of the Ohio") —Breckinridge Co. (or Hardin).

Mill Creek—Carroll and Henry Cos.

Mill Creek ("Waters of Licking")—Bourbon Co.

Mill Creek ("Waters of N. F. of Licking")—Mason or Fleming Co.

Miller's Creek—Clark Co.

Mud Lick—Bath Co.

Muddy Creek—Butler Co.

Muddy Creek—Ohio Co.

Muddy Creek—Madison Co.

Muddy Creek—Trigg Co.

Muddy River—Logan Co.

Mulberry Creek—Branch of Breashears in Shelby Co.

Murray's Run—Mercer Co.

Nolin's Creek—Hardin Co.

Ohio River—Northern boundary of Kentucky.

Otter Creek—Madison Co.

Otter Creek—"Waters of Salt River."

Otter Creek—McLean Co.

Paint Creek—Johnson Co.

Paint Lick Creek—Garrard Co.

Panther Creek—Daviess Co.

Pine Lick—Lincoln Co.

Pitman's Creek—Pulaski Co.

Pleasant Run—Marion and Washington Cos.

Pleasant Run—Morgan Co.

Plumb Creek—Spencer and Shelby Cos.

Plumb Run—Fayette or Jessamine Co.

Pond Creek—Jefferson Co.

Pond River—Hopkins and Muhlenberg Cos.

Pottenger's Creek—Nelson Co.

Quirk's Creek—"Branch of the Salt River," Mercer Co.

Red River—Powell Co.

Rock Dunda—"On Indian Shore."

"Rocky Ford on Licking River."

Rolling or "Rowling" Fork of Salt River—Nelson, Larue and Marion Cos.

Rough Run or Creek—Hardin, Grayson, Hancock and Ohio Cos.

Salt River—Mercer, Anderson, Spencer and Bullitt with branches in Washington, Nelson, Shelby, Jefferson, &c.

Shannon's Run—Woodford and Fayette Cos.

Shawnee Run—Mercer Co.

Shawnee Spring—Mercer Co.

Silver Creek—Madison Co.

Simpson's Creek—Spencer and Nelson Cos.

Skagg's or Skegg's Creek—Rockcastle Co.

Slate Creek—Bath Co.

Small Mountain Creek—Same as Little Mountain Creek, Montgomery Co.

Severin or Sovern Creek—Hardin Co.

Soverin's Creek—"Branch of Hingston's Fork of Licking."

Sovern Creek—Owen Co.

St. Asaph's Spring Branch—at Logan's Fort near Stanford.

Station Camp Creek—Estill and Jackson Cos.

Steel's Run—Woodford and Fayette Cos.

Stewart's Fork of Salt River—Nelson Co.

Stoner's Creek—Bourbon Co.

Stoney Creek—Boone Co.

Strodes Branch of Licking—Bourbon Co.

Sugar Loaf Lick—Madison or Lincoln Co.

Summer's Run—Branch of Licking.

Tate Creek—Madison Co.

Ten Mile Creek—Grant Co.

Town Fork of Elkhorn—Fayette Co.

Town Fork of Salt River—Mercer Co.

Townsen's Fork—Bourbon Co.

Twin Creeks.

Two Mile Creek—Clark Co.

Upper Blue Lick—Nicholas Co.

Wheatley Creek—Same as Whitley, Lincoln Co.

White Lick—Garrard Co.

White Oak Springs—Hart Station in Mercer Co.

Whitley Creek—Lincoln Co.

Wilson's Creek—Bullitt and Nelson Cos.

Wilson's Run—Branch of Dick's River.

Wolf Creek—"About 70 miles below Falls of Ohio," Meade Co.

Wolf Creek—Branch of Stoner's Fork of Licking.

Woods Creek—Campbell or Kenton Co.

For map - see copy in map Drawer (Filson Club) under "Kentucky" - LJK

ELIHU BARKER MAP OF KENTUCKY

By Dr. Willard Rouse Jillson,

Director and State Geologist, Kentucky Geological Survey

There is presented herewith a faithful reproduction of the rare second edition of the Elihu Barker map of Kentucky. This map was published by Debrett in London, England, June 1, 1795, and appeared in the third edition of Imlay's "A Toporgraphical Description of the Western Territory of North America . . . 1797," which was also published by Debrett. The first edition of the Barker map was published in Philadelphia and bears the following title: "A Map of Kentucky from Actual Survey, by Elihu Barker, entered as Act directs. Engraved and sold by Matthew Carey, Phild.[a] Scale American Miles 45 (4½") 17 3/8x38/4 (1793)." A reduced copy, the third edition of the Barker map, appears also in Carey's American Atlas, which was published in 1796. The first, second and third editions of this map as above described are on file in the Library of Congress, Washington, D. C.

The original unpublished Elihu Barker map was advertised for sale by Oliver Barker, possiby a relative, in "Dunlap's American Daily Advertiser" January 8th to 10th, 1793. The advertisement was as follows:

FOR SALE

A large and Elegant MAP

Of the State of Kentucky:

Comprehending also the principal Parts of the Cumberland, Tennessee. Kaskeskies, Wabash, Miami, and Siota Countries, never yet published.—Almost the whole taken from actual Survey, and accurately laid down by Mr. Elisha Barker, late of the State of Kentucky, deceased.

Any person inclining to purchase said Map, and the Copy Right to the same, on application to the Subscriber at the City-Tavern (who is fully authorized to dispose thereof) may see the said Map and the Recommendations accompanying it, and receive such reasonable Terms of Sale as may make it an Object of Attention.

OLIVER BARKER

Evidently this advertisement gave the impression that a published map was meant, for on January 11th, it was changed to read:

FOR SALE, A

Large & elegant unengraved Map

Of the State of Kentucky:

Comprehending also the principal Parts of the Cumberland, Tennessee, Kaskeskies, Wabash, Miami, and Siota Countries, never yet published—Almost the whole taken from actual survey, and accurately laid down by Mr. Elihu Barker, late of the State of Kentucky, deceased.

Any Person inclining to purchase said Map, and the Copy Right to the same, on application to the Subscriber at the City-Tavern, (who is fully authorized to dispose thereof) may see the said Map and the Recommendations accompanying it, and receive such reasonable Terms of Sale as may make it an Object of Attention.

OLIVER BARKER

Philadelphia, Jan. 4, 1793.

Little is known concerning the life of Elihu Barker, and nothing is to be found after a search of the records of the Library of Congress, though data might possibly be procured elsewhere. He was evidently an Englishman born who had good connections there as well as in America, and was particularly interested in the western country. His map of

Kentucky was preceded by John Filson's much distorted map of Kentucky and other of the Eastern Mississippi River Valleys, but it is by far the most accurate of the early maps of this State. It is so well done that it could be used today with satisfaction for general purposes.

There are some interesting cartographic features on this map, chief among which are representations of mountains in Eastern Kentucky, and also between the Cumberland and Tennessee Rivers in Western Kentucky. The fact that there a number of isolated knob areas in different places in the State, particularly in what is known as Campbell, Pendleton and Kenton counties, and again in Jefferson and Bullitt counties, as well as in Russell, Casey and Simpson counties, points without doubt to the fact that Barker made use of the available published sources, and took the written and verbal statements of others in compiling his map. He circles an area East of Science Hill in Pulaski County on the waters of what is now Buck Creek, but was then called Caney Fork or "the Glades."

The various known salt licks throughout the State are indicated, and the principal trails and settlements. At this time, according to the Barker map, the principal towns in Kentucky were Washington and Charleston in Mason County, Bourbon Court House, Lexington, Frankfort, Versailles, Louisville, Bardstown, Danville, Harrodsburg, Madison Court House, Stanford, Crab Orchard, Petersburgh, Balclutha, Bealsburgh, Georgetown and Vienna. The State was divided into nine counties, which were: Jefferson, Fayette, Mercer, Nelson, Lincoln, Madison, Bourbon, Woodford and Mason.

The "Henderson Grant" is also indicated in the vicinity of the mouth of Green River. The "Barrens" are indicated as at that section between Great Barren River and Green River, and the Little Barren River in South Central Kentucky; while the region between the Tradewater, Ohio and Cumberland Rivers in Western Kentucky is designated as "barren naked land." The territory in the vicinity of Irvington in Breckinridge and Meade counties is also designated as "barren naked land."

A number of outlying stations, such as Moddrel's Station in Laurel County and Shaw's Station in Grayson County, where Leitchfield now stands, Barnett's Station on Rough Creek and Hardin's Fort on Hardins Creek, where Hardinsburg is now located, are also indicated. Making due allowances for the paucity of data at this early date the Elihu Barker map of 1795 may be regarded as a very good one, containing a great fund of information, particularly with respect to the several drainage basins and the names of the tributary creeks. The wonder is that it was done as well as it appears to have been at this early time.

INDEX
Certificate Book of the Virginia Land Commission 1779-80

Compiled by
Colleen M. Elliott